JAMES C. RILEY

International Government Finance and the Amsterdam Capital Market, 1740–1815

During the eighteenth century European governments began systematically using an international credit structure whose center was the Amsterdam capital market. This book reconstructs that system and surveys its principal effects on the European, and especially the Dutch, economies. Eighteenth-century states borrowed chiefly to finance wars and, increasingly toward the century's end, debts from earlier wars. Military and naval spending and debt service together consumed up to eighty percent of peacetime revenues and more in war. Borrowing on international markets stabilized previously disruptive deficit financing techniques and moderated the economic consequences of sharply irregular war spending. This development, however, eased the problems of war-making more than it developed national economies or enhanced prosperity.

The Dutch, heretofore seen as having squandered the advantage of cheap credit, actually faced the difficult problem of finding productive uses for their savings at satisfactory returns. Dutch rentiers searched for domestic and foreign outlets and proved willing to lend to both risky and dependable borrowers, but the credit those rentiers might have provided Dutch industry was not widely used because it was not sufficiently cheap to counterbalance high labor costs. By the time the relative importance of high wages had diminished, during the nineteenth century, credit was no longer cheaper in the Dutch Netherlands than elsewhere.

INTERNATIONAL GOVERNMENT FINANCE AND THE AMSTERDAM CAPITAL MARKET 1740–1815

INTERNATIONAL GOVERNMENT FINANCE AND THE AMSTERDAM CAPITAL MARKET 1740–1815

JAMES C. RILEY
Indiana University

CAMBRIDGE UNIVERSITY PRESS
Cambridge
London New York New Rochelle
Melbourne Sydney

CAMBRIDGE UNIVERSITY PRESS
Cambridge, New York, Melbourne, Madrid, Cape Town, Singapore, São Paulo, Delhi

Cambridge University Press
The Edinburgh Building, Cambridge CB2 8RU, UK

Published in the United States of America by Cambridge University Press, New York

www.cambridge.org
Information on this title: www.cambridge.org/9780521226776

First published 1980
This digitally printed version 2008

A catalogue record for this publication is available from the British Library

Library of Congress Cataloguing in Publication data
Riley, James C
International government finance and
the Amsterdam capital market, 1740–1815.
Bibliography: p.
1. Loans, Dutch – History.
2. Capital – Netherlands – History.
3. International finance – History. I. Title
HJ8707.R54 332.4′5′09492 79-152

ISBN 978-0-521-22677-6 hardback
ISBN 978-0-521-10110-3 paperback

Portions of Chapter 7 were originally published in the following articles by the author: "Dutch Investment in France, 1781–1787," *Journal of Economic History,* XXXIII, no. 4 (December, 1973), 733, 736–9, 743, 744–51, and 753–5; "Foreign Credit and Fiscal Stability: Dutch Investment in the United States, 1781–1794," *Journal of American History,* LXV, no. 3 (December, 1978), 656–7, 659, 660, 662, 663, 664, 665–6, 667–8, 669–71, 677, and 678.

To

John McConnell

and

Julia Clifford Riley

CONTENTS

TABLES AND CHARTS

Tables

Tables and charts

Charts

ACKNOWLEDGMENTS

A number of people have earned my gratitude for their part in this book. Mej. W. van der Burg, formerly curator of the Economic History Archives in The Hague, introduced me to uninventoried parts of the collection, since dispersed. In Amsterdam Dr. Simon Hart, formerly director of the Municipal Archives, acquainted me with the notarial records and a number of specialized collections, and shared his rich insights into the holdings in his care. I was also assisted by the present director, Dr. Wilhelmina C. Pieterse, and Mevr. drs. C. Gravesteijn, librarian at the Economic History Library, Amsterdam. For another kind of help I wish to thank Prof. dr. Pieter J. van Winter, who criticized my earliest work and some of my later as well, and Prof. dr. J. H. van Stuijvenberg, who provided every possible aid. In addition to referees, who remain anonymous but to whom I am grateful, several scholars suggested improvements after reading part or all of the manuscript at one stage or another. For the mistakes and the problems they pointed out, I wish to thank Prof. dr. Johan de Vries, Professor Paul W. Kuznets, Prof. dr. Marten G. Buist, and Prof. dr. W. M. Zappey.

Research trips in 1968–9 and 1971 were supported by a Waddell Fellowship from the University of North Carolina at Chapel Hill, by the University of Houston, and above all by my generous parents. For that and better reasons also I have dedicated this book to them. My wife, Sharyn, has encouraged and helped me in direct and subtle ways as well. And finally George V. Taylor, in whose seminar I trained in 1965–8, deserves a special expression of thanks for what he did then and since.

1

INTRODUCTION

Financing deficits in the eighteenth century

The competitive state system of early modern Europe was characterized by political and military aggressiveness whose costs exceeded the traditional revenues available to rulers. Taxation authority, elaborated simultaneously with the development toward centralized states, distributed the burden of furnishing resources for dynastic rivalries beyond princely domains but did not provide sufficient revenues. In the same fashion as their predecessors, early modern states employed auxiliary financial devices often marked by arbitrariness and by disruptive consequences for political stability and economic activity. Supplies, manpower, and money were requisitioned; coinage was debased; voluntary and involuntary loans were raised; liabilities were renounced or left unpaid. The fundamental feature of this system of government finance was instability: financial instability in the sense that taxation programs were oriented chiefly toward meeting peacetime rather than wartime requirements, economic instability in the sense that neither taxation nor auxiliary financial techniques was generally used in such a way as to assist economic development, and political instability in the sense that inadequate tax and domain revenues led to tensions surrounding attempts to increase the rate of assessment or exact resources that could not be secured by consent.

To increase tax revenues necessitated, in the first place, conflict with taxpayers, from whom resistance was mounted by numerically small political and social classes with disproportionately large economic resources. Following the path of least resistance, governments turned to social classes whose resources were inadequate to furnish sufficient revenues. Redistribution was theoretically possible but politically inexpedient. Second, the authority to tax was acquired before the construction of administrative structures capable of exploiting tax levies efficiently. Into the eighteenth century many states maintained administrative systems based on venal office holding rather than rigorous central control. But the principal reason for inadequate tax revenues was the extent to which the financial demands of a competitive state system increased more rapidly than the resources of an agrarian economy and the proportion of private resources that subjects had yet been coerced to sacrifice in taxation.

Requisition, debasement, involuntary borrowing, and repudiation were unavoidable so long as tax revenues regularly or consistently fell short of expenditures, and so long as a more reliable system of supplementing those revenues had not yet been devised. But each yielded diminishing returns whenever used extensively because of resistance from those whose assets were depleted and because of the depletion of private resources itself. The consequences of arbitrariness in financial policy could be modified by those whose property was threatened, as may be illustrated in the case of borrowing. Early modern government credit shared the feature of annuity yields including both interest and a sizable risk premium, a form of insurance under which paper was amortized for the very reason that it might be repudiated before redemption. In other words, to borrow, governments were obliged to offer such high returns that servicing loans was difficult or impossible. Over the long run periodic bankruptcies damaged lenders' interests only when the risk premium was not sufficiently high. Nevertheless, the institutionalization of default left states with neither stable nor reliable credit resources.

In the absence of economic growth sufficient to increase tax revenues without higher rates of assessment, and given the continued political inexpediency of redistribution, revenues could still be expanded and made more predictable by an efficient exploitation of credit. Traditional practices stressing emergency borrowing from a narrow pool of lenders could be replaced by credit planning and an expanded pool of lenders. Such a shift, accompanied by a transition from yields including a risk premium to those composed principally or exclusively of interest, occurred first in the Dutch Republic, a small state whose impressive economic resources were, despite high per capita taxation, insufficient for participation in international rivalries dominated by larger powers. During the seventeenth century the Republic devised a system of credit exploitation and management that gradually reduced credit costs. By the end of that century the chief public institutions could borrow without any significant risk premium. Personal savings that could not be tapped through increased or redistributed taxation were tapped through voluntary loans. As long as returns included a significant risk premium, high service payments restricted the potential size of government debts. But Dutch debtor institutions managed to inspire confidence in their ability to service and redeem liabilities, and, in a painstaking process complicated by the erratic credit demands of wartime, the province of Holland expanded its debt by more than 225 percent without increasing its allocation for debt charges.

The seventeenth-century transformation of public credit in the Dutch Republic was duplicated thereafter with greater or lesser rationality in other states. Creating reliable public credit facilities necessarily involved major refinements in credit practices. But because capital availability among greater and lesser powers fell short of demand, it also involved the creation of an international long-term credit structure. The foundation of that structure in the eighteenth century was the Amsterdam capital market, a channel through which passed into European and American government finance the savings of a people noted for parsimony, and a significant part of the resources of an economy marked by stagnating or declining returns in previously strong sectors.[1]

What is at issue here is neither the origin of government borrowing nor its complex development in the sixteenth and seventeenth centuries, but the use of credit raised on the primary eighteenth-century capital market in lieu of reorganization of financial management or overt reform in tax assessment, and in lieu also of sufficient gains in revenue from economic growth. Although Dutch investment capital did not single-handedly cover deficit spending by European states, the transfer of Dutch savings abroad financed part of the conflicts from the War of the Austrian Succession to the wars of the French Revolution, tended to reduce credit costs for governments borrowing on domestic capital markets, and supported an expansion of the money supply in states whose domestic capital markets were not adequate for large-scale borrowing. By bringing Dutch savings into use European governments leveraged tax revenues and other credit resources and, with simultaneous inflation, leveraged them over the long term. Paradoxically, the international credit structure permitted both a heightened degree of conflict with larger unproductive spending than would otherwise have been feasible, and helped stabilize credit exploitation so that the disruptive economic consequences of past deficit-financing practices were replaced by policies that appear to have had expansionary effects among debtor states.

Nevertheless, the new credit structure was no more than an expedient response to continued, more frequent, and more substantial deficits. Its management was entrusted to a capital market inexperienced in such matters, a market that, because lenders failed to become informed about inflationary patterns, debt levels, and other trends, could not perform its regulatory charge satisfactorily. Although the Amsterdam market was adept at improving access to savings and at rapidly mobilizing large sums, it was not adept at manipulating capital availability and credit cost to restrain deficit spending. By the eve of the wars of the French Revolution cumulative debts among borrowing powers were many times larger than the sum of each year's current revenues. It is difficult to project the extent of still stable leveraging that might have been managed after that point had capital supply in Amsterdam and on other markets not been curtailed by the outbreak of war. As events took place, however, capital supply declined on the ascending side of demand. On the European continent, where economic growth was not yet sufficient to compensate for unreformed tax programs, the war and its costs made default unavoidable.

Format of exposition

Organizing this book has been difficult because several topics seem to demand simultaneous explanation and because a satisfactory account involves both very detailed reconstruction and generalization. Three subjects – the Amsterdam capital market, international government finance and credit exploitation through the Amsterdam market, and the consequences for the Dutch economy of foreign lending – require lengthy exposition. Comprehensiveness rather than brevity is necessary because the secondary literature lacks an overall treatment of the Amsterdam market and because much of the literature dealing with aspects of the market is in Dutch, a language unfamiliar to some scholars who may nevertheless be interested in the market and its role in government finance.

Market structure will be taken up first, with the objective of providing institutional and human background to Dutch foreign investments. But government borrowing cannot be treated solely from the perspective of Amsterdam. Financial practices introduced first in the Dutch Republic and later duplicated and refined by Britain provided a model for the reformulation of credit policies in other states. The important features of that model will be discussed in tandem with credit demand among Dutch public institutions. Although the Republic first shifted to a rationalized program of credit inflation, it was also the first state to approach the exhaustion of the resources thus gained. That occurred not because savings were consumed or because lenders refused to extend more credit, but because the costs of a great-power role in the wars of 1667–1713 nearly exhausted the revenues that could be made available for debt service.

Reduced demand from Dutch public institutions was a necessary prelude to the creation of an international credit structure with sufficient resources to permit a general European shift toward public finance stability through foreign borrowing. But the transition on the Amsterdam market was not abrupt. Although European governments had tapped Dutch savings early in the seventeenth century, returns and risks remained relatively unattractive to lenders until the 1740s. By that point stable or declining demand for capital from other sectors of the Dutch economy made foreign investment attractive even though returns from British securities, the principal kind of paper bought in the 1740s, were declining toward interest-only yields. The subsequent development of foreign lending, and in particular changes in the rate at which Dutch investors are estimated to have converted other assets into loans to foreign governments,[2] may be tied to long-term trends in the Dutch economy. Foreign loans were increasingly attractive during most of the second half of the eighteenth century because capital demand and yields were declining in other investment sectors.[3]

On the Amsterdam market banking intermediaries and investors alike were poorly informed about financial policies, debt levels, and the frequency of deficits among debtor states. Therefore it is not documents about the market that will reveal why European governments found foreign borrowing more attractive than tax reform. Nevertheless a general understanding of credit practices among borrowing powers is necessary background for the bilateral relationships between the Amsterdam market and the nine states that were the principal exploiters of Dutch savings. Those practices will be surveyed as a prelude to a series of case studies in which the general discussion of credit demand will give way to a more detailed discussion of borrowing in public finance among the nine debtor states, concentrating on periods when Dutch lending was particularly significant. By no means comprehensive in their coverage of public finance in debtor states, the case studies attempt to bring the national history of public finance together with the role played by Dutch capital markets in the international credit structure.

Lending to governments was the chief activity of the Amsterdam capital market but, led by aggressive intermediaries, investors allocated savings elsewhere as well. Capital abundance in the Republic, demonstrated by low returns on domestic and foreign government loans, represented an asset that might have been exploited to regain competitiveness in European markets for Dutch shipping, fishing, and industry and thus arrest the eighteenth-century stagnation or decline of traditionally strong sectors of the economy. The most important issue in the problem of Dutch economic revitalization arises from what has previously been portrayed as a missed opportunity. Investment capital, it has been argued, could have been employed to build an industrial infrastructure that would not only have reversed retardation but also have led to an industrial revolution a century or more in advance of the actual course of events. Lending to foreign governments is made to appear detrimental because resources allocated in that direction were either not used or were unavailable for investment in industry. That case is built on one of two hypotheses that cannot be verified. First, it has been assumed that lending to a modern sector of industry at returns prevailing in government finance would have overcome other factors impeding industrial revitalization, and that earnings in a modern sector of Dutch industry would have been sufficient to compensate investment capital at rates equal to or greater than those paid in government finance. Second, Joel Mokyr has argued that links did not exist between otherwise highly developed Dutch capital markets and an incipient sector of modern industry, so that the problem of comparative returns is specious.

The "absent-links" contention arises from the need to explain what seems otherwise inexplicable–high aggregate savings along with industrial retardation. It is a plausible interpretation in theoretical terms, but does it agree with what is known about the Amsterdam market and, moreover, is it necessary? Insofar as there was little investment in industry through the market, such a hypothesis is difficult to prove or disprove. But what can be established about the market leads to a more plausible and less strained explanation of Dutch failure to invest in industry. A shift in government annuity yields around 1795, when exogenous factors were more favorable to industrial modernization, indicates that the problem of comparative returns is anything but specious and that links failed to develop not because the market was incapable of furnishing capital to industry but because industry could not compete with other borrowers.

The setting of borrowing

This survey of themes, necessary because of the problem of organizing this book, is still not a sufficient introduction. It must be supplemented with a discussion of the supply of Dutch capital for foreign lending, the demand for credit and for an international credit structure, and the economic background in the Dutch Republic. Each of those topics is allied to the three principal subjects of concern here, but what should be known about them transcends those three subjects and is a foundation for what follows.

Capital supply. In the second half of the eighteenth century a number of European commercial and banking centers provided markets for the issue of loans and offered management services for direct investment in government paper. Some of those capital markets specialized geographically, organizing issues principally on behalf of neighboring states. In certain periods Geneva rivaled Paris as a source of capital for French loans.[4] Genoa as well invested large sums in French royal loans,[5] but that city was chiefly a continental rather than a regional capital market. In comparison to Amsterdam, Genoa was of secondary importance, but it appears, until the 1790s, to have surpassed other markets in both the volume and frequency of foreign loans issued. In Germany, Frankfurt was the most active market in foreign lending in the last two decades of the century, whereas Vienna marshaled resources for the empire throughout the century. The leading European capital market after 1815, London, engaged in foreign lending early in the century and again during the 1790s, but its principal orientation was toward exchequer borrowing. Although its resources equaled or exceeded those of any other market, London constituted a domestic rather than an international market.

Among those cities Amsterdam was preeminent in having the necessary volume of capital for large-scale lending and in combining access to capital with the market structure and entrepreneurial sophistication that could mobilize resources and, to appearances at least, safeguard the interests of borrowers and lenders alike. The hinterland from which Amsterdam drew investment capital was made up for the most part by the Dutch Republic, particularly the province of Holland, but some foreign capital also moved through the city into European government loans.[6] Furthermore, on ancillary capital markets in Utrecht, Rotterdam, and The Hague firms competed for intermediary positions and sometimes managed to become agencies for issuing loans.

The sums lent by Dutch capitalists to foreign governments were drawn from savings accumulated as the result of a social imperative encouraging parsimony, from the reinvestment of earnings from prior foreign loans, and from a conversion of existing assets and new earnings from investment sectors offering less attractive returns.[7] If reconstructing the precise rate or volume of capital accumulation permitted by seventeenth-century Dutch supremacy in the European carrying trade remains difficult, there is no doubt that commerce, and especially the Baltic grain trade, had yielded huge profits and that those profits were customarily husbanded with care. Inflationary price movements in the first half of the seventeenth century were particularly beneficial to Dutch merchants, who bought grain in Baltic ports at prices that lagged behind those in western European and Mediterranean cities.[8]

The commission trade, which gained momentum over the century from 1650 to 1750, returned more modest yields on a given transaction than had the carrying trade. But commercial finance offered a potentially larger scale of transactions and thus equal or greater ultimate profits. In trade, credit instruments tended to be employed in a pattern tied to the rhythm of goods moving from points of supply through distribution centers to consumption centers. When Dutch staple market merchants granted credit they did so on the security of commodities in commercial exchanges set in motion at the same time. Elimination of the Dutch entrepôt as a distribution center reduced the lag between production and consumption and increased the potential velocity of credit. Furthermore, in commission trade short-term drafts ceased to be useful merely for buyers and sellers wishing to settle their respective interests after completion of a given transaction and became more flexible credit tools. No longer restrained by the need to tie credit to commercial exchanges, the commission intermediary could expand the value of paper he put into circulation and the number of bills he guaranteed up to the limit to which the market would absorb his drafts. The thoroughness with which Dutch intermediaries exploited commercial finance opportunities is still obscure because of wholly inadequate data about changes in the scale of Dutch credit participating in European trade. But savings accumulation clearly was not disrupted and probably not even disturbed by the transition from the carrying to the commission trade.

Political, demographic, and social structures in the United Provinces were suited to the preservation of wealth acquired in commerce, commercial finance, and elsewhere. Political authority was decentralized. The States General, the national legislative authority, depended upon the unanimous consent of delegations from provincial states, which in turn were selected in municipal and social corporations. By tradition the stadholder held executive authority, but in practice the power allotted to successive stadholders by the seven provinces varied inversely with the influence of the regent oligarchy in the seaward provinces, especially Holland, in what was an ingrained rivalry. Conflicting interests, for instance those separating landward and seaward provinces, often retarded progress in any direction on controversial issues, but the underlying premise of government was compromise.

Access to seats in the provincial states or the States General and to high-level government appointments was largely reserved in the seaward provinces, where both population and wealth were concentrated, to commercial and professional classes that had emerged in the sixteenth and seventeenth centuries. Demographic trends supported static rather than dynamic political, social, and economic structures. The very low rate of population growth characteristic of most of Europe in the late seventeenth and early eighteenth century persisted in the Republic after mid-century, when neighboring areas went over to higher growth rates. A nearly stable population meant that social and economic tensions sometimes accompanying demographic expansion elsewhere were absent and posed no hindrance either to the preservation of wealth by classes already enriched by commerce or to an increasing maldistribution of wealth in their favor. In the eighteenth century, especially in Holland and Zeeland, those classes resisted social infusion as well. Even new men who followed traditional avenues in building fortunes often found the path to political power and social preferment blocked.[9]

The transition from the carrying trade and a coincidental withdrawal by many members of the regent oligarchy from active roles in trade meant that economic mobility was growing at the same time that entrepreneurial success no longer sufficed for entry into the regent class. In the commercial and financial community the reorientation of the market after about 1650 was accompanied by growth in the number of entrepreneurial roles. Wholesale merchants, still socially the most prestigious members of that community, did not control ancillary roles in commercial finance or lending to governments, with the result that those who would previously have merely provided services to merchants found structural restraints reduced. At the same time the shift toward banking led to new occupations as profitable as those in wholesale trade. The commercial hierarchy did not disappear in the eighteenth century, but its traditional rigidities were relaxed.[10]

Like the abovementioned political and economic trends, the Dutch tax system also encouraged capital accumulation and investment in commercial finance and foreign loans. Municipal and provincial governments drew income chiefly from indirect taxes on items of everyday consumption. Those revenues were supplemented by assessments on certain kinds of fixed property and by occasional levies on the long-term paper of domestic government loans and on some Dutch joint-stock-company shares. Commercial profits were not themselves taxed, while import and export duties and a levy on larger ships increased indirect taxes insofar as they were passed on to consumers. Income was subject to extraordinary levies, but until the end of the century such assessments were extremely rare. To the extent that this tax system encouraged investment in any area it did so particularly with respect to foreign lending. Those investments were not taxed except when estates passed out of the direct line of succession or in occasional extraordinary income or property levies that included them. In addition, some Dutch government loans were not taxed and the long-term notes of joint-stock-company loans also remained free from direct assessment except in the cases mentioned for foreign loans.

As early as the mid-seventeenth century there was a strong tendency toward concentration of wealth in the hands of a small segment of the populace, a group that could afford high savings.[11] For the seventeenth century Violet Barbour found "the saving and investing habit of Hollanders of moderate or even small means" an important feature of capital accumulation.[12] That propensity was more than matched among wealthy classes. Indeed Sir William Temple thought the "common Riches" among the Dutch to lie "In every Man's spending less than he has coming in, be that what it will."[13]

Although it was long fashionable to find an increasing incidence of ostentatious display in the eighteenth-century Republic and to trace that to moral decay and an enervation of the entrepreneurial spirit, the savings habits of the earlier period did not give way to full consumption or deficit spending on the part of individuals in commercial and financial classes, whether or not they were part of the regent oligarchy. The increasing concentration of wealth after 1650 presumably reduced aggregate savings, but modern and eighteenth-century economic analysts both suggest that the savings capacity of the 10 percent of a population with the highest income is the most significant area of capital accumulation.[14]

The observation concerning savings habits that has gained the widest currency for the latter part of the eighteenth century is drawn from Henry Hope, leading partner in the most heavily capitalized and one of the most prestigious commercial and banking firms in Amsterdam, and a knowledgeable source. Writing in 1791, long after it had become commonplace to lament the Republic's commercial decline and at the height of foreign government lending, Hope reported to Lord Auckland: "Tho we have many in this Country who spend their incomes, I believe the people taken in a body do not consume above ⅝, or at most ¾ of their Revenues."[15] The American diplomat Gouverneur Morris gave a similar if more impressionistic judgment. Visiting Amsterdam in 1790, Morris was invited to dinner by Willem Willink, a prominent banker associated in raising loans for Congress who might be thought to have had some reason to try to impress Morris favorably. But at Willink's house the dessert was "a little better [than the main course] as to Quantity but the Quality shews that the Principles of a rigid oeconomy have been duly attended to. The Wines, however, might give that Indigestion against which the due Precautions have been taken in the Dinner."[16] Comments on Dutch parsimony appear repeatedly in travel accounts and other sources, and not all observers found such a trait as lamentable as did Morris.

Although the evidence that can be cited reflects the habits of only a few individuals and the time span of an entire century, Hope's estimated savings rate appears to have balanced the greater capacity of wealthier individuals active in entrepreneurship against the lesser capacity of groups that suffered from political and economic trends. For example, between 1685 and 1709 Cornelis de Jonge van Ellemeet, a receiver general for the United Provinces and thus a man singularly well placed to take advantage of an expanding income to indulge an inclination to save, increased his savings from about half of income to 67 percent.[17] Holding one of the choice plums of the regent oligarchy, van Ellemeet was atypical of many of his peers in enjoying rapidly increasing income. Still, what he did could be matched by merchants, bankers, and others.

At the apex of the commercial and financial world of late-eighteenth-century Amsterdam stood Hope & Co., a remarkably successful house whose partners persistently reinvested profits to expand the firm's capital.[18] Between 1762 and 1769, for example, Hope & Co.'s capital grew from about f. 4.3 million to more than f. 6.8 million. Average annual distributed profits totaled f. 458,335,12, or some 8.25 percent of mean capital. The average annual growth rate in the firm's capital was 8.64 percent, part of which resulted from reinvestment of earnings and part from investment from other sources. Interfamily inheritances contributed to capital expansion, but Henry Hope, the most aggressive partner, more than matched income from such sources by reinvesting earnings. His share in the firm's capital, little more than f. 57,000 in 1762, amounted to over f. 4.75 million in 1801 when he withdrew. For the firm as a whole the profits distributed annually advanced with fluctuations to a plateau of over f. 1 million between 1801 and 1806, at which point the house was capitalized at nearly f. 5.5 million. Even so, neither Henry Hope nor the other partners reinvested all earnings in the firm, where it was difficult to keep such substantial sums occupied profitably. Hope's other assets included an estate near Haarlem, paintings and sculptures, and a private account for ventures outside the firm.[19]

Although by the 1780s Hope & Co. stood in a class apart from other banking and commercial houses, there were other firms whose partners or directors managed affairs with similar skill and accumulated capital at an impressive pace. Pieter Stadnitski, grandson of an immigrant cloth presser, married in 1763 at the age of twenty-eight at the beginning of his business career. In their marriage contract Stadnitski and his wife declared their wealth not to exceed f. 50,000.[20] Bequests subsequently added to Stadnitski's assets, but his most significant income came from investment operations in which Dutch capital flowed toward France and, later, the United States. At his widow's death in 1799, Stadnitski's estate appears to have amounted to something in excess of f. 1.6 million in nominal values.[21] In 1791, when a partnership agreement was struck, he had had only f. 400,000 invested in his firm.[22] Other cases, too, reveal a similar pattern among entrepreneurs and the investment of excess profits outside the firm in lower-yield areas.[23]

Those three examples reflect successes that must be balanced against venal officeholders who suffered from the midcentury curtailment of tax farming, firms that failed to make the transition from the carrying trade to commercial finance or overextended themselves and were called to account, individuals whose wealth was concentrated in fishing and industry where decline prevailed, and rentiers who forwent altogether the higher earnings of active entrepreneurship. Still, "conservatism was the principal trait in the lifestyle of the Dutch merchant in the middle of the eighteenth century,"[24] and that characteristic was preserved thereafter.[25] The apparent paradox between venturesomeness and aggressiveness in commecial and government finance and conservatism in life-style was not in fact a paradox at all. A social imperative in favor of saving complemented another imperative toward the keen pursuit of business opportunities.

Credit demand. The first large-scale foreign outlet for Dutch loans appeared with expanded British borrowing on the London market during the War of the Austrian Succession. Dutch investors bought funded debt through intermediaries in London, bypassing Amsterdam agents and thus operating largely outside the management of Dutch capital markets. With the restoration of peace new English borrowing was suspended, but the initiative displayed by Dutch investors pointed up the possibility of expanding foreign investment outlets. No evidence has been uncovered to link the collapse of demand from England with the appearance in the early 1750s of loans to planters in the Dutch West Indies and the development of an outlet managed by intermediaries rather than rentiers, but it is plausible to assume that Dutch firms began to explore foreign opportunities because they recognized that large sums were available for returns of some 4 to 6 percent. There was not, however, an immediate shift. After the first loan organized for Dutch West Indian planters in 1753, a decade passed before the field was developed to the potential offered by planter demand or by the returns that could be realized in the West Indies.

Plantation loans were managed by merchants seeking to combine a novel investment outlet with commercial redevelopment in an area in which the Dutch were losing ground to competitors in France and Germany.[26] The technique was to organize credit secured on plantation assets and serviced by revenues obtained from the expanded coffee and sugar production permitted by that credit. In retrospect it is obvious that the high yields of plantation loans still did not reflect the risks involved, but lenders were so eager during the 1760s that some planters inflated the value of their assets, and even manufactured fraudulent assessments that could be used to secure loans.[27]

Those and other defects became evident only after the plantation loans had fostered greater foreign lending, a pattern further encouraged by increased credit demand from Britain and Austria during the Seven Years' War and from other governments toward the end of the war. With the return of peace in 1763 Britain suspended loan issues but other powers, in financial disorder because of wartime deficits and, in some cases, disruptive monetary policies adopted to cover deficits, began to search actively for foreign credit.

European capital markets found the 1760s a period of expanding foreign lending, but prospective borrowers turned in particular to Amsterdam because there capital was abundant and credit costs as low as or lower than elsewhere. Before the end of the decade Sweden, Denmark, Austria, several of the lesser German states, and Russia had all floated loans in Amsterdam and signaled an intention to continue to use foreign credit for deficits and postwar financial restabilization. The terms of loans raised on the Amsterdam and subsidiary Dutch markets, and on the other capital markets of Europe, were preferable to the reorganization of revenue systems or to tax reform, and could be combined with the exploitation of domestic credit. By the 1780s every major power in Europe, with the sole exception of Prussia, and many of the secondary powers had found it expedient to supplement ordinary revenues either with loans raised directly in the Dutch Republic or by attracting Dutch capital to domestic issues.[28]

Between 1763 and 1770 the balance of Dutch loans to foreign governments and direct investments abroad in government loans appears to have increased from some f. 200 million to between f. 230 and 270 million, of which the largest part was in British government annuities and bank and company stock.[29] From then to the 1790s there was steady growth in the volume of credit outstanding and a relative redistribution away from Britain. Evidence given or cited in later chapters indicates a balance in the early 1790s of f. 500 to 650 million,[30] of which f. 150 to 220 million was composed of debts arising from loans negotiated in the Republic and the remainder of direct investment abroad, principally in England and France. In terms both of the frequency of issue and the volume of capital moving abroad, Amsterdam's most intensive activity occurred between 1780 and 1793. The average net annual addition to the sum outstanding increased from between f. 11 and 14 million in the 1760s and 1770s to some f. 20 million between 1780 and 1793.[31]

Eighteenth-century commentators who were willing to estimate the extent of Dutch foreign lending usually exaggerated.[32] By the end of the 1770s borrowers were customarily deferring the settlement of outstanding credits by means of prolongation loans, new issues of equal or greater size. The larger contemporary estimates were cumulative, counting all issues as loans involving new capital outlays. But some evaluations were reached with more care. In 1782 the secretary to the states of Zeeland, L. P. van de Spiegel, suggested that f. 475 million was outstanding in government and plantation loans, and more than half of that in Britain.[33] Van de Spiegel's estimate is plausible for that date. Even though it includes too large a sum for the plantation loans, it clearly underestimates the total outstanding in Spain, Germany, Denmark, Sweden, and Russia.

By the 1790s Dutch observers widely but incorrectly believed that foreign loan assets equaled about a billion guilders, with most of that in loans to governments.[34] Especially after the French invasion of 1795, when Dutch wealth became a major issue in French plans for extracting an indemnity and subsidies, wild figures were bandied about. A more realistic appraisal was given by Rutger Metelerkamp, who, in estimating capital assets of inhabitants of the Republic as of 1804, put the present value (*valeur actuelle*) of the income from foreign debts at f. 650 million, with an annual return of f. 40 million.[35] Although Metelerkamp claimed to have taken the French annuity reduction of 1797 into account, his figure still exceeds slightly the estimated nominal value balance outstanding and exaggerates the market value of that balance by a larger margin.

Although each state drawing upon Dutch savings followed some unique usages, those particular features should not divert attention from common elements in credit exploitation and public finance policy. Despite variations from state to state, tax structures made foreign borrowing generally attractive. Taxation was everywhere distributed regressively and everywhere to a greater or lesser degree administered inefficiently. Indirect levies on consumables and import and export duties were widely preferred to direct taxes on income or assets, and in most states social privilege had real benefits in tax law.[36] In spite of inefficient and regressive qualities, such a system could still gain from expanding production and consumption. But on the continent government expenditures tended to increase more than production. In general taxation revenues were not adequate to meet the spending commitments assumed by the second half of the eighteenth century, and where budgetary data are available they reveal frequent and sometimes annual deficits.

European states were particularly likely to face deficits in wartime, but in the period after 1740, which was marked by frequent international conflict, indebtedness increased because of both wartime spending and a high incidence of peacetime deficits. To deal with deficits, which officials in most states were aware of in general rather than precise terms, government had recourse to what may be termed a mercantilist expedient approach to state finance. The underlying assumption of mecantilist expedient fiscal policy, that the prosperity of a state, its tax revenues, and its power, could be enhanced by an expansion of the money supply, may be traced to seventeenth-century ideas about the role that an increase in the volume of precious metals in circulation could play in economic expansion and the growth of political power. In the earlier period fiscal policies designed to increase money supply concentrated primarily on expanding imports of bullion and specie and on seigniorage via coinage debasement. Paper currency experiments revealed the potential for increasing money supply independently of trade and bullion flows, but as long as nothing was done to support the value of bank notes, large-scale paper seigniorage significantly increasing the quantity of money in circulation left notes prey to rapid devaluation, with counterproductive fiscal and economic consequences.

What had been lacking was a technique of manipulating the market value of paper currency that permitted value to be kept at or close to par with specie over the long term. Such a technique was provided by foreign credits, and specifically by a systematic use of foreign loans that bolstered paper currency value by countering the tendency of paper to drive specie abroad or into hoards. In furnishing solid commercial drafts or actual specie shipments, foreign loans could modify or eliminate the tendency of paper currency to lose value against specie, thereby permitting an expansion of the quantity of stable media in circulation (although that stability might mask relative price changes in commodities). At the same time loans supplemented paper issues as a means of covering deficits. But credits raised in Amsterdam and on other European capital markets supported paper currency issues without becoming an explicit part of monetary policy in all states issuing such notes. In general the impact of foreign borrowing on money supply was poorly understood or neglected and monetary stability gained by borrowing abroad was fortuitous rather than planned.

Because debtor states did not use capital imports to subsidize industry, trade, or agriculture, any link to increased economic production remained indirect, the uncertain product of decreased credit costs, increased capital availability resulting from an enlarged yet still stable money supply, or expansionary spending by the borrowing state. Taxation did not increase in proportion to foreign borrowing, with the result that deficit spending had a generally expansionary impact. But currency inflation was ultimately fragile. That policy depended on the continued accessibility of foreign credit, that is, on a state's ability not only to prolong loans already outstanding but also to increase the balance owed in the event that further gains in taxable wealth were sought or that deficits obliged yet additional paper issues.

States using paper currency both to enhance prosperity and to supplement revenues were those without domestic capital markets able to provide adequate sums for deficit spending or those which, like Austria, exhausted the domestic capital supply without having resolved the elementary problem of deficits. Other states, and in particular Britain, France, and the Dutch Republic, followed an alternative mercantilist expedient program because they had access to a large enough volume of long-term credit to support a secular trend of increasing deficits and indebtedness. Persistent use of the long-term loan tactic depended on the accessibility of investment capital, but among states regularly borrowing on domestic markets only the United Provinces had an abundant supply.[37] Britain and France continued to rely principally on domestic borrowing, which was possible because foreign and especially Dutch investors were attracted to loans issued in London and Paris.

As in the case of paper currency issues, foreign investment in domestic loans enlarged the amount that could be borrowed. But the flow of investment capital to London or Paris represented an attempt by investors to secure higher returns. Such a movement shifted capital from an area of abundance and thus lower interest rates to an area of higher returns, and in the case of Britain it modified pressure toward higher returns and toward the devaluation of paper paying lower yields. There such flows both increased the total that could be borrowed and reduced credit costs. Governments did not need to borrow abroad or attract foreign capital to domestic loans in sums matching or even approaching the volume of paper currency or interest-bearing notes issued internally but instead, with or without an appreciation of the mechanism in operation, needed to use foreign credit to leverage domestic resources.

When securities could be transferred among investors without technical hindrance, and when the value of those notes was sufficiently predictable to inspire confidence in them, long-term borrowing approximated another way to enhance money supply. Thus, in the mercantilist conception, borrowing contributed to the expansion of prosperity and tax revenues. Issues of long-term notes increased money supply without, however, increasing its velocity. They did not necessarily lead to a greater supply of capital for commerce or industry but merely to a means of payment for the borrower. To the degree that increased spending made possible by borrowing led directly or indirectly to increased production of goods and services, the overall effect was expansionary. But any detailed interpretation of the economic effects of borrowing depends, among other matters, on projections of spending and employment levels in the absence of borrowing, which are beyond the scope of this study.

Although the economic consequences of exploiting foreign

credit through paper currency or interest-bearing note issues must remain unsettled, it is apparent that tax revenues increased substantially in most debtor states after midcentury. Budgetary data, which will be furnished in the bilateral studies, indicate that and, given the absence of significant tax reforms, lend credence to (but do not, of course, prove) the hypothesis that fiscal policies had an expansionary economic effect. Because that was also an inflationary period the question arises whether tax revenues increased more than the cost of goods and services acquired by government. Price data are not comprehensive enough to answer the question for Europe as a whole, but revenues appear in most states to have increased in constant values between the conclusion of the Seven Years' War and the wars of the French Revolution, when price increases were comparatively moderate. Thereafter, however, credit policies were formulated on the continent in fashions dictated by war. Even vaguely enunciated economic objectives gave way altogether to programs intended to create revenues regardless of economic consequences.

Both before and during the Revolutionary and Napoleonic wars governments employing either mercantilist expedient tactic derived important financial advantages from credit inflation. In the first place, they got the revenues from an issue of paper currency or interest-bearing notes. In the former case that sum amounted to the difference between the very minor administrative and material costs involved in printing and distributing paper currency and what was realized from putting notes into circulation. Against that the state had to balance its obligation ultimately to redeem those notes, and the costs of accepting paper in lieu of specie for tax payments, a necessary measure if the value of paper were to be retained against specie. Where paper currency carried interest the state also faced service charges. In domestic or foreign interest-bearing note issues there were also minor administrative and material costs to be deducted from the sum raised. Against the gross yield the state had to pay interest and, sooner or later, in theory, redeem its obligation. Like paper currency issues, domestic and foreign loans were not always put into circulation at prices equivalent to their par value, and whenever a discount was involved the obligation remained to redeem at full face value. Britain often issued domestic loans substantially below par, but most governments generally avoided discounts. On the Amsterdam market interest rates and commission charges were customarily adjusted so that loan notes could be marketed at or near par.

Where revenues increased significantly the inflationary trend of prices after midcentury was advantageous in terms at least of the theoretical ability of governments to redeem their debts. Increased revenues enhanced the state's position with respect to prior indebtedness, which had a fixed nominal value. In such circumstances the ratio of prior indebtedness to tax revenues was reduced, resulting in an inflation-induced expansion in the total debt supportable by tax revenues. The full benefit of that process could be enjoyed only where there was little or no allocation for amortization and where, therefore, debts were permitted to depreciate in real value at the highest possible rate.

Once in circulation both paper currency and interest-bearing notes tended to depreciate. That was true of the latter because price and credit inflation favored higher interest rates. Paper currency tended to depreciate because it was based neither on disposable assets that inspired confidence nor on an economy's ability to absorb a larger money supply. Financial policy rather than economic policy determined how much paper would be put into circulation and fresh issues occurred when governments needed to raise funds. Depreciation had both attractive and unattractive features for the issuer. It decreased the yield of later paper currency issues and of taxes in terms of specie or foreign currencies not disturbed to the same degree by monetary inflation, and it increased the cost of later interest-bearing note issues. But it could also reduce the theoretical and actual liabilities of the debtor whenever those liabilities could be computed in terms of the cost of buying paper. Prolongation of outstanding debts during monetary and price inflation, with or without depreciation from nominal values, also reduced the ultimate cost of redeeming paper currency or interest-bearing notes. Both inflation and depreciation, if the latter were taken advantage of through redemptions, transferred a share of the amortization cost to noteholders and thus acted as a tax. As Benjamin Franklin explained the process, paper currency "pays and clothes troops, and provides victuals and ammunition, and when we are obliged to issue a quantity excessive, it pays itself off by depreciation."[38] Since most paper was absorbed by wealthier classes, classes that otherwise benefited from regressive tax systems, monetary inflation shifted taxation partially toward agreement with wealth. Government could also write off part or all of its liabilities through bankruptcy, and thus redemption costs could be calculated largely or exclusively in terms of the economic and financial consequences of partial or complete bankruptcy. Repudiation of liabilities, gains from depreciation, and as-yet-unrealized advantages produced by inflation together involved a transfer of taxability to domestic and foreign investors. Dutch rentiers were, therefore, unwitting taxpayers to all the states of Europe that acquired credit from the Republic.

Both mercantilist expedient tactics, together with demographic expansion during the second half of the century and a coincidental increase in bullion imports from the New World, contributed to the inflationary trend of prices. Had taxation revenues increased ahead of prices without a coincidentally higher growth in spending, the international credit structure would presumably have led to decreasing deficits, even to surpluses sufficient to reduce outstanding debts. That is to say, if the states of Europe had limited nonproductive spending and pursued monetary and credit inflation with restraint, then those policies might reasonably be expected to have satisfied the objectives of enhancing prosperity, tax yields, and power. But in most states tax revenues did not increase as rapidly as spending. Where mercantilist expedient policies expanded credit use at a faster rate than growth in the productive capacity of preindustrial economies, their adoption led to a situation in which any significant reduction in credit supply would be critical. During the Revolutionary and Napoleonic wars, when wartime spending grew more than the resources available through the capital markets of Europe, the Dutch repository of capital and mercantilist expedient policies failed.

That situation provoked both a reappraisal of revenue systems and attempts at increasing income through reform in tax administration and distribution. Without having entered a crisis itself, Britain shifted taxation toward agreement with wealth by introducing an annual income tax that permitted the percentage of expenditures drawn from borrowing to be reduced. France, having successively repudiated most of its liabilities in interest-bearing notes and paper currency, reorganized its tax retrieval system to reduce collection costs and transferred assessment to client states in the form of war indemnities. But both the British and French cases were unique, the former because Britain enjoyed expanding production and productivity, and the latter because France could implement a supranational system of taxation. Elsewhere, in the face of indemnities imposed by France and expanding military spending and borrowing costs, deficits increased despite any administrative rationalizations or tax increases.

The network of international credit exploitation that had been adopted in Europe in the middle of the eighteenth century provided a period of grace during which a significant part of expanding government spending was shifted temporarily to domestic and foreign creditors. But the transition to using that network as the foundation for funding deficits did not coincide on the continent with significant tax reform and expanding productivity. When the margin of stable credit was exhausted, there was no alternative but an overextension of credit, which, because it was unsupported by foreign capital, led to financial crisis. Together with price inflation, that crisis made permanent much of the temporary shift of deficits onto lenders.

Trends in the Dutch economy. In the seventeenth century, the golden age of the Dutch Republic, investment capital was created by and flowed toward the commodities trade, fishing, shipbuilding, agriculture, transport, and textile and other industries in a diversified economy. In the most important of those areas, wholesale commodity trade, Dutch preeminence was built essentially on entrepreneurial aggressiveness, a central location for entrepôt distribution, and business and technical skill rather than upon natural resources or effectively controlled sources of supply. The market area for commodities dealt in by Dutch merchants and carried in Dutch bottoms extended over the continent of Europe along a curved line stretching from the Baltic to the Mediterranean, with important linkages to the German North Sea and Baltic hinterland and to the East and West Indies. But the core market area was much smaller, stretching inland from the North Sea into Germany.

International finance and the Amsterdam market

The aggressiveness and skill that, along with their central location, made Dutch merchants paramount in the seventeenth century carried over into the eighteenth century. But their preeminence did not last. Even before the eighteenth century had begun, commercial traffic patterns had shifted to their disadvantage. British, French, and German competitors established trade channels that, by linking sources of supply directly with markets, bypassed Dutch ports. The transition away from an entrepôt function was not abrupt, and indeed the chronology of that change remains imprecise. Continued expansion in European commerce left Dutch merchants able to contest their rivals in trade, but the core market over which the Dutch held a geographical advantage was inadequate to sustain the existing volume of commerce, much less to permit continued expansion. The result was stagnation in the quantity of goods carried and a relative deterioration of the Dutch position. Although there were periods of revival, such as between the outbreak of the Seven Years' War and the Fourth Anglo-Dutch War, those were not characterized by long-term growth equal to that which had prevailed in the first half of the seventeenth century.[39]

While trade volume stagnated, European textile industries with access to cheaper labor and otherwise at-least-equivalent factor costs came to rival Dutch producers, and the important fishing industry entered a long period of absolute decline. Of all major sectors of the Dutch economy in the second half of the eighteenth century only agriculture and finance enjoyed conditions favorable to growth.[40]

If aggressiveness and skill no longer sufficed to secure the customary volume of commodities for Dutch bottoms or maintain the former relative position in wholesale trade, the leadership of the seventeenth century had nevertheless provided its own solution to declining opportunities in foreign trade and industrial production for foreign markets. In their heyday Dutch merchants had fashioned for themselves an integral role in bullion and specie transfers and in transactions in commercial drafts. Amsterdam, the leading Dutch port, was the center of a European network of trade settlement. Even while Dutch trade was declining in relation to rivals, the volume of commercial paper passing through Amsterdam continued to expand.

What occurred between 1650 and 1750 was a transition from

commerce to commercial and government finance. Investment opportunities in traditional sectors, shares in commercial voyages, in ships themselves, and in marine insurance, commodity storage, futures transactions, textile production, and other industries such as shipbuilding and the herring and whale fisheries, were giving way to growing opportunities in commission transactions, short-term commercial credit, commercial settlements and the bill trade, and lending to governments.[41] Dutch merchants remained active in the carrying trade and marine insurance, but the share of their resources and energies devoted to commercial finance increased.

Nineteenth-century Dutch historians saw this drift from wholesale commodity trade to commercial finance, the shift from commercial entrepreneurship to banking, and the incipient development of large-scale lending to foreign governments as fundamental reasons for the political and economic decline of the Republic after the seventeenth century. But, as recent scholarship has maintained, those changes arose from efforts to take advantage of available opportunities embraced out of recognition that the Dutch position in trade was on the wane.[42] Conversion to commercial and government finance involved a loss of economic diversity, but that process was a symptom and not a cause of the stagnation or decline of traditionally strong sectors of the economy.

A persistent high savings level among at least the wealthiest part of the population resulted, however, in the accumulation of wealth that might lose purchasing power as a result of the secular inflation of prices. Investments in business firms, commercial transactions, marine insurance, urban real estate, and productive agricultural land were in some measure protected from the depredations of inflation because the value of goods and services produced, and thus of the assets themselves, may be assumed generally to have advanced with the price of agricultural and industrial goods.[43] But a progressively greater allocation of savings to lending to governments entrusted resources to assets that did not retain real value and therefore led to persistent although not entirely appreciated losses. The eagerness with which financial intermediaries and investors alike exploited government finance during the inflationary period indicates that both entrepreneurs and rentiers were unable to avoid the erosion in purchasing

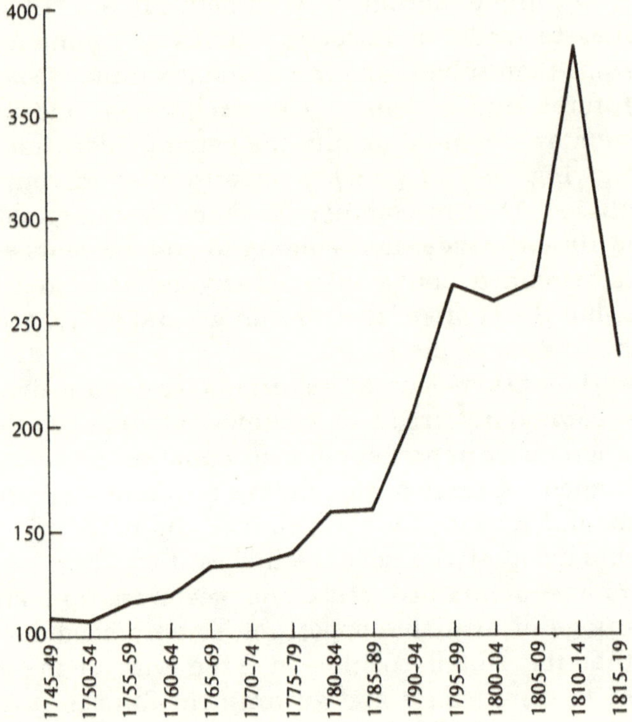

Chart 1-1. Weighted averages of the relative prices of 44 commodities, 1745–1819 (1721–45 = 100).

power of returns and cumulative holdings that inflation entailed.[44] That was true to whatever degree investors were able to bring an understanding of inflation to their choice of investments because alternatives in growth sectors could not absorb available resources. Continued expansion of government lending also indicates that perceived inflationary losses were not deemed large enough to outweigh lower returns in other areas.

Although a general European inflation extending to about 1815 is evident, there is not as yet any composite index of price movements and existing national and regional indices have been constructed by different standards. The index for the Dutch Republic, developed by N. W. Posthumus, is based on wholesale prices of a wide range of selected commodities traded on the Amsterdam exchange. Posthumus's index, reproduced for 1745–1819 in Chart 1-1,[45] is suggestive of price movements in the Republic.

But because it is based on wholesale commodities it may not reflect trends in areas of particular importance to investors, such as urban and rural real estate, and it clearly does not represent a market basket of all goods acquired by any group of Dutch consumers. Nonetheless, that index is the closest available approximation of changes in the purchasing power of fixed assets, and it will be used here, sometimes with an adjusted base period, to calculate changing real values in government finance.

To explain Dutch inflation is another matter. Money supply, the increase of which was an important contributor to inflation elsewhere, is difficult to reconstruct for the Republic because coins, the officially authorized type of money, were minted for an international rather than merely a national market and because sources on unofficial types of money are wanting.[46] A major change in the velocity of circulation, on the other hand, appears unlikely because Dutch prices followed a European and perhaps world trend and because no unique Dutch readjustment that would account for much greater velocity is evident. Rather than looking for an explanation within the Republic it may be more fruitful to consider that prices recorded by Posthumus were those of international trade goods, that increasing money supply elsewhere affected Amsterdam, the chief center of commercial finance, and that expanding European trade permitted a larger Dutch supply of such unofficial money as commercial drafts. Following that line, strictly local Dutch markets, if such existed at all, would appear to have been less affected by the inflation evident in Amsterdam because some forces contributing to higher prices outside the Republic, such as demographic expansion, were less significant in the Dutch interior.

Chart 1-1 shows a marked expansion in inflation during the second half of the 1780s. The height of foreign lending through the Amsterdam market fell within the early stages of that surge, but even during the 1790s inflation discounted only a small part of the annual savings of 25 percent or more of income, which, as Henry Hope claimed, was characteristic of the Dutch populace. Although sometimes contradictory in their impact, the social imperative favoring savings and secular inflation both contributed to the accumulation of wealth that could be converted into government loans, and fed the development of the Amsterdam capital market.

2

THE AMSTERDAM CAPITAL MARKET

The bequest of commerce and commercial finance

As Amsterdam's preeminence as a European entrepôt waned in the late seventeenth century, the importance of financing trade grew. An adaptable banking system eased that shift, although credit facilities in the city were independent and often highly individualistic. The Exchange Bank of Amsterdam, founded in 1609 and administered under the supervision of municipal authorities, emerged as a source of stable media of exchange, a secure depository where payments could be made by book transfers, and a central clearinghouse for international payments.[1] The monopoly over exchange initially given the bank was soon relaxed, permitting the reemergence of private cashiers (*kassiers*), whose activities had been curtailed in 1609. To Amsterdam's monetary system the bank contributed a unit of account, the bank-money guilder, which traded at a premium (agio) or discount (disagio) against current money. Until the disagio crisis of 1789 the eighteenth-century bank-money premium was usually between 2 and 5 percent. Although the bank was dominant early in the eighteenth century in bank-money transactions, Amsterdam's cashiers, who acted as agents of collection and payment, exchanged bank- and current-money drafts, and issued transferable receipts for clients, controlled the increasingly important field of current-money transactions.[2] Together bank, cashiers, and, by midcentury, bankers specializing in the bill trade formed the Amsterdam clearinghouse of commercial finance. Especially after a change in regulations in 1683 permitting the bank to accept specie in return for transferable bank-money receipts, Amsterdam's role in bullion trade was enlarged.

Thus European draft and specie settlements tended to be concentrated there, to the advantage of both commercial and government finance.

From the heyday of the carrying trade the eighteenth-century Amsterdam market also drew commercial precedents for large-scale capital accumulation through the sale of stock. (Capital formation by analogous means appeared in government finance in the seventeenth century, but its potential was not fully exploited until the second half of the eighteenth century.) And in company stock the Amsterdam market found a new object to which sophisticated speculative techniques developed first in commodity exchanges could be applied.[3] In the seventeenth century investors and speculators traded stock actually held in an attempt to profit from price changes, and also entered wagers on future prices without ever acquiring any of the paper whose price was at issue. Given the closed structure of large-scale commerce and the difficulty of penetrating the ranks of established merchants and legally supported monopolies, futures trades appealed to ambitious men without large resources as well as to other groups. The comparative dearth of literature on futures transactions after 1720 may suggest either that what had once been novel had become commonplace, or that such transactions were of diminishing importance on the eighteenth-century market, where there was a broader context of activity.[4] In any case speculation was concentrated in the eighteenth century on a restricted part of the stocks and annuities traded in Amsterdam, being limited to the paper of the Dutch East and West India companies, the British East India and South Sea companies, the Bank of England, and some British government annuities.[5] Prices on those securities often responded to political, diplomatic, and financial news, and were thus sufficiently volatile to attract speculators. After the Fourth Anglo-Dutch War the futures trade was curtailed even in those securities without any apparent shift to other paper.[6]

Although futures trading concentrated on a few securities, the notes of foreign and domestic government loans and of an increasing variety of stock-substitution undertakings based on government paper were as readily subject to nonspeculative trading as joint-stock-company paper. During the eighteenth century trading impediments were gradually reduced, and by midcentury most government paper in circulation was held by the bearer (*in blanco*) rather than, as formerly, in the name of the investor (*op naam*).[7] As early as the 1690s foreign government loans were issued in bearer shares whose sale did not have to be recorded,[8] a necessity for *op naam* paper. And substitution ventures issued either type of paper, at the pleasure of the investor. These and other changes, which reduced the cost and trouble of trading, have been interpreted as evidence that speculative transactions were growing in importance. Certainly the shift toward bearer paper was an aid to futures deals, but it also assisted such non-speculative sales as estate liquidations. Fragmentary evidence on portfolio management practices suggests that during the second half of the century the dominant pattern was acquisition and retention.[9] Because, in known cases, neither rentiers nor the managers of stock-substitution ventures focused on trading for speculative or capital gains,[10] bearer paper may have been preferred for reasons altogether divorced from the greater ease of its use in futures transactions.

In addition to establishing an Exchange Bank to facilitate commerce, early-seventeenth-century Amsterdam authorities authorized the formation of a Municipal Loan Bank (1614) to regulate credit extended by private lombards and to control usury.[11] But early on in Amsterdam and slightly later in the case of the loan bank formed in Rotterdam, lending was oriented toward small sums on personal property and on modest quantities of commercial goods.[12] Because the Amsterdam loan bank granted credits of f. 500 or more on single transactions, merchants could return several times for fresh advances and thus raise large sums. But commercial credit could be obtained in commercial drafts and advances arranged between individuals on more attractive terms than those demanded by the loan bank.[13]

As these brief descriptions demonstrate, the tenor of public banking institutions in Amsterdam remained conservative throughout the period of expansion in trade and commercial finance. The Bank of Amsterdam was never intended to manipulate credit costs or extend credit to merchants and bankers; indeed its original ordinance provided penalties for overdrafts. Within the first two decades of its existence, the bank granted loans to the East India Company, the municipal treasury, and other public bodies, but the prohibition against private lending was maintained.[14] Public bank credit facilities remained restricted because requirements in the private sector were met through a highly individualistic structure of commercial and personal credit.

The preeminent instrument of commercial finance was the draft secured on commodities, for which large-scale exchange facilities were, by the middle of the eighteenth century, provided by a few leading merchant bankers specializing in the bill trade and for that reason able to charge low commission rates on remittances.[15] By about 1700, if not earlier, commercial practice in Amsterdam included discounting bills and the circulation of such paper far beyond the original parties by endorsement.[16] Conservative commercial practice permitted merchants to allot some overdraft credit on anticipated commodity exchanges or commodity and security speculations, but not all firms adhered strictly to such restraints. During the periodic crises of the century there were, consequently, failures tied directly to the overextension of acceptance credit.[17] In a similar fashion Amsterdam cashiers, who sometimes permitted clients short-term overdrafts, found greater difficulty in meeting their commitments during crises.

Another important credit source was composed of short- and long-term advances arranged among individuals on the security of commodities, stock and annuities, and real estate, but also granted in personal loans secured by notes. The evidence on this sector, which served principally internal needs, is fragmentary, but rentiers were involved on a larger scale than were merchants.[18] The sources – estate inventories, the records of the Office of Insolvent Estates (Desolate Boedelskamer), and merchant and rentier accounts – do not permit an estimate of either magnitude or trends, but it is clear that some rentiers devoted a large part of their resources to such advances.[19] Insurance underwriters also offered loans on security on more attractive terms than did the Municipal Loan Bank.[20]

Although evidence on interest rates charged in such transactions is also fragmentary, the downward movement characteristic of annuity rates in government borrowing was clearly also a feature of commercial credit.[21] From about 1750 into the 1780s longer-term personal and secured advances were customarily extended at returns of 2.5 to 4 percent,[22] so that credit could be raised on promissory notes and re-lent to foreign governments at a profit. Discount rates are seldom encountered for the Amsterdam market. In Paris in the latter decades of the century the discount varied between 4 and 6 percent in normal times,[23] and the ties between Amsterdam and Paris in short-term paper were close. The range in Amsterdam may by then have been slightly greater, perhaps 2 to 6 percent.[24] Advances on commodities, personal loans, and long-term loans to domestic governments all offered yields below those available in most loans to foreign governments, whereas the discount rate probably fluctuated within the range encompassed by all those transactions.

The private credit sector found no difficulty in broadening the security regarded as acceptable to include foreign government annuities, and thus proved adaptable to the shift of the Amsterdam market toward government finance. But its individualistic character made Amsterdam susceptible to liquidity crises that tended to be prolonged because of the lack of effective management in their early stages.[25] The sharpest crises experienced between 1740 and the wars of the French Revolution were those of 1763 and 1772–3. In both cases, and in a commercial depression during the Fourth Anglo-Dutch War (1780–4), merchants and speculators found it difficult to raise cash on satisfactory terms because assets used to secure credit had lost value and because of a general crisis of confidence in credits outstanding. Creditors responded to price movements by calling in secured and unsecured advances or by demanding an increase in loan backing. Firms and individuals unable to meet those demands were forced into bankruptcy, provoking a backward chain of attempts at settlement. The traditional response to such a situation within the European commercial community was to mobilize outside resources for at least those houses whose assets inspired confidence in terms of precrisis values, thereby diminishing anxieties among creditors and encouraging the restoration of precrisis margins and interest rates. Such support was generally slow and difficult to gather and it was seldom summoned before failures in one center had begun to provoke anxiety elsewhere.

During the Seven Years' War the credit structure, oriented in peacetime toward commodity exchanges, expanded to meet wartime government needs, and the commercial paper supply rose sharply. Britain and France used drafts to forward subsidies to allies, and although those bills were backed by bullion shipments their introduction encouraged the appearance in Amsterdam and Hamburg of credit instruments divorced from shipments of bullion or other goods. Simultaneously, peacetime trade channels were disrupted, to the advantage of merchants in neutral states, who were able to expand transactions in bullion and deliveries of war matériel. Shortages in some commodities increased prices. The conclusion of the war, a sharp fall in commodity prices, and disarray in the bullion trade produced by wartime monetary debasement by some belligerents provoked a crisis.[26] Houses that had taken advantage of acceptance credit possibilities available during the war found their positions untenable, and hastened to call in their assets. Late in July 1763 two major Amsterdam firms (A. Joseph & Co. and Gebr. de Neufville) suspended payments, and even some houses that had resisted tempting credit opportunities were faced with the threat of having to liquidate assets on unfavorable terms to satisfy creditors.

In the end Amsterdam was cleansed of some overly ambitious houses and the panic restricted to a few Dutch and German commercial centers. A rapid recovery restored confidence in the inherent strength of existing credit practices, and as a result proposals advanced during the crisis for a local credit cooperative came to nothing.[27] But the idea of calling on stable houses and rentiers to build a public fund to assist firms caught short by a decline of commodity prices did not die.

In fact existing credit practices were more fragile than was recognized in 1763. Within less than a decade the Amsterdam market faced another crisis, this one provoked by overextensions in British East India Company stock, reproducing developments in London where a speculative boom had collapsed in 1772, and by short-term deterioration in the West Indian trade, which led to the suspension of service on many plantation loans negotiated during the 1750s and 1760s on coffee and sugar anticipations. The speculative boom in East India Company stock coincided with an expansion in acceptance credit and, when both commodity and stock prices fell, overextended firms were forced into liquidation. On this occasion the failures began in December 1772 in spectacular fashion with the suspension of payments by Clifford & Zoonen, one of the most prestigious banking houses in the city.[28] Once again international support was mobilized to save other threatened firms, but Amsterdam merchants turned also to a cooperative fund organized within the locale. In January 1773 a circle of houses led in the formation of a subscription loan bank styled the "Fonds tot maintiën van het publiek crediet," and that institution, with municipal support, extended short-term credit on commodities and domestic government securities.[29] The lesson of 1773 was taken to be that acceptance credit was hazardous, and there was substantial contraction in that area. But the conclusion of the crisis restored confidence in the individualistic structure of private credit, and the subscription loan bank was dissolved later in 1773.

Because the crisis had called to account a number of firms overextended in speculations and threatened investors overcommitted in plantation loans, it is plausible to suggest that rentiers may have put another interpretation on it. During the 1770s stock-substitution ventures moved away from portfolios concentrated in plantation loans, domestic government annuities, or the British funds and toward diversification. Such a trend represented an obvious response to the collapse of both West Indian commodities and British East India Company stock, but it also had the effect of channeling attention toward other investment sectors, and in particular toward loans to foreign governments. Diversification was further encouraged by unfavorable comments on British credit worthiness that appeared more frequently during the 1770s.

In 1781, during the Fourth Anglo-Dutch War and more general North Atlantic tension, disruption of Dutch commercial routes led to trade depression. The subscription bank of 1773 was revived under the style "Stads-Beleeningkamer," and on this occasion maintained after the depression faded.[30] But the resources assigned to it would not permit it to supersede private credit channels even in short-term lending. There was, therefore, no fundamental alteration in Amsterdam's credit structure and no correction of the basic instability of commercial finance in that city. Because the Stads-Beleeningkamer did not become a central bank able to manipulate credit practices or costs,[31] future corrective measures remained focused on the mobilization of international assistance. Dutch houses were sometimes called on to lend support to other centers, and apparently for that reason Amsterdam merchants remained confident in the reliability of international cooperation out of self-interest.[32]

As the capital market shifted toward government lending, the individualistic credit structure of commercial finance remained intact. Crises and depressions underscored the weaknesses of unsecured credit and of advances backed by too low a margin on commodities subject to sharp price fluctuations, but the domestic and foreign loans of the same era were themselves not secured on more reliable assets. A shift away from acceptance credit was a step toward stability, but in assimilating securities into the assets acceptable for mortgages, creditors accepted backing that had a more fragile foundation than commodities or real estate, for government securities rested only on the good faith of the borrower.

Government finance

The Amsterdam market apparatus. Eighteenth-century European governments used credit instruments that resist unqualified translation into twentieth-century terms.[33] In the *obligatie*, the most common type in the Dutch Republic, an advance was raised through the issue of bearer shares on stated security and at a specified yield, but there was not necessarily any fixed term. When the redemption date was unspecified or when a loan with a specified term was prolonged, the *obligatie* was in fact a perpetual annuity, redeemable at the will of the borrower and thus similar to the British perpetual redeemable annuity and the French *rente perpétuelle.*[34]

On the other hand, governments opening foreign loans were not customarily permitted such latitude in specifying redemption terms. In Amsterdam foreign governments were usually obliged to establish ultimate reimbursement dates in debentures.[35] In most cases loans were extended for eight to fourteen years, with reimbursement spread over the four to six years preceding the due date. Nominally the notes of such issues were bonds, long-term paper secured on specified assets, usually tax anticipations or amortization funds based on tax or other revenues, with a given due date. But foreign borrowers copied the practice of prolonging loans either by deferring settlement at the due date or by absorbing the old loan in a fresh issue. Such prolonged loans led to the accumulation of debts of the same type maintained by borrowers with access to domestic capital or to foreign capital channeled through domestic markets. In practice if not in legal theory prolongations were redeemable at the will of the borrower and were thus perpetual annuities.[36]

Investors and borrowers alike distinguished perpetual-annuity loans from term and life annuities, both of which included interest and reimbursements in annual or semiannual payments, the former over a specified term and the latter during the life of a nominee. Those loans were "self-liquidating" in that there was no separate reimbursement of principal, and the sum of the annual payment of course exceeded the interest yield of a perpetual annuity.

In each of the three broad types of long-term credit instruments used by government – perpetual, term, and life annuities – the nominal cost of borrowing could be made identical in given issues, but contemporary practice did not use those formulas interchangeably. The term annuity could be equalized in cost with the perpetual annuity more readily than either form could be made equal in cost to the life annuity because of the tie of life annuity loans to the longevity of nominees. Term-annuity loans cost the sum of the annuity paid out, an altogether predictable amount when a loan term was established and adhered to, but in the eighteenth century there were advantages in shifting costs to the future. Insofar as service on the term annuity included payments of interest and principal, it was by its very nature less attractive to borrowers facing financial stringency. That was perhaps sufficient reason to prefer the perpetual annuity except where the borrower could confidently predict revenue surpluses. But the domination of the perpetual annuity over other loan formats during the second half of the century suggests that debtors were at least intuitively aware of the degree to which the real cost of service and reimbursement could be diminished in an inflationary period by the prolongation of loans or the issue of very-long-term loans.

Both debtors and creditors found it difficult to calculate the return that should be established in a life annuity in order for its interest to equal that of a term or perpetual annuity. The crucial factor absent in the seventeenth century was accurate information about life expectancy. Toward the end of that century mortality records and the probability theory necessary to interpret them for annuitants of different ages became available, and governments that had used life-annuity loans and variations thereon learned that they had been paying higher-than-necessary returns. Governments in relatively sound financial positions tended thereafter to abandon that format, but some states and municipalities issued life annuities throughout the eighteenth century.

On the Amsterdam market lenders distinguished among borrowers, demanding, for example, higher returns on loans negotiated for foreign governments, and varying the return required in the issues of both domestic and foreign borrowers according to their perceptions of financial stability and credit worthiness.[37] With the advantage of hindsight it is clear that those distinctions did not reflect actual differences among borrowers, and it is also clear that in general lenders fared poorly in protecting themselves against defects in the information to which they had access about government budgets and accumulated indebtedness.

In commercial finance the key factors influencing interest rates, the availability of capital and the demand for credit, were reflected in the range of current discount rates on commercial drafts.[38] Although the discount rate served commercial finance as an index of capital supply, that short-term commercial credit standard could not be applied to long-term government lending without an adjustment for which the quality of information was seldom as sound as that for drafts. Like variations from the current discount rate for good paper, returns on individual government loans responded to capital availability. Those returns also reflected investors' images of the solidity of the borrower and sometimes that of the banking house managing a loan and the agents selling notes in it. In government lending interest rates varied upward from the return on paper of the highest quality, represented by the notes of certain domestic borrowers. But it was often more difficult to assess the credit position of states than that of parties liable in a given bill, whereas capital supply, evaluated daily in the discount market, was hard to project because large-scale loans were comparatively infrequent.

A limited number of firms, in some cases the same houses dominant in commercial paper transfers, controlled the issue of most loans to European governments. But loans to domestic government remained chiefly in the hands of public officials, whereas houses outside the select company of bankers managing most foreign loans were active in organizing stock-substitution ventures, loans to trading, industrial, and agricultural enterprises, and advances to some governments. Had the few firms exercising nearly monopolistic control over advances to foreign governments been informed about the market's receptivity to the issues of all borrowers, then the information necessary to adjust long-term interest rates in response to capital flow and to the financial integrity of borrowers would have been concentrated in those houses. To the degree that each firm specializing in the issues of a given state became knowledgeable about the financial position of that debtor and about investors' responses to that debtor's loans, that was the case. But much vital information remained unavailable to those firms and to investors.

The periodical press of the Dutch Republic devoted substantial attention to dispatches about domestic and foreign political developments, and such news, and in particular informed speculation about the prospects of war or peace, was important for investment planning. In the latter decades of the eighteenth century the important journals for the business community were the *Amsterdamsche courant*, which appeared three times weekly, and the *Maandelijkse nederlandsche mercurius*[39] and *Nederlandsche jaarboeken* (from 1766 the *Nieuwe nederlandsche jaarboeken*), both of which appeared monthly.[40] Those periodicals published information of direct value in commerce and finance. The *Courant* usually listed prices on securities involved in futures transactions,[41] but not until the autumn of 1792 did any journal regularly include prices on a wider range of securities.[42] Both the *Courant* and the *Mercurius* published notices or lists covering the securities, real estate, and personal property sold in weekly public auctions, and both also included notices or lists of notes drawn for liquidation in the lotteries that settled due dates on individual shares in government loans. All three journals also published official notices about domestic government finance, announcements of public loans or lotteries, and the text of legal decrees and municipal, provincial, and Generality decisions affecting commerce and banking. Foreign loan announcements were rarely included, although notices of changes in management and of upcoming dividend or interest payments were entered by the responsible firms.

Not until the *Prijs-courant der effecten* appeared on 2 August 1796 did regularly published securities quotations covering something approaching the broad range of paper in active trade become available. Before that point, and before 1792 for the more restricted list in the *Mercurius,* investors depended for current prices on direct contact with the *beurs,* on personal contact with their brokers, and on occasional lists compiled by brokers and booksellers, such as in the event of extraordinary tax levies.[43] Some brokers circulated printed lists of selected securities with current prices filled in by hand, but only a few of those survive. It remains possible that there was a more extensive exchange of such information than is suggested by fragmentary survivals, but the absence of any *beurs* periodical before 1796 indicates that there was insufficient demand for regular price quotations. Except for the stocks and annuities that were the usual objects of futures transactions, neither investors nor firms managing loans required news on short-term fluctuations,[44] and thus little attention was given to price shifts and disparities among foreign loans.[45]

Neither the political nor the commercial news available in Dutch periodicals was sufficient to evaluate credit worthiness among debtor states. Nor were government revenue and expenditure accounts often published elsewhere. Budget projections sometimes appeared in political-economy tracts and in the journals of inquisitive travelers,[46] but these estimates do not consistently agree with subsequent reconstructions. Without access to privileged information writers were obliged to be satisfied with data gleaned from unreliable sources, usually from one another. Where they deal with both revenues and expenditures, their projections tend more frequently to cite surpluses than deficits.[47] If bankers or investors consulted such sources, and there is no evidence either way, they did not gain trustworthy information.

Incomplete data on government finance could also lead to misappraisals, as is most strikingly demonstrated by comparisons in the 1770s and 1780s portraying Britain as a weaker debtor than France. Britain alone in Europe then used accounting procedures that permitted accurate annual budget statements and tallies of the scope and cost of long-term debts.[48] In a market accustomed to defective information at best, accurate balances revealing substantial deficits were detrimental. Elsewhere such data were not so much jealously guarded as seldom assembled. In the Dutch Republic, for instance, British government accounting methods were never adopted completely. When the Batavian regime, which came to power in 1795, appointed committees to investigate the financial position of Amsterdam and the province of Holland, those committees discovered that public accounts were muddled to the point that even retrospective balances could not readily be struck. Moreover, in most states public revenues remained the preserve of absolutist rulers. Where the assets of the state were the personal assets of the king investors had little or no accurate information about the budgetary situation. Secrecy and sloppy accounting procedures prevented lenders and Dutch firms managing foreign loans from getting information that would have permitted them to distribute states along a scale of credit worthiness in the fashion that individual debtors paid higher or lower interest rates according to estimates by their peers of the risks involved in any particular transaction.

Accurate data were also wanting about capital supply. No independent indexes of investment capital existed, and contemporary statements about capital supply usually took the form of imprecise comments referring without elaboration to abundant or tight credit.[49] More precise estimates are occasionally available, such as in a 1788 memorandum by Thomas Jefferson. Citing the merchant banker Jacob van Staphorst of N. & J. van Staphorst, Jefferson indicated that "there are about 14. millions of florins, new money, placed in loans in Holland every year, being the savings of individuals out of their annual revenues &c. Besides this there are every year reimbursements of old loans from some quarter or other, to be replaced at interest in some new loan."[50] Gouverneur Morris was told in March 1790 that Dutch capitalists received annually some £2 million (or f. 23.3 million at current rates) in interest from foreign loans.[51] If it is taken to reflect all foreign government loans and not merely issues negotiated in the Republic, Morris's information, implying a return of 3.6 to 4.7 percent, falls at the lower end of the range of probable earnings on the estimated balance in the early 1790s, f. 500 to 650 million. Other accounts exaggerated reality, reaching f. 50 to 60 million plus whatever was received from British and French annuities.[52] Annual proceeds from foreign government loans at that point more likely totaled about 4.5

percent of the outstanding balance or, according to the estimate reached here, f. 22.5 to 29.25 million.

Until 1793 the long-term trend on the Amsterdam market was toward an increasing capital supply, a situation that eased considerably the task of projecting resources available for a given issue. But short-term fluctuations, often associated with diplomatic events,[53] sometimes forced the adjustment of interest rates, the addition of premiums, or an extended period of subscriptions. Both borrowers and intermediaries understood that lenders regarded the subscription experience of a loan as a measure of credit worthiness and financial standing. But when subscriptions lagged, or when the managing house had to close an issue without having raised the sum sought, such information was sometimes withheld from the public. As a consequence none of the parties in such transactions, neither borrowers nor intermediaries nor lenders, had a reliable grasp of trends across the market. Information about the success of recent issues could be centrally important in establishing new loan terms, but as long as the secular trend of capital supply was toward abundance and evidence of failures was obscured, market conditions favored low returns.

Information defects affected borrowers in that loans were sometimes opened on more generous terms than necessary to attract capital, as evident in issues filled in a few days or weeks rather than more gradually over the several months during which most loans were left open. But in government finance the Amsterdam market was biased in favor of borrowers so that, with much greater frequency, lenders suffered from defective or piecemeal information.

The fundamental agents of international government finance were three – the banker, the broker, and the commission agent.[54] Each of those intermediaries requires some elaboration before returning to the matter of market bias toward borrowers.

In eighteenth-century usage a firm was designated a banking house because it dealt on a grand scale in commercial paper, drawing, accepting, transferring, and perhaps also discounting bills. Banking houses seldom restricted their activities to the bill trade, dealing also in commodity and bullion exchanges and speculations, executing orders for clients, and, on the Amsterdam market, floating loans for foreign states, rulers, large landowners, and trading and industrial enterprises.[55] As opportunities for negotiating foreign loans broadened after midcentury any earlier precision in the use of the term "banker" to indicate a house engaged in the bill trade seems to have faded. In the meantime, however, firms successful in raising loans for foreign powers did not withdraw from commerce but maintained established ties and, when possible, added to them.[56]

In commercial finance as in commodity and bullion transactions merchants and bankers sometimes developed geographical specializations while still maintaining peripatetic interests. With the transition to government lending, houses experienced in a given area had an obvious advantage when states, landowners, or commercial and industrial enterprises in that area sought to negotiate loans. The pattern established in Austrian loans managed by the Widow Jean Deutz & Co. in 1695 and thereafter was duplicated not only in the forms used but also in the tendency toward monopolistic control by one house or a limited circle of houses. In that instance control was acquired as a result of Deutz's agency for selling mercury from the imperial mines. More general commercial contacts permitted other firms to control the loans of other states, and by the 1780s most foreign governments seeking credit had settled on the banker or bankers to whom they would customarily apply.[57] There was little leeway for firms excluded from that circle to acquire entry to it, although there was sometimes intense competition within the circle to acquire or retain agencies.

The banking house with the advantage of long-standing expertise and contacts in a given area had still to meet certain requisites before it could secure a loan agency. First and foremost was the reputation that a firm acquired only after several years of prudent enterprise in which even the suggestion of rash business practice was absent.[58] A house also had to meet standards concerning the scale of its activities, and thus to be able credibly to suggest that it could market and administer a large-scale loan. Lesser firms occasionally secured loan agencies, but borrowers appear generally to have understood that there were only a few houses that could handle issues competently. Investors also preferred firms meeting these and other standards. According to an insider's memorandum of 1790, investors distinguished among houses on the basis of the confidence which a firm inspired, that arising from the "soins que ces maisons prennent à n'offrir que des emprunts solides & a veiller à l'èxécution de toutes les formes."[59]

For practical reasons the banker had to be accustomed to commercial credit usages, of course, but also able readily to transfer large sums to the borrower. In some loans a house was persuaded in return for better terms to guarantee the success of part or all of the issue, and there the prudent firm had to have the capital or credit necessary to cover that guarantee if the loan failed to find subscribers. Furthermore, subscriptions were usually paid in over several months whereas anticipated proceeds might be due at or soon after the date of issue. In some cases the banker had to arrange short-term credit to transfer sums not yet paid in.

The large banking house with long-standing integrity met these conditions, but to them was added a requirement focusing on the pace at which subscriptions could be secured. To test the market for a given issue the banker engaged one or more brokers, firms specializing in this area of their activities as wholesale intermediaries not for the sale of notes but for evaluating the availability of capital and its readiness to flow toward a projected loan. The broker also organized the coterie of commission agents, firms that had behind them investors prepared to follow their advice in the selection of securities, and that actually marketed notes.[60] The functions of banker, broker, and commission agent were not, however, as distinct as this description implies. The banker also acted as broker and commission agent, and brokers occasionally marketed small blocks of notes, serving therefore as commission agents.[61]

Sales were arranged in contracts with commission agents, although those were sometimes concluded only after a period of public subscriptions at the banker's office. In those contracts, which might be settled at the opening of a loan or might stretch over a series of consecutive compacts, the commission agents agreed to place a block of notes.[62] But such arrangements were not inviolate, for their terms could be altered when placements were more rapid or slower than originally forecast. In the contracts the terms of an agent's participation were established: the commission, the period during which subscriptions were to be paid in,[63] and any provision on rebating or on the distribution of interest accruing between the opening of the loan and the date or dates on which subscriptions were due.

Late-seventeenth- and early-eighteenth-century marketing details are unclear, but it appears that bankers relied principally on direct contacts with investors, on sales conducted in the firm's own offices, and, in some cases, on receivers general who had developed links with investors by marketing loans for the Generality, the provinces, and other bodies. Such methods were increasingly unsatisfactory as foreign lending expanded. By the 1780s the largest houses had evolved a system that combined exploitation of the firm's own links with investors with large-scale sales through commission agents who marketed paper within their own circle of investors or enlisted intermediary brokers, particularly for sales outside Amsterdam itself.

Banking houses able to mobilize brokers and commission agents more readily than competitors had an advantage in issuing loans because they had readier access to investors. Although brokers were systematically employed to circularize commission agents, some firms that, year after year, opened large-scale loans accumulated what was effectively a clientele of commission agents participating in issues under their management. And in small loans and negotiations the managing house's success was often tied closely to previous commission agencies in which the firm had expanded its following among investors.

The most active house in organizing foreign government loans during the 1770s and 1780s was Hope & Co., which, in different periods, controlled or shared control over the management of issues for Sweden, Poland, Russia, and Spain. The available lists of Hope's commission agents indicate that that house and its associates used a circle of some fifty agents all told, of whom about twenty-five were markedly more active than the others.[64] Although most of Hope's agents operated small firms with limited activities, the more active twenty-five included ten firms – J. Menkema & Zn., A. van Ketwich, P. Stadnitski, Isaac van Eyk, Albert Strockel, Widow E. Croese & Co., S. & D. Saportas, D. W. van Vloten (of Utrecht), van Maurick & Willink, and H. van Maarseveen – which at one time or another between 1770 and 1801 opened loans on their own account. Moreover, some firms less active in marketing notes, among them J. Bouman, A. Brinkman, and A. & S. Boas (of The Hague), and the broker H. Volkmar, also opened loans or stock-substitution undertakings on their own account. These were most of the up-and-coming firms on the Amsterdam market,[65] the energetic and ambitious houses exploiting openings in government lending, municipal finance, and stock substitution from the foundation provided by their commission agencies. Hope & Co. thus built a circle of industrious entrepreneurs able to market loan paper more rapidly and on a larger scale than other agents, and to an important degree that firm's prominence in government finance was the product of its adeptness in attracting such a coterie of agents.[66] Other bankers also used such intermediaries, and thereby participated in a marketing system with broad and effective links to investors.

The negotiation of terms between borrower and banker was customarily handled by special envoys dispatched to Amsterdam or in correspondence between the banker and treasury officials.[67] In all cases the banker was more knowledgeable about market conditions and for that reason had an advantage in such negotiations. On the other hand, it was a firm's task to build a relationship of trust with the borrower's agents so that the borrower would accept the banker's advice. Where that developed, the banker dominated loan negotiations. But most borrowers occasionally sought advances on other capital markets, with the result that markets were to some degree brought into competition with one another to provide credit on terms attractive to debtors.

Increasingly during the 1760s and 1770s the scale of resources required for deficit finance forced most states to concentrate on Amsterdam. Other markets could absorb loans only on a smaller scale and with less frequency, and such conditions were attractive only to powers whose overall requirements were comparatively modest. Sweden, for example, was a peripatetic borrower, employing several markets and sometimes several houses in the same market. Although Amsterdam remained the chief source of foreign credit, Sweden provoked competitiveness there more successfully than did most states. Between 1775 and 1789 Sweden raised fifteen Dutch loans totaling about f. 24.5 million (including prolongations) at an average annuity of no more than 4.16 percent,[68] a level that reflected neither its financial position nor the risks assumed by lenders as a result of Gustavus III's ambitious foreign policy.[69]

But no state secured more favorable terms than the United States. Loans raised by Congress early in the 1780s paid premium yields and especially generous commissions. Even so those terms hardly reflected the financial position of the Confederation. With the adoption of the Constitution the federal government extracted still more favorable conditions. Unlike most other states, the American republic handled credit negotiations through its regular diplomatic agents. The first of those, John Adams, established the precedent of informing himself about trends on the capital market and about terms accorded other borrowers.[70] That knowledge was then used to press bankers for better conditions. Although Adams had turned at first to firms whose political affiliations were congenial, he had in the process assigned the American agency to particularly aggressive houses anxious to secure and retain a position in the lucrative world of organizing loans for foreign governments. For that reason and because of a threatened transfer of America's affairs to another market, the bankers opened on their own initiative in 1790 a loan whose terms were dramatically more attractive than had been customary.[71] In the process they anticipated an improvement in Congress's financial position that did not materialize until later in the decade. Although Sweden and the United States deviated from established custom to gain leverage in loan negotiations, all debtor states benefited from a bias in the structure of the Amsterdam market that favored them.

The principal matters at stake in loans were the amount of the loan; the term; the interest rate; and the level of commission to be awarded the banker, broker, and commission agents together for the issue of a loan, the marketing of shares, and long-term management.[72] The amount to be sought could be arrived at by comparing the borrower's needs to judgments about capital availability. Although a borrower might have in mind a range within which a loan was to be sought, such a consideration by no means always determined the size of an issue. The banker might discourage too great expectations of the market, but a firm was equally likely to discourage too modest expectations.

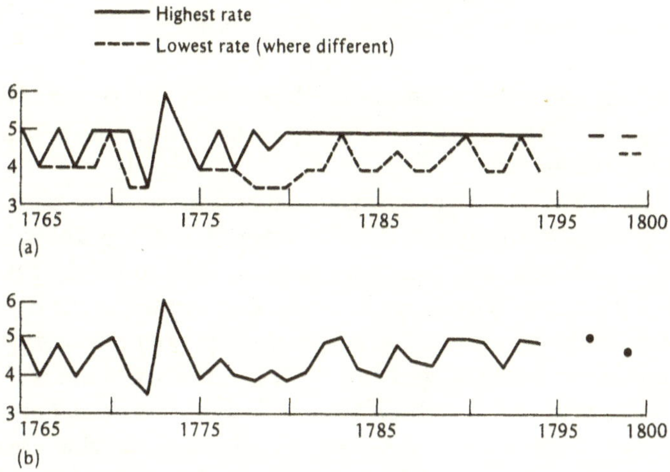

Chart 2-1. (a) The range of annuity rates in loans to foreign governments, 1765–1800. (b) Average annuity rates in loans to foreign governments, 1765–1800.

Because European governments tended to redeem old loans out of fresh issues, the minimum amount to be sought was the amount coming due, to which might be added enough to cover costs. But bankers sometimes encouraged borrowers to avoid repeated small-scale loans in favor of impressively large issues. The sum preferred by some houses for individual issues, even when a series of loans could be anticipated, was f. 3 million, and by the end of the 1780s that had become the most common denomination of loans.

Having settled on the sum to be sought, a fixed amount stated in loan announcements and not thereafter increased without public notice, the negotiators had still to fix other matters. The term was usually established within the range of eight to fourteen years, although some borrowers preferred shorter or longer periods, up to twenty years. Interest rates were generally determined by the return on prior issues of the same borrower or other borrowers in a similar position.[73] During the second half of the century foreign government loan yields fell almost exclusively between 3.5 and 5 percent (Chart 2-1).[74] Average returns (also in Chart 2-1) reflect fluctuations that, over most of the period, were produced by differences in the assumed credit worthiness of individual government borrowers and changes in the incidence of loan issues by more or less credit-worthy states rather than by shifts in capital supply. Both the narrow range of annuity charges and the tendency to move toward stability apparent in Chart 2-1 are evidence of defects in the information acquired by bankers and investors about the financial resources of borrowing states.

The prevailing range of annuity rates was narrow because investors generally found returns between 4 and 5 percent acceptable. To some measure that was because of the flexibility left to bankers by customarily larger commission charges, the percentage of the loan amount allowed by the borrower to compensate intermediaries. Brokers dealing with loans on a wholesale basis got ¼ to ½ percent for their part, whereas commission agents usually got from 1 to 2 percent, depending on the ease with which a loan was placed.[75] Because total commission charges usually came to between 4 and 7 percent, the largest share was clearly reserved to the banker, who determined the allocation of percentages. But commission agents could be allotted a higher percentage when placements moved slowly, and it was by that inducement that bankers could spur agents to greater efforts among investors. Even so the largest portion usually fell to the banker and was his source of profit. To that the banker could add brokerage and commission-agent percentages on any part of a loan arranged and marketed without the aid of intermediaries. Once established, the amount, term, interest and commission rates, and security behind a loan and any other provisions were recorded in a debenture, which, after approval by the borrower, formed the contract among borrower, lender, and intermediaries. Theoretically negotiable as the debtor's pledge, debentures were deposited with notaries for safekeeping.

The terms of a given loan were announced in printed notices that were solicitations for subscription.[76] Those prospectuses conveyed the information in the debenture to which investors were to have access – amount, interest, term and redemption provisions, security, and any other features peculiar to a particular issue. Commission charges and their allocation were always omitted, leaving both investors and borrowers without data that would have permitted them to compare the actual cost of raising loans faced by various borrowers. As a result there was imperfect correlation between the sum of annuity rates and commis-

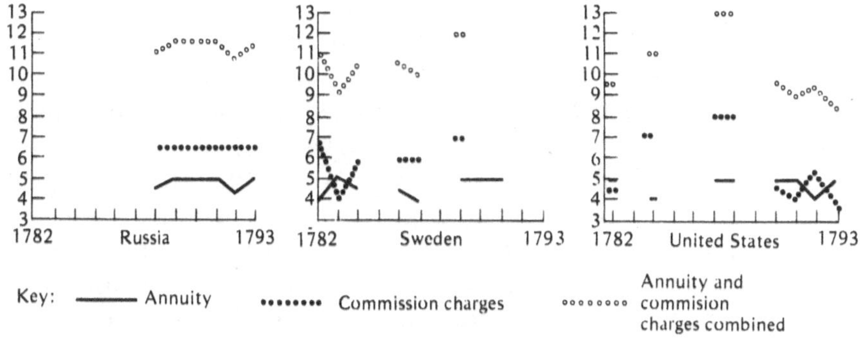

Chart 2-2. Average commission charges and annuity rates in Russian, Swedish, and United States loans, 1782–93.

sion charges and the credit worthiness of different borrowers. Some states achieved substantial savings in one area whereas the other remained stable.[77] Nor did commission charges alone or commission charges and annuity rates together consistently indicate the relative volume of capital available for foreign loans. As Chart 2-2 indicates, these rates, taken singly or together, did not respond in unison to any one set of stimuli.[78] Even when such factors as differences in the security behind loans are taken into consideration no consistent rationale behind variations can be found.

The Russian loans of 1788–93, all managed by Hope & Co., reflect a rational approach in that commission charges were stable, suggesting fixed costs and reasonable commissions, whereas the annuity varied with capital supply and a changing perception of Russia's credit standing. In the cases of Sweden and the United States, however, interest rates varied little despite sharp changes in solidity, and commission charges fluctuated widely. There loan intermediaries appropriated for themselves benefits drawn from what were, from the perspective of the investing public, no more than slight changes in capital supply, credit standing, or security.

Pressure toward low returns produced by capital abundance and information restraints was strengthened by that appropriation out of commission charges. Moreover, even limited competition among bankers for control of the issue of loans created additional pressure toward lower annuity rates. All governments borrowing in Amsterdam raised loans that, in light of the secular inflation of the period and arbitrary service and redemption suspensions during the Revolutionary and Napoleonic wars, paid returns below what was necessary to maintain real value and cover interest. The advantage of retrospective knowledge put aside, some borrowers were still distinctly more favored than others. Domestic governments usually paid between 1.5 and 5 percent, that is, less than what was demanded of foreign borrowers. In fact the preference for domestic government loans was more pronounced than those percentages suggest because most issues of that type paid between 2.5 and 4 percent. There was more variation in foreign loan returns, but over the period examined the annuity paid by foreign borrowers judged initially to be more secure moved toward that paid by less secure debtors without the latter group paying higher returns. Thus by the 1780s all foreign loans were grouped at 4.5- to 5-percent annuities, although there were still significant differences in financial standing among the governments raising loans in Amsterdam.

Posthumus's index of wholesale commodity prices indicates an annual inflationary rate during the decade from 1780–4 to 1790–4 of not quite 3 percent, a higher rate thereafter, some 6 percent per annum to 1795-9, and then approximate stability until 1810–14. The average effective return on a portfolio distributed across a selected group of domestic and foreign loans (Chart 2-3) increased between September 1792 and January 1797 from 3.97 to 6.66 percent, or at an annual rate above 10 percent.[79] But only new investments enjoyed those increasing effective returns. Since most investors bought to hold rather than to seek turnover gains, they benefited little from inflating effective yields. For the stable portion of portfolios the annual inflation of prices was greater than the average effective return of 1792 and returns on new loans were appreciating behind commodity prices.

Credit tightened in 1793 and the characteristic features of the earlier market became muddled. Distinct congregations of domestic borrowers regarded as secure (the Generality, the provinces of Utrecht and Holland, and the Dutch East India Company) and, separately, of foreign governments (Russia, the United States, and Austria) evident in 1792 (Chart 2-3) were con-

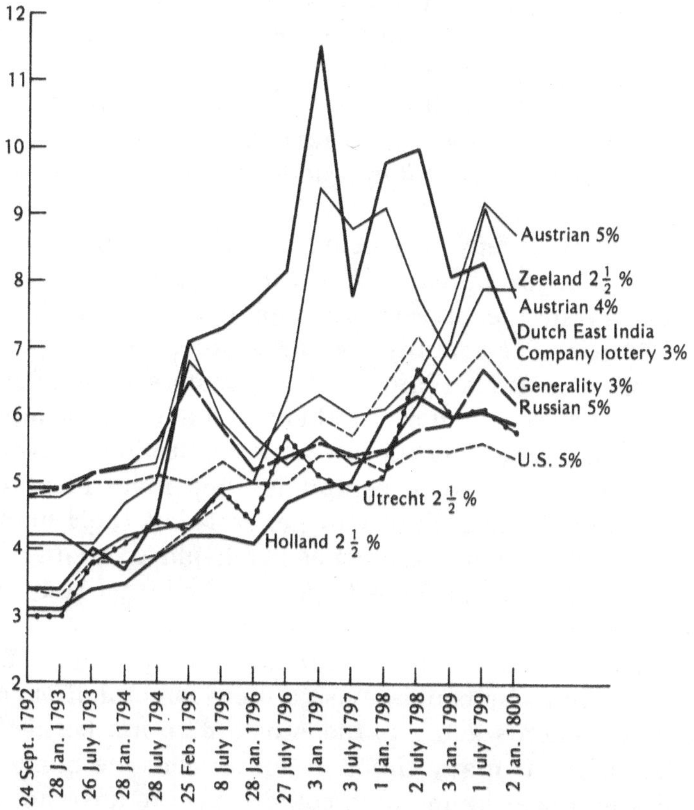

Chart 2-3. Effective annual returns on selected foreign and domestic loans, 1792–1800.

fused thereafter when the traditional preference for all Dutch governments collapsed in the face of wartime financial pressures and uncertainties. By 1796 investors were distinguishing among borrowers according to more realistic appraisals of credit worthiness, preferring stronger domestic institutions like the provinces of Holland and Utrecht and the Generality, and foreign powers as yet little affected by the European conflict (like the United States and Russia). In the meantime there was some improvement in the budgetary data available to lenders, particularly for the Republic itself, and that together with the war, which began in 1792, favored higher returns on outstanding paper and on new loans.

In the prewar period Dutch investors had suffered from a structural relationship between bankers and borrowers that favored the interests of debtors. In negotiating annuity yields, bankers were the agents of both borrower and lender. Had the pressure that each party was able to exert been more or less equivalent, then foreign loan yields would have represented an equitable compromise of interests. But in practice those pressures were not equivalent.

Bankers were chiefly interested in the profit that could be made from negotiating loans. The ultimate source of gain from any issue lay in the investment capital mobilized for it, but lenders did not allot commissions or pursue their interests collectively. On the Amsterdam market investors were seldom organized beyond the extent of the clientele following the advice of a commission agent. There were some institutional investors – estates in trust, insurance companies and investment trusts, and substitution undertakings in general – but their managers neither controlled enough securities nor displayed enough expertise in manipulating portfolios to protect the larger body of individual investors.

The borrower, on the other hand, not only could offer the banker more but also could devise a more forceful offer. As European governments going to the Amsterdam market for credit went not once but many times in succession, the banker who satisfied a borrower in one loan could expect to have an advantage in subsequent issues. Moreover, the banker bargained with the borrower's agents on two percentages, the annuity and the commission. A low commission and a high or a low annuity yielded little for the banker because other intermediaries were customarily paid minimum percentages that did not necessarily decline when the total commission was reduced. A loan paying a high return and a high commission was entirely satisfactory to the banker but unappealing to the borrower. But an issue paying a low yield and a high commission satisfied both banker and borrower, and that was the most common formula.

A borrower might seek to reduce both the annuity and the commission rate, but the difference in long-term costs made the annuity a more important consideration. A ½-percent reduction in yield counterbalanced even a 2-percent increase in commission, as a calculation will show. In a f. 3 million loan a 2 percent greater commission cost f. 60,000 whereas a ½-percent decrease in annuity saved f. 15,000 each year over the term of the loan, rarely under four years.

The borrower's influence on commissions sufficed by itself to incline a banker toward serving the borrower first, but that was not the only feature favoring debtors. There were also commercial and financial inducements, such as insider's information on policies that would influence commodity or security prices or the outright grant of commercial privileges, which could be dangled before the firm that served a borrower well. In addition, particularly in wartime, bankers might be given control over the large-scale transfers necessary to pay troops or provide military supplies abroad. And there were, moreover, private favors to be dispensed, the prestige conveyed by personal contact with royal personages, even patents of nobility.

Although there were skillful rentiers who followed market trends carefully and managed their portfolios in such a way as to modify this structural bias, loan intermediaries generally disparaged the acuity of investors. One of the prevailing fictions on the Amsterdam market was that a given loan was the last contemplated by a borrower. In the Russian loans of 1788–93, Hope & Co. took particular care "to make each loan appear to be the last and to convince the public that peace between Russia and her enemies would bring the whole affair to an end."[80] But the partners knew that Russia wished to open an extended series of issues, and in fact preparations for subsequent loans were usually underway before the completion of the one current. The ease with which a banker could deceive the investing public created only disdain for it.

The investor's principal contact with foreign loans was through the commission agent or securities broker. Although notes could be bought directly from the banker or from one or another agent without a rentier having to join that agent's clientele, a substantial part, perhaps the majority, of total sales was handled between commission agents and their clienteles or subclienteles, that is, investors to whom they had access through intermediary brokers. Just as the relationship between banker and borrower was built on trust, so the tie between agent and investor evolved out of the confidence that the agent's investment advice inspired. Without intending to be the guardian of investors' interests, commission agents filled the only role that might have served investors effectively on a collective scale. But, like bankers, some commission agents realized that investors often followed advice without independent inquiry and also adopted a disparaging view of their clientele, regarding them as so many sheep content to follow a bellwether.

A 1788 memorandum probably written by Pieter Stadnitski, a commission agent of wide experience, indicates that "the wealthy public" seldom compared investment opportunities.[81] Habit counted more than rational appraisal in determining the direction in which money would flow. Moreover, "the small capitalist in the Netherlands did not as a rule ask the purpose for which money was raised" although there were certain signs, such as repeated attempts to raise small sums, that aroused suspicion.[82] The American diplomat William Short, describing the Amsterdam market to Alexander Hamilton, secretary of the treasury, found that after placing the block of notes allotted to them, commission agents "are not further concerned in the solidity of the borrowers or the profits of the lender, & of course high premiums with them are the first motive."[83]

There were still minimum standards that a commission agent had to meet to accumulate and retain a clientele, but the expectations investors settled on their agents were not demanding. Again according to William Short: "The money lenders in general are a class of heavy dull men, the sum of whose ideas consists in a few constant habits. Obstinate & incapable of being influenced so long as they are within that narrow circle, when out of it they become mere automates in the hands of their directors. Their extreme ignorance which renders them fearful of every change, would prevent their ever transgressing it, if they were not tempted by their excessive avarice to enter sometimes into new combinations in the hopes of greater gain. It is this conflict between their ignorance & their avarice which puts them under the direction of another class of men called undertakers."[84] Short's image of the Amsterdam market is expressed in acerbic tones, but it is still apparent that commission agents could satisfy customers with the lower returns toward which the banker-borrower relationship militated as long as service was reliable. There were also benefits in yielding to lower annuity rates, in that higher commission charges and other inducements could increase the agent's income.

Numerous sources indicate that investors judged borrowers chiefly by the regularity of annuity payments and the punctuality of reimbursements.[85] Those satisfied, Dutch rentiers were confident in the integrity of their investment and, when service was paid regularly, generally willing to reinvest in prolongations or take up fresh loans. Punctuality in meeting commitments can be an effective measure of credit worthiness, but Dutch investors relied more heavily on that yardstick than was warranted. Because the financial data available to borrowers were incomplete, punctual service sometimes reflected no more than a short-term availability of revenues. In other cases punctual payments did not reflect even that. Some borrowers customarily used the proceeds of fresh loans to service outstanding debts, and when that was the case intermediaries took care to shield the investing public from such disturbing information. Annuity payments might also be drawn from other credit sources and, because accounting techniques were sometimes faulty, that could be done without even the debtor realizing that credit was being used instead of tax revenues. Such practices did not penetrate the literature to which Dutch investors had access, nor apparently did they figure in word-of-mouth exchanges about borrowers.

From the 1760s to 1793 government borrowers usually met annuity payments punctually enough to satisfy investors, so that the commission agents' task in recommending investments was hardly difficult. Their ability to please investors with minimal benefits contributed to an expansion in the scale of commission-agent transactions and to the development of the commission agency as an avenue of entrepreneurial mobility. Firms excluded because of inexperience or inadequate reputation and credit from competing for banking agencies could build reputation, capitalization, and credit access in large-scale commission transactions. By the late 1780s several houses had exploited that avenue to the point at which they could organize substantial negotiations on their own account and manage loans for Dutch institutions that no longer found the traditional technique of raising credit through revenue officials adequate. Among those were two firms in particular that are prominent in this narrative because both left papers that have survived and because both were involved in a wide range of financial enterprises.[86] Each house was originally under the direction of a single man, Pieter Stadnitski and Abraham van Ketwich, but in each the number of partners and associations increased as the range of activities grew.[87]

Stadnitski, the grandson of a cloth presser and the son of a small-scale textile merchant, began business in the 1760s dealing in cotton and perhaps other commodities. His capital was modest, less than f. 50,000, but he was ambitious and able, and successive testaments reveal a steady increase in assets. By the 1780s his firm, operating under the style Pieter Stadnitski, was active in securities speculations and brokerage, in guaranteeing commercial transactions (a kind of bonding), and perhaps also in commodity trade. In securities transactions Stadnitski specialized in the French royal debt, although he also dealt widely in the paper of Dutch government loans. The rapid growth of his firm during the 1780s may be explained by the combination of commission agencies for loans floated for Sweden, Denmark, Russia, and Poland with investment ventures that Stadnitski organized on his own account.[88]

His first independent negotiation, a small venture on French life annuities opened in 1782, was followed by a series of larger ventures organized in association with Hendrik Vollenhoven. In 1787 Stadnitski opened his first undertaking based on the domestic debt of the United States and simultaneously expanded his commission agencies. Although he never obtained and may never even have sought a loan agency for any European state, Stadnitski was able nonetheless to accumulate large profits and a wide clientele of investors. Together those permitted him to buy large tracts of unsettled American land for resale to the investing public in negotiations rivaling major government loans in the amounts involved.

The available accounts from Stadnitski's commission agencies are not comprehensive, but data for the Russian loans indicate the size of his profits.[89] In 1788–93 Stadnitski agreed to place f. 4,295,000, or 8.67 percent of the total marketed through agents in seventeen issues in which he participated and for which contracts survive. The commission on those various agreements ranged between 1 and 2 percent, averaging about 1.8 percent, and yielded some f. 77,000, of which part may have been rebated to investors but which may also have been increased by sales at premiums. Commissions on Swedish, Danish, and Polish loans in which Stadnitski was involved were smaller, but the net income from all agencies together probably exceeded f. 100,000.

In launching negotiations on his own account Stadnitski risked his capital in acquiring paper or land for resale at a profit. At the same time, however, he was a commission agent engaged in a solid and secure area of enterprise. That combination balanced comparatively speculative but potentially lucrative negotiations with reliable commission agencies selling paper that already had an established market. Both activities succeeded handsomely.

Commission agent contracts for the Russian and Swedish loans included several firms that, like Pieter Stadnitski, combined underwriting with the issue of negotiations in areas not already preempted. Several agents had backgrounds in trade, but that was not the only possible path toward a goal of organizing large-scale negotiations. During the 1770s Abraham van Ketwich, an innovative financial entrepreneur, organized a series of stock-substitution undertakings, negotiations that pooled subscriptions to buy preexisting securities, and in which the organizer's profit was drawn from the commissions charged participants. His first venture appears to have been a single-unit investment trust (viz., a trust holding only one type of security) with a life-annuity feature, formed in 1770. Subscriptions totaling f. 50,000 were invested in a plantation loan, an unfortunate choice in view of the upcoming deterioration of plantation commodity prices. After the crisis of 1772–3 van Ketwich tried to take advantage of what must have looked like temporarily discounted plantation loan securities by forming a multiple-unit investment trust. But that paper did not recover and the foreign government securities van Ketwich added to the trust's portfolio could not make up for losses on the plantation loans. As a consequence that venture, which attracted subscriptions totaling nearly f. 1 million, and other trusts organized on the same types of paper benefited participants far less than had been promised,[90] and left the multiple-unit trust discredited in the eyes of investors.

Because it was no longer possible during the 1780s to organize multiple-unit trusts, van Ketwich turned to large-scale sales of notes in foreign government loans. His success there provided him with the capital and clientele necessary to form further substitution undertakings during the 1790s and thereafter, and in 1802, together with two other firms, to introduce the administrative or trustee office as a format for managing investments in a given sector, in this case in French consolidated annuities.[91]

Both Stadnitski and van Ketwich owed their success to having built clienteles of rentiers willing to follow their advice. On a rising market they looked like financial geniuses, and they took full advantage of opportunities permitted by that market. Like rentiers they were content when investment ventures paid service regularly, and like rentiers they failed to perceive ways in which the long-term interests of investors might be better protected.

Each state floating loans in the Dutch Republic offered certain security for annuity and redemption payments. In the seventeenth and early eighteenth century foreign borrowers had been obliged to transfer real property that might be sold in the event of default or to secure loans on commodity shipments.[92] Such practices were suitable enough for occasional loans but awkward for large-scale use. After raising advances on mercury and copper anticipations, early in the eighteenth century Austria shifted in part to mortgages based on tax anticipations.[93] That practice was adopted by other states, and from midcentury most foreign loans were issued on the security of debentures outlining the revenues mortgaged for the advance and giving other information as indicated above. Somewhat later there was also a shift away from personal guarantees on the assets of rulers toward backing provided by central banks under the control of representative institutions or by representative institutions themselves.

Whereas loans negotiated around the turn of the eighteenth century by Austria, some lesser German states, and the Spanish Netherlands commonly carried guarantees from the States General, that practice was abandoned after 1713, when the Republic adopted a policy of neutrality.[94] The divorce of international finance from the diplomatic considerations that had led the States General to make such guarantees was a progressive step for the Amsterdam capital market, and especially for firms involved in negotiating and managing foreign loans. But for investors it was a perilous step, for they lost both the ancillary support of the guarantee, based on domestic revenues, and the assurance that in case of default the States General could intervene to encourage resumption of payments or negotiate a settlement. The 8-percent return offered by Austria in a 1714 loan (as opposed to 5 percent in the most recent prior issues) undoubtedly reflects a very much changed perception of imperial credit worthiness in the absence of a Generality guarantee. As long as the annuity rate remained high, investors' interests were protected by a return that ensured them against the greater risk of loss. But, as we have seen, yields tended to move toward those current on the Amsterdam market for the most solid domestic borrowers, with the result that the risk premium paid in foreign lending declined. What received inadequate notice in 1714 and thereafter was that firms active in negotiating foreign loans had done nothing to improve the creditors' claim upon mortgaged assets. The States General could no longer be expected to intervene, which left the maintenance of payments subject to the whim of the debtor and to the leverage that could be applied through the prospect of future credit extensions.

In theory debentures were equivalent to more concrete types of security because, by implication, default would permit creditors to take over the revenues specified. In practice, however, things were not so simple. Debentures usually cited some specific tax sources and added a mortgage on the general revenues and assets of the borrower.[95] The sums raised annually from the sources cited or from general revenues were occasionally given for less credit-worthy borrowers, but generally were not included, indeed perhaps not known. Such instruments implied that mortgaged assets were adequate for service and redemption and that, in the event of default, investors would have priority over other claimants against the state. In no case, however, did a debenture describe any mechanism for transferring collection to the bankers or other representatives of the lenders. This suggests the existence of a fiction that debentures had a value of their own, equal at least to the amount lent. But there was no market in debentures and, when put to the test by annuity suspensions and defaults, a market did not develop. As long as a loan was serviced regularly the debentures behind it might have had a market, but an interruption in service damaged the value of those instruments and of loan notes.

Rentiers failed to grasp that, at the heart of matters, loans to governments were settled on confidence in the integrity of the borrower, on the assumption that the borrower's tax revenues were adequate, on the expectation that political events would not force an interruption of service or a deferral of redemptions, and on the notion that a desire to maintain a good credit standing was as persuasive a force in the realm of government finance as it undoubtedly was in the realm of the firm. The unrealistic quality of those expectations and assumptions became evident during the Revolutionary and Napoleonic wars, when defaults underscored the worthlessness of debentures. Even then Dutch investors sometimes accepted foreign loans secured in the old fashion, presumably because of a lack of investment options and out of an effort to salvage earlier investments by maintaining the leverage offered by the prospect of further loans.

That investors were credulous is confirmed by the implicit instability of government lending. Because loans were used chiefly to pay for wars, borrowers, and especially defeated powers, gratified aggressive proclivities but got very little out of borrowing that might be construed as "value." But lenders appear to have been little bothered by the purpose for which loans were raised. There is no evidence to indicate that they were disturbed when two or more states seeking credit went to war with one another, although intermediaries generally felt obliged to make a choice if one client declared war on another. Because conflict was the chief occasion for loans, the market's interest was favored by numerous although not oppressively expensive wars. A limited number of major borrowers – ten including the Republic – and a competitive state system made conflict within the group inevitable and encouraged investors to appear to be neutral. Even when partisanship was influential, as it probably was around 1780 in a shift away from British and toward French loans, it joined with other causes and did not prevent anglophiles from following the francophile trend.

Investor characteristics. Who were the investors who saw government lending through rose-colored glasses? They are difficult to identify individually. The issue of notes *in blanco* eased transfers but removed the need for maintaining lists of subscribers and recording transfers. A few such lists survive nonetheless, but the names in them are often those of agents collecting interest or dividends for clients. For the rest it is only in estate and collateral-succession tax inventories that such data are numerous, but those sources involve substantial problems in interpretation and in identifying significant traits of individuals whose assets are listed. At present any analysis of those who invested necessarily has an intuitive and impressionistic quality.

According to *De Koopman* in 1768, the rentier was "usually a capitalist [*kapitalist*] . . . interested in different branches of business affairs [*negotie*]," someone who lent money and discounted commercial paper.[96] But rentiers, individuals living securely on their investments, were not the only investors. There were others among a class vaguely labeled the greater bourgeoisie who accumulated portfolios in domestic and foreign government loans, and they included wholesale merchants, insurance underwriters, bankers, large-scale manufacturers, and the wealthier members of the commercial oligarchies dominating municipal and provincial government in the most prosperous parts of the Republic.[97]

There were also investors among the lesser bourgeoisie, another vague group composed of members of the liberal professions, including attorneys, notaries, professors, clergymen, physicians, and lesser government officials; smaller-scale merchants and rentiers; the intermediaries of foreign loans themselves, that is, brokers, commission agents, and the cashiers who handled disbursements on order; and probably shopkeepers and artisans as well.[98] In both categories there were also widows who sometimes combined management of an estate with control over the direction of the firm left by their husbands.[99] Female life expectancy exceeded male for every age group in the eighteenth century, with the result that widows were prominent as investors.[100]

Institutional investors, such as religious and charitable organizations,[101] and even governments also bought notes. The most common institutional investor was the estate in *fideicommis*, a practice providing that part of an estate would be reserved from use by the heirs in favor of a third party, usually the second generation of heirs. Income on that part of the estate was assigned to a first-generation heir, but the principal was managed by trustees.

Substitution negotiations were another common type of institutional investor and one in which securities were generally withheld from the market for long periods. That category included private tontines, life-annuity associations, prebends, and widows' funds, all of which enabled individual investors to join a cooperative whose assets were used to settle annuities on their dependents. Numerous beneficial societies were formed in the seventeenth and eighteenth centuries, but during the 1750s and 1760s, with the growth of plantation and foreign government loans, brokers tended to replace notaries as organizers. They introduced a more ambitious scale of operation and formed substitution undertakings in which the lifespan of a nominee was no longer a part and subscriptions far surpassed that which had been customary earlier.[102]

In order to understand the image conjured up in the eighteenth-century Republic by the term *kapitalist,* it is necessary to realize that value and gain were not measured principally in monetary terms but in a combination of economic value with the security and social and political status preserved, gained, or enhanced. In the seaward provinces an aristocratic bias toward certain types of property did not function in the same fashion as elsewhere in Europe. There land was not the central feature of high-status assets, not only because the class that can be identified as aristocratic had at least arisen out of commercial entrepreneurship, but also because land was in too short supply to permit numerous income-producing estates. After the revolution of 1747–8 venal office-holding opportunities narrowed in the Republic. But in other respects the Dutch investor resembles a French counterpart distinguished by George V. Taylor, the exploiter of proprietary wealth whose assets were centered on land, venal offices, urban property, and government securities.[103]

For land and venal offices the Dutchman managing proprietary wealth substituted promissory notes from individuals, silent partnerships, marine insurance, bill discounting, and a larger allotment to urban real estate and to government and company loans. The assets of such investors thus differed in important respects from those of the French counterpart, but management attitudes were strikingly similar. A distinguishing feature of this attitude was concern for security, the concentration of wealth in areas whose yields were low partly because of their security. The most obvious alternative for the Dutch investor was active entrepreneurship, but because the quantity of capital that could be employed profitably in the firm was limited, even entrepreneurs were obliged to become managers of proprietary wealth. Without therefore responding exclusively to an imperative grounded in the status qualities of investments, the eighteenth-century Dutch investor allotted an increasing part of his assets to areas requiring little active management and paying secure yields. Government loans in particular suited this pattern because they were long-term affairs, stretching over a decade or more and, with prolongation, subject to being renewed with little administrative difficulty for an indefinite period. Thus the Amsterdam market's shift toward government finance assisted the acquisition of proprietary wealth.

The objective was to build an endowment safe from most of the risks of active entrepreneurship, an endowment that had social value and could be passed on from generation to generation. The *fideicommis* portion of an estate was therefore the core of a broader pattern of capital accumulation with social and economic rather than legal hindrances to alienation.

Proprietary wealth or, as Ralph E. Giesey has labeled it, "lineage property," was wealth invested in assets that either were not productive (in the sense of fostering a higher level of economic activity) or that were not attractive because of the possibility of productive gains. But it does not necessarily follow that a preference for such types of property stifled a novel type of capitalism, as Giesey has argued,[104] or hindered economic development. In the seventeenth-century Dutch Republic practices similar to those identified with proprietary wealth in old-regime France had existed simultaneously and in the same individuals along with investment, innovation, and productive gains in commerce and manufacturing. In France wealthy classes with the capacity to save at significant levels often aspired to withdraw from active entrepreneurship when it became possible to endow retirement, and a pattern of withdrawal from commerce can be discerned in the eighteenth-century Republic. But in both societies the chief means of accumulating such assets was active entrepreneurship. The emphasis given that avenue was a generator of risk taking and a source of the infusion of new men and perhaps also of new skills and aptitudes. Entrepreneurial aggressiveness was therefore assured by a system that militated toward investments in land, public offices, urban real estate, and government securities. Once an endowment was built there was little disposition to reenter active entrepreneurship, but managers of proprietary wealth in both France and the Dutch Republic invested some of their savings in productive assets like mining, industry, agriculture, and trade. That is to say, wealthy individuals were willing to some degree to take profits where they could find them as long as investment could be separated from the loss of social status attendant on active participation in trade, manufacturing, and similar activities.

In the Dutch Republic endowments built by the managers of proprietary wealth were one of two types, very secure properties (such as urban real estate and domestic government securities) paying the lowest yields, and less secure or somewhat venturesome properties (such as sleeping partnerships, marine insurance, loans to commercial, mining, and industrial enterprises, and foreign government securities) paying higher yields. The point is that managers of proprietary wealth did not invest only in the lowest-yield and most-secure areas. This distinction is important because it reflects three broad investment attitudes: (1) rentier allocation; (2) venturesome rentier allocation; and (3) entrepreneurship, which might be more or less venturesome but which in any case involved active participation in business affairs. The second category was the chief area of increasing capital accumulation in the Dutch Netherlands during the second half of the eighteenth century. That it thrived, and especially that foreign lending thrived, is evidence that market intermediaries could draw capital into risky enterprises and that the risk averse behavior of investors accommodated both low-risk low-profit assets and significantly higher-risk higher-profit choices.

From another perspective a distinction among capitalists may be drawn between large-scale investors with established commercial and banking connections in investment areas, able to buy without using market intermediaries, and smaller investors who were by and large dependent on intermediaries.[105] Direct investment abroad dominated some areas, certainly the British funds and French government loans, but in other cases the Amsterdam market offered an access that was difficult to obtain otherwise. The stock-substitution format extended the advantages of direct acquisition abroad to smaller investors, so that by the 1780s there was no sharp boundary separating these two groups in terms of access to paper.

Although some differentiation between the two groups is useful, perhaps particularly in accounting for the development of substitution negotiations as a means of reducing overhead costs in direct foreign investments, it is difficult to settle on even an approximate sum that may be said to have separated them. Using collateral-succession tax inventories to reconstruct investment distribution between foreign and domestic loans, Alice C. Carter established three levels of estates–below f. 20,000, f. 20,000 to 89,999, and f. 90,000 and over.[106] Distribution of portfolios was found to vary among those categories, with the latter two, for example, displaying increased holdings in the British funds from 1739–40 to 1769–70 and from 1739–40 to 1779–80, respectively. But to place investment capital abroad directly on a scale sufficient both to build a diversified portfolio and to submerge acquisition costs probably required assets substantially greater than f. 90,000.

The rise of the stock-substitution undertaking and in particular the development from the 1770s of large-scale single-unit investment trusts demonstrate that investors appreciated savings in transactions costs. But that same kind of attentiveness was not evidently given to managing portfolios for capital gains. The expansion of foreign lending indicates that investors bought initially to satisfy such expectations as high yields or to diversify assets, but available *beurs* quotations do not show that investors consistently traded in response to opportunities presented by price fluctuations.

A secular series of biweekly or monthly quotations is available for the British funds traded in Amsterdam. Although the dates of quotations do not always coincide with dates on which news of dramatic international events probably arrived in Amsterdam, it is possible to analyze prices in terms of selected events that might be expected to have been influential. In some cases prices responded predictably. At the conclusion of the Treaty of Vienna on 16 March 1731, and the dissolution of the Ostend East India Company, there was a sharp rise in British East India Company stock and other funds.[107] In similar fashion the landing in Scotland of the Pretender, Charles Edward, on 25 July 1745, and his advance into England in the autumn coincided with and presumably provoked an initial decline and then a steady fall in prices on all British stocks and annuities. Other events, however, were not reflected on the *beurs*. The outbreak of the War of Jenkins' Ear in October 1739 and even the major French victory over the allies at Fontenoy on 11 May 1745 had no impact. In these and other cases tested there is no consistent pattern of response and thus no trend of fluctuations even in the terms to which eighteenth-century investors were thought by contemporaries to be attuned – political news.[108]

With the appearance of quotations in the *Maandelijkse nederlandsche mercurius* it is possible for the first time to test whether *beurs* prices reflected portfolio management aimed at adjusting price disparities. When the *Mercurius* began to include quotations, on 24 September 1792, the effective return of notes issued by different foreign governments at the same nominal return fell close together. Thus the effective return for the 5-percent notes of Russia, Spain, Austria, and Sweden was between 4.82 and 4.93 percent, whereas notes that had been issued at 4 percent (Spain excluded) yielded 4.05 to 4.08 percent. Those four states were then regarded as virtually identical in credit worthiness but, since the movement toward higher yields during the 1780s, there had not been an adjustment of prices on lower-yield notes to correspond with the more recent higher-yield emissions. Nor was that a temporary phenomenon. It persisted through the remainder of 1792 and indeed into the autumn of 1794. Even then it was not corrected, for 5-percent notes moved temporarily below 4 percent in terms of effective returns.[109]

The market situation of 1792–4 was not necessarily typical of the second half of the century. Nonetheless, had investors customarily managed portfolios to maximize returns, prices should, even and perhaps especially in a period of wartime disruption, reveal no more than minimal variations of this type. Such inattentiveness may have been a feature of the rising market. In any case it was not sustained after the French invasion of 1794 and the more frequent extraordinary income and property levies of the Batavian regime because those developments obliged a reconsideration of portfolio management practices.

Dutch lenders, even bankers and commission-agents who were the best informed, were overconfident about their position. The market structure, their own habits, and a naive belief in the reliability of government borrowers made credit raised on the Amsterdam market indeed attractive. And its attractiveness to borrowers increased with inflation and government debts. On the level of both institutions and individuals the market was fundamentally unprepared to regulate and adjust terms and costs in order to counter the advantage held by borrowers, unprepared because of information defects and a profound inattentiveness to those defects. What most strikingly distinguishes Dutch capitalism from the entirely rationalized pursuit of gain is neither aversion to risk nor a preference for unproductive property grounded in social values, but the problem of recognizing the need for and acquiring important information pertinent, in this case, to government finance.

3

PUBLIC CREDIT IN THE DUTCH REPUBLIC

Foreign government borrowing in Amsterdam became significant long after Dutch governments had begun to tap the savings of the Dutch public. Indeed the methods used by Dutch governments to raise credit preceded the appearance of capital markets capable of providing a link to investors. Subsequently, as the Amsterdam market shifted from commercial to government finance, most government borrowing remained independent of the market apparatus. Public institutions drew on the same pool of savings that foreign governments utilized either through intermediaries in Amsterdam or in direct Dutch investments in loans opened at home. But they raised credit through parallel organizations managed by revenue officials, who sometimes called on brokers for assistance but for whom the chief importance of the market was presumably its function as a source of information about capital availability and interest rates. Despite that measure of independence from the Amsterdam market, credit exploitation by the Dutch Republic was not basically dissimilar to the practices of other states, although Dutch practices anticipated usages adopted elsewhere.

Fragmentation of authority and sharp rivalry between seaward and landward provinces are evident in the Dutch system of taxation, in the distribution of assessment among various corporations carrying fiscal responsibilities that transcended their borders, and in the management of public finance. The strongest segment of the whole was not the Generality, which for all practical purposes was merely the fiscal subordinate of the provinces, nor all the provinces together.[1] It was instead the wealthiest of the seven provinces, Holland. But to divide public finance only among the Generality and the provinces is to obscure other public corporations that had important taxation powers. Five admiralties were charged with collecting import and export duties and with the maintenance of the Republic's navy.[2] In theory they fell under the control of the States General, but in practice they were managed in the provinces where they were located, Holland (three), Friesland, and Zeeland. Likewise the drainage network of the Republic was maintained by dispersed public corporations with taxation rights. The municipalities of the most highly urbanized society in Europe also exercised taxation powers, and were in some respects the foundation of the larger whole of the Dutch fiscal system.[3] The data available on public finance in the Republic are, however, scattered and incomplete. Although the importance of other public corporations must be acknowledged, it is necessary to concentrate on the province of Holland, the principal part of the whole and the part about which data are most extensive.

Decentralization and its consequences

National financial requirements were met through assessments on the provinces and Generality lands that respected provincial particularism. Under a structure formulated in the late sixteenth century and revised last in 1616, the provinces were given quotas, percentages of the annual estimate of necessary revenues prepared by the council of state in The Hague and approved by the States General.[4] In the early years of the Republic those quotas reflected variations in wealth and resources, but the formula adopted in 1616 was not revised until 1792. In the meantime the division of wealth moved further in Holland's favor, and long before 1792 the 1616 distribution was recognized as inequitable. Attempts to adjust it failed, however, in the face of resistance from Holland, whose share remained about 58 percent until 1792, when it was enlarged to about 62 percent.[5]

Although collection and management methods varied from province to province, the structure of public finance in the larger provinces was similar to that in the Generality. There two officials directed the apparatus under council-of-state oversight. The treasurer general supplied the council with information for preparing spending estimates and managing expenditures, and the receiver general served as central accountant in the collection of quotas and managed loan subscriptions and interest and redemption payments.[6] The provinces carried the principal weight of tax collection and borrowing, but they too could subdivide responsibility. In Holland the municipalities controlled a network under which quotas were assigned separately to southern and northern sections of the province. Within each of those, revenue offices were established in major cities to oversee tax collection and market loan paper.[7]

As the fiscal subordinate of the provinces, the Generality was essentially a bookkeeping unit, managing income from the provinces and Generality lands, a minor area of the Republic under direct control of the States General.[8] In wartime sums administered by the council of state increased as the States General approved higher expenditures and convinced provincial assemblies to accept their part of the larger outlay. But the determination of Generality spending remained in the hands of provincial assemblies, and the Generality could not force quota collections. The central government had no other independent authority than to levy taxes in areas under its direct control and to raise loans serviceable out of those revenues and the rather modest income that could be projected from peacetime quotas.

During the seventeenth century the United Provinces assumed a role in European affairs whose costs exceeded taxation resources. Acquisition of major-power status was possible because of the Republic's commercial and industrial development. With a smaller territory and population than its principal rivals, Britain and France, the Republic exploited the greater per capita wealth of its inhabitants. The gap that remained between tax revenues and the costs of major-power status was covered by a financial program relying on long-term credit. In addition to higher per capita wealth, which also permitted greater individual investment in government loans than in other seventeenth-century states, the components of the Dutch fiscal formula were low service costs (and thus a higher level of supportable indebtedness against any given level of revenues) and a mystique of solid public credit based on obscurantism in the development and exposure of information about assets and liabilities.

In comparison to the public finance system introduced in England between 1660 and 1714, the Dutch structure may appear inefficient and ineffective. The two states used basically the same kinds of taxes, a mélange of excises and direct property levies, and, during the 1690s conflict with France, similar loan formats as well. But in England the treasury had by 1688 gained control over tax collection and in the process management and record keeping had been centralized at the exchequer. In the Dutch Netherlands these functions remained decentralized. On the other hand, per capita taxation in the Republic was significantly higher than in England. It is of course true that Dutch per capita income and assets exceeded those of the English, but it may also be true that the percentage of income taken in taxes substantially surpassed the English level.[9] In concentrating assessment in excise taxes to an even greater extent than did the English, the Dutch system was particularly suited to an economy specializing in production for foreign consumption and in carrying goods from domestic and foreign areas of production to foreign areas of consumption.

Moreover, improving financial information by centralizing management and record keeping did not, in the early modern period, enhance control over taxpayers or access to lenders. Decentralized taxation and borrowing brought Dutch fiscal authorities and their associates, the tax farmers, into direct relationship with the inhabitants of the Republic and may have been partially responsible for the high rate of per capita taxation. At the same time there was superior access to investors through the Republic's dispersed system of revenue offices than through the central issue of loans in London. Per capita holdings of public debt instruments were higher in the province of Holland and probably in the Republic as a whole around 1700 than in England and remained higher throughout the eighteenth century.[10]

In other respects too the Dutch Republic already had an effective system of public finance, one in which the measures of centralization and consolidation adopted in Britain would have had negative consequences. If the central ingredient in any system of public finance relying on credit is acknowledged to be the dependability of the borrowing apparatus, then it is evident that by the middle of the seventeenth century the Republic had the most dependable system in Europe. Without ever centralizing management, without even systematically specifying the tax revenues being mortgaged in a loan, the Republic built and maintained high debts at modest cost and was able consistently to raise fresh loans.

Both the annuity paid in new loans and that paid to service outstanding debts were reduced during the seventeenth century despite the secular expansion of government debts. In the 1590s the province of Holland paid 8.33 percent on redeemable annuity loans, but that fell in 1608 to 6.25 percent, and in 1611 outstanding redeemable annuities were converted to the lower return. In 1640 the yield on redeemable annuities was reduced further to 5 percent, and in 1655 to 4 percent. By the latter decades of the century some loans were raised at 3.5 percent, and during most of the eighteenth century public corporations could borrow at net returns of 2.5 to 3 percent.[11] Because some debt had been marketed at higher rates, and because the debt included self-amortizing annuities, service costs exceeded the return paid on new loans after the deduction of taxes on such assets. For Holland gross service averaged about 4 percent of the outstanding debt in the second half of the eighteenth century.[12]

Although Dutch capital markets were international, returns demanded by Dutch investors remained as low or lower than those required outside the Republic in government or private borrowing. The difference was costly to investors, but it benefited other parts of the economy because it lowered factor costs, and it benefited the government because it reduced service costs. That advantage for public finance appeared no later than the early seventeenth century and, short-term fluctuations aside, persisted into the last decade of the eighteenth century. Such a situation resulted from a secular abundance of investment capital, the sustained preference of rentiers for domestic government paper, and defective information about the relative standing of Dutch governments as debtors. Nonetheless, the Republic used that resource to create and maintain lower proportional service costs than those paid by other states relying exclusively or principally on long-term loans (as opposed to paper currency issues).[13]

One of the advantages of a centralized fiscal system lies in the greater ease of drawing retrospective balances. In Britain public finance reorganization after 1660 led to reliable statements on revenues, expenditures, and accumulated indebtedness. In the province of Holland, however, such steps would certainly have been deleterious because the existing debt was immense and could never be redeemed out of existing resources. Gaining retrospective knowledge, the province would have lost the benefit that the absence of such information gave it – the benefit drawn from the ignorance of its creditors that bred confidence among them.[14]

There is no intent to imply conspiratorial maneuvering to obscure financial realities, but a suggestion that Generality and provincial authorities failed to gather and reveal information that they knew or had good reason to suspect would have undercut public confidence in government credit. In Holland and in the Generality officials prepared spending estimates and maintained accounts of current revenues and expenditures. In neither, however, were those current accounts used to draft retrospective deficit totals. Although authorities had partial information about long-term liabilities in the irregular taxes assessed on domestic government paper and in debt-service cost estimates, the total amount of accumulated debt remained a seldom-asked question.[15] On the other hand, it is rather Britain that was the anomaly in having converted to management techniques that readily yielded such information. Other states remained uniformly content with traditional usages, the most progressive of which were oriented toward annual projections of spending requirements rather than toward cumulative accounts. As long as there was no monitor of government overdrafts outside an investing market that had only fragmentary information, British accounting methods were in fact detrimental to maximum borrowing.

Borrowing formats

The credit formats used in the seven provinces and the Generality in the seventeenth century were an adaptation of the practices of medieval Flemish municipalities that sold annuities to raise money. Even some Dutch villages anticipated revenues to meet fiscal requirements. Nor were such techniques peculiar to government corporations, for during the seventeenth century, if not earlier, religious and charitable organizations also borrowed, using proceeds to fund eleemosynary projects and for building costs.[16] In short, the exploitation of public credit was a pervasive feature of government and institutional finance by the time the northern Netherlands gained independence from Spain.

Nonetheless, the loan formats introduced first by institutions with primarily local responsibilities were refined by the provinces and the Generality. Early practice in the issue of redeemable (rather than self-amortizing) annuities followed a *losrente* formula under which paper was issued in varying denominations in the name of the investor.[17] During the seventeenth century Dutch governments altered that format to the *obligatie*, under which notes represented parts in a larger total liability and were issued either in the name of the lender or to the bearer. Toward the end of that century there was also a shift away from life annuities, and during the eighteenth century the most common form of certificate expressing indebtedness was the *obligatie* of a uniform denomination. Strictly speaking, both *losrente* and *obligatie* loans were redeemable but in practice loans that were not self-amortizing were usually prolonged and thus became perpetual annuities. The ability of Dutch fiscal units to treat redeemable liabilities as perpetual credit and, in the long run, to expand indebtedness without having to renegotiate outstanding paper, was another element in the relative superiority of the seventeenth-century Republic's credit system.

A discussion of life-annuity loans and the shift away from them may clarify the advantages gained by debtors from adopting a loan format that was not self-amortizing. In a life annuity a fixed annual yield is paid as long as the nominee or nominees designated in a contract survive, a period that varies with the lifespan of different individuals. The interest portion can be established only if information about the age and probable longevity of the nominees is sufficient to permit the calculation of the life annuity as though it were a term annuity. A close approximation of life-annuity value became available in 1671 when probability theory was used to analyze yields.[18] Because the interest portion of the life annuity could then be estimated, it can be assumed that new issues of excessively generous life annuities by some borrowers prevented more credit-worthy public corporations from reducing life-annuity returns to a level equivalent to redeemable annuity returns plus amortization calculated with life expectancy taken into account. On the other hand, self-amortizing loans are undesirable whenever accumulated indebtedness has reached the point at which debt charges require a substantial part of revenues. The conversion to perpetual annuities expanded the overall debt that government could carry not only because it reduced average interest rates but also because it shifted more service appropriations to interest and away from amortization.

The refinement in understanding of loan types produced by the segregation of interest and amortization occurred on the eve of the French invasion of the Republic in 1672, and thus on the eve of intermittent conflicts that stretched to 1713 and required vastly expanded borrowing. In the province of Holland the public debt has been estimated at f. 140 million in 1655.[19] In that year service on the redeemable debt was reduced from 5 to 4 percent, but the average cost before the reduction exceeded 5 percent because some life annuities issued earlier were still active. If the average before conversion totaled no more than 6 percent, a conservative estimate, then the appropriation necessary for service would have been about f. 8.4 million per annum. That same sum could have serviced a debt of f. 210 million (a level apparently reached during the War of the League of Augsburg) if the average cost were as low as 4 percent. In other words, by shifting away from life-annuity loans Holland gained a substantial margin of additional supportable indebtedness without increasing service expenditures. Self-amortizing loans did not disappear from the province's repertoire of credit devices, but thereafter preference was given interest-only annuities and the part of the outstanding debt composed of such paper increased apace.

That trend was accompanied by a shift in capital access on the part of government borrowers. Until the seventeenth century municipal and provincial credit utilization relied chiefly on inhabitants of the governing unit. Thereafter borrowing shed its local or regional character and, with the assistance of institutions devised to assist commercial growth, Amsterdam emerged as the principal national market in government finance.[20] By the last quarter of the seventeenth century Amsterdam's market was the major source of information about annuity rates and the arbiter of value. Most Dutch governments continued to borrow through local fiscal authorities, but the revenue office of issue was no longer an indicator of a restricted region from which capital was being raised. Amsterdam brokers exploited their contacts with rentiers to market paper throughout the Republic, becoming in the process secondary fiscal agents for the borrowing units. That function was particularly important when it expanded the market for paper already in circulation and thus broadened the pool of investors involved in lending to government.

Myth and reality in the public's appraisal of credit worthiness

Throughout this period the staple commodity of the Dutch investor's portfolio remained the long-term loans of public corporations in the Republic, even though those assets were less visible than the East and West India companies and English paper involved in speculation. The high regard that investors continued to show for the obligations of public corporations was justified by the care those bodies took to service their debts. It was not unheard of for a municipality or a province to fall into arrears in service payments, or for fresh loans to fail in part or altogether because investors were suspicious about the soundness of a borrower or reluctant to lend at the returns offered.[21] But the contrary was more typical; public corporations generally met their obligations promptly and preserved their ability to borrow. In the absence of information to the contrary, investors appear to have believed government to be financially reliable.

In truth the debts accumulated during the Eighty Years' War with Spain and added to in seventeenth-century conflicts with England and France left the Republic in a more precarious position than is suggested by the low annuity rates paid. Competing with states that, despite lower per capita wealth, had greater latitude to expand tax revenues, the Republic's debts mounted until their ratio to annual revenues far exceeded the ratio current in Britain, the only other state for which comparative data are available. Table 3-1 gives available estimates of outstanding debts, debt-service costs, and taxation revenues for the province of Holland through 1794.[22]

There is only one reliable estimate of provincial revenues between 1689 and 1768. Taken together with debt service figures for 1721 and 1728, that estimate permits the approximation of provincial indebtedness in 1721 and 1728 (in parentheses in the table) and a calculation of the debt–revenue ratio. Average service on the debt had declined in the seventeenth century, but it

Table 3-1. *Estimates of outstanding debts, debt service, and tax revenues in the province of Holland, 1652–1794 (in millions of guilders)*

Date	Outstanding debt	Service costs	Tax revenues
1652	132		
1655	140		
1667	132		
1678	160	7.1 (4.44%)	
1689			13
1713	343		
1721	(304.4–362.5)	13.7–14.5	
The 1720s			19 per annum
1728	(300–337.5)	13.5	
1761	350	14.4 (4.11%)	
1768			20
1780	317.5	13 (4.09%)	
The 1780s			23 per annum
1787–8	359–60	14.4–14.6 (4–4.07%)	
1788–94			24.24 per annum
1794	422	16.7 (3.96%)	

may not yet have reached the level characteristic of the second half of the eighteenth century, about 4 percent. Nevertheless, as life- and term-annuity loans amortized themselves, average service fell until it was close to 4 percent. At the 1721 level of debt service, provincial liabilities probably totaled f. 304.4 to 362.5 million, the respective products of calculating from service charges of 4 and 4.5 percent. At the lower figure the debt–revenue ratio would have been 16:1, at the higher figure about 19:1. In either case debt service required more than 70 percent of annual tax revenues.

Some progress was made in reducing liabilities during the 1720s and again after 1761.[23] In the interim tax revenues do not appear to have increased much, but the only estimate available between the 1720s and the 1780s is for 1768, at f. 20 million. If that amount is assumed to be appropriate for 1761, the debt–revenue ratio would then have been 17.5:1 and debt service would have required 72 percent of tax income. Although there was certainly some fluctuation in that ratio and in the percentage of revenues required for debt service between the 1720s and 1760s, the province did not benefit much from the Generality policy of neutrality followed since the War of the Spanish Succession except in the negative sense of thereby avoiding debts that might otherwise have been contracted. Provincial liabilities rose slowly during the 1730s and more rapidly during the War of the Austrian Succession, in which the Republic was involved during some eighteen months in 1747 and 1748.[24]

What these estimates and ratios indicate is that by the end of the Spanish Succession conflict the Dutch Republic had already mounted a program of intensive credit exploitation and consumed the additional resources made available by it and by the low annuity rates permitted by continuing public confidence. There was, therefore, no choice for the Republic but to reduce sharply its role in European politics in the postwar period because no capability remained for the costly naval and military forces required to compete.[25] As long as the province of Holland had to allocate approximately 70 percent or more of its revenues for debt service, and in the absence of marked growth in taxable resources, the Republic was automatically a second-rate power or less.

On the other hand, the Republic's financial position in 1714 could be sustained indefinitely as long as no significant new demands were made of it. The length of the period over which the province and the Republic maintained reputations not only of solvency but of solidity is an indication of the effectiveness of the public credit structure devised in the seventeenth century. That was still, however, a fragile system, for it offered little latitude to meet new spending demands. Any further reduction in service costs was possible only to the increasingly modest extent to which old life annuities were amortized and to which the remaining portion of revenues could be used to retire old debts or service new. The annuity demanded by investors was already the lowest in Europe, and the economic situation that had favored decreasing credit costs in the seventeenth and early eighteenth century gave way around 1750 to an inflationary trend in commodity prices that exerted pressure toward higher yields. Likewise, in the absence of economic growth and given an already heavy per capita tax burden, significantly increased revenues could only be obtained by taxing the wealthy. Such an innovation would have been opposed by rentiers, who were both government creditors and the personnel of public offices.

The principal issue in tax-reform proposals after midcentury was not redistribution among individuals but among the provinces. That elementary problem, one of the consequences of political decentralization, could not easily be resolved, and as long as the quota system remained unrevised any reform in other spheres of public finance was more difficult. There was presumably some scope for reducing overhead in tax collection and management, but most of the gains possible in that realm had already been achieved by the curtailment of tax farming into which municipal and provincial authorities were forced by popular uprisings in 1747–8.[26]

Those deficits upon whose absence the financial stability of Holland and the Republic depended appeared during the Fourth Anglo-Dutch War and continued to mount through the remainder of the 1780s. In the interim, since the 1760s, the province had made some progress in reducing its liabilities. In 1771 the periodical *De Koopman* could give a laudatory view of the soundness of public credit in the Republic.[27] But *De Koopman*'s case was built on the fallacy that had long misled investors – defective information about debts and revenues. It was assumed that public borrowing must not yet have exhausted available resources, and indeed that would certainly have been the case had tax revenues approached the level projected in that periodical, f. 244 million for the Republic as a whole in about 1770. Obscurantism clearly had its rewards.

Between 1780 and 1794 the provincial debt increased from f. 317.5 to more than f. 422 million.[28] Debt reductions in the 1760s and 1770s, due both to economies and to the continuing lapse of life annuities,[29] had reduced the debt–revenue ratio to about 13.8:1. But there had not been any appreciable change in service costs as a percentage of debts. By 1794 the debt–revenue ration was once again about 17.4:1, and 69 percent of revenues was required for debt service. The latitude for additional borrowing gained in the 1760s and 1770s and extended somewhat by increased tax revenues in the 1770s and 1780s had been consumed by 1793, when the Republic entered the War of the First Coalition. On the eve of the Batavian Revolution of 1795 the province's debt exceeded f. 422 million and required nearly 10 percent more of tax revenues for service than had been the case in 1787. According to retrospective revenue estimates compiled in the Batavian period, Holland's revenues from 1788 to 1794 had totaled about 81 percent of the Republic's revenues (of some f. 30 million).[30] Debt estimates for Holland in 1796 and for all seven provinces together in 1795, respectively f. 455 and f. 610 million, indicate that the province had shouldered about 75 percent of provincial debts and that Holland may therefore have been in a slightly stronger position than other fiscal subdivisions.[31]

Public finance and the Dutch economy

As other manufacturers and merchants learnèd to mimic the skills and duplicate the technological devices that had contributed to making the Dutch Republic preeminent in European trade and an important center of manufacturing, and as those merchants and manufacturers were assisted by legislation designed to impede the Dutch, the concentration on excise taxes that had benefited the Republic in the seventeenth century became an anachronism. Whether there was any alternative to a gradual withering of the Dutch economic and political position is not clear, although such steps as the recruitment of cheap foreign labor and tariffs or higher duties on certain imports competing with Dutch industry might have been beneficial. Aided in those fashions the traditional sector of industry might have found feasible the application of mechanized techniques that enhanced productivity. In the absence of those or any other positive steps, Dutch industry succumbed as the Republic fell back upon safeguarding a carrying trade whose relative position could not be maintained and upon a jealous preservation of a fiscal structure that was no longer appropriate or inappropriate to economic growth, but simply an anachronism.

At the same time, however, the fiscal system that had fostered commercial and industrial development had also, coincidentally, encouraged the growth of lending to governments. Maldistributed taxation safeguarded savings, including those in government paper, and notwithstanding intermittent levies on domestic government notes. While Dutch public corporations were expanding their borrowing, that is to say, until about 1720, investment capital gravitated toward their loans. After 1720 there was a shift toward foreign lending, one that became marked during the 1740s. Forces that contributed to the growth of the Amsterdam capital market as a center of capital export ultimately weakened the position of domestic governments. When, during the 1780s, large-scale borrowing was again necessary, there was enough competition for available capital to force annuity rates upward in advance even of public disquietude about the credit worthiness of domestic governments. The resulting contraction of the debt supportable on a given amount of revenues, a reversal of the prior trend, further weakened the financial position of Dutch governments.[32]

Although new deficits in the 1780s and 1790s led inevitably toward insolvency because of the overly slender credit margin remaining to be exploited, there was one area where other states could take advantage of economic trends to reduce the real burden of debts. Outside the Republic government revenues expanded sharply after midcentury,[33] and the foremost growth occurred in indirect taxes. Estimates distinguishing between direct and indirect tax income in France from 1715 to 1773 show that indirect tax revenues increased from 37 to 52 percent of all revenues.[34] In Britain in the same period indirect tax income grew less strikingly as a percentage of net revenues, but still rose from 69 percent in 1715 to 77 percent in 1775.[35] A similar division between tax types cannot be made for the Republic, but there clearly overall revenues expanded more slowly than elsewhere and indeed so much more slowly that, taking into account the inflating cost of goods and services, real revenues probably declined significantly.[36]

Other states found a temporary remedy for secular deficits and a method of compensating for revenues lost under regressive tax structures by expanding long-term debts and paper currency issues that were absorbed chiefly by classes benefiting from tax maldistribution.[37] Any loss in the purchasing power of annuities or paper currency converted into specie or commodities was absorbed by the rentier. Because the inflation of government credit instruments coincided with an inflation in commodity prices *and* increased tax revenues, other states enjoyed revenues that expanded against prior obligations. Their income did not have to increase at a rate sufficient to maintain real value according to an index of goods and services acquired by the state based on the period prior to inflation, but merely to increase in comparison to outstanding debts from an earlier time. In the Dutch Republic, in contrast, tax revenues expanded so much more slowly that the real value of outstanding debts declined without a proportional improvement in the state's relative position with respect to those obligations.[38] In other words, whereas other states transformed lenders into taxpayers in a covert fashion, in the Dutch Republic lenders suffered all the losses inherent in holding assets of fixed nominal and declining real value without at the same time delivering a useful portion of their losses to the state.

4

SUPPLY AND DEMAND PATTERNS

The period of British domination

Dutch foreign lending shifted orientation around 1780 when the British public debt, which had been dominant, ceased to attract the customary volume of new wartime investment. The first indication of that shift was a reduced rate of investment in British loans during the War of the American Revolution in comparison with earlier wartime experience. During the Fourth Anglo-Dutch War rentiers by and large suspended new lending to Britain, dispersing their investments among a number of clients. In the following decade British liabilities in the Republic grew slowly or not at all in sterling values, whereas loans to other foreign governments increased rapidly and came to surpass the British total (Table 4-1).[1]

Throughout the period from about 1720 to Dutch entry into the French Revolutionary wars, credit demand from domestic governments remained less than demand from all foreign borrowers taken collectively. The balance owed by Dutch governments continued to exceed foreign assets, but to a diminishing degree (Chart 4-1),[2] and domestic governments did not, except in the latter 1780s and early 1790s, compete with foreign borrowers. Chart 4-2 portrays foreign lending over a longer period and illustrates its concentration in the second half of the century.[3] Although the volume and velocity of Dutch capital exports grew after 1740, practices and usages developed in the preceding half century remained influential.

1695–1740. In the earlier phase, Dutch lending to foreign governments assumed two patterns. The first of a series of loans

Table 4-1. *Distribution of the estimated balance of foreign government loans (in millions of guilders)*

	Estimated balance	British liabilities	Liabilities of other states
1770	250	205	45
1780	350	255	95
1790	575	265	310

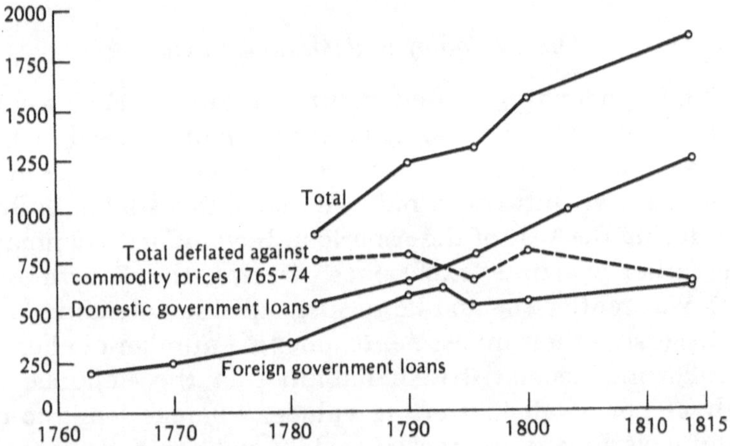

Chart 4-1. Estimated total Dutch investment in foreign and domestic government loans, 1763–1814 (in millions of current guilders and in nominal values). French liabilities have been treated as if the repudiation occurred when annuity payments were suspended (1793).

organized for Austria between 1695 and 1740 by the firm of the Widow Deutz & Co., long-standing imperial agents for marketing mercury, was based on joint-stock-company methods of capital mobilization.[4] In the process Deutz furnished borrower and lenders with services that were attractive enough to institutionalize a similar intermediary role in subsequent Austrian loans. Such a function was necessary because commercial and financial relations between the empire and the Republic were not sufficient to provide the necessary range of direct contacts.

Within the same period the Dutch began investing in the British public debt, but the avenues they employed largely bypassed the foreign loan apparatus Deutz had helped develop. Certain

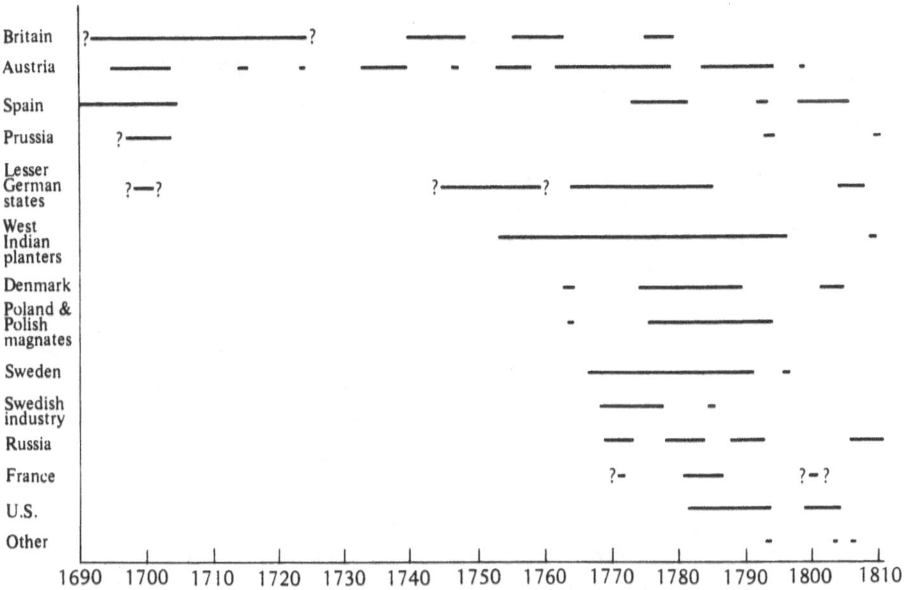

Chart 4-2. Lending patterns on the Amsterdam market.

parts of the apparatus assisted investors by managing transfers and returns, but individual rentiers developed the habit of using London agents for their purchases. As investments in Britain grew, a market in British paper appeared in Amsterdam, and in 1723 the *Amsterdamsche courant* began publishing current prices. Although some brokers in major Dutch cities handled transactions in British paper, and although Dutch rentiers were able to buy from previous Dutch holders, the most important avenue of investment remained the direct path to London agents, often members of the Dutch business community in that city.

By the 1690s commercial contacts with England were long-standing and varied. No single firm was dominant and no Amsterdam house managed to establish links with the British government that were of any particular value in the developing transfer of Dutch savings. Deutz, on the other hand, exploited its imperial mercury agency to establish a novel pattern of capital mobilization and management. Prior Dutch advances to European rulers and governments, dating at least from a 1616 loan to the electoral heir of Brandenburg,[5] had generally been managed by tax receivers, officials who were well placed for such transactions because of their involvement in domestic public finance. Pieter Martensz. Hoefijzer, the receiver for the Amsterdam admiralty who organized the 1616 loan, appears to have extended a total of f. 248,000 out of his own resources, but the techniques used by subsequent receiver-bankers included merchandising loans through intermediaries in Amsterdam. Deutz, however, marketed the 1695 issue in notes or shares, thereby expanding capital access.

Because customary practice regarding the size of subscription units or the number of subscribers no longer restricted foreign government lending, Deutz's method of raising capital resembled a joint-stock technique. But the benefits thus acquired by organizer and borrower were not matched on the side of investors. Deutz's role as banker differed significantly from that of the managing director of a joint-stock commercial enterprise because the firm's responsibilities were clearly demarcated only with respect to the debtor. Charged with handling the receipt and sale of mercury shipments, making annuity and redemption payments, and remitting to Vienna, Deutz's ability to satisfy the interests of subscribers was dependent on a continuation of shipments. The firm did not acknowledge any liability to subscribers, so that although Deutz might have been expected to represent creditor interests in Austria in case of default, there was no explicit or implicit obligation beyond that. Aside from the 5 percent return, investors were apparently attracted by the notion that a Dutch firm, one whose name was familiar and respected, was managing the advance, and perhaps by an ancillary guarantee in the form of a general mortgage on revenues and properties of the emperor. That those features had an implied rather than an actual value was not deemed a matter of consequence, for the loan was raised and its proceeds forwarded to Vienna.

From Deutz's perspective the commercial aspect of the 1695 contract was more important than the credit feature. In place of the joint agency that had long been used in Austrian marketing, Deutz gained exclusive management over sales and thus control of what was at the time a European monopoly.[6] The firm's compensation was also based principally on the mercury anticipations, for 2 percent was earned on mineral sales and a smaller commission on the credit component.[7]

Deutz clearly understood where its own advantage lay in the opportunity before it. In place of using the firm's own assets to extend credit on future commodity shipments, an element of the shared mercury agency, Deutz substituted the savings of Dutch rentiers, enlarged the scale of credit supply, and extracted an additional commission. No evidence has been uncovered concerning the understanding or attitude investors brought to the contract. The commercial element was presumably reassuring, in the sense both that mercury prices had been predictable and that commodity shipments stood behind the advance, if in a different rhythm than in short-term commercial credit. But the Austrian loan was a wartime advance and the purpose behind it was to assist the empire in its intermittent conflict with Turkey (1682–99) and in the War of the League of Augsburg (1688–97). There is no hint that any part was intended for expanding mercury production or in any other fashion influencing Austrian output or Austro-Dutch economic ties. Since Austria also raised loans in the same period in London and Genoa,[8] the Amsterdam issues may have represented to Deutz a means of safeguarding a commercial tie otherwise in danger of being lost. Even if that were the case, the precedents established in 1695 were essentially financial rather than economic. Subsequent loans to Austria and other states were not organized with the aim of expanding Dutch trade or increasing production in debtor states in a fashion that might benefit the Republic.[9]

As other states joined Austria and England in drawing on Dutch savings, the dual pattern that evolved in the 1690s was maintained. England and, later, France attracted a multinational clientele into loans floated at home, whereas most other debtor states relied on Dutch intermediaries.[10] Well beyond 1740 Britain dominated Dutch foreign lending, chiefly because British financial practices gave real and important assurances to foreign lenders. But the flow of savings across the Channel was determined in part by opportunity itself. Austria's loans of 1695–1740 imply that a public credit apparatus emphasizing foreign borrowing might have evolved earlier than it did in the empire. In the event, however, Austrian finance retained a hand-to-mouth quality. Wartime policy included requisitions, the deferral or suspension of payments, forced levies in occupied territory, and domestic as well as foreign borrowing. During the

Spanish Succession conflict deficits were covered chiefly by nonpayment and, beginning in 1705, by credit organized through the Bank of Vienna. Foreign credit, although important enough to have been treated carefully in order to preserve its availability, did not have a dominant role. That was true not only of the six issues dating from 1695 to 1704,[11] in which a total of f. 7,275,000 was raised, but also of the entire series through 1740. Even the f. 13 million borrowed during Austria's conflicts of the 1730s (the Polish Succession War of 1733–5 and the Austro-Turkish War of 1737–9) appears to have accounted for only a small segment of overall spending.[12]

In the meantime Austrian mortgage practices had shifted from commodity anticipations (mercury and copper) to a combination of mineral and revenue anticipations. Revenues from Silesia were used until 1737 when, having mortgaged them to exhaustion, the empire offered income from Bohemia. When Prussia seized Silesia in the War of the Austrian Succession, Austria proclaimed that its liabilities had changed hands with the territory. But Prussia refused for more than fifty years to acknowledge any logic in that stance,[13] and payments were suspended on those loans. Because imperial income from Silesia had been mortgaged so extensively, the loss of that province was, in the short run, less damaging than has sometimes been supposed. Austria abrogated part of its foreign debt and sacrificed revenues that would, at least in the immediate future, have been claimed by the Dutch in any case.

In an important sense Austrian utilization of Dutch credit early in the eighteenth century was premature. Because lending to foreign governments was still of limited attractiveness, the quantity of capital available was still modest and an entirely disproportionate part was claimed by a government (Britain) in which investors felt more secure. Gradually declining credit costs on the Amsterdam market reflect an economic setting in which investment opportunities outside government finance were slowly shrinking in volume and yield. Through the 1730s, however, marine insurance, bill discounting, shipping, manufacturing, fishing, and other areas remained generally more attractive than loans to foreign governments.

The most plausible reconstruction of Dutch investment in the British debt does not find growth marked until the 1740s.[14] Such timing fits neatly with what is known about trends in the Dutch economy. Although the expansion of trade slowed by the mid-seventeenth century, Charles Wilson maintains that the Republic's merchants preserved their superiority to rivals until about 1730.[15] English and French transport and commerce may have quickened their pace of growth at about the same time, but the Republic's position shifted in relative rather than absolute terms. The volume of goods carried declined only slightly. However, once in an approximately stable position, commerce was decreasingly able to absorb its own profits and those earnings in other sectors that, in earlier times, would have flowed into trade. In terms of the availability of capital for foreign government lending, the shift was gradual rather than immediately noticeable. Somewhat greater Dutch lending to Austria in the 1730s may be attributed in part to increasing capital supply, but there is less doubt about explaining the surge of investment in British loans in the 1740s by referring first to deteriorating opportunities in commerce and then to the coincidental collapse of Austrian credit in Amsterdam.

1740–80. Dutch foreign lending during the War of the Austrian Succession marked the first substantial reorientation of investors' interests toward international government finance, but it did not establish an invariable pattern. At the end of the war British credit demand waned without alternative borrowers appearing. In contrast, capital exports once again increased sharply during the Seven Years' War and in its aftermath a suspension of new British borrowing coincided with high demand from continental governments. The estimated annual addition to the Republic's foreign loan balance averaged some f. 14 million during the Seven Years' War. Between 1763 and 1780 annual capital exports averaged between f. 11 and 12 million when loans to West Indian planters and foreign commerce and industry are excluded, and more than f. 15 million when included.

Because demand was not constant, the flow of Dutch capital was not as steady as these averages suggest. Governments floated loans as compelled by erratic spending requirements rather than in an effort to exploit capital-supply and credit-cost trends in Amsterdam. Britain sometimes renegotiated debts in peacetime to reduce charges, but such operations depended on little new investment from the Republic, and other borrowers were generally content with the possibility of using cheap Dutch credit to reduce their own costs. Even if financial authorities had watched the short-term movement of Amsterdam charges, several factors militated against taking advantage of any changes. States relying on the market's government loan apparatus were bound by redemption schedules specified in their debentures. Renegotiation of outstanding credits could not ordinarily occur except within the temporal framework of the debenture. Furthermore, such a step required fresh commission payments that might, because long-term credit costs fluctuated within such a narrow spectrum, equal or exceed any savings. On the other hand, states also borrowing on domestic markets sometimes used cheap Dutch credit to reduce domestic debts,[16] or attempted to lower overhead costs for Dutch lenders and thereby increase capital imports.

To an important degree the Amsterdam market was organized so that short-term shifts in capital supply would have little impact on annuity rates. Loans customarily remained open for several months or longer, and thus short-term supply changes could occur without influencing an issue. Loan subscriptions moved in spurts,[17] but not in a wholly unpredictable fashion. Information about capital supply was defective, and this was further confused by investment flows that bypassed the market's foreign loan apparatus. Presumably because they wished to overcome information problems, bankers used methods of mobilizing credit that enabled them to disregard unpredictable shifts within a subscription period. They retained the flexibility to make minor modifications in commission fees and, by seldom guaranteeing subscriptions, to inform borrowers that the terms initially established had proved inadequate. But the most common pattern was to leave an issue open until it was fully subscribed and, if necessary, to sell notes gradually as the loan waxed and waned in attractiveness. In a few cases remnants of loan notes were placed with foreign brokers, usually in Antwerp.[18]

Issues remaining open for several months encompassed some important and largely predictable shifts in capital supply. Although the conversion of commercial assets toward foreign government lending might be expected to have occurred as appealing opportunities were announced on the Amsterdam market, other sources yielded investment capital in a more regular pattern. For example, government debtors usually scheduled annuity and redemption payments for the first of the month. Actual payments stretched over months or years, as some investors responded tardily to public notices. But disbursements were concentrated toward the first and brokers found buyers more readily then than at other times.

Seasonal irregularities in annuity and redemption payments also influenced capital supply, but again in a predictable fashion. Some governments distributed loan initiation and thus payment dates throughout the year, but others set formal opening dates more frequently in one month than another. The general distribution from January through December was concave, although the number of loans formally opened in the first four months of the year exceeded the number opened in November and December. In the interim, from May through October, issues were less frequent than in either peak period. Late summer was labeled the *konkommer tijd* (cucumber period), signifying the doldrums when everyone who could escaped the humidity, heat, and stench of Amsterdam for country homes. The impact of such a pattern increased over time, but because subscription periods were several months long and because in the long run the volume of available capital was growing, supply proved to be predictable.

When the prevailing annuity rate trend shifted during the 1780s, that change responded principally to the reemergence of large-scale borrowing by domestic governments. In the interim, from the mid-1750s into the 1780s, demand was more regular than irregular even though often dispersed among several borrowers. As Chart 4-2 shows, the British suspension of new borrowing at the end of the Seven Years' War coincided with increased borrowing by other governments and by West Indian planters. By about 1766 these together had pushed capital exports above the wartime level.

The shift away from lending to Britain was uneven, but the only available measure of annuity rates, Amsterdam prices on the British funds, does not indicate any significant change in realizable returns that should not be accounted for by other factors. The 3-percent consolidated annuities trading in Amsterdam advanced toward par at the end of 1762 and from then until 1770, despite a decline associated with the crisis of 1763, were exchanged at prices giving effective yields of 3.1 to 3.6 percent.[19] An inflexible pattern of capital supply would presumably have led to competition for British paper, and thus to a reduction of realizable returns. In the event investors altered the rate at which they converted assets from other sectors into government finance, a step eased by high liquidity preference during and immediately after the crisis of 1763.

Average returns in all foreign investment areas increased as the plantation loans, which offered high yields, became more numerous. Although plantation loans paying as little as 4 percent were introduced in 1769, average returns remained between 5 and 6 percent.[20] Aggressive Amsterdam and Rotterdam merchants, aware of the commercial possibilities in organizing long-term credit for the West Indies, sharply expanded attempts to mobilize savings. But the higher returns offered to attract capital reflected a sense of the risk premium required of such extensions rather than a shift in the intensity of pressure on capital supply. Stable returns paid in other foreign investments once again indicate flexibility in the rate at which investors could convert assets into foreign lending.

Lenders probably did not leave savings unemployed in periods of comparatively slack foreign demand, such as in 1771, thereby hoarding resources in anticipation of a resurgence. A likelier but still tentative explanation would account for such flexibility by referring to the liquidity crisis of 1763 and more generally to the importance of short-term credit and lending to individuals. Because foreign lending offered higher returns or more attractive management arrangements, investors may have moved in and out of the short-term and individual credit sectors as the demand for foreign loans waxed and waned. Moreover, since in the long run government finance drew capital out of traditional investment areas, which were less attractive rather than unattractive, the process of conversion could be quickened or slowed with variations in demand.

In 1771 the number of issues and volume of capital sought by foreign governments fell and, until about 1775, remained less than during the late 1760s.[21] After opening 1771 with an effective yield of 3.8 percent, British 3-percent consols traded through 1775 at prices giving yields of 3.3 to 3.6 percent.[22] Once again, therefore, a short-term decline in demand did not produce competition for British paper. Both the crisis of 1763 and that of 1772–3 occurred when few borrowers were seeking loans, although demand conditions were coincidental to rather than products of high liquidity preference in Amsterdam and a contraction of capital supply.

The latter crisis threatened the solvency of overextended planters, and lending to the West Indies declined for the remainder of the decade. But demand from continental states, and in particular from Austria, Russia, and Spain, increased. When Britain renewed borrowing with the opening of hostilities in America, the Amsterdam market faced simultaneous pressure from nine of the debtor areas identified in Chart 4-2. Dutch prices on British annuities declined into 1780, but it does not follow that increasing realizable returns on those securities should be taken to indicate unusual pressure on capital supply. Prices commonly fell during war. Moreover, there was only a slight increase in average annuity rates in loans negotiated for foreign governments between 1775 and 1776 (Chart 2-1), and for the remainder of the decade the average stood at or close to 4 percent. As the velocity and volume of loans increased after the crisis of 1772–3, investors appear to have expanded conversions toward government finance, thereby accommodating the surge. Annuity rate changes continued to be related chiefly to the idiosyncrasies of borrowers rather than to shifts in credit demand.

Certain Dutch banking customs influenced the annuity paid by given borrowers and the range of returns available in any particular year. In addition to practices already discussed in Chapter 2, it is evident that bankers usually brought the initial loan of a new borrower onto the market at returns near or identical to the maximum prevailing for borrowers of that type. The Russian loans, for example, opened in 1769 with 5-percent returns, at which level Russia was grouped with other first-time credit seekers, including Sweden and some of the lesser states of Germany. The correspondence and records of the firm that introduced the Russian issue, Raymond & Theodore de Smeth, have not survived, and it is impossible to establish what steps were taken to evaluate Russian finances. Neither in that nor any other case, however, is there evidence of a detailed inquiry. As a result it seems reasonable to conclude that bankers dealt with this aspect of aversion to risk among investors in the simplest way they could. The operative principle, already mentioned, was that the borrower that serviced debts punctually would be able to reduce credit costs in later loans. For Russia the loans of 1769–73 were prolonged in 1778 and thereafter, and new advances also negotiated. Both credits and prolongations paid 4 to 4.5 percent.[23]

In summary, both the Amsterdam marketing structure and the ability of investors to shift between loans to governments and to planters or others, among government borrowers, and between short- and long-term credit sectors diminished the incidence and effect of variations in capital supply and demand up to about 1780. Insofar as they are evident in new loan issues, long-term annuity rates moved only within the narrow range shown in Chart 2-1. Even such variations exaggerate changes in what was demanded of borrowers generally regarded as secure and credit worthy. The practice of offering returns including a risk premium of no more than 1 to 1.5 percent over the annuity paid by the most highly regarded foreign borrowers suggests that variations in rates tied to demand pressures (as opposed to perceived differences in credit worthiness) may have been little more than incidental. In any case, annuity rates for the most preferred borrowers entering the market in a given year do not appear (with the possible exception of 1773) to have varied by more than ½ percent.

The period of dispersal

The suspension of new lending to Britain around 1780 coincided with a decline in Austrian borrowing. Other investment sectors remained active (Chart 4-2), but an oversupply problem was unavoidable. Oversupply is not reflected in realizable returns on British annuities, however, for such paper moved to high yields as demand for it declined and as British credit deteriorated in Dutch appraisals. Nor is it evident in average annuity rates on foreign government loans negotiated through the market apparatus, for yields increased slightly from 1780 to 1781 and more sharply from 1781 through 1783. But it is apparent in revived aggressiveness on the part of banking intermediaries and investors seeking to mobilize credit demand. Such aggressiveness had last been evident in the aftermath of the Seven Years' War, when West

Indian planters and continental governments were simultaneously drawn to Amsterdam in search of credit. Since the crisis of 1772–3, in contrast, the trend had been more restrained.

Oversupply was particularly noticeable in 1780 and 1781. In the latter year, however, there were signs of a commercial depression and a liquidity crisis of the sort last experienced in 1773. That no crisis developed after commodity flows contracted abruptly during the Anglo-Dutch war may be ascribed at least in part to the coincidental decline in foreign lending and therefore to greater liquidity among rentiers. On the other hand, Dutch participation in a European conflict for the first time since 1748 led to tax increases and high domestic government borrowing. In January 1781 the province of Holland introduced a levy on some types of securities, public offices, and real estate, among other tax increases. But the war with Britain did not draw the united support of political factions within the Republic, and for that reason it was pursued with less than utmost vigor. As a result credit demand from domestic government did not take up the slack created by a shift in foreign lending patterns.

Quite fortuitously the search for alternative outlets was not difficult. Both France and the United States were eager to draw on Dutch resources and, although investors were at first reluctant to lend to the United States, they had no such qualms about taking advantage of the lucrative terms of French loans. By 1783 large sums were moving toward Paris and between then and 1787 Dutch investment in France increased more rapidly even than earlier lending to Britain.

During the 1780s the pace at which assets were converted toward government finance quickened. To be precise about that process requires information that is not available, but there are clear indications of a change in the conversion rate. The estimated average addition to the balance of Dutch assets in foreign government loans increased between 1780 and 1793 from the prior range of f. 11–12 million to some f. 20 million per year. Within the same period stable or declining domestic government debts gave way to expanded borrowing, although that trend is particularly noticeable only toward the late 1780s. Annuity rates on domestic and foreign government loans reveal pressure on capital supply, although there too the increase is more evident at the end of the decade.[24] But credit costs did not rise proportionally with the balance of government loans and, in 1792, annuity rates in the foreign sector declined from the high levels prevailing in 1789–91 (Chart 2-1).

To a significant extent capital accumulation in lending to governments was self-generating, not merely because prolongation loans were common but because annuity earnings were often reinvested. In the long run the foreign government loan balance grew at a pace approximately equivalent to that permitted by foreign-exchange earnings from annuity payments.[25] Actual annuity reinvestments amounted only to that share of earnings that rentiers allocated to governments rather than saved elsewhere or consumed. Combining at the more conservative level of 25 percent Henry Hope's estimated savings rate with estimates of the nominal value balance of Dutch investments in foreign government loans in 1770 and 1793 (f. 250 and f. 610 million, respectively), and assuming that average returns increased from about 4 percent in 1770 to about 4.5 percent in 1790, the proportion of additions to the balance covered by annuity income appears to have grown from about 22 percent of f. 11.5 million in 1770 to some 34 percent of f. 20 million in 1793.[26] At that rate, however, new investment from other sources would have increased from about f. 9 million to slightly more than f. 13 million per annum.[27] In fact the interim rate of conversion was higher than these calculations suggest because annuity earnings increased more slowly than foreign assets. Between 1780 and 1792, therefore, the average rate of conversion increased to an annual level that reached or slightly exceeded f. 15 million before falling to about f. 13 million in 1793.

As long as domestic government borrowing was increasing slowly, part of the sum required to account for greater foreign lending was provided by annuity income from domestic loans. Nevertheless, adding those estimated earnings to the computation leaves a growing sum that was supplied out of other sources. And of course when domestic government borrowing expanded, it too required infusions at a greater rate than that permitted by savings out of annuity receipts. Apparently the annual rate at which assets were converted (after accounting for annuity income from all government loans) increased from about f. 5 million during the early 1770s to between f. 15 and f. 20 million in the latter 1780s and early 1790s.

Supply and demand patterns

As tentative as those figures are, they correspond with what we know about Dutch economic trends after 1780. The Dutch share of Europe's carrying trade decreased absolutely during the Anglo-Dutch War, whereas fishing and manufacturing continued their earlier decline. Investment opportunities and the profitability of new or old holdings in those spheres shrank. In the short run, at least, converting assets toward government loans was a sensible procedure. But the success of foreign and domestic governments in raising credit at net returns of between 2.5 and 5 percent underscores a longer-term problem of finding productive uses for capital. That the rate of conversion to such yields increased markedly from the 1770s to the 1780s points dramatically to the pace at which Dutch competitiveness in trade, manufacturing, and fishing was being lost, and to the impotence of cheap credit to reverse that development.

A trend that would not have developed without a simultaneous increase in credit demand was, however, spurred by government borrowing. Available evidence points to growing momentum in the incidence and magnitude of peacetime deficits without any coincidental reduction in wartime deficits. By the latter 1780s demand applied persistent if still rather slight pressure to Dutch capital supply, but it would be improper to characterize that decade as one of unremitting competition among borrowers. The sharpest increase in new foreign lending may be dated from 1783, when Dutch investment in France expanded. Elsewhere on the continent deficits were funded in the mid-1780s chiefly from domestic resources. Then in 1787, having come unexpectedly to realize that its financial position was grave, the French monarchy by and large suspended new loan issues. France actually withdrew from the market before it had exhausted the willingness of investors to extend credit, although loans projected after public revelation of the monarchy's position were generally unsuccessful in attracting foreign or domestic subscribers.

France's withdrawal coincided with increased demand from other states and with an aggressive exploration of investment opportunities in Russia and the United States. Between 1788 and 1791 Russia, Austria, the United States, Poland, and Sweden returned to the Amsterdam market in earnest,[28] where they found themselves in competition with the domestic government, in particular with the forced loan adopted in the aftermath of the Patriot Revolution. It was only then that capital demand clearly exceeded supply, even in terms of the sustained subscription periods that remained customary. The average annuity in new foreign loans (weighted according to the sums raised at different rates) rose from some 4.3 percent in 1788 to 5 percent in 1789 and 1790, and declined only slightly (to 4.9 percent) in 1791 (Chart 2-1).[29] Yet the 5-percent barrier was not broken, as borrowers regarded as less reliable continued to attract lenders with returns at that level whereas the more creditworthy governments increased the yields they offered. In short, pressure on capital supply in 1788–91 can too easily be exaggerated unless the reaction of investors – an increase in the rate at which assets were converted from other sectors – is kept in mind. In 1792 the average annuity on twelve issues seeking nearly f. 35 million (including prolongations) fell to 4.3 percent.

In 1787 Hope & Co. secured management of Russian borrowing in the Republic.[30] The Hope archives, exploited carefully by Marten G. Buist, provide evidence about the firm's appraisal of market conditions and of the prospects of filling what turned into a series of large loans. The firm's attention was occupied not by an effort to evaluate Russian finances, for that was in any case unnecessary because Russian public credit was established in the eyes of Dutch investors.[31] What concerned Hope & Co. was capital availability in Amsterdam in the aftermath of the Patriot Revolution and in the face of a renewal of Russia's war with Ottoman Turkey. Although the firm urged caution in setting amounts to be sought, Russian loan proposals met an eager response from commission agents circularized by Hope's brokers.[32] Before the end of December 1787 contracts were signed with agents for f. 6 million, far more than the f. 1.5 million for which authorization had arrived in Amsterdam.[33] The response from agents was in turn matched by investors who, in Henry Hope's estimation, were drawn by an annuity ½ percent higher than that available on competing foreign loans. In a subsequent assessment Hope also suggested that capital had been more abundant than had been realized, and that the discredit of domestic government at all levels had inclined investors toward foreign loans.[34] Some explanation was important, for within six years Russia raised no less than f. 53.5 million.[35]

Supply and demand patterns

Buist ties changes in loan terms to domestic and international political developments.[36] Hope was as well informed as anyone about forces influencing the Amsterdam market. Had his reports to Richard Sutherland, the court banker in charge of negotiations from St. Petersburg, been completely frank, they might be accepted as the authoritative statement on the causes of market oscillations between 1787 and 1793. But Hope was, after all, bargaining with Sutherland, and bargaining from a position in which the information at his command about capital supply was defective. It was certainly in the Dutch firm's interest to serve Russia satisfactorily, especially because Hope did not stand above the threat of competition. Russia had successfully negotiated loans in other financial centers, and had on at least one occasion approached another Dutch firm. And of course profits were no niggling consideration. As Buist interprets the Hope–Sutherland correspondence, it appears that Hope wished to exaggerate the deleterious impact of domestic and international events on capital supply. Despite the fact that the Russian loans, floated for larger sums than ever before attempted by a single foreign borrower through the market apparatus, succeeded beyond expectations, Hope always stressed hindrances and anticipated problems. Once each loan was underway, however, he managed readily enough to find reasons for its unexpected success.[37]

An attempt to test the impact of international events upon the price of British securities in Amsterdam suggests that the market did not respond consistently in one direction or the other to events that might be expected to have influenced it.[38] Because secular quotations are unavailable for Russian securities until September 1792, that theory cannot be tested here.[39] But it is plausible to suppose that Hope, serving the interests of the firm, distorted his portrayal of forces affecting the Amsterdam market. Such a strategy amounted to a psychological ploy that, while the loans continued to succeed, made Hope look singularly adept at overcoming adversity.

In short, the slightly increased yields that Hope advised Russia to adopt and the high commission charges of those issues (Chart 2-2) attracted subscribers despite unprecedented competition among borrowers. What Hope failed to understand, or at least to explain to Sutherland, was that capital supply was malleable because investors were willing to convert other assets to 4.5- and 5-percent yields.[40]

It is uncertain how long a high conversion rate could have been maintained without reviving more profitable opportunities in Dutch trade, industry, or fishing. But such a situation did not arise. The 5-percent barrier, so appealing to bankers and investors while capital supply was increasing, proved with the War of the First Coalition to be attractive to investors no longer. Bankers were reluctant to increase the returns they recommended to prospective borrowers to levels that would have captured subscribers.[41] But, with Dutch entry into the war in 1793, domestic governments increased their demand for savings that might otherwise have flowed abroad. European governments may plausibly be supposed to have been willing to increase returns, but the particular financial pressures that would have made 6-percent yields, for instance, attractive, were encountered only after domestic governments had taken over the allocation of investment capital and made it largely involuntary.

5

INTERNATIONAL GOVERNMENT FINANCE

Resources

The core of the financial means available to eighteenth-century states was made up of tax revenues, the magnitude of which varied from state to state with the number and economic resources of taxpayers and the comprehensiveness and efficiency of tax assessment and collection. Although the construction of a time series of revenues and expenditures among all states for the whole century is not possible, sufficient data exist to approximate the relative position of revenues in seven governments during part of the second half of the century. Chart 5-1 gives tax-revenue estimates using current exchange rates and converting into Dutch guilders.[1]

The general pattern of increasing revenues evident in the chart should be interpreted in the light of both simultaneous inflation in the cost of goods and services acquired by government and frequent international conflict between 1740 and 1815. Tax income advanced, but lagged behind increasing expenditures.[2] Chart 5-2 portrays deficits in Great Britain and Austria during the years within the period 1763–1800 for which data are available.[3] Where similar information exists for other states it indicates that the Austrian pattern of almost perennial deficits was more common than the British pattern of small-scale peacetime surpluses interspersed with massive wartime deficits. In any case there is no question that deficits were regularly larger than surpluses among all major powers except Prussia (until the 1790s) and among many secondary powers as well.

Because the incidence and volume of deficits increased during the eighteenth century and because deficit spending became a

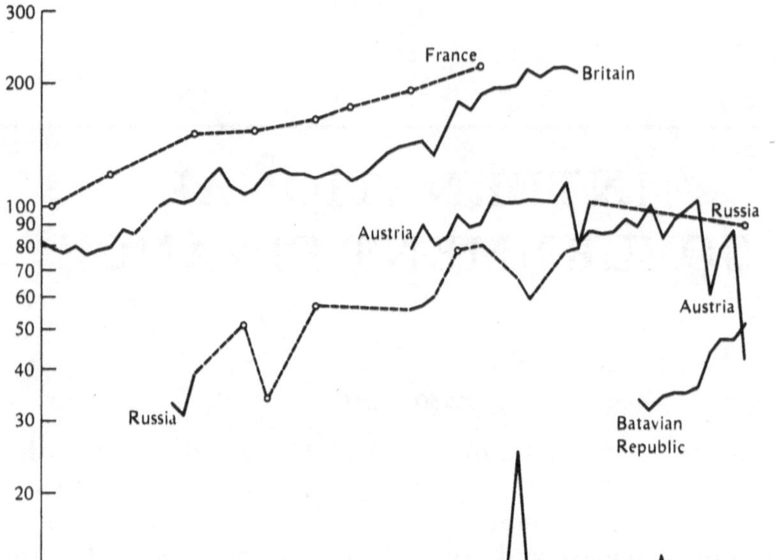

Chart 5-1. Tax revenues in some states, 1750–1809 (in millions of current guilders, semilog scale).

peacetime as well as a wartime phenomenon, finding reliable taxation supplements became an increasingly acute problem. During the second half of the century a number of states temporarily resolved that problem by shifting away from the deleterious and unstable measures that had traditionally been used to meet

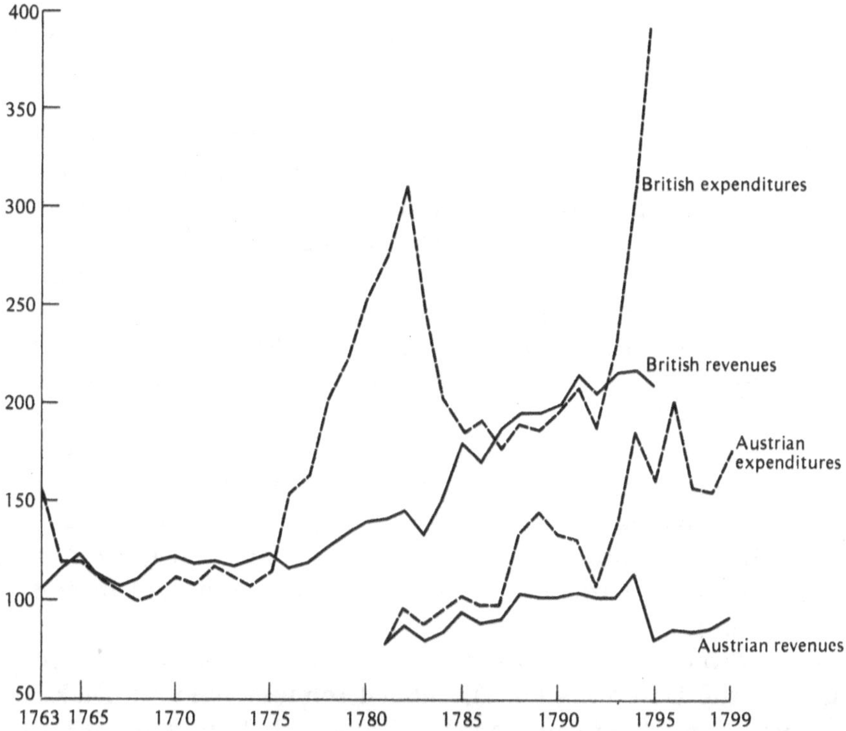

Chart 5-2. Revenues, expenditures, and deficits in Great Britain and Austria, 1763–99 (converted into millions of current guilders).

deficits and toward mercantilist expedient programs based on long-term credit exploitation.

Considered as a resource analogous to tax revenues, the volume of credit that could be raised varied from state to state, and therefore the overall resources of states differed according to two indexes. There were vast differences among eighteenth-century states in domestic credit resources, but there were also significant differences in the efficiency and expertise with which those greater or lesser resources were brought into use. Both the taxation and the credit component of financial power might therefore vary according to differences in resources and in the relative efficiency of exploitation but, because long-term credit could be raised in a supranational system, territorial limitations usually inherent in taxation could be superseded.

International finance and the Amsterdam market

Credit exploitation was by no means novel in the eighteenth century, but it is important to distinguish two types. In a pattern widely employed in seventeenth-century Europe, states raised short- and long-term loans by paying annuities that included interest and recapitalization. What may appear to have been usurious returns were in fact an acknowledgment of relative capital availability and the riskiness of lending to government, and their justification is evident from periodic repudiations. It has been shown that the seventeenth-century Dutch Republic adopted an alternative mode under which the part of an annuity serving to recapitalize a loan was gradually reduced until, toward the end of the century and with the assistance of a secular decline in credit costs in the private sector, Dutch governments were able to borrow by means of long-term redeemable (but in practice perpetual) annuities at rates equal to the lowest interest returns demanded in the private sector. The United Provinces had shifted to a program of credit exploitation that gave investors guarantees sufficient to convince them to accept interest-only lending formats.

During the wars of 1689–1714 Britain adopted the basic features of the Dutch system and added refinements to it. Dickson and Sperling have estimated that France, Britain, and the province of Holland met between one-third and one-half of their expenditures during those years by borrowing, but that Austria borrowed only about one-tenth of its outlays.[4] With higher per capita but more modest overall wealth than some of their European rivals, Britain and the Dutch Republic tapped domestic resources more effectively than either France or Austria. They emerged in 1714 with what appeared to be staggering debts, but in more stable financial positions than their rivals because they had seized the benefits of low-cost credit, comparatively efficient financial structures, and methods of borrowing that shifted debt maintenance charges to as large a degree as possible to the distant future while avoiding default. At that point the Republic had nearly exhausted its ability to continue credit exploitation, but Britain retained a significant margin between actual and potential credit use. Other states had, in the Anglo-Dutch credit structure, a model after which to fashion their own practices. Change toward that model, with or without the adoption of the rationalized management practices instituted in Britain, would play an important role in determining power relationships in Europe during the eighteenth century.

As France demonstrated, extensive internal resources could still be exploited without a rationalization of credit usages or an early entry into supranational borrowing, but a more efficient fiscal system, and the one most attractive politically, was that which took full advantage of low-cost credit. Outside the Dutch Republic inadequate domestic credit resources prevented sustained self-sufficiency in deficit financing or low debt maintenance costs. In order to compete among political units whose economic and credit resources varied substantially, other states, including France, found sooner or later that they were obliged to expand credit access. Because low interest rates in the Dutch Republic helped reduce credit costs, the state taking advantage of Dutch credit earlier than its rivals enhanced its position with respect to those rivals.

An international mechanism was available before the eighteenth century for mobilizing short-term credit. But such a method of borrowing tended to cost more in interest charges and management overhead than did long-term credit, and the continual requirement to renegotiate advances left the debtor prey to short-term fluctuations in capital supply and cost. During the 1720s Britain combined an efficient domestic public finance program with increasing use of long-term foreign credit, and managed thereby to reduce proportional debt-service costs. In other states, where financial planning was absent or inadequate and where domestic capital supply was also insufficient to permit a shift to low-cost credit, such developments awaited the appearance of a domestic market that could attract foreign capital or financial pressure sufficiently intense to oblige an active search for foreign capital. In the meantime costlier short-term credit and long-term loans encompassing recapitalization continued to be used. So long as there were intermittent periods of peace of sufficient length to permit recovery from the disarray of wartime deficits, both credit rationalization and tax reforms could be deferred. Between the War of the Spanish Succession and the War of the Austrian Succession (1714–40) there was just such a sustained period of peace, interrupted only by comparatively minor conflicts. Monetary and credit experimentation in Britain and France around 1720 aside, a period of years in which ordinary revenues appear to have matched or exceeded expenditures brought restabilization without significant reform or financial reorganization in states that had not already gained access to low-cost credit.

Had the same rhythm prevailed during and after the Seven Years' War, the financial disruption caused by that conflict would gradually have given way to stability and the reestablishment of a position that would permit renewed war. But that rhythm did not persist. Instead both the states involved in the conflict and the secondary powers that remained neutral found the postwar era a period of international tension and higher peacetime military spending more difficult to bear because of cumulative deficits. At the end of the war in 1763 the major powers of Europe, and many of the lesser powers as well, attempted to regain stability,[5] but were unable to reach their objective through tax reform alone. Furthermore, there were more frequent and more expensive regional conflicts between 1763 and 1792 than there had been between 1714 and 1740. Intermittent war was especially costly for states relying heavily on indirect taxes because revenues from such levies were more susceptible than property taxes to wartime shrinkage from contracting commercial activity. At the same time secular inflation produced higher nominal revenues from most tax sources, but revenue inflation lagged behind the higher cost of goods and services required by government. Where indirect taxes were farmed for collection, the practice of using leases of several years' duration could reduce wartime shrinkage but it accentuated the lag between rising prices and receipt of assessments at inflating levels.

If postwar reforms are evaluated in terms of the additional revenues produced, it will become apparent that they were, in general, failures. In 1765 Britain entered a decade of overall budgetary surplus (Chart 5-2) and, from a position of relative financial strength, attempted to shift more of the cost of servicing the public debt and of defense onto the American colonies. Although that effort was perceived at the time as being of critical importance, Britain had already succeeded in reversing a wartime trend to restore the potential cost of new credit (measured by realizable returns on current paper) to a rate below that paid by any other state, excepting only the Dutch Republic. The failure of the attempted transfer, the alienation of the American colonists, even the initiation within the British Empire of a civil war that turned into a European conflict, all had financial consequences of less significance than those following the failure of tax reform in other states.

Austria had more ground to make up than Britain in rationalizing its administration of revenues, but in comparison to other states on the continent the empire already enjoyed the benefits of low-cost credit to the limited degree to which foreign and domestic resources were in use. After 1763 the Austrian clergy and nobility were made to pay higher sums into the imperial treasury, but the nobility was able to resist tax redistribution that drew directly from its assets and thus to diminish the effectiveness of an attempt both to expand revenues and reallocate taxation away from the peasantry. Maria Theresa's reforms enhanced income but during the period for which budgetary data are available, from 1781 (Chart 5-2), Austrian expenditures exceeded revenues in every year but one to 1818. Tax reform efforts subsequent to those introduced after the Seven Years' War did not restore balance, and as deficits mounted Austria was forced to expand its utilization of domestic and foreign credit.

In France the *parlements* defeated reform in the assessment of the *taille*. There short- and long-term credit had long played an integral part in a revenue system marked by the absence of rationalization and even of some of the most elementary information necessary for financial management. Faced with no alleviation in its need for credit, France shifted toward an increasing emphasis on attracting international investment capital into government loans. That policy gained more resources, but large-scale capital imports during the 1770s did not decrease yields paid in new loans. Foreign capital was simply exploited on terms established in the Paris market, where a developing speculative frenzy and perhaps also an inadequate money supply contributed to high credit costs. Greater overall resources, vastly incomplete information about the size of the debt and its costs, and some comparatively minor economies and reductions in maintenance costs on the short-term debt deferred financial collapse, but throughout the period from the mid-1770s to the Revolution France was paying annuity yields so high that they stand in retrospect as evidence of an inevitable crisis of solvency.

Mathias and O'Brien have demonstrated that taxation in France was significantly less on a per capita basis (measured in constant prices) than in Britain at the same time.[6] Although much uncertainty remains about differences in the distribution of taxable wealth and about relative rates of economic growth in the two states, France appears after about 1735 to have permitted an increasing disparity to develop between actual tax levels and the potential taxability of an expanding economy.[7] The significance of that margin grew over the years and reached a peak during the 1780s.

What those and other states shared was reluctance or inability to redistribute taxation to reduce the most obvious inequities in a system that left the American colonies and powerful social and religious corporations undertaxed. It is tempting to assume that revenues sufficient for budgetary surplus or balance could have been gained through reapportionment of taxes toward accordance with wealth. But it may be more plausible to assume that redistribution would not by itself have permitted Britain, France, Austria, or other states to reach financial stability.[8] Britain benefited from sustained real economic growth that was reflected in tax revenues despite the absence of significant reform in the distribution of assessment. As long as a low-cost credit structure could be preserved without a higher rate of taxation at home, Britain could compete with continental rivals from a superior position while subsidizing the war efforts of allies. And it was Britain's military and naval spending that set the standard against which other states had to compete.

The absence elsewhere of equivalent economic growth in the latter decades of the eighteenth century or of a proportional reflection of growth in tax revenues left the margin of resources that could be seized through redistribution or higher taxation inadequate. That may have been true in terms solely of the absolute tax-paying ability of privileged groups still charged with costly social, political, and religious functions, but it was certainly true in terms of the balance between the social and political costs of redistribution and the relative benefits that might be derived from higher taxes paid by privileged groups and corporations.

International government finance

Fiscal alternatives

Parsimony. Denied, in practical if not also in absolute terms, from achieving stability by redistributing or otherwise reforming taxation, the states of the continent had two alternatives, credit inflation or strict economy. A frugal structure of household finance with deflationary effects had served Prussia before the Seven Years' War and was adopted again after that conflict.[9] The consistent objective was to accumulate a state treasury of sufficient size during years of peace that in war that asset, in combination with subsidies from allies, an even more rigorous exploitation of crown domains and indirect taxes, and coinage debasement, would permit Prussia to pursue more ambitious political goals than were warranted by the extent of its economic resources in comparison to those of other major powers. Prussia employed a fiscal system that was conservative both in its orientation toward serving the absolutist state while maintaining a tax distribution that burdened the lower classes and hampered the middle classes,[10] and in peacetime monetary restraint juxtaposed with wartime spending and debasement. A state treasury was not, as was often argued by eighteenth-century theorists, necessarily so much money taken out of circulation, but the accumulation of a war chest did presumably reduce the volume of circulating media and hinder economic activity. Nevertheless, for the time being that system succeeded for Prussia, if success is measured in terms of the state's ability to pursue its political objectives and not in terms of the economic consequences of such a pursuit through deflationary means in an inflationary era.

Credit inflation via long-term loans. The Prussian model was not, however, attractive to states that no longer had either extensive royal domains or an administrative structure capable of wringing the last drop out of levies on consumables. Other governments turned instead to credit inflation, a fiscal policy that complemented price trends and, if often unwittingly, seized some benefit from them. That approach was not novel to the post-1763 era, for most states had by that time used either long-term loans or paper currency issues to cover deficits. What was novel in the postwar era was the extent to which governments across Europe grasped foreign capital as a means of expanding the credit that could be raised through long-term loans or paper currency issues without counterproductive consequences while reducing the proportional cost of credit exploitation. That program was both politically expedient, in that it deferred or avoided a clash with privileged social corporations, and financially expedient, in that access to foreign credit in substantial volume reduced annuity rates in new loans and retarded the devaluation of paper currency. Fiscal authorities did not have to understand the mechanism in use, and were led to adopt it not because they understood all its implications but because they could gauge adeptly the financial options left open by political circumstances.

Significant differences existed among states inflating credit in the efficiency with which credit devices were employed. Two areas in particular, credit costs and the degree to which amortization was shifted to the distant future, require some elaboration. Short-term fluctuations aside, the Dutch Republic and Britain consistently paid the lowest annuity rates and exploited credit most efficiently. The margin separating them from France, which exploited credit in the least efficient fashion, was substantial. Whereas government borrowers in the Dutch Republic raised loans on net returns of as little as 2.5 percent, France continued into the 1780s to indulge lenders with annuity rates reminiscent of those paid by Britain and the Dutch Republic during the latter part of the seventeenth century.[11]

Throughout the eighteenth century French authorities, captivated apparently by its "self-liquidating" character, preserved a loan format, the life annuity, which had by and large been rejected by other borrowing powers because of its excessive costs. In the 1770s and 1780s most *rente viagère* issues were opened without regard to the age of nominees on whom contracts were settled, and thus in disregard not only of available information about the average longevity of nominees in prior loans but also of any attempt to separate interest from principal payments in the *rente*, or annuity.[12] Those loans were expected to amortize themselves over an average of twenty years,[13] a span more or less appropriate to life expectancy at the median age of the French population as a whole but one inappropriate to a situation in which investors would constitute contracts with care and on some nominees with a life expectancy that reached or exceeded forty-five years.[14] A calculation of the simple interest paid under such a format depends on the number of years assigned as the average span during which all contracts may be expected to have remained active. At an average longevity of twenty years the interest paid on an issue with a net yield of 9 percent was only 4 percent, although with the additional bonus that lenders could begin from the first year to shift the recapitalization portion of their annuity to new interest-bearing investments. As the remaining capital committed to the contract diminished, the yield would increase until in the twentieth year the holder of a 1,000 livres tournois (l.t.) contract returning 9 percent net would receive a yield of 80 percent (40 l.t. on a remaining capital of only 50 l.t.). At a span of forty years, more appropriate to longevity under the assumption that most investors chose nominees with care, the interest yield would increase from 6.5 to 260 percent. If the return the French treasury had to offer to raise long-term loans without a self-amortizing feature is estimated at 5 percent, a rate actually paid in some perpetual-annuity issues and a return commonly demanded on the Amsterdam market of the least credit-worthy governments, then the formula for capitalizing an income stream may be applied to establish the life-annuity yield necessary to match that return and amortize the principal over forty years. That calculation indicates that France was paying an interest yield of some 8.7 percent when it needed to pay no more than 5 percent, and that France might have paid only some 5.8 percent to cover both interest and amortization when the prevailing interest rate was 5 percent.[15]

On the overall royal debt France was paying an average net yield of 6 to 6.5 percent[16] whereas the province of Holland was paying an average net yield of between 2.5 and 4 percent. But in reality the margin separating the two ends of the debtor-state spectrum was even greater because France was paying a 6- to 6.5-percent return on the nominal value of a debt whose life-annuity portion had already been partially amortized. Other governments generally employed interest-bearing loan formats closer to the Anglo-Dutch model. The share of revenues required for debt service was thereby reduced whereas the volume of indebtedness that could be sustained was enlarged.

Like a rationalization of credit-exploitation techniques that lowered interest rates, measures that reduced the proportion of amortization payments in debt service increased the debt that could be accommodated without any increase in revenues. Higher spending for amortization could be used, as it was in the sinking fund established in Britain in 1786, to enhance public confidence in government credit. Yet the state allotting the greatest absolute and proportional amount of debt charges to retirements, as France did in the tontine and life- and term-annuity part of its debt, at the same time paid the highest interest rates, whereas the Dutch Republic, which met an insignificant portion of retirement expenses in the present year's expenditures, enjoyed the lowest credit costs.[17] Nor did French amortizations improve the monarchy's credit standing. Since states raising loans on the Amsterdam market commonly deferred amortization by renegotiating their debts, those governments shifted retirement to the distant future and thereby approximated the Dutch rather than the French approach.

The significance of these differences can be illustrated by comparing British and French allocations for debt service. In the second half of the 1780s Britain's revenues and expenditures both averaged about £16 million per annum, whereas French revenues in 1787 totaled a substantially larger sum, 474 million l.t., or about £19.1 million. For 1788 France budgeted 318.3 million l.t. (some £12.8 million) for debt service, or 67 percent of 1787 revenues. Britain's funded debt, amounting to £239.7 million at the end of 1786, was larger than the debt projected for France in 1788, nearly 5 billion l.t. (about £201 million).[18] But at the rate of British debt charges, approximately 3.7 percent in 1787 on the nominal sum of the funded debt, France could have supported a debt more than half again greater than the size estimated for 1788 before presumably having reached the point at which, in the eyes of financial authorities, it was necessary to consider the suspension of payments or summon the States General to attempt a general reorganization.[19]

Credit inflation via seigniorage. In Sweden and Denmark, where credit inflation was based on bank note issues, experts explicitly assumed the key to economic growth to lie in money supply. An increase in the volume of coins and bank notes was expected, when combined with a balance-of-payments surplus, to assist industrial and commercial development. The supply of paper currency was regulated by taxation, payable in such notes, and by controls over the convertibility of notes into specie exercised through central banks. But because recurrent deficits were sometimes met by an unbalanced program of credit expansion concentrating on monetary creation, both economies experienced violent price fluctuations. That unbalanced program, one of particular importance both before states experimenting with paper currency credit linked monetary programs to foreign borrowing and during the Revolutionary and Napoleonic wars, may be illustrated by Swedish policies during the conflict with Russia of 1740–3.

To finance the war, the quantity of notes in circulation was expanded, but with the expanded issues notes that had exchanged at a small premium against bulky copper coins in the 1730s depreciated against specie. In 1745 convertibility was suspended, replacing a copper and silver standard with a paper standard, and the resulting depreciation effectively canceled part of the debt incurred by note issues. The inflation that coincided with the war and with the expanded issue of notes was viewed as a product of the decline of the Swedish daler on the international exchange, not as a product of the overissue of paper.[20] The real crisis of inflation and depreciation of notes was thought to lie in exchange rates that mirrored the balance of payments.[21] Equilibrium was restored by persistent depreciation that tapered off gradually as notes were withdrawn from circulation.

Even if they did not acknowledge the inflationary pressures applied by an overissue of paper,[22] Scandinavian fiscal authorities understood the mechanism of meeting extraordinary expenses by the subtle form of taxation involved in depreciation. But there was an alternative technique for dealing with secular deficits while bolstering the exchange rate, and that consisted of adding foreign credit to the fiscal mechanism. In the 1760s Denmark and Sweden, facing both budgetary deficits and a critical overextension of paper in circulation, turned to the capital markets of Europe for credit.

In terms of debt-service charges the most efficient mercantilist expedient technique was a combination of paper currency issues with foreign loans, a system that was adopted and sometimes used in conjunction with domestic borrowing not only by

Denmark and Sweden but also by Russia, Austria, and Spain.[23] Overt costs amounted essentially to charges on interest-bearing credits, so that states with smaller financial or economic resources than their rivals could, by issuing interest-free paper, meet persistent deficits while paying comparatively little to service debts. In Sweden, for example, service on foreign loans absorbed less than 15 percent of projected revenues during the 1780s. On the other hand, precisely because such states did not have economic infrastructures capable of absorbing large-scale interest-bearing loans, they were susceptible to an overextension of currency credit. The relative advantage gained by note issues depended on the rate at which such paper was accepted in transactions. The ceiling beyond which paper currency issues began to lose their effectiveness was reached when such notes were discounted in trading to the extent that tax revenues collected in notes declined significantly in specie values and to the extent that note depreciation sponsored inflation in the cost of goods and services acquired by government. Foreign loans served to manipulate exchange rates between monetary systems based on specie and commercial drafts and systems based on specie, commercial drafts, and paper currency, and enabled the borrower to reduce note volume and diminish the pressure of monetary inflation while continuing to cover deficits.

National debts

The temporal pattern under which various states shifted to an intensive utilization of long-term credit may be established by comparing foreign and domestic debt totals with current revenues (Table 5-1).[24] The ratios given in the table indicate a general trend toward large-scale debts, but by themselves do not represent precisely the relative efficiency with which various states used domestic and foreign credit to move toward the Anglo-Dutch model of public finance. Although it is generally true that larger debt-revenue ratios reflect both more efficient credit techniques and an expanding use of the international network centering on Amsterdam, all states retained some practices that reduced the sum of revenues that could be appropriated for interest and thereby limited potential indebtedness. Nonetheless, there was a general shift toward the practices first brought into use in the Dutch Republic and thus toward a maximization of credit use. Whether debtor states used long-term loans or a combination of long-term loans and paper currency issues, they accumulated debts that assume staggering proportions when compared with the liabilities of twentieth-century developed states.

There was no common threshold beyond which states could no longer expand debt–revenue ratios, but there was a range within which liabilities could be accumulated through the international credit structure without producing an unacceptable discount on new borrowing. That range had several components, among which the comparative accessibility of domestic and foreign credit, the capacity of an economy to absorb paper currency issued for financial reasons, credit costs, and the relative level of spending for redemption or amortization have already been mentioned. Together with the sum of tax revenues that could be raised without counterproductive consequences, those were the most important elements of the credit formula in each state and in Europe as a whole.[25] At the same time, however, it is necessary to recognize that the absolute and relative levels of spending regarded as essential for the performance of administrative and military functions varied from state to state, and that such variations influenced the share of revenues that could be allotted to debt service. In the province of Holland, for example, proportionally and absolutely smaller military and naval appropriations (through the Generality) during most of the period from the conclusion of the War of the Spanish Succession to the Fourth Anglo-Dutch War released revenues for debt service and permitted the province to maintain a higher debt–revenue ratio than had yet been approached by other states and to spend about three-fourths of its revenues on service. In similar fashion variations in administrative spending could influence the comparative solidity of a debtor state. Military and naval spending was the area in which the greatest potential savings might be made to release revenues for debt service, but of course such spending was the preeminent cause of debt accumulation in the first place.

These, then, are the general features of credit exploitation by European states in the second half of the eighteenth century. The case has been made that an international credit structure enabled those states to sustain deficit financing while avoiding undesirable economic, political, or financial decisions and con-

Table 5-1. *Approximate debt–revenue ratios, 1689–1811 (all figures are ratios to unity)*

	Province of Holland	Britain	Austria	France	United States	Russia	Sweden	Denmark
1690	13 (1689)							
		.8 (1692)						
1700		3.3						
1710		4.1						
				6.4 (1713)				
1720	17	8.5						
1730		8.2						
1740		8.3						
1750		10.4						
1755		10.4						
1760		11						
	17.5 (1761)							
1765		12.2						
			8.5 (1768)				4.1 (1766)	6.9 8.5 (1769)
1770		11.5						
						.86 (1773)		
1775		11.5						
							8 (1777)	
1780	13.8	13.4					2.7	
1781		14.3	4.3 4.5				2.6	
1782		15.6	3.8 4			1.4	2.6	
1783		18.3	4.4				2.8	
1784		18.4	4.2			2.5	2.7	

1785		15.8	3.9	4				2.9		
1786		16.1	4.1					3.4		
1787		14.9	4.1		10.5			3.6		
1788	15.6	14.6	3.8					3.9		
1789		14.7	4	4.3				5.3		
1790		14.3						2.1		
1791		13.1						4.8		
1792		13	4.3	4.7		21		9.3		
1793		13.4				17.3		8.5		
1794	17.4	13.3				14.4	3.2	8.8		
1795		14				13.2		9.2		
1796		16	6.2	6.9		10		7.5		
1797		16.8	6.6	7.6		9.4		8.9		
1798		14.5	7.1	8.3		10		8		
1799		13.4	7.6	9.3		10.4		8.1		
1800			8	10.4		7.6		8.5		
1801		14.4	8.1	10.9		6.4				
1802		12.8	9.2	13.1		5.4				
1803		12.5	7.9	11.2		7				
1804		12.4				6.5				
1805		10.7				6.4		3.8		
1806	23.5[a]	10.3				5.3			8.1	13.1 (1806–7)
1807		9.7	4.5	8.1		4.6				
1808		9.1	3.9	7.1		4.1				
1809		8.8	6.1			8.4	6	5		
1810		8.8	4.8	12.2		6.1				
1811		8.4	9.5	12.5		3.7				

[a]The Batavian Republic.

sequences until the wars of the French Revolution. That structure has, to this point, been described in terms of capital supply and the techniques used in raising loans on the Amsterdam market, and in terms of the temporal pattern of demand for Dutch credit. There remains the task of furnishing evidence of a more detailed nature about bilateral relationships between the Amsterdam market and the major debtor states drawing upon Dutch savings. And there remains also the matter of the exhaustion of the international credit structure during the Revolutionary and Napoleonic wars. In the bilateral studies that follow, the discussion will concentrate on periods in which Dutch savings were employed by each state at a significant level.

The pattern of converting assets toward foreign lending, which developed on the Amsterdam market over the period into the 1790s, was disrupted in the early stages of the wars of the French Revolution. After 1793 capital exports through the market apparatus decreased markedly, but some European states were able to draw on Dutch credit intermittently during the conflict of 1792–1815. For that reason and because the bilateral studies have been designed both to reconstruct Dutch lending and to place foreign credit use within the context of financial policy among debtor states, the studies are incomplete. For continental states the narrative has been carried only to the point of financial crisis. The crisis itself will be taken up under the rubric "the collapse of solvency."

6

THE DEBTOR STATES: I

Great Britain

Dutch investment in the British public debt dated from the 1690s, when the royal debt was transformed into a public debt and Parliament guaranteed loan issues, securing them on specific sources of public revenue. British financial practices were partly fashioned after techniques introduced earlier in the Dutch Republic, although Britain made significant improvements.[1] But the British debt may have attracted Dutch investment not so much because of reforms in progress in account keeping and other administrative practices as because the debt was made the responsibility of a representative institution and thereby came to resemble the public debts of major government institutions in the Dutch Republic. There bodies that claimed to have a representative character had long carried the principal burden of raising credit under a more appealing framework than the princely responsibility identified with absolutist monarchies.

Other factors, too, may explain the attractiveness of the British debt. Dutch rentiers were familiar with the loan formats employed in Britain: life and term annuities and, from 1715, redeemable (but in practice perpetual) annuities. The principal agencies administering the public debt were also familiar, the exchequer for its resemblance to the receivers general of the provinces and the Generality, and the Bank of England for its extensive involvement in discounting commercial paper. Moreover, the financial links necessary for direct investment in loans issued in London were available in long-standing contacts between the two states in commerce and commercial finance.

As early as the 1740s some investors recognized that both Brit-

Table 6-1. *Borrowing as a percentage of expenditures in wartime*

1688–1697	33.6%
1702–1713	31.4
1739–1748	31.1
1756–1763	37.4
1776–1783	39.9
1793–1815	26.6

ain and the United Provinces drew in part on a common pool of capital.[2] Nevertheless the flow of investments to Britain was not sufficient then or at any time before 1780 to close a gap between the cost of long-term government credit in the two states.[3] That continuing margin reflects Dutch preference for domestic over foreign loans and the higher costs of managing foreign investments. But the returns on new British loans and on stocks and annuities already in circulation were generally below those available in the Republic from other foreign investments. In short, in the eyes of Dutch investors British public credit occupied a position of strength, one warranted by financial policies that shunned arbitrary depredations against investors' interests. It might also be appealing to describe Dutch investment in the public debt in terms of a bond of sympathy between two peoples, but the evidence, admittedly impressionistic, suggests otherwise. In the era of Dutch diplomatic dependence on Britain, stretching to 1780 and the Fourth Anglo-Dutch War, the argument might be made that Dutch investors, although perhaps antagonistic toward Britain because of their dependent position, felt greater confidence in a state that perceived its interests as being tied to those of the Republic against France. But Dutch investments in Britain did not spring from sympathy with the British people, and among individual merchants there was bitter rivalry.[4]

As is evident from Chart 5-2, British borrowing over the last four decades of the century was war oriented. The same pattern had characterized the earlier part of the century (Table 6-1).[5] In peacetime revenues matched or slightly exceeded expenditures, but surpluses were seldom sufficient to reduce significantly the balance of debts outstanding. However, the resulting accumulation of indebtedness was managed with skill and in such a fashion that the relative burden of the public debt was mitigated by long-term trends in credit costs, taxation revenues, and prices.

The average yield on the long-term debt declined from a range of 7 to 14 percent during the 1690s to 3 percent or less in the mid-1730s, moving (although not so quickly) in the same direction as deflating credit costs in the Dutch Republic.[6] Peacetime annuity trends were influenced both by attempts to reduce the cost of debt service, thus lowering the overall level of expenditures, and by a combined government and private effort based on the assumption that broad economic benefits could be realized from the tax decrease that would be made possible either by a reduction of the debt or of its maintenance costs.[7] In 1717 and again between 1727 and 1730, for example, the return was lowered on part of the debt. By the mid-1730s the average annuity stood at or below 3 percent, a decline of more than 2 percent in some twenty years. Similarly the Pelham conversion of 1749–57 reduced the annuity on the funded debt first from 4 to 3.5 percent and then to 3 percent. Such measures were generally accepted by domestic and foreign creditors because returns available in alternative investment areas were also falling.[8] Britain was able therefore to renegotiate loans contracted under wartime pressure on capital supply, and to conduct those renegotiations on terms acceptable to creditors.

When confronted with rising credit costs, Britain generally preferred to issue loans at a discount. In that fashion capital was raised on terms that granted creditors notes of higher nominal value than their cost or than their immediate market value. This technique implicitly acknowledged the impact of secular inflation on the long-term debt because the government managed thereby to hold annuity rates down as a percentage of nominal values. When credit costs fell, the advantages of that method were apparent, for then realizable (or effective) yields moved toward, reached, or fell below nominal yields. In the process the debt maintenance costs that were incurred in the early years of a loan were reduced at the same time that eventual redemption was made less costly by inflation. At the end of the 1790s an increasing national product permitted Britain to introduce new taxes that sharply increased revenues in constant values, and which thereby both reduced the part of overall expenditures funded out of loans and further decreased the relative significance of the debt accumulated over the period since the 1690s. There is, therefore, really no paradox in the observation that the seemingly staggering debt levels reached during the Revolutionary and Napoleonic wars were less burdensome than the much smaller levels of eighteenth-century conflicts.

The skill with which public finances were administered in Britain should not, however, be taken to suggest that there was steady improvement in the public credit position of the state over the century. Annuity-rate renegotiations and discounts on wartime issues were useful devices for reducing the relative burden of accumulating debts. But the debt was expanding and, during the Seven Years' and American wars, the share of expenditures covered through loans was increasing in comparison with earlier conflicts (Table 6-1). In the absence of a national product expanding in real value or, by the 1780s, in the absence of a tax program benefiting at the same rate as earlier in the century from gains in taxable assets, the British credit position was deteriorating.

Its rate of deterioration was modified significantly by the development of an international pool of investment capital from which loans might be raised, and, during the two major conflicts between 1739 and 1763, by expanding use of that pool.[9] Foreign investment in the public debt became particularly important in the 1740s. Between 1742 and 1748 the long-term debt increased by some £20.7 million and the funded debt as a whole by £25.4 million.[10] There are no satisfactory estimates of foreign holdings in the public debt outside bank and company stock before mid-century, but investment during the 1740s may be estimated on the assumption that holdings in bank and company stock in 1723–4 were approximately proportional to contemporary holdings in the public debt as a whole. On that basis foreign holdings would have increased from slightly over 9 percent in 1723–4 to slightly less than 15 percent in 1750, the latter proportion indicated by estimates and surveys dealing with the entire national debt.[11]

Expanded investment was probably concentrated between 1742 and 1748, when the public debt was increasing, rather than in the preceding period, when there was a net reduction.[12] If foreign holdings still totaled no more than about 9 percent of the public debt at the end of 1739, and reached nearly 15 percent in 1750, then the increase during the 1740s would have totaled almost £6.9 million.[13] At that level foreign capital from all sources would have accounted for about 24 percent of the net addition to the funded debt in the 1740s and for slightly more than 7 percent of net expenditures.[14]

Even if the addition to the funded debt covered by foreign investors was less than 24 percent (and therefore fell somewhere between 15 and 24 percent), foreign credits still eased pressure on domestic capital supply and thus modified the wartime tendency toward rising interest rates. The effective yield on 3-percent notes increased from 3 percent in 1742–5 to no more than 4 percent in 1746–8, and fell again thereafter. A similar movement appears to have characterized Dutch government loans,[15] although the effective return on notes of the more creditworthy Dutch governments remained far enough below the annuity offered in wartime Britain to favor capital export.[16]

Estimated foreign holdings in the public debt toward the conclusion of the Seven Years' War (1762) vary from 14 percent to more than 25 percent. The lower figure is drawn from a computation made by Sir John Sinclair, and the higher from a survey of a wide range of eighteenth-century estimates.[17] At the end of 1762 the funded debt amounted to about £121.9 million, which would make foreign holdings between £17 and 30 million or more.[18] A reliable estimate for the late 1770s, when the funded debt totaled between £131 and 144 million, puts Dutch holdings alone at one-sixth to one-eighth (12.5 to 16.5 percent).[19] Taken at the mean, Dutch assets would have equaled some £21 million (about f. 240 million at current rates) and all foreign holdings something in excess of that. Unless there was significant (and unobserved) disinvestment in the interim, foreign holdings in 1762 probably did not exceed £25 million.

Estimates of Dutch holdings in the public debt in the late 1770s indicate that the Republic was the dominant source of foreign investment. In paper tested by Dickson for 1750, when all foreign holdings were slightly less than 15 percent, Dutch assets accounted for 77.8 percent of that share,[20] or some 11.7 percent of the total. That ratio was maintained and expanded (to between 12.5 and 16.5 percent of the total) while the funded debt increased from £71.8 million at the end of 1749 to £144.1 million at the end of 1779.

During the Seven Years' War (when £57.3 million was added to the funded debt) Dutch investment appears to have equaled some 7 percent of net expenditures totaling £122 million.[21] Van Dillen's compilation of Amsterdam prices shows that the effective yield on the 4-percent annuities of 1760 rose as high as 5.3 percent during the conflict. But in 1763 when, according to prior experience, the yield should again have peaked, it averaged only about 3.9 percent. The entire wartime pattern once again reflected a substantial flow from an area of capital surplus and lower borrowing costs, which reduced borrowing and service costs.

During the early stages of the War of the American Revolution previous Dutch investment levels were maintained but the gap between Britain's ordinary revenues and expenditures did not widen as rapidly as it had in the previous conflict. Between the end of 1775 and the end of 1779 £19.8 million was added to the funded debt. Thereafter the deficit increased and the funded debt rose at a sharply higher rate than did new investments from abroad.[22]

Dutch action, amounting to a relative withdrawal, accentuated pressure on capital supply in Britain. But because the Dutch image of British credit worthiness was changing,[23] the parallel rise of yields on British securities to an effective return of more than 5.25 percent in early 1785 did not restore the previous flow of Dutch capital. Disenchantment with British securities developed both as the result of the existence of profitable alternative outlets and from political antagonism. Higher returns had been available to Dutch investors before 1780, but their accessibility had not caused a flight from British funds or even a relative withdrawal. Other sectors could not absorb the volume of capital that an absolute withdrawal would have produced. In the early 1780s, however, enhanced availability of outlets lent added attraction to the threat to public credit that Britain's war with the United States, France, Spain, and the Republic seemed to pose, and to antagonism sharpened by the war. Still, Dutch investors did not sell off their British assets. To do so only invited loss because the funds were discounted from pre- and early-war levels, and because of the problem of finding somewhere else to place large sums.[24] But they did sharply reduce placement of new savings in Britain and the reinvestment of remittances on existing holdings.[25]

The part of the funded debt in British hands moved above 85 percent during the 1780s, and the sum outstanding grew from £144.1 million at the end of 1779 to £228.7 million at the end of 1784. It was in that period in particular that strain on the British public credit system became evident. As measured by the effective yield of 3-percent consols in Amsterdam prices, new loan costs advanced from an average of 3.5 percent during the 1760s to 3.7 percent in the 1770s, and then to 4.9 percent from 1779 through 1784.[26] There was some improvement after 1785, when the debt fell slightly, but the cost of credit increased again after 1792. Other governments also found borrowing more expensive during the 1780s, but credit costs increased earlier and more sharply in Britain. The American war was the immediate cause of that, but the trend was aggravated by greater relative scarcity of capital after Dutch suspension of new investment.

By 1785 the cost of servicing the public debt was more than double what it had been in 1775, and there was some uneasiness about fiscal stability.[27] Subsequent surpluses (Chart 5-2) provided some relief, but service remained at or above 50 percent of revenues through 1792. An ambitious sinking fund was established in 1786, allocating £1 million per annum for purchase of securities on the market, preferably at prices below par. That program took advantage of inflationary losses to creditors but ultimately cost the treasury more than it saved and was funded in part out of short-term advances. Nonetheless, the funding program provided some evidence of careful attention to public credit and helped strengthen market prices.

That did nothing, however, to reduce the amounts that would have to be raised from domestic resources in the event of future deficits. With the renewal of war in 1793 the threat to Britain's system of low-cost credit reappeared. Foreign capital was no longer available to retard the familiar wartime annuity-rate increase, so that in order to save the system tax revenues had to be increased and the pressure on loans as a revenue source diminished. Britain had the latitude to do that, and the income tax introduced in 1799 preserved low-cost credit at the proportion of all expenditures subsequently covered from such sources, permitting the public finance structure devised at the end of the seventeenth century to be maintained through the Napoleonic wars. The long-term debt grew from £229.6 million in 1793 to £684.6 million at the end of the war (plus £60.3 million in unfunded debt, a relatively minor category before 1792).[28] But that represented a smaller part of expenditures than during any eighteenth-century conflict (Table 6-1), and Britain emerged from the war in a public credit position superior to all continental rivals.

Within the same period foreign investment in British securities reached a level of "marginal importance."[29] Although the ratio of foreign holdings declined, it does not follow that their absolute volume also fell. The sum of liabilities owed to Dutch creditors may still have exceeded f. 200 million, perhaps by a substantial margin.[30] And in any case British annuity payments during the war formed one of the most important sources of foreign exchange earnings remaining to the Dutch.

Austria

Competing in a European state system in which some rivals enjoyed substantially superior resources, Austria developed a varied program of credit exploitation. In the second half of the eighteenth century the empire negotiated long-term domestic and foreign loans and issued a variety of paper currency instruments, including interest-bearing bank notes. Although those revenue supplements were used with some skill, the empire did not in the long run improve its position in comparison with its most important rivals. The foundation of its system, tax revenues, was significantly weaker than that of major rivals, although the reasons for that are not altogether clear. In territory and population Austria, like Russia, had greater resources than indicated by its place in the distribution of tax revenues among major states (Chart 5-1).[31] Manufacturing and commerce were less developed than in France or Britain. But Austria may have been exploiting its existing taxable resources with significantly less efficiency than either France or Britain. Certainly Austria stood far behind Prussia in the comprehensiveness of its taxation system. Nevertheless, the judgment of impecuniousness that has been reached to characterize the empire during the entire century is, to some degree, too sweeping for the period from the 1760s into the 1790s. Austrian credit utilization, assisted by Maria Theresa's tax reforms, enabled the empire more or less to keep pace until the mid-1790s with rival states blessed with greater resources and apparently higher rates of economic growth as well.

The chief issue of concern here is loans negotiated in the Dutch Republic, but those credits were part of a diversified program. Domestic borrowing was managed chiefly by the Bank of Vienna, organized in 1705 to regain access to credit after the collapse two years earlier of a short-term network based on the court banker, Oppenheimer & Co. In theory an agency of municipal government but in practice part of the imperial administration, the bank administered and serviced part of the empire's debt, using excise taxes assigned to it and drawing upon greater public regard for municipal than for imperial credit. After mid-century the bank remained the principal institution of imperial finance, although other agencies were also assigned revenue anticipations to secure loans.

Beginning in the 1760s debentures drawn on the bank secured large foreign loans. In 1762 bank notes were introduced, although part of the 12 million Rhenish florins then put into circulation was soon retired and outstanding paper did not exceed fl. 20 million until 1788.[32] Those notes traded at or very close to par until the late 1790s but, given the small sum outstanding, long-term interest-bearing loans obviously remained Austria's chief supplementary revenue source.

The data available about the imperial debt in the 1760s and 1770s (Chart 6-1) are piecemeal, but it is clear that Austria's liabilities more than doubled during the Seven Years' War.[33] In the first decade after that conflict tax reform expanded revenues, and service charges on the imperial debt were reduced.[34] By 1768 debt service required only 34 percent of expenditures on liabilities of fl. 252 million,[35] a manageable figure by eighteenth-century standards. But postwar tax-revenue gains could not readily be repeated. Domestic borrowing remained the chief means of financing deficits. Of fl. 38 million owed abroad in 1768, only some fl. 21 million was due wholly outside the empire, the difference having been raised in the Austrian Nether-

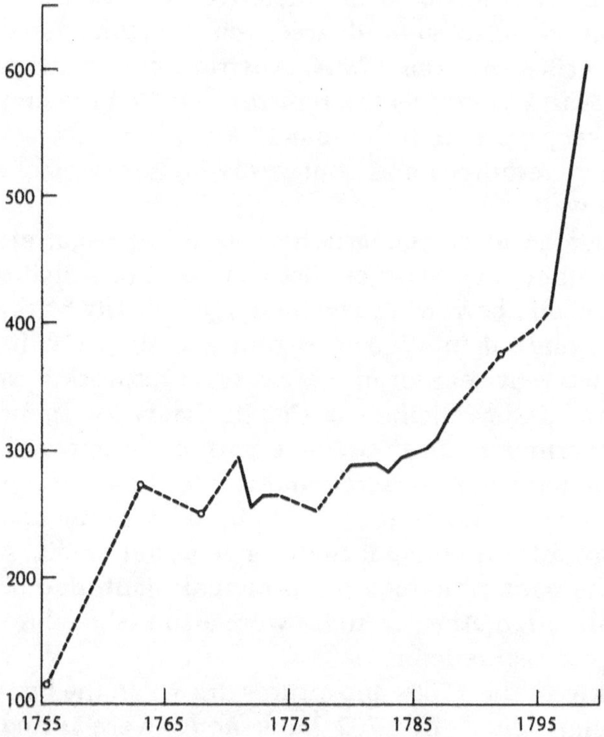

Chart 6-1. The combined imperial foreign and domestic debt, 1755–99 [in millions of gulden (fl.)].

lands.[36] During the War of the Bavarian Succession (1778–9) liabilities increased once again, and thereafter perennial deficits, financed increasingly with foreign credit, led to what appears to have been an almost unbroken path of debt accumulation lasting until slightly after the Napoleonic wars.

Nevertheless, neither the Bavarian Succession conflict nor deficits in the 1780s imposed any particular strain on imperial finances. Charges on the part of the debt owed domestic creditors averaged 4 percent in 1781.[37] The debt–revenue ratio, 4.3:1 (revenues of fl. 66 million on a debt of fl. 287 million), was still appreciably lower than levels prevailing among some other major powers. Interest on the imperial debt, but not service as a whole (for those data are lacking), cost slightly more than 17 percent of 1781 revenues, in contrast to British annuity and redemption payments of 52 percent of revenues. Although the sav-

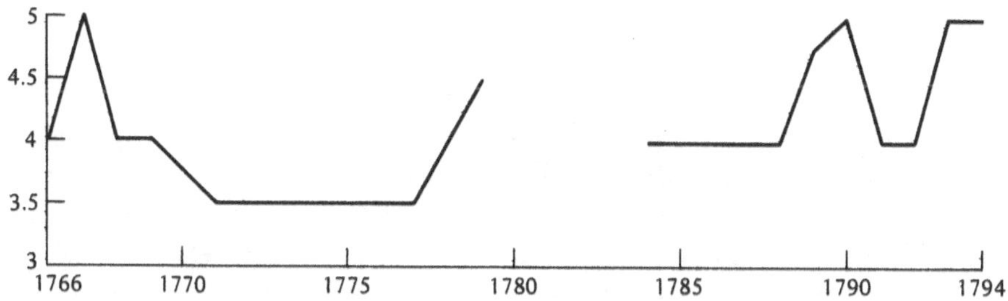

Chart 6-2. Annuity rates in Austrian loans, 1766–94.

ings available for government lending were far less substantial in Vienna than in Amsterdam, London, Paris, or Genoa, Austria could borrow on the Viennese market at rates only slightly in excess of the average charges paid in Amsterdam (Chart 6-2).[38] Overall imperial credit resources were no match for those of Britain, but Austria does not appear to have been as close to the limit of its resources in the 1780s as Britain, France, or the Dutch Republic.

The tertiary element in Austrian deficit financing through the 1780s was foreign borrowing. Between 1765 and 1779 Austria averaged at least one loan issue per annum in the Republic and managed, for the most part, to borrow on highly advantageous terms. Attractive conditions must have been available on other capital markets, for the empire also raised credit in Genoa, Florence, and Bern.[39] Because the overall interest-bearing debt in 1777 (fl. 253 million) was only fl. 1 million more than it had been in 1768, Austria had adopted a policy of redeeming part of its internal debt by shifting that onto foreign creditors. Such a program presumably responded to at least temporarily lower credit costs abroad.

The Amsterdam banking houses that had managed imperial loans early in the century were no longer much involved by the 1760s. Willem Gideon Deutz died in 1757, and early in the 1760s George Clifford & Co., Deutz's rival, became involved in loans to Denmark.[40] In their stead appeared first the Utrecht firm of Tiberius Beeldsnijder Matroos and, in 1758, Verbrugge & Goll (from 1778 Goll & Co.), which was assigned the imperial mercury agency and thus given a competitive advantage.[41] Other firms were occasionally allowed a role in subsequent Austrian issues, but the mercury agency gained Verbrugge & Goll a virtual monopoly, which it held into the 1790s.[42]

The available data on Dutch loans, a fractured series of debt totals and information on individual issues but not on the annual balance outstanding, will not support an accurate distribution of annual credit usage, but general images can be formed. In 1774 the secretary to the Prussian ambassador in The Hague answered a request from Frederick II for information on totals borrowed by Austria and Russia with a figure of f. 22,670,000 for advances to Austria.[43] That sum included, however, some loans of the 1730s backed by Silesian revenues. Without those the 1774 balance would appear to have been f. 21.5 million (fl. 19.4 million at current rates), or about 7 percent of the combined domestic and foreign debt of the empire. Austria was floating new loans and simultaneously prolonging outstanding issues, so that the debt was growing. According to the Prussian ambassador, the empire raised f. 20 million during the Bavarian Succession War,[44] although most of that merely prolonged advances from the 1760s.[45] By 1780, when there was a brief interruption in Austrian borrowing in the Republic, at least f. 25 million was outstanding in recognized loans, that is, excluding the old Silesian credits. Even so only about 7.5 percent of the debt was owed in the Republic. The earlier policy of shifting liabilities abroad had been suspended during the war in favor of borrowing on all fronts. The interest-bearing debt grew to fl. 287 million in 1780, an increase of fl. 34 million over the 1777 figure, while an additional fl. 2.4 million in paper currency was put into circulation.[46]

If the net amount owed the Dutch increased by f. 3.5 million, as appears to have been the case, then less than 10 percent of the wartime deficit was funded by Dutch loans. Supplementary advances were raised in Frankfurt and Bern, but the contact with Genoa appears to have lapsed in 1778 or 1779.[47] Although neither borrowing in the Dutch Republic nor foreign borrowing in general funded the war, Austria's ability to defer redemptions helped maintain a strong public credit position. Furthermore, Verbrugge & Goll organized two substitution undertakings during the war, using subscriptions to buy an assortment of Austrian paper in Vienna.[48] These together raised f. 586,000, a comparatively modest amount in itself but suggestive of direct investment by Dutch rentiers that may have been more extensive than is indicated by the two ventures.

During the 1770s, if not earlier, Austria emerged as the preferred foreign borrower negotiating loans through the Amsterdam market's government loan apparatus. Such a position is reflected in annuity rates and in the available evidence about the pace at which Austrian paper was sold. The annuity rate the empire paid (Chart 6-2) fluctuated, and in both the War of the Bavarian Succession and the Turkish conflict of 1788–91 higher returns were demanded than of some other foreign borrowers. In general, however, Austrian returns were near the low end of the spectrum of rates paid by all foreign governments. Indeed imperial loans appear usually to have set a standard against which other foreign loan proposals were weighed, and to have served informally as the best available guide to the prime rate of foreign lending.

Austria's financial position remained in some respects superior to that of its rivals into the early 1790s. Charges increased to an average of 4.36 percent on the interest-bearing debt in 1796, but interest itself (still excluding redemptions, about which information is unavailable) required only 27 percent of revenues (fl. 66 million) and the debt–revenue ratio had climbed no higher than 6.2:1. As long as Austria could borrow large amounts abroad on terms as attractive as those prevailing in 1781, and as long as paper currency issues could be increased without provoking a decline in confidence in that paper or specie flight, the empire would occupy a position of relative strength.

Debt service costs cited above are based on the assumption that Austrian loans were issued at par, and an explanation of that assumption is necessary. Direct evidence about the price of issue on the Amsterdam market is seldom available, but prices can be extrapolated from occasional *beurs* quotations and other sources. In July 1774, for example, the secretary to the Prussian ambassador informed Frederick II that securities in the most recent Austrian loan were trading at a 3-percent premium.[49] Since Verbrugge & Goll was an experienced banking house it is not likely to have so misjudged the market as to have offered investors a discount in initial sales. Other equally piecemeal evidence supports the suggestion that Austria customarily avoided discounts. During the War of the Bavarian Succession, Prussia tried to undercut Austrian credit in Amsterdam, as Thulemeyer indicated in a dispatch of 16 June 1778: "Je fais de mon mieux pour discréditer les négociations pécuniaires de la cour Impériale."[50] The campaign was opened with the assistance of one Chomel, a merchant from Berlin who had relocated in Amsterdam. But Thulemeyer was not content with direct tactics and mounted a sly flank attack by seeking to insert in a French-language gazette published in Cleves "quelques réflexions sur l'état peu favorable des finances autrichiennes."[51] He and presumably Frederick II too understood that foreign credit resources were of some consequence in the Austrian war effort, and expected that derogatory news reaching Amsterdam from a foreign periodical would be effective. In Thulemeyer's view Austrian credit was fundamentally precarious.

Whatever the progress of the flank attack, the campaign had little success. Price currents for single trading days in 1778, 1779, and 1780 indicate a very modest decline on Austrian paper secured on mercury and bank debentures from 1778 to 1779, and an advance in 1780 to and slightly above par.[52]

Thulemeyer quite simply misjudged the soundness of Austrian credit in the eyes of Dutch investors. The Bavarian war forced Austria to issue additional loans, but before the conflict such favorable terms had prevailed that the pressure of more numerous loans and any war-induced caution among investors could be met by a slight modification of annuity rates. Thus in 1778 and 1779 Austria increased the return from the 3.5 percent paid in 1775 to 4 and then 4.5 percent. Despite Thulemeyer's machinations, the 1779 loans traded at a premium in June of that year and earlier issues held their market value.[53]

On a state visit to the United Provinces in the summer of 1781, Joseph II asked Austria's banker in Amsterdam, Johann Goll, what state had the highest credit standing in the city. Goll, who certainly had a stake in his answer, replied that Austria and Russia had.[54] On 6 October 1783, the nearest date for which *beurs* quotations are available, Austrian securities traded slightly higher than Russian paper offering the same return.[55] Goll could have claimed confidently enough that Austrian credit was premier among foreign governments, but such an answer might not have been as convincing as the response that linked Austria to its Russian ally against the Ottoman Empire.

Lacking the papers of Verbrugge & Goll or of any large-scale investors in Austrian loans, there is no contemporary explanation of Dutch investors' preference for Austria over other states. No fundamental differences in borrowing policy separated Austria from other debtors. All states commonly prolonged old loans with new issues, and other states took as much care as Austria to provide for regular service. There may have been some attraction in the Austrian practice of using proceeds from mercury sales to pay annuities but, in view of the decline of mercury prices in the 1750s, 1770s, and early 1780s, grounds for continued confidence on that point were lacking. Dutch rentiers were creatures of strong habits, disinclined to investigate investments on their own and inclined to rely on the advice of market intermediaries. Those characteristics favored Austrian retention of the favorable terms established in the 1760s. No evidence was discovered to indicate that Dutch rentiers had any trustworthy information about imperial revenues or debts, but the confidence they displayed in Austria was, at least in the 1780s and early 1790s, justified by the indexes that have been used here to measure credit worthiness.

Austria's solid position in 1781 did not deteriorate despite a brief suspension of annuity payments in 1784 resulting from controversy over reopening the Scheldt River.[56] But as long as redemptions could not be provided out of the annual deficits that the empire faced after 1781, the Austrian debt required infusions from prolongation loans.[57] Between 1780 and 1787 only one advance was sought, a 1784 issue for f. 2,500,000.[58] But in 1787, with the renewal of the Turkish war, Austria returned to the Amsterdam market in earnest. Two loans were negotiated in 1788 for a total of f. 5 million; three (of which one failed in part) in 1789 for f. 6,150,000; one in 1790 for f. 4 million; another in 1791 for f. 2.5 million; and, with the War of the First Coalition, three in 1792 for f. 8,125,000 – a total of f. 25,775,000 within five years.[59] Between 1784 and 1799 Austria borrowed some f. 39,525,000, of which as much as f. 35.5 million may have consisted of fresh advances and the remainder of prolongations.[60] These extensions are projected against imperial revenues and expenditures in Chart 6-3, which includes information on loans raised in England in the same period.[61] Credit from those two sources together accounted for slightly more than 6.8

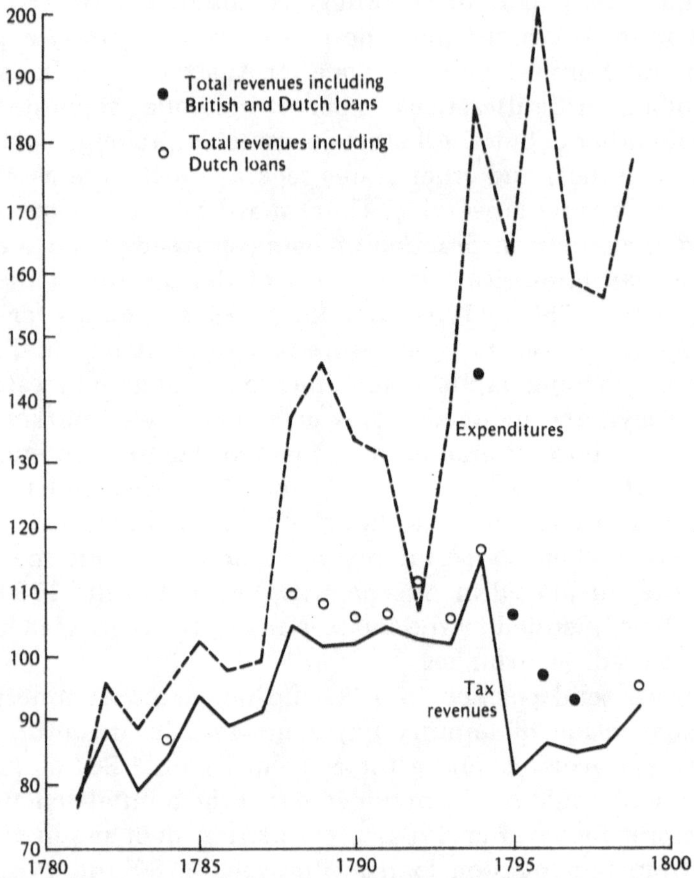

Chart 6-3. Austrian revenues, expenditures, and deficits, and net proceeds of Dutch and British loans, 1781–99 (in millions of current guilders).

percent of all expenditures from 1788 through 1797, and about 20 perçent of the deficit accumulated in that period. Net proceeds from the Dutch loans covered about 3.3 percent of all expenditures from 1788 through 1794, when most of these loans were floated, but as much as 27 percent of the net addition to the imperial debt between the end of 1787 and the end of 1796, dates for which data are available.[62] Together Dutch and British loans, with net proceeds of about f. 100.7 million, accounted for some 55 percent of the increase in the imperial debt between the end of 1787 and the end of 1797. The brunt of long-term borrowing was therefore shifted abroad, but the empire simultaneously increased paper currency issues. The total in circulation, fl. 17.9 million at the end of 1787, reached fl. 74.2 million by the end of 1797, an increase of fl. 56.3 million.[63] Even with that additional resource, foreign loans accounted for some 40 percent of the combined total of new liabilities.

The scale of government credit operations altered sharply in that period. In the first half of the 1780s imperial revenues averaged fl. 70.2 million and expenditures fl. 75.8 million, but these increased, respectively, to fl. 84.6 and fl. 121.2 million in the first half of the 1790s. Tax-revenue gains achieved earlier could not be duplicated in the 1790s, and in specie values revenues actually declined after 1794.[64] An increasing gap between receipts and expenditures could be sustained only as long as domestic and foreign borrowing and paper currency issues could be exploited simultaneously at such a rate. Failure of any one of them would inevitably force a reduction in spending and in Austria's role in the coalition against France.

The empire's credit position in Amsterdam began to slip in 1793, when the annuity on new loans was increased from 4 to 5 percent to attract subscribers. But that change reflected not so much a deterioration of Austria's position as the constriction of capital supply on the Amsterdam market after France declared war on the Republic. *Beurs* quotations declined during 1793, but at the end of the year 5 percent securities were still quoted at 97½ to 98½.[65] Nevertheless, new loans could not be issued in the necessary velocity and volume. A constriction of capital supply and continued credit demand from other states prevented the Amsterdam market from accommodating the enlarged scale of credit required during the Coalition war. Even as the Amsterdam market contracted, however, Austria expanded borrowing elsewhere, particularly in London. In 1793 negotiations were opened for £3 million, or some f. 36 million at current rates. A loan that was subsequently expanded to £4.6 million was opened in May 1794 and secured on revenues from the Austrian Netherlands, collaterally on bank debentures, and on a guarantee offered by Parliament.[66] Although Austria returned to Amsterdam in 1794 to raise f. 2.5 million, and again in 1799 for f. 5 million,[67] the vast requirements of the war against France could not be met there. Because loans on the London market were tied to the Austro-British alliance, that source was dependable only insofar as Austria could service its debts and acquire additional advances in order to pursue the conflict with France. At the end of the 1790s, sharply expanding expenditures, a conflict with Britain over the nature of prior credits (which Austria professed to view as subsidies), and the exhaustion of all other foreign credit sources led to an abrupt deterioration in Austria's financial position and withdrawal from the war.

Denmark

Denmark and Sweden pioneered in introducing the lowest-cost technique of mercantilist expedient finance – the combination of foreign loans with paper currency issues. In both states, however, the integration of foreign credit into programs intended to support recurrent deficits was preceded by a long period of experimentation with paper currency issues. During the years of experimentation money supply was expanded according to the demand for supplementary revenues, and regulated by taxation and by controls over the convertibility of notes into specie exercised through central banks.[68] Because deficits were recurrent and large scale, those devices did not produce stable monetary programs. During the 1760s both states shifted to policies that included foreign borrowing, thus improving their ability to finance deficits and gaining a new means to regulate money supply and foreign-exchange rates.

In Denmark paper currency was introduced to supplement tax revenues and proceeds of domestic loans during the Great Northern War, with provision for its retirement made in permitting it to be used to pay certain taxes.[69] By 1728 those notes had been withdrawn, and the experiment concluded satisfactorily. A new cycle began with the formation of the Copenhagen Kurantbank in 1736, but its loans to the royal treasury, which were based on the issue of notes convertible into specie, were marred by the suspension of convertibility briefly in 1745 and for a longer period from 1757. Although uninvolved in the conflict, Denmark again resorted to bank note issues during the Seven Years' War, when circulation was expanded from 2.4 million rixdollars (rdl. cour.) in 1760 to 5.3 million in 1762,[70] and when domestic and foreign long-term borrowing was also sharply increased.[71]

To deal with the wartime decline of the Danish rixdollar on

the international exchange,[72] the government of Frederick V arranged for the Danish Asiatic Company to import silver from Mexico. Christiaan van Orsoy & Zoonen of Amsterdam was approached for short-term advances, and seems in 1762 to have arranged credits totaling something in excess of f. 1.3 million. But that was inadequate, and in the following year fresh loans were arranged through A. & S. Boas of The Hague and Clifford & Zoonen of Amsterdam.[73] Advances to the company and Kurantbank in 1763 are more difficult to reconstruct; one source suggests that Clifford and Andries Pels & Zoonen arranged a loan of f. 2.5 million, but another puts loans at f. 12 million from Amsterdam plus a further f. 2.6 million from the Bank of Hamburg.[74] Whatever was raised was inadequate and further sums, perhaps exceeding f. 10 million, were borrowed in 1764 and 1765.[75] During 1765 the exchange responded to that flow of specie and drafts, moving seven points in Copenhagen's favor.[76]

At Frederick's death in 1766 the new king, Christian VII, was a minor, and six years passed before he took the throne. In the interim, under the guidance of Struensee, Christian's physician, a state lottery was established to augment revenues. Whatever assistance that gave the royal treasury was quickly dissipated after Struensee's execution in 1772 and the seizure of power by a cabal guided by hopes of self-enrichment. Christian was only intermittently lucid and did not resist the depredations of his advisers. Earlier stabilization measures thus had a short-lived effect, and the exchange rate again moved against Copenhagen.[77]

During the 1770s and early 1780s loans were opened with increasing frequency in Amsterdam and on other European capital markets, and that part of the state debt composed of foreign credits grew (Tables 6-2 and 6-3).[78] In 1774 the crown arranged with Jacob Dull & Zoonen, which had taken over management of the 1765 loan, to open the first in the series of issues listed in Table 6-4.[79] That contact enabled Dull to build a virtual monopoly that was maintained through 1785 and, in the management of service payments, through the Napoleonic era.

The first loan of the series was secured on revenues from the capitation tax levied in the crown dominions of Schleswig, Holstein, and Ploen, but thereafter Denmark reverted chiefly to its practice in the 1764 and 1765 loans, mortgaging toll revenues,[80] and those issues were differentiated from other Danish paper as

Table 6-2. *Danish state debt (in millions of rdl. cour.)*

	Interest-bearing debt	Foreign debt as % of total
1730	3.161 (or f. 6.9 million)	
1746	2.43 (f. 5.33)	
1754	1.055 (f. 2.35)	
1766	20.25 (f. 42.72)	39.5
1771	16.23 (f. 33.43)	
1774	16 (f. 32.16)	
1784	21 (f. 40.86)	66.7
1800	28.32 (f. 54.88)	38.8
1807	42	
1814	126	

Table 6-3. *Danish foreign debt, 1781–8 (end-of-year totals converted to current guilders, in millions)*

	Total foreign debt	Part owed in Dutch Republic
1781	f. 25.43	f. 21.63 (85%)
1783	24.53	18.29 (75%)
1784	27.25	16.68 (61%)
1785	27.74	18.01 (65%)
1786	27.46	18.09 (66%)
1787	27.37	17.21 (63%)
1788	27.38	16.91 (62%)

"the Danish tolls." Between 1774 and 1777 the annuity demanded of Denmark declined from 5 to 4 percent, bringing the monarchy into line with states whose financial reliability was most highly regarded. By the end of the 1770s, if not earlier, Danish issues were trading near par or at a premium.[81]

Simultaneously with the foreign loans Denmark expanded the volume of bank notes in circulation. A dual program was necessary because of continued deficits despite a general trend toward increased indirect taxes.[82] After a reduction in notes outstanding in the mid-1760s, new issues occurred at first gradually and then more rapidly, as Chart 6-4 indicates.[83] This cycle, one of expanding domestic and foreign liabilities, came to a climax at the end of

Table 6-4. *Danish loans in the Dutch Republic from 1774*

Date	Director	Amount, f.	Security	Return, %	Due date
1 Apr. 1774	Dull	2,000,000	Capitation taxes	5	1778
1 July 1777	Dull	2,500,000	Holstein tolls	4	1781 or 1783
1 Mar. 1779	Pye Rich & Wilkieson	700,000	For the Asiatic Co.	5	1784
1 Jan. 1780	Dull	3,000,000	Sound tolls	4	1789–91
1 Jan. 1785	Dull	3,000,000	Sound tolls	4	1796–1805
1 Jan. 1788	A. & S. Boas	(2,000,000)	For the Bank of Copenhagen	4	—
1 Dec. 1788	Dull	1,000,000	For the Asiatic Co.	5	1800
1 Oct. 1805	Dull	1,000,000	For the Asiatic Co.	5	1811

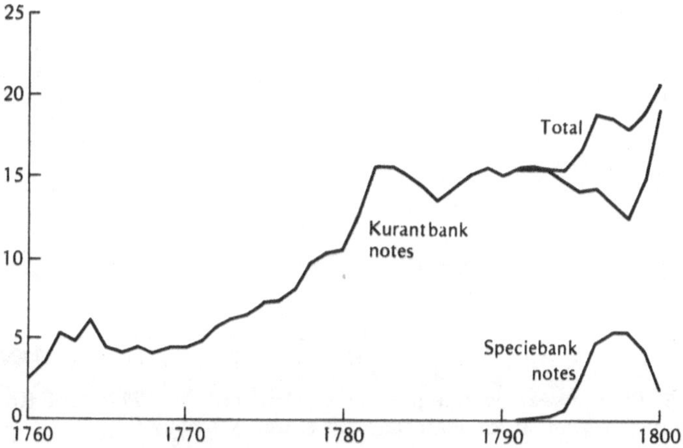

Chart 6-4. Bank notes in circulation, 1760–1800 (in millions of rdl. cour.).

the War of the American Revolution. During the conflict Danish shipping, like that of other neutrals, thrived. The war's end suddenly halted commercial prosperity and reduced the kingdom's tax receipts, requiring further foreign loans at a moment that coincided with what to that point was the apex of note supply.[84] At the same time war with Sweden threatened. First-of-year quotations in Amsterdam (Chart 6-5) indicate that a favorable ex-

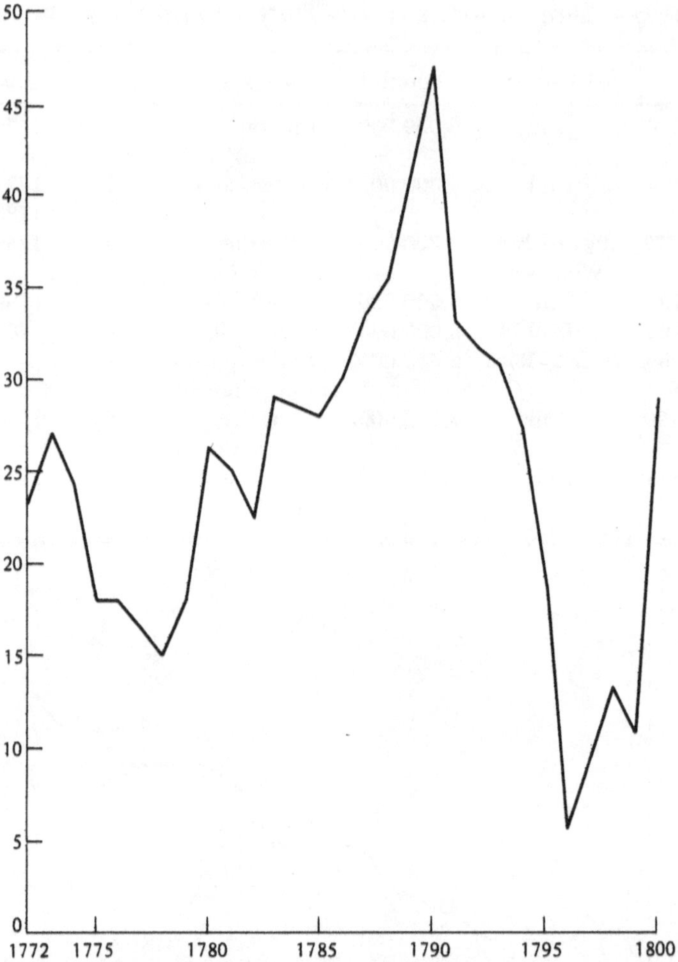

Chart 6-5. First-of-year exchange rates on Amsterdam, 1772–1800 (in percentage premium of Danish rdl. cour. against Dutch rdl. cour.).

change rate was maintained through the 1770s, when foreign loan proceeds exceeded redemptions.[85] Thereafter, and markedly in the late 1780s, the rate moved against Copenhagen.

Heavy indebtedness in the 1780s (Tables 6-2 and 6-3 and Chart 6-4) sparked a debate among Danish mercantilists on the classic problem of mercantilist monetary and fiscal policy – balance-of-payments deficit, depreciating paper currency, falling exchange rate, and inadequate revenues. After the ministerial revolution of 1784, management of the crisis was entrusted to

Count Andreas Peter Bernstorff, the new minister of foreign affairs, and Ernst Heinrich Schimmelmann, the minister of finance. Under Schimmelmann revenue administration was rationalized and a reform of the monetary system begun. Bank note circulation was reduced slightly, and a sinking fund established to service the foreign debt.[86]

The antagonists in the debate generally agreed on the efficacy of increasing means of payment over deflationary programs.[87] Thus a credit institution was established to make commercial loans and, in 1788, a bank was created in Altona to assist the economic recovery of Schleswig and Holstein. The monarchy also assumed some debts of Danish West Indian planters, using proceeds of the 1785 loan floated in Amsterdam,[88] but in general the committee directing reform of the fiscal system preferred note issues to foreign loans.[89] With economic expansion foremost in mind, the policies of the mid-1780s did not significantly reduce money supply or the foreign debt. By 1789 bank notes had regained the level of 1783 and new foreign loans were raised at the same time that loans falling due were prolonged.[90]

Toward the end of the 1780s both the Kurantbank and the Danish Asiatic Company returned to the Amsterdam market, the bank for a conversion loan and the company for an advance of f. 1 million.[91] In the same period the monarchy completed its conversion of West Indian planter debts, issuing notes in 1787 to cover still outstanding obligations.[92] Those credits coincided with slightly expanded bank note issues and an extraordinary income and property levy, necessitated by the Swedish war of 1788–90.[93] After the war Denmark again tried to reduce domestic and foreign liabilities. Monetary reform was begun in 1791 with the formation of the Dansk–Norsk Speciebank. Officials planned to withdraw nonconvertible Kurantbank notes gradually in favor of convertible specie bank paper, thus restoring Denmark to a silver standard for the first time since 1757. But specie bank issues exceeded retirement of Kurantbank notes, which remained nonconvertible, with the result that money supply continued to rise.[94] Exchange rates after 1790 (Chart 6-5) nonetheless reflect economic stabilization and Danish commercial benefits resulting from neutrality during the War of the First Coalition.

Until halted by a commercial crisis in 1798, some progress

was also made during the 1790s in reducing the foreign debt.[95] The crisis forced prolongation of outstanding liabilities as the monarchy allocated resources toward short-term domestic loans that were called in and for purchases of silver to redeem specie bank notes presented for conversion.[96] Kurantbank note issues were also increased and the earlier decline in foreign currency cost gave way to a sharp rise in 1799.

Despite stabilization of foreign and domestic indebtedness earlier in the 1790s, Denmark remained saddled with a larger debt than could be sustained by what was customarily available for debt service among small states, for which military and administrative expenses were a relatively heavier burden than for large powers. Spending economies might have relieved the problem, but instead the financial crisis was aggravated early in the nineteenth century. Denmark's armed neutrality of 1801–7 demanded fresh domestic borrowing, and the domestic debt increased from just over 28 to 42 million rdl. cour. Simultaneously note circulation was expanded from 16.5 to 26 million.[97] Small advances were arranged in Amsterdam, f. 600,000 in 1802 and f. 1 million in 1805, the latter by the Asiatic Company,[98] but foreign credit was no longer available in volume.

In 1807 Britain, reacting to French pressure on Denmark to join the Continental System, bombarded Copenhagen's harbor and carried off the Danish fleet, an indignity that provoked Denmark to ally with France. As a result toll revenues, on which most of the debt to the Dutch Republic was secured, dropped sharply. In Amsterdam a hodgepodge of paper, some of it decades old, still circulated, and in Denmark fresh currency issues contributed to hyperinflation between 1810 and 1814.[99]

The diminishing effectiveness of deficit financing by means of paper currency issues alone required new taxes, and in 1810 Denmark inaugurated an income tax to be assessed for eight years.[100] Besides arousing discontent, that measure failed either to increase revenues to the necessary level or to halt depreciation of bank notes. Until 1811 Denmark met annuity payments and such redemptions as had been scheduled on the foreign debt, but by 1810 and perhaps earlier the technique used involved a covert prolongation. Notes turned in for redemption by investors who refused prolongation were reissued at discounts ranging up to 16 percent.[101]

Under wartime pressure Denmark also considered new loans in Amsterdam. But in 1811 redemptions on Dutch loans were suspended, and paper circulating in Amsterdam plunged from the high trading prices maintained until that time.[102] By autumn, after the suspension, new loan proposals were refused. Preparations for the Napoleonic campaign in Russia occasioned new demands on residents of the empire which, from 1810, included the former kingdom of Holland. Moreover, 1808 and 1809 decrees had restricted the freedom of Amsterdam bankers to open loans. By 1811 Napoleon's authorization was required for any new issue, and that was problematic, even for an ally.

Denmark also considered a consolidation of Dutch liabilities of some f. 9 million and the creation of additional paper for a total of f. 12 million.[103] The new paper might then either have been sold, if market prices recovered, or have been used to secure short-term advances. To draw investors into the conversion and extension, the crown was prepared to pay premiums ranging from 3 to 10 percent. In truth the plan was nothing more than a proposal for a new loan for something less than f. 3 million, and it too had little chance of success in 1811. Having broached those various proposals, Frederick VI settled on a simple notice informing investors of the suspension of redemptions. To this bad news was added a firm pledge of Denmark's intention to resume payments when possible.[104]

The consolidation proposal reveals the status of Danish loans in the Dutch Netherlands in the second half of 1811:

Notes unredeemed in 1811	f. 424,000
Notes due in 1812	687,000
Notes with no scheduled redemption	5,417,000
Crown obligations	1,130,400
Notes from bank loans	1,167,000
	f.8,825,400

According to draft notes on this plan, Denmark had redeemed about two-thirds of its debt in the Netherlands before 1811. That would suggest that Danish loans had totaled some f. 27 million, a figure within the range of information presented here,[105] and that the outstanding balance of 1781 (f. 21.63 million) was probably the highest sum owed the Dutch Republic at any point.

For Denmark, then, foreign and especially Dutch loans were

particularly important between 1762 and 1784, when they permitted use of the most efficient formula of mercantilist expedient finance, the combination of foreign borrowing with bank note issues. In 1784 Denmark reverted to an unbalanced monetary and fiscal program, relying principally on paper currency issues to meet deficits. Monetary manipulation could still be beneficial, as the introduction of convertible specie bank notes in 1790 indicates. But the declining cost of foreign currencies over much of the 1790s was also influenced by exogenous factors such as the War of the First Coalition and, in the case of Dutch guilders, by the effect of the war and the French indemnity on the Dutch balance of payments. In the longer run the unbalanced program could not furnish enough resources.

Sweden

Swedish bank notes appeared initially as receipts for non-interest-bearing accounts in the Riksens Ständers Bank, the Bank of the Estates of the Realm or the Bank of Sweden. In 1701, early in the Great Northern War, the bank began issuing transfer notes, that is, notes that were negotiable and could pass from hand to hand in settlement of debts. From 1726 this paper, backed by specie reserves, was accepted by tax collectors as equivalent to coin, and transfer notes gradually replaced other bank notes and were used by the bank for credit extensions to the crown, state agencies, and private individuals. The volume in circulation was increased during the early 1740s to assist in financing the Russian war, and contracted after the war. The same technique was used during the Seven Years' War, when notes were expanded from 13.8 million dalers in 1755 to a high of 44 million in 1763. At that point the Bank of Sweden, with bullion reserves of some 2.2 million, had nearly 79 million dalers outstanding in credits to the crown and private individuals. As the issue of notes swelled, certain commodities reached prices double those of 1755 and bank notes depreciated sharply against silver. Domestic tax revenues expanded but more slowly than note supply and the cost of living.[106] At the same time the rate of the daler in exchange transactions fell.[107]

Toward the end of the war the crisis of depreciating bank notes, a falling exchange rate, and inflation led the Estates, controlled by the political faction known as the Hats, to seek foreign loans in Amsterdam and elsewhere, but that effort was only partially successful.[108] The unfavorable outcome of the war, in which Sweden was allied with France, favored the Hats' opponents, the Caps, who advocated a more restrained foreign policy and opposed inflationary monetary and fiscal policies. In the 1765 session of the Estates the Caps replaced their rivals, who had failed repeatedly to regain for Sweden the prestige and territory lost since the seventeenth century. Upon taking office the Caps initiated a financial inquiry and discovered the extent of the crisis engendered by Hat policies. They introduced retrenchment, taxation reform, new levies on previously undertaxed groups, and general deflationary policies.[109]

But the crisis demanded more immediate relief than the Caps' program could provide, and in 1766 that faction sought and received from the Estates authorization to raise extensive foreign credits. Thus the Caps turned to the least costly and most efficient means of dealing with secular deficits, the combination of long-term foreign borrowing with domestic paper currency issues. Within the year about f. 1 million was raised in Genoa.[110] The contact with Dutch capital, with which we are primarily concerned, was renewed in 1767 when, at the request of the Estates, Adolphus Frederick signed a royal patent for a loan of f. 750,000 to be managed by Hope & Co.[111]

The Caps' internal efforts to deal with the economic and fiscal crisis were largely nullified by opposition from economic groups more heavily taxed in new levies and by continuing factional strife with the Hats. Until the royal coup d'état of 1772 ended the so-called Days of Liberty, the Caps and Hats alternated in controlling the Estates. Partly because neither faction retained power more than temporarily, the financial crisis and the economic disorder associated with it persisted. But fresh foreign loans were raised, and those tended to ameliorate conditions. Four issues were arranged in 1770, one in Genoa for about f. 1 million, two in Amsterdam for f. 1.25 and f. 1 million respectively, and one in Amsterdam and Rotterdam that was eventually expanded to more than f. 1.25 million.[112] With foreign credit deflationary policies could be avoided while bank note supply was reduced from the high of 1763 to 31.8 million in 1769. Sweden's balance-of-payments position improved with the influx of commercial drafts and specie, and the Hamburg rixdollar banco, which had risen from an adjusted annual average of 41.8 Swedish marks copper in the 1750s to a high of 85.1 in 1764, fell to 50.1 in 1769.[113]

Continued factional strife, however, impeded restoration of the prewar equilibrium. In August 1772 Gustavus III seized power, restoring royal absolutism. The problems attacked first under a revised constitution were political, but in 1775 Gustavus took up financial and economic issues. He adopted a fiscal program designed to redeem the still depreciated notes of the Bank of Sweden while reducing the volume of paper in circulation, pursuing policies advocated by Johan Liljencrantz, director of the newly created department of finance.[114]

The reforms of 1775 and thereafter reintroduced convertibility, restoring Sweden to a silver standard. Depreciated daler notes were redeemed at 50 percent, while the quantity of newly issued Swedish rixdollar (rdr) specie notes was gradually reduced over the following decade.[115] Foreign loans were required to finance the transition from a depreciating to a stable currency while avoiding sharp deflation, and the reforms of 1775–7 were based on credit acquired in Amsterdam and Genoa and used both to buy silver for coinage and to cover deficits.[116] Reconversion to a silver standard was also eased by the commercial benefits of Swedish neutrality during the War of the American Revolution.[117]

Supplemented by some small-scale domestic credits, foreign loans permitted continued deficit financing and a simultaneous reduction in note supply. But, as newly minted silver coins were issued, the total supply of notes and coins remained for the most part above the 1776 level and commodity prices generally increased, fluctuating above 1776 levels.[118] The restoration of monetary order was not therefore accompanied by deflation, but instead by very nearly the same inflationary cost-of-living trend that had been characteristic since the mid-1760s.[119]

Toward the end of the 1770s Gustavus began to shift attention to an ambitious foreign policy, and from that point loan proceeds were allocated for military and naval uses. The redirection is first apparent with the Genoan loan of 1779,[120] but became increasingly evident as rearmament was stepped up in 1783 in preparation for a campaign planned against Denmark.[121] As events took place conflict with an ally of Russia, which Denmark was, had little chance of success as long as Russia was free from other entanglements. The threat of a renewed Russo-Turkish conflict passed, and it was not until 1787 and the Second Russo-Turkish War that Gustavus could implement his military plans with a revival of the ancient conflict with Russia.

In the meantime royal absolutism proved an expensive form of government and war preparedness required fresh loans. The Estates remained obsequious before Gustavus until, taking an opportunity presented by the Russo-Turkish war, he ordered an attack on Russian Finland in July 1788 and violated terms of the revised constitution of 1772 dealing with authorization of offensive war. After some initial successes the Swedish campaign faltered, encouraging opposition to Gustavus. But a constitutional crisis was averted by patriotic response to the Danish declaration of war on Sweden. Thus with substantial foreign loans Gustavus preserved a free absolutist hand throughout his reign, using loans to underwrite military adventures that could not otherwise have been afforded.

The sums raised abroad after 1765 amounted to more than f. 56.7 million, of which Dutch investors supplied over f. 32.5 million.[122] But Swedish practice included prolongation of loans falling due, so that outstanding foreign or Dutch debts (Table 6-5) never approached those figures.[123] The cumulative effect of foreign borrowing after the reforms of 1775–7 was the creation of a manipulable drawing power that could be expanded or contracted as circumstances warranted. Between 1762 and 1794, when foreign borrowing was integrated into overall Swedish financial policy, projected ordinary and extraordinary taxation revenues consistently fell short of expenditures.[124] Sweden met deficits chiefly through paper currency issues and foreign loans, but formal domestic loans and uncovered shortages were also used. Revenue and expenditure projections had been in use since 1722 but they did not, despite frequent deficits, lead to a highly rationalized program of deficit financing. Instead a hand-to-mouth approach prevailed and, although it generally served fiscal requirements at lower outright cost than was the case in other states, it was subject to intermittent crises and devaluations.

Foreign loan incidence is indicated by Table 6-5, which gives the annual balance of the Swedish foreign and overall debt from

Table 6-5. *Swedish foreign debt as percentage of total debt, 1777–1809 (end-of-year figures converted into millions of current guilders)*

	Domestic and foreign debt (1)	Foreign debt (2)	Dutch debt (3)	% foreign (1)÷(2)
1766	46.3	1.2	.74	2.6
1777	39.4	13.6	10.25	34.5
1778	37.3	11.8	9.5	31.6
1779	18.7	13.8	11.25	73.8
1780	17.5	12.8	10.25	73.1
1781	17.2	12.6	10.13	73.3
1782	17.8	13	10.25	73
1783	21.6	16.6	11.73	76.9
1784	21.2	16.6	11.72	78.3
1785	22.4	17.8	12.73	79.5
1786	23.7	19	14.23	80.2
1787	26.9	22.3	14.74	82.9
1788	28.7	22.7	15.24	79.1
1789	58.1	25.9	16.5	44.6
1790	58	26	15.95	44.8
1791	55.2	30.2	22.31	54.7
1792	77.3	34.8	21.29	45
1793	77.1	33.1	20.25	42.9
1794	77.2	31.5	19.28	40.8
1795	76.3	27.9	16.61	36.6
1796	76.6	28.6	15.93	37.3
1797	75.1	29.5	15.94	39.3
1798	78.2	29	16.62	37.1
1799	78.6	29.4	16	37.4
1800	80.8	28.2	15.13	34.9
1801	81.2	28.6	14.82	35.2
1802	81.1	29.7	14.04	36.6
1803	41.6	29	13.55	69.7
1804	37.7	28.6	13.06	75.9
1805	36.2	26.6	12.56	73.5
1806	34	26.6	12.05	78.2
1807	32.4	26.8	11.83	82.7
1808	30.9	27.5	11.97	89
1809	38.7	28.6	11.53	73.9

1777. Slightly more than half the 1777 foreign debt had been accumulated in 1776 in connection with currency reform. After Liljencrantz's program was completed and domestic liabilities were reduced sharply by partial liquidation of debts to the Bank of Sweden, foreign indebtedness increased more gradually, as redemptions lagged behind new advances. Between 1779 and 1787, when the balance outstanding abroad rose from 73.8 to 82.9 percent of total indebtedness, Sweden was shifting toward a fiscal program that relied principally on foreign credit and that, consequently, was costlier in the short term than the combination of measures employed previously. Nonetheless, approximate service costs on foreign liabilities (calculated at an average of 5 percent, and thus by estimation taking commission charges into account) rose no higher than 11.4 percent of expenditures during the 1780s and at no time exceeded 20 percent of expenditures. Up to the eve of war with Russia, Sweden therefore retained a greater ability to exploit credit in comparison to states where service costs reached or exceeded 50 percent of expenditures, and the restoration of monetary stability reinstated the option of currency inflation.[125] But the Russian war required that all supplementary revenue sources be used. The currency supply was enlarged from 6.1 million rdr at the end of 1788 to 12.8 million in National Debt Office and bank notes at the end of 1792, and both foreign and domestic long-term borrowing also increased (Table 6-5).[126]

New bank note issues were begun in 1789 through the National Debt Office,[127] foreign loans scheduled for redemption in 1789 and 1790 were prolonged, and an ambitious program of credit mobilization was organized through the Amsterdam firms of Hogguer, Grand and Hasselgreen. After the war credit instruments issued by the debt office were transformed from interest-bearing notes into paper currency, a measure that effectively replaced the silver standard reintroduced in 1775 with a paper standard.[128] But in the meantime Sweden had come to the verge of insolvency. Because of systematic prolongations, Sweden was by 1790 doing nothing more than meeting annuity payments in the Dutch Republic, at a cost of more than f. 850,000 per annum. Proceeds of fresh loans, needed for the war, were being eroded by service requirements rising toward the point at which the annual sum that had to be transferred to Amsterdam would equal what Swedish authorities could reasonably expect to draw from the Republic in new loans. Although redemptions might still be deferred by prolongation, the need for fresh advances led Sweden to seek a renegotiation of outstanding obligations on terms preferable to those embodied in the mere prolongation of all loans falling due. In 1789 suggestions were solicited from Amsterdam about reformulation, and the bankers asked to devise a funding procedure that would lengthen the term over which payment of Sweden's debt was due while maintaining the monarchy's credit so as to permit fresh loans.[129]

With those questions before them, Hogguer, Grand and Hasselgreen asked their commission agents to assess the situation and offer recommendations. The first agents approached were apparently Pieter Stadnitski and Abraham van Ketwich,[130] both of whom suggested a continuation of existing arrangements together with reformulation of the term of redemption, that to be tied to a funding program.[131] Reassurances of Sweden's intent to meet its obligations and the addition of premiums or the conversion of old notes paying 4 and 4.5 percent to 5-percent returns would reassure investors. According to van Ketwich, it would be useful "dresser le programe de ces Emprunts de façon a prevenir le public que ce n'est pas pour accroître la dette du Royaume, mais pour la determiner sur un pied plus regulier & plus stable."[132]

Van Ketwich also recommended the creation of a secret fund to buy up Swedish notes when market prices dipped, with the necessary money being drawn from a covert reissue of notes taken in for redemption. The notion of manipulating the market in such a fashion was not novel in 1789, and van Ketwich presumably understood that such practices, involving as they did a particularly fragile kind of leverage, could be no more than temporarily useful. This part if his plan responded to the immediate problem, but van Ketwich also looked to long-term interests, advocating the f. 1 million be spent annually for annuity and redemption payments. That would have been a solid funding program and would have served investors well, but the key problem at hand was Sweden's need for fresh loans. Redemptions, even spaced over thirty years as van Ketwich proposed, could not be afforded. Such funding plans were popular mathematical exercises for eighteenth-century Europeans captivated by the apparent power of mathematical progression, but when applied to swollen national debts they suffered a common defect–drafted usually in time of crisis, they assumed a steady source of revenues for funding when in fact no such stability prevailed.

How serious the committee of finances was in soliciting such proposals is open to question. The principal concern of the moment must have been solely that of preserving Sweden's ability to borrow abroad. An appearance of willingness to reformulate the entire debt on whatever terms the bankers recommended could only assist such a goal. In any case nothing was done in 1789 or 1790. The loans of 1788–93 cleared more than f. 12 million in the United Provinces and elsewhere and although Ruuth, Liljencrantz's successor, fell into disgrace briefly in 1790 for his inability to produce revenues needed for the war, those loans enabled Sweden to carry on.[133] At the conclusion of the conflict the Hogguer, Grand–Hasselgreen association was dissolved, but Sweden continued to expand its search for foreign credit.

In Amsterdam the opportunity provided by the committee of finances to reflect on Sweden's credit standing might have occasioned misgivings, but there is no indication that the bankers took alarm or that they shared with investors the disquieting information available to them. A life-annuity loan of 1790 managed by A. & S. Boas of The Hague aside, the return paid on Dutch loans increased in 1789 to 5 percent, which was perhaps a reflection of some anxiety about Sweden's position, but other borrowers also found credit costs higher that year. Still, intermediaries might have realized at that point that Sweden's outstanding balance was secured only by the leverage provided by anticipated advances. Such a situation was not contrary to their interests, as long as Sweden's credit standing could be preserved, but it involved a kind of financial brinksmanship turning on matters beyond Dutch control–the size of future deficits and the relative adequacy of alternative credit sources to meet those deficits.

Late in 1791 Stadnitski and van Ketwich were approached again about a reformulation, this time together with one of the partners in S. & D. Saportas. At that point Sweden's debt in the Dutch Republic amounted to some f. 22.3 million, all of which fell due by 1803. The loans of the 1780s had not been arranged with staggered redemption dates so that, according to their original terms, they were scheduled to fall due in clusters. On this occasion the agents recommended only an extension of the term of reimbursements combined with new loans, dropping the notion of offering investors the inducement of a conversion to a higher return and substituting a suggestion that credits outstanding at 5 percent be converted to 4.5-percent yields. That striking reversal of opinion may be attributed to the termination of the Russian war and to a simultaneous but brief expansion of capital supply on the Amsterdam market.

Gustavus's assassination in 1792 and the conclusion of his adventurous foreign policy fell on the eve of the contraction of capital supply in Amsterdam, but there was no coincidental reduction of Swedish deficits. As a result Sweden was forced to shift back to bank note issues. Frugal policies introduced under Gustavus IV Adolphus gradually reduced the foreign debt from its high point in 1792, but they failed to eliminate continued deficits and enlarged currency issues. In 1797 Sweden reverted to foreign loan prolongations, and in 1798 deferred heavy outlays falling due by a consolidation and extension of the debt in the Dutch Republic.[134]

A limited supply of long-term credit available on the domestic market and the constriction of foreign capital access obliged Sweden to return to the unbalanced fiscal program employed before the 1760s. Acceptance of debt-office credit notes for tax payments reduced real revenues because notes depreciated as their quantity was expanded to cover deficits. During the years of increasing advances from abroad, that is, into 1792, the discount of nonconvertible notes against convertible notes did not exceed 12 percent, but during 1792 it advanced to 20 percent. Thereafter the disagio fluctuated, moving to 22 percent in 1794, then falling to about 10 percent from mid-1795 to early 1798. In that year, however, the discount expanded once again and reached about 50 percent in 1803.[135]

The rising discount on nonconvertible debt-office notes was attacked in 1803 by devaluation at the rate of 1 rdr in convertible paper for 1.5 rdr in nonconvertible paper in a program that reintroduced the silver standard. But Sweden was forced to suspend convertibility again in 1809, and in 1812 to declare null two-thirds of the foreign debt. The War of the Third Coalition, the Russo-Danish War of 1808–9, and then the conflict against France of 1812–15 left Swedish finances in chaos.

7

THE DEBTOR STATES: II

Russia

Revenue and expenditure figures are available only intermittently for the second half of the eighteenth century, but it is apparent that Russia confronted almost perennial deficits (Chart 7-1) during the reigns of Catherine II and Paul I.[1] The response followed a pattern typical in central and western Europe, centering first on attempts to increase existing taxes, introduce new levies, and reorganize the administrative system of revenue management in order to reduce overhead and improve control. Catherine pursued reforms both in the administration of tax collection and the centralization of account keeping over the entire period stretching from the conclusion of the Seven Years' War to the end of her reign in 1796.[2] Those efforts did enhance revenues and led to marked improvement in the information available to the central administration of the empire. Catherine also added allocations from her personal resources. Nonetheless revenue gains did not keep pace with expenditures even in peacetime, and after the Seven Years' War Russia turned to more flexible means of expanding income.

The first attempt to borrow abroad in this area, initiated by Empress Elizabeth during the Seven Years' War, failed.[3] But during the First Russo-Turkish War (1768–74), and in a period of growing Russian involvement in the internal affairs of Poland, Catherine arranged the simultaneous issue of paper currency through the Assignat Bank formed in 1768 and the negotiation of foreign loans in Amsterdam and Genoa. Bank notes were seen both as a supplement to imperial tax revenues and as a means of expanding production by circumventing a restrictive specie

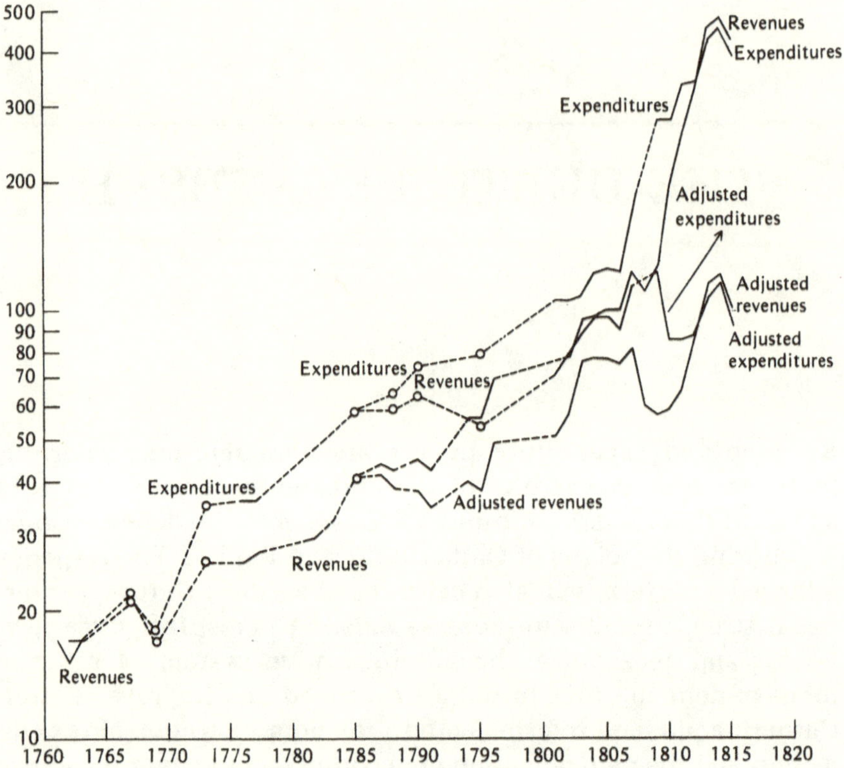

Chart 7-1. Tax revenues and expenditures, 1761–1815 (in assignat rubles and adjusted to specie, semilog scale).

money supply.[4] An increase in money supply was expected to enhance general prosperity and, presumably, to enlarge taxable resources while producing a more rapid turnover among commodities subject to indirect taxes.

The model of mercantilist finance adopted in Denmark and Sweden was thus duplicated in Russia, although with the difference that Russia began bank note issues and foreign borrowing at the same time rather than borrowing abroad to salvage an already-damaged money system. Without an internal capital market able to organize investment in interest-bearing notes, and without malleable tax resources, that was an attractive fiscal alternative. In its first year of operation the Assignat Bank limited note issues to the amount of its specie reserves, but that policy was sacrificed in 1770, after which money supply was governed by spending requirements rather than by the bank's resources or the absorptive capacity of the economy. The assignat issues, projected in Table 7-1,[5] mirror deficits and the financial tensions of intermittent foreign wars. This was nonetheless an efficient device for supplementing revenues as long as the market rate of the assignat remained close to par, so that the purchasing power of the share of tax revenues received in assignats was retained. Such a situation prevailed up to the Second Russo-Turkish War (1787–92). Until 1787 the premium that assignat holders had to pay for silver rubles appears never to have exceeded 5 percent and to have averaged slightly over 2 percent.[6] Even so there was some concern about the foreign-exchange rate of the ruble during the 1780s, resulting presumably from an expatriation and hoarding of specie that threatened to exacerbate depreciation.

Anxiety about the value of the ruble against the principal foreign monies of account in the Russian commercial sphere was justified. Against the Dutch guilder the ruble declined from an annual average of 47.25 stuivers in 1750 to 29.6 in 1797 (Chart 7-2),[7] a loss on transfers to the Republic of nearly a guilder per ruble. In other words, whereas a hundred rubles would have brought f. 236 in 1750, the same sum in 1797 would have brought only f. 148. As Chart 7-2 indicates, marked decline began in the late 1780s, that is, when the first particularly substantial block of assignats was put into circulation. Because from 1788 through 1793 there were also large advances from the Dutch Republic that tended to redress the effect of expatriation and hoarding of silver rubles and to increase demand for ruble bills, the ruble's devaluation was more restrained than would have been the case without those loans.[8]

Russian borrowing in the Dutch Republic coincided with the first and second Turkish wars and, between 1778 and 1782, with the credible threat of war in the diplomatic tension between the League of Armed Neutrality and Britain and an alliance with Austria directed against Turkey. Access to Dutch capital was acquired initially through R. & Th. de Smeth, one of the most substantial firms operating in Amsterdam.[9] Between 1769 and 1773 Russia raised f. 10 million, or slightly less than 5 million rubles figured at current exchange rates after deduction of costs.[10] Those loans covered only about 5 percent of revenues

Table 7-1. *Assignats in circulation and market rates 1769–1815*

	Volume in circulation (in millions of rubles)	Average rate against silver
1769	2.6	98.3
1770	6.3	98
1771	10.6	96.9
1772	14	96.2
1773	17.8	97.3
1774	20	98.5
1775	21.5	98.3
1776	23	98.3
1777	23.5	98.8
1778	23.5	98.9
1779	23.5	98.9
1780	24.5	98.3
1781	27.4	98.5
1782	33.3	99.5
1783	36.7	96.4
1784	40.1	97.7
1785	45.3	97.6
1786	46.2	97.3
1787	100	97.1
1788	100	92.2
1789	100	88.7
1790	111	85.5
1791	117	82.3
1792	120	78.7
1793	124	73.5
1794	145	71.2
1795	150	68.5
1796	157.7	71.7
1797	163.5	80.3
1798	194.8	73
1799	210	67.5
1800	—	65.3
1801	221.5	66.2
1802	230.5	72.5
1803	250	80
1804	260.7	79.4
1805	292.2	76.9
1806	319.2	74.6
1807	382.3	67.1
1808	477.4	53.5
1809	533.2	44.5
1810	579.4	30.9
1811	581.4	25.4
1812	646	25.8
1813	749.3	25.2
1814	798.1	25.3
1815	825.8	23.8

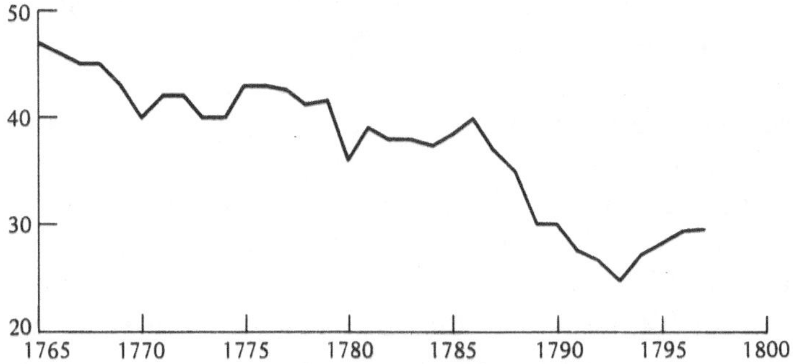

Chart 7-2. Average exchange rates against the Dutch guilder, 1765–97 (stuivers to the ruble).

(Chart 7-1), but the flow of guilder drafts appears to have contributed to a recovery of the ruble (Chart 7-2). Moreover, considered as a factor against estimated deficits of about 23 million rubles, Dutch loans covered some 22 percent and assignat issues the remainder.

Those loans fell due beginning in 1779, by which time Russia had opened another series intended both to prolong the earlier advances and raise fresh sums.[11] The amounts involved in individual issues of 1778–82 remain uncertain, but the net addition to the debt appears to have amounted to between f. 6 and f. 9 million (or 3 to 4.5 million rubles at current rates after deduction of costs).[12] Those were significant supplementary revenues, particularly because the alternative was higher expenditures to repay the f. 10 million outstanding from 1769–73, but deficits were still being covered chiefly out of assignat issues. Bank note volume reached 40.1 million assignat rubles in 1784 against foreign liabilities of 9.7 million, or 19 percent of the total state debt.[13] Once again, however, guilder drafts bolstered the ruble.

The earlier foreign loans were particularly useful as a source of foreign currency that moderated the tendency fostered by assignat issues toward hoarding or expatriation of specie. But as long as the assignat rate remained close to face value, foreign loans were a secondary means of supplementing revenues. During the second Turkish war, however, an unprecedented issue of 53.8 million assignat rubles depressed the market rate from 97 in 1787 to 78.7 in 1792. A projection against approximate deficits (using Chart 7-1) indicates that bank notes covered shortages in 1787, 1788, and part of 1789. But the deterioration of the assignat must have underscored the fragility of such heavy reliance on paper currency. After 1787 the Dutch loans, which by 1793 raised f. 53.5 million, provided an equally important source of supplementary revenues. At average annual exchange rates and distributed according to the date of availability to Russia, gross proceeds totaled some 36.5 million rubles and net proceeds slightly over 34 million. Because those credits were used in part to prolong 1778–82 loans, new proceeds amounted to between 22 and 24 million assignat rubles, a quantity approximately equivalent to the assignat issues of 24 million rubles from 1788 through 1793.

Foreign loans were especially attractive when the ruble was trading at declining rates because each successive loan yielded a larger sum in rubles. The prolongation of earlier loans delivered in lower ruble sums and continued devaluation of the ruble against the guilder combined, however, to increase the cost of retiring the foreign debt whether or not new sums were added to it. Russia had not anticipated such a development, and the provisions of the Russian loans in the Republic, like those of loans raised by other states, called for reimbursement in guilders.

As long as Russia could borrow at competitive rates, Dutch issues were still an efficient and expedient source of credit. By 1788–93 interest rates equaled those charged the foreign governments that Dutch investors judged most credit worthy. After the loans of 1788–93 and the prolongation of earlier advances, Russia was paying 4.75 percent in interest, appreciably closer to the current charges on British or Dutch debts than to what France paid its creditors. As of 1794 the Dutch part of the foreign debt, still far and away the largest share of the total, claimed only 3.3 percent of revenues (f. 2.54 million, or 1.86 of 56.3 million rubles). To that point Russia had benefited from a fiscal policy combining paper currency issues and foreign loans, but drawing an advantage from the same system in the future depended on continued access to foreign credit and to revenues from assignat issues at real values that did not continue to fall, thereby reducing tax revenues in terms of their purchasing power.

The close of foreign credit availability in 1793 threatened Russia's financial position because the stoppage both removed a source of pressure toward higher exchange value for the ruble and encouraged an increased rate and volume of assignat issues. Russia had shifted toward a paper standard without having anticipated the consequences of such a move, and after 1793 alternative deficit-financing methods were narrowing. In the meantime little progress had been made toward developing domestic capital markets, although Russia was able to raise small sums internally. The almost singular dependence on bank note issues was in fact encouraged by the still acceptable market rate of the assignat against silver. Adjusted according to that rate, revenues continued to expand until 1807. Although imperial fiscal authorities do not appear to have made a retrospective evaluation of Russia's position or of the assignat issues in those terms, the increase of revenues in constant values suggests that the expectation held in the late 1760s of enhancing general economic prosperity and taxable wealth had been met.

In 1807 more than 382 million assignat rubles were in circulation. That quantity had not been reached by a steady accrual, but the annual average issue had remained less than 8 million through 1802. In the following decade more than 415 million was added (to reach 645.9 million in 1812), and by the conclusion of the Napoleonic wars the supply totaled 825.8 million. Even adjusted according to the market rate of the assignat against silver, those expanded issues represented a significantly greater reliance on paper currency as a revenue source. When adjusted revenues declined, as they did sharply from 1807 through 1809 (Chart 7-1), Russia had exhausted the productive features of assignat issues for economic growth, but because of the Napoleonic wars there was no alternative save bank note inflation.

Poland

Sums borrowed by Poland in the Dutch Republic between 1777 and 1792 were both large enough and sufficiently concentrated in time to suggest that they supplemented revenues in much the same fashion that Dutch credits served other states. But the information available about revenues of the monarchy and the Polish Republic and their management is inadequate for an analysis of foreign credits as a factor in overall spending or fiscal policy. There is nonetheless a reformist political framework to which most of those advances appear to have been tied. Loans were raised in two periods of attempted constitutional reform: after the reorganization of the Polish state in 1775, which sought to deal with financial and political consequences of the first partition, and during part of the Four Years' Diet of 1788–92, which introduced political reforms centering on a constitution converting an elective into a hereditary monarchy and which also sought to reorganize the administrative apparatus and enlarge the army. In neither case, however, were the political or fiscal reforms adopted by the sejm adequate to stabilize Poland's position with respect to neighboring powers.

The Polish loans began during the political revival that followed the first partition. A revised constitution was introduced in 1775, and in the same year the newly created permanent council, composed of sejm members, renewed a program of financial reform begun in 1764.[14] The first partition had cost the state nearly half its annual revenues, seriously aggravating the prepartition problem of deficits.[15] The sejm's first step was to remodel taxation and, in accordance with increasing emphasis on direct taxes, to extend a chimney tax from Lithuania alone to the entire nation.

The reforms of 1764 (modified in 1766) and 1775 were designed to centralize the administration of republican finances and increase revenues. Although substantial gains were made in both areas, revenues remained inadequate to meet military requirements. Royal income was based chiefly on crown property, mining rights, port taxes, and customs (which were shared with the republican treasury), but it too was insufficient in some years to carry the king's responsibilities. Poland had earlier supplemented income through debasements, and during the Seven Years' War had been inundated by poor-quality Prussian coins. Under Stanislas (1764–95) the monetary system was reorganized and proposals considered for acquiring credit through paper currency issues.[16] Not until the Kościuszko insurrection of the early 1790s, however, was paper seigniorage invoked. In the interim both the Republic and the monarch turned to foreign loans.

In 1776 the sejm authorized the issue of a royal loan in Amsterdam, and in 1777 f. 2,625,000 was successfully negotiated at 5 percent through Hope & Co.[17] That advance was settled on a

Table 7-2. *Polish loans in Amsterdam, 1786–92*

Date	Debtor	Amount f.	Return %	Issuing house	Commission, %	Due date
1 June 1786	King	2,000,000	5	Hope & Co.	6	1796
1 Nov. 1790	Republic	2,100,000	5	R. & Th. de Smeth and Hogguer, Grand	—	1802
1 Jan. 1791	Republic	955,555	5	R. & Th. de Smeth and Hogguer, Grand	—	1803
1 Mar. 1791	King	1,500,000	5	Q. W. van Hoorn and Theodoor Gülcher & Mulder	—	1801
1 June 1792	Republic	3,500,000 (760,000 subscribed)	5	Pieter de Haan	—	1807

special amortization fund, on revenues assigned the king from the grand duchy of Lithuania, and on income from crown lands.

In a departure from customary practice, the annual amount of the revenues mortgaged was specified (at a sum that may be converted to about f. 1,240,000),[18] and both principal and annuity were guaranteed by Catherine II. In 1777 and again in three smaller loans opened in the early 1780s (totaling f. 1,662,500),[19] there appears to have been little or no discount to investors.[20] Other governments seeking loans in Amsterdam were then paying up to 5 percent, and debtors regarded as reliable about 4 percent. Poland was therefore offering a risk premium amounting to an additional f. 10 per annum on a f. 1,000 note. The high return, the specification of security and its annual yield, and, in 1777 but not thereafter, the ancillary guarantee from Russia all suggest that a cautious reception was expected. Whatever misgivings might have been felt among investors, the inducements sufficed.

As Table 7-2 indicates, subsequent loans were opened under the terms established earlier.[21] Over the years to 1792, however, annuity rates generally increased as more secure debtors were forced to offer yields equivalent to those of Polish issues. There remained in the Polish loans the more careful specification of backing that Hope had originally arranged, but in other respects that firm's 1777 evaluation of Polish credit had not subsequently been reassessed.[22]

In the interim King Stanislas had made little progress in consolidating Poland's political position, whereas lavish court expenditures had increased royal indebtedness. One source puts royal income in 1786 at 6,143,000 złotys, approximately one-third of total government revenues. But the king's debts amounted to some ten million, raised abroad and through royal bankers in Warsaw.[23] The marathon sejm of 1788–92 extended the financial reforms begun in 1764 and continued in 1775, but those same sessions approved additional military spending for which taxes were inadequate.[24] A loan broached with Genoan bankers was rejected in February 1790, but Poland succeeded in raising f. 4,555,555 in Amsterdam within the following thirteen months.

If a well-informed rentier had chosen that moment to strike a balance on Polish credit, he or she might have realized that the factors that had forced Poland to offer more lucrative terms than other borrowers in 1777 and the early 1780s remained in force and indeed had been aggravated. Given the gulf separating Poland from more politically stable debtors, it is surprising that Dutch investors did not demand higher returns in 1790. In effect that happened finally in 1792 when the wartime loan opened by Pieter de Haan fell far short of being fully subscribed, perhaps chiefly because of pressure applied by Russia in Amsterdam. But for a year and a half investors accepted Polish paper paying a return equal to or less than that available from other foreign debtors.

Poland's retention of a 5-percent return after that return had ceased to provide investors with a risk premium reflects the importance of habit in investment choices among Dutch rentiers. The initial loan had been managed by Hope & Co., a house superior in capitalization to all its competitors, and superior also to some competitors in the care it took in formulating loans. Terms established by that firm had substantial weight, but it is not clear why they should have been maintained after Hope shifted to organizing loans for Russia. Of the houses directing loans in 1790 and 1791, Hogguer, Grand & Co. was solid, but neither R. & Th. de Smeth nor Q. W. van Hoorn had for several years brought a loan before the public. For that reason they might have been suspected of too great eagerness to regain their former position.

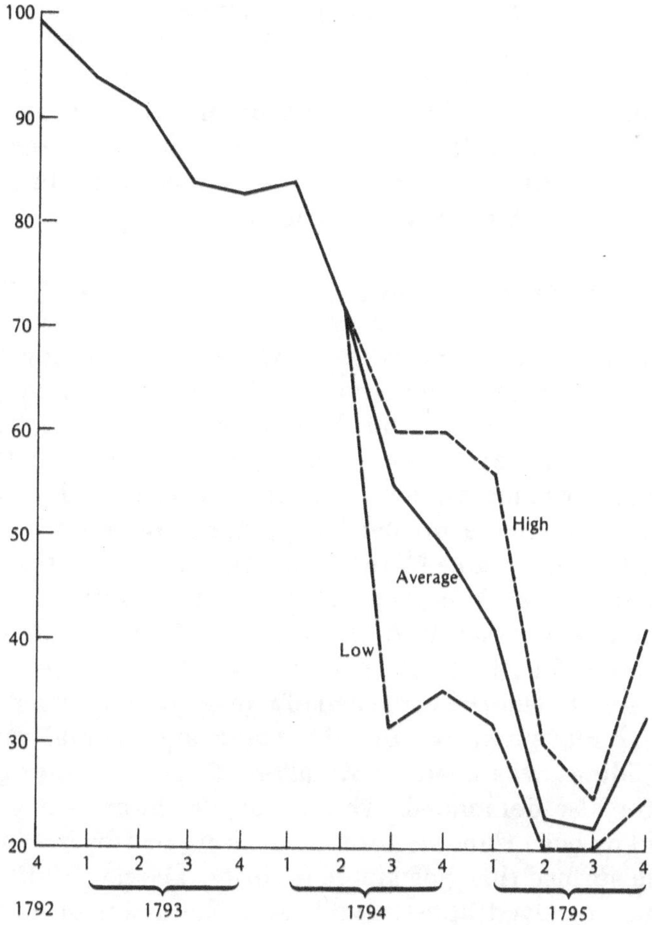

Chart 7-3. The quarterly average of Polish 5% notes, Oct.–Dec. 1792 through 1795.

The last issue, that of 1792, was entrusted to de Haan, a house whose standing, as reflected in market prices on loans it directed for both the government and Polish landowners, was unreliable. Particularly the instability of Poland's banking agency in Amsterdam might have aroused caution, but that was a frame of mind alien to the Amsterdam market in 1790 and 1791.

Despite their misgivings about the de Haan loan, Dutch investors remained confident in Polish securities already in circulation in 1792. As Chart 7-3 reveals,[25] it was not until 1793 that prices fell, and not until the second quarter of 1794 that serious depreciation occurred. Polish paper declined in advance of that of other borrowers, reflecting the disintegration of the state, but the sharpest fall was produced by the suspension of annuity payments rather than by the second partition.[26] Rumors about Russian and Prussian willingness to assume part of the Polish debt probably account for the comparatively modest decline during 1793, when the partition was carried out.[27]

Dutch investors in general paid little heed to the value that might, in the event of default, be realized from assets mortgaged in loans, and that oversight is nowhere more striking than in credits raised in Amsterdam on behalf of some Polish magnates, among them Stanislas and Alexander Lubomirski, Michael Ogiński, Adam Czartoryski, and Ignatius and Jean Potocki. These loans became numerous during the 1780s, when some of those magnates were involved in forming industrial establishments on their estates.[28] In terms and structure the issues, which were floated for a total of more than f. 9 million, followed precedents established in loans to the king and the Republic.[29] In all but one for which information is available the annuity rate was 5 percent. Security consisted of mortgages on landed estates and other real property, and the value and annual return of those holdings was customarily given. Supplementary guarantees were also demanded, which took the form of assurances extended by one or another of four banking houses in Warsaw.[30]

On the surface this was stable security. The negotiating firms sometimes received impressive lists of the assets of mortgaged estates, including even the number of serfs thereon,[31] and such evidence presumably confirmed the reputation for wealth and political influence enjoyed by that small group of families at the apex of Poland's nobility. What was not immediately apparent was that those estates could not readily be sold in the event of default. First, of course, the mortgage holder had to secure title to the estate in question in a society unusually solicitous of the interests of its nobility. Moreover, the second partition confused the issue because some estates fell within areas taken over by Prussia and Russia, and some of those were sequestered by the partitioning powers.[32] Finally, the supplementary guarantees offered by Warsaw bankers depended on the solvency of those houses. Tepper and Blanc fell into difficulties during 1793 and were forced to suspend payments.[33] Tepper's bankruptcy proceedings revealed that business standards in Warsaw fell substantially below what Amsterdam firms regarded as responsible. Tepper was seven years behind in maintaining accounts.[34]

Service was suspended on most of the advances to magnates in 1793 and 1794, leaving Dutch noteholders with paper that could not be realized without heavy losses.[35] The anxieties produced by those defaults and by the sequestration of some estates were mitigated somewhat in 1796 when Robert Voûte, an associate in Hope & Co. acting for bankers involved in the issues, put forward a case for Russian assumption not only of the foreign debts of the Polish state but also of the landowners' debts.[36] Voûte's argument, that the empire could defer the redemption of its own debt in the Republic by assuming those obligations and converting them into longer-term annuities, was sufficiently convincing to persuade Russia to agree in 1797. There was, moreover, the attraction of gaining some hold over a nobility that had previously been recalcitrant and might be so again. Thus Russia assumed principal and annuity arrears. The total sum taken over in the conversion adopted in 1798, including loans to the king, Republic, landowners, and private advances to the king and some landowners, was nearly f. 16 million.[37] With that step those liabilities were merged with the Russian imperial debt.

Spain

Exploitation of the international credit structure by Spain began during Charles III's efforts to regain some of the economic might that had shriveled during the previous century.[38] The plan for revival included ambitious Atlantic trading enterprises and construction of an extensive irrigation and navigation system centering on a canal paralleling the Ebro River. Because domestic resources were insufficient for the enormous expense of canal building, Spain turned to foreign capital markets in 1770 and 1773, in the latter year contracting with Adolf Jan Heshuysen & Co. of Haarlem and Amsterdam and A. & S. Boas of The Hague to float a loan for f. 2.4 million.[39] The terms agreed to reveal the caution with which those bankers expected investors to approach the issue. In addition to an annuity of 6 percent, a high rate for the 1770s, Spain agreed to redemption premiums on a substantial segment of the notes issued.

Such caution was warranted. Earlier Spanish monarchs had perfected the technique of periodic repudiations. And in general the states of southern Europe were less attractive borrowers because they lagged behind their counterparts in northern and central Europe in the comparative efficiency of their taxation systems and general financial stability.[40] The 1773 loan was secured on revenues from a part of the Tauste canal, a branch of the imperial canal that had not yet been built. Nonetheless, neither the problematic nature of the security nor warnings offered in the commercial periodical *De Koopman* altogether deterred Dutch investors.[41]

Proceeds were, however, inadequate for the overall canal project, and Spain sought vigorously to expand financing. In 1775 the firm of Jean Soret of Madrid floated a life-annuity loan for 15 million livres tournois, with shares marketed throughout Europe.[42] The annuity was to be paid in Madrid, Genoa, Bern, and Hamburg, all except Genoa second-class financial centers at best, suggesting that Pradez y Cía, holders of the canal concession, may have intentionally bypassed the more discerning first-class markets.[43] Still, the venture captivated Dutch investors, who were attracted by the lottery-ticket size of notes – 60 1.t., or less than f. 30 (which may have appealed to economic groups usually excluded from government loans by the standard f. 1,000 price of paper) – and the high return. *De Koopman* once again pointed out its defects, principally the division of the loan into 250,000 small shares, a measure necessarily involving greater expense and difficulty for the debtor and increasing the possibility of fraud, but also the fact that the loan was secured only by a canal project that might not be completed or that might fail to provide the revenues necessary for service.[44] But such arguments failed to stifle Dutch interest.

Eighteenth-century canal-building costs could not easily be projected, and in Spain the grand projects of the 1770s assumed the character of bottomless pits. In 1778 fresh credits were once more sought in Amsterdam even though the terms that had to be offered were onerous. In each of the years 1778, 1779, and 1780 Nicolaas Echenique & Sanchez of Amsterdam floated loans nominally paying 3.5 percent, but subscriptions could be paid half in cash and half in old notes, then trading in Amsterdam far below par.[45] To raise loans that would bring in at best no more than f. 3,208,000, less commissions and other costs, the Spanish court was willing to issue paper totaling twice that sum.[46]

In fact these were conversion loans that at the same time kept afloat the canal projects and met other financial needs arising from Spanish entry into the War of the American Revolution in 1779 and from the wartime disruption of trade and bullion imports. They were also forced conversions. Holders of old notes were informed in the prospectus of the 1780 issue that those notes would cease to have any value after the expiration of the subscription period for the current loan, 1 May 1781.[47] Although the loans of 1778 and 1779 appear to have been subscribed in full, the issue of 1780 fell slightly short nonetheless, attracting f. 2,298,000.[48] Total net proceeds would then have been f. 3,149,000 (some 1,810,000 pesos vellon) less costs.[49]

Spain's initial extraordinary expenses in the conflict with Britain, which brought to a conclusion the effort at economic expansion using foreign capital, were met principally through a 1780 decision to finance the war by means of currency inflation in the form of interest-bearing notes termed the *vales reales*. That paper, declared receivable for tax payments, was intended to circulate as legal tender for large-scale settlements. No specific provision was made to support public confidence in the *vales* until 1782, when the Bank of Spain was founded and given the charge of maintaining value in the 30 million pesos in *vales* then in circulation by trading in them with revenues from commissions on military contracts and specie exports.[50] But by October 1782 the *vales* were discounted by 22 percent, so that the program of currency inflation was losing its effectiveness as a source of revenues. Following the practice adopted by other states, Spain turned to Amsterdam for further credit. A loan for f. 3 million (about 1,780,000 pesos vellon) was raised beginning on 1 November through Hope and Fizeaux, Grand.[51] That was of particular assistance at a time when wartime interruption of bullion shipments and Spain's inability to circulate *vales* abroad increased the cost of paying for military expenses or debt charges in foreign currencies. But the principal assistance in that direction had been provided by a Dutch, French, and Spanish syndicate of merchants who supplied funds against the first two issues of *vales*.[52]

The conclusion of the war in 1783 and the renewal of silver imports from Mexico brought a respite to Spanish finances and enabled the monarchy to take the unusual step among government debtors of redeeming the 1782 loan according to its original conditions, between 1789 and 1792.[53] As a result confidence in Spanish credit worthiness was buoyed during the decade of peace that followed 1783, and paper that had traded at deep discounts on the *beurs* moved toward and reached par. In Spain itself the *vales* recovered from their wartime depreciation and advanced to a 1- to 2-percent premium over specie.[54] For the moment Spain warranted greater confidence, both because of postwar financial recovery and the relative economic prosperity that marked the decade after 1783.[55]

In 1792 the monarchy took advantage of its strong standing in Amsterdam by placing a loan for f. 6 million (about 3,500,000 pesos vellon) through Hope & Co. at 4.5 percent, and at the same time making preliminary arrangements for two further issues each of the same sum.[56] Growing diplomatic tension and the likelihood of being drawn into the War of the First Coalition appear to have been the immediate factors leading Spain to organize fresh foreign credits.[57] But the prospect of a series of issues faded with the downturn of the Amsterdam market in 1793, only months after Spanish entry into the conflict.

Dutch capitalists were deterred for the time being from granting further credit to Spain not by any insight they had gained into the inevitable effect of war on its financial position but by the coincidental threat to the Republic from France. To deal with war costs Spanish authorities resisted increasing regressive taxes and turned instead to direct levies on the wealthier elements of society and renewed domestic credit inflation. The quantity of *vales* in circulation reached about 100 million pesos in February 1795, and by the early summer they were again trading at a discount of some 22 percent.[58] With the conclusion of the war in June Spain's position improved, as is reflected in the ascent of *vales*, despite nothing more than fractional retirements, to a rate of 95 percent against specie. In Amsterdam market quotations show that Spanish credit began a revival at about the same time.[59] Despite the fact that the peace lasted only sixteen months, Spain retained its credit standing in Amsterdam even through the war with Britain that began in October 1796. At home, however, that war forced the adoption of measures that revealed the increasingly desperate straits of royal finances.[60]

Fresh domestic loans and the sale of property in entail provided some assistance, but foreign credit was again necessary. The *vales* fell against specie even though no new issues were organized until the spring of 1799. Measures designed to hold value close to par failed because the taxes assessed for that attempt could not be collected. Interest payments on the *vales* were suspended temporarily, and by 1802 that paper was being discounted up to 75 percent. In the interim four new loans were opened in Amsterdam, one each in the years 1798–1801, for a total of f. 13 million.[61] The first was only partially subscribed and absorbed into the subsequent issue. For the rest, of f. 10 million sought, Spain appears to have raised some f. 8 million (about 8,750,000 pesos vellon).[62] That was no more than a drop in the bucket against *vales* outstanding, nearly 146 million pesos after the issue of April 1799. But against their market value, ranging apparently from a discount of 43 percent in April 1799 to one of 75 percent in 1802, as a current account credit in Spain's balance of payments, and as a source of solid exchange value against the faltering ducat, the Dutch loans assume more importance.[63] Proceeds from those loans were evidently used for the War of the Oranges against Portugal, the continuing naval conflict with Britain, and for servicing the loans themselves.[64]

Although Spain had managed, by careful attention to service and redemption payments during the 1780s and 1790s, to build a position of strength in Amsterdam, and to maintain that position after the point at which deterioration in its domestic credit program was evident, the terms of the issues of 1798–1801 reflect growing caution in the Republic. In addition to an annuity of 5 percent and a conversion operation in which outstanding notes were exchanged with bonuses, the monarchy also offered premiums and lottery prizes. *Beurs* prices show that investors were considerably more sanguine about the short-term than about the long-term reliability of Spain as a debtor. Between 1798 and 1807, when earlier loans were falling due, notes scheduled for redemption in a given year were bid up toward par from sometimes substantial discounts whereas paper with some years to run continued to trade at a discount.

Spain was still able to meet debt charges in Amsterdam, but by 1800 the monarchy's position was fundamentally precarious and it did not improve after the conclusion of European peace in

March 1802. Spain emerged from the war in alliance with France and, although the monarchy remained aloof from the renewal of Anglo-French conflict in 1803, that stance had to be bought with subsidies to France set initially at Fr. 6 million per month. The exploitation by France of resources that Spain did not possess led to an intensified search for foreign credit and to highly imaginative techniques for transferring silver produced in Mexico for use in Europe. Those measures ultimately involved Spain, France, Britain, and Dutch and British bankers in a Milo Minderbinder-style operation that permitted the opposing sides in the European war to pursue hostilities all the more vigorously and enabled Spain to meet part of its obligations to France. Hope & Co. was involved in both elements of Spain's financial program but, because of Buist's careful reconstruction of Hope's role, nothing more than a summary is necessary here.[65]

Spanish plans to float new loans in Amsterdam were hindered after 1801 by regulations under which the Batavian regime had to sanction all foreign loans. In the interim, before permission was secured for an issue, a stopgap measure was arranged through French military contractors led by Gabriel Ouvrard. As a result Ouvrard gained an entrée to Spanish finances and laid the foundations for an 1805 agreement with Hope & Co. providing for the use of commercial exchanges among Europe, the Spanish colonies in America, and the United States to arrange shipments of piastres (the peso of eight reales or piece of eight, a coin then worth about f. 2.3) from Mexico. Late in 1804 Ouvrard, ingratiating himself with Charles IV's prime minister, Godoy, agreed to deliver a series of advances to Spain, among them a loan of f. 10 million to be floated in Amsterdam. In return he was promised a monopoly over imports to and exports from the Spanish colonies, to be shared with the crown. That gave Ouvrard access to Mexican silver and thus to the means to expand his role as financier to France. But there remained the problem of safe passage of silver to Europe. Even before Spanish entry into the War of the Third Coalition, early in 1805, Britain had resumed seizures of Spanish ships. There was, however, the common interest that Britain, France, and Spain shared in the need for specie, and Ouvrard appealed to Pitt for permission to ship piastres to Europe, leaving a portion of them in England. Pitt refused, but the notion of serving the common interests of warring states did not die.

To explore that end Hope & Co., brought in by Ouvrard in May 1805, approached Baring & Co. in London. Sir Francis Baring was to sound out the British government, pointing out the twofold attraction of securing precious metals while British trade expanded at the expense of American merchants. Anticipating agreements that would launch the project, Hope & Co. set out to establish the framework of agents in the United States and Mexico necessary to handle transfer of piastres and other commodities. Ouvrard was removed from the scheme in 1805 when Napoleon launched an inquiry into the accounts of French financiers, but Hope had already begun to receive piastre drafts on Mexico. Those were consigned to agents in the United States, and the venture was launched without Ouvrard's direct participation.

Shipments of European and American goods to Vera Cruz, the port of exit for piastres, were arranged by Hope's agents, with return cargoes composed of piastres, and other ships were dispatched to Vera Cruz in ballast. The value received in the United States was then exported to England, for the most part in cargoes of American goods, and Hope collected from the consignees of those cargoes. Sums due Paris for Spanish subsidies were then either remitted directly or through intermediaries in Hamburg, Rotterdam, Antwerp, and Frankfurt.

This system, based on a triangular trade in silver and general commodities, was interrupted in 1807 by the Continental System and an American embargo on all foreign commerce. But at the same time Baring's efforts to secure British permission to ship piastres from Vera Cruz without hindrance succeeded, as did Hope's efforts to reach terms with France on Spanish piastre drafts that it held. Hope and Baring agreed on the provisions of their association in July 1806, and in March 1807 Napoleon came to terms and Baring secured the necessary authorization from Britain. The first shipment of piastres under the revised project, for the most part excluding cargoes and relying on British warships to carry the silver, arrived in England in October 1807.

In the meantime Ouvrard's agreement with Spain to arrange a loan in Amsterdam was, after some delay, fulfilled. In 1805, having secured authorization from the Batavian regime, Hope opened a loan for f. 10 million at 5.5 percent for ten years.[66] Once again the Dutch government was manipulated by France. Opposition to the Spanish loan was overcome by pressure applied from Paris.

But the new loan did little to arrest the deterioration of Spain's financial position. Its proceeds were diverted in part to France after Ouvrard's embarrassment in 1805, and a new loan was immediately necessary.[67] De Smeth was approached first, for the unprecedented sum of f. 30 million, but was unable to make headway. Then in August 1806 Hope was contacted, but that firm insisted on including a conversion of all existing notes, excepting only those of 1805, and more stringent safeguards for investors.[68] Had conditions permitted Spain might have resisted those terms, but pressure from France obliged Spain to accept them. Thus in the spring of 1807 Hope opened a loan for f. 30 million at 5.5 percent.[69] The necessary government permission was at first refused, not because of opposition to the loan but because Louis Napoleon wished to issue a loan for the kingdom of Holland. After Hope agreed to assist in a consortium raising f. 40 million for Holland, the Spanish loan was approved.

Placement of notes on the scale demanded by the Spanish loan was a difficult charge for 1807. Since 1793 the sharp decline in new emissions, the normal turnover in firms, and strains on the Amsterdam market had driven many commission agents out of business. There was still money in Amsterdam for investment in foreign loans, but there was also in circulation a great volume of depreciated paper, both obligations and annuity coupons, and investors preferred to update that paper in conversions when possible. Because Hope had bargained to have notes from Spanish loans before 1805, amounting to some f. 10.5 million, converted in 1807, subscribers could exchange a combination of depreciated old notes, past-due annuity coupons, past-due redemptions, and cash for new notes. Altogether the claims on the loan, including unpaid drafts drawn by Croese on Spain in connection with loans managed by that house, a 10-percent discount on the issue price, the commission, and conversion, totaled nearly f. 20 million, leaving Spain with a maximum potential income of slightly over f. 10 million. To compound those deductions, proceeds were to be dispatched not to Spain but to France, to which subsidies were perennially past due.

Although notes moved well enough at first, by the end of 1807 the commission agents had ceased taking further parcels. At that time 23,000 shares had been placed with the agents, with no net proceeds to Spain. On the side of Dutch investors even the fractional cash subscriptions necessary proved to have been good money after bad. In the summer of 1808 the French puppet Joseph replaced Charles IV, initiating a period of internal disorder in Spain. Both Spanish governments, that of Joseph and that of the loyalist regime, were impecunious and, although Hope had provided for annuities due in 1808 to be paid out of subscriptions, there was the problem of future service payments. Moreover, in the change of government in Spain Hope was shut off from the Mexican piastre shipments and thus prevented from presenting for payment drafts on the Mexican treasury given as security for the loans of 1805 and 1807.

Hope exploited what avenues remained to it to find funds for service but was hindered by conflict within Spain and continuing French control over the finances of Joseph's government. With the abdication of Charles IV, Dutch investors had lost most of their leverage. A loan for Joseph's government was broached in 1809, to be secured on sequestered church property, but Hope resisted. "Amsterdam had lost three-quarters of its resources and also its influence on the investors."[70] But more important, Amsterdam had lost its influence over debtors. Notes from 1807 remained unplaced and, although they might still have been sold if annuity payments were met, Amsterdam had virtually dried up as a source of foreign loans. It was the eve of a new crisis, one that in 1810 and 1811 would consume several of the major firms still in operation, including de Smeth. This state of affairs is reflected by the Amsterdam stock exchange, where transactions had fallen to no more than f. 50,000 a day.[71] A capital market unable to meet the needs of borrowers was a market without leverage over borrowers.

By 1809 Spanish credit had held up far longer than was warranted by that state's financial and political instability. One important prop was the attachment of Hope & Co. to the loans of 1805 and 1807. That firm's integrity and solidity inspired wholly unrealistic confidence. Hope covered the annuity due on the 1807 loan in July 1809, in anticipation of finding funds for that from the sale of unsold notes. But authorization for that sale was withheld by Spain, and no other resources were available. Thus Hope was obliged to announce that the annuity due in November could not be met, and that redemptions scheduled for 1809 would be deferred. That announcement was the signal for Dutch investors to give up their long and fondly held notion that Spain might meet its commitments.[72]

France

A rational program of debt conversion or renegotiation, under which returns were adjusted to reflect major changes in pressures on the money market, was an element of government policy and most of Europe by the end of the eighteenth century. Such a policy both mitigated the effects of high credit costs commonly encountered in war and postwar restabilization loans and enabled debtors to take advantage of the secular trend toward lower long-term annuity rates. But in France partial repudiations of indebtedness, reductions of returns on long-term paper, and suspensions of payment on short-term obligations had an arbitrary character.[73] Indeed the public credit element of the financial system was marked by a degree of irrationality and unpredictability unmatched by any other major power. The French treasury relied on both short-term advances to anticipate tax revenues paid over by venal officeholders months after collection and long-term loans for the extraordinary expenditures of wartime. In the latter case in particular France paid excessive yields to attract credit during the second half of the century. Those yields were partly a product of the insecurity of advances to a debtor that dealt arbitrarily with its obligations and thereby had to pay a risk premium. But in the life-annuity format, the preferred technique of raising credit during the 1770s and 1780s, France paid returns that exceeded any reasonable estimate of what was necessary.[74]

There was at least intermittent foreign investment in French loans throughout the eighteenth century, but the scale of foreign assets reached a level of particular significance only during the 1770s and 1780s. In Geneva, Genoa, and the Dutch Republic investors found attractive the earnings of the complex assortment of instruments used by the monarchy. Although France seldom issued loans on foreign capital markets, foreign rentiers bought heavily through Parisian agents. The major shift in French access to foreign capital was apparently the product of a conscious policy, adopted by Terray in conjunction with a suspension of payments on certain short-term paper in 1770 and 1771. A large life-annuity loan was issued in Amsterdam in 1772,[75] on the eve therefore of the crisis that led potential investors to attempt to increase liquidity. Few contracts were placed, but the loan was later transferred to Paris and eventually oversubscribed. Although Dutch rentiers remained for nearly a decade little interested, Genevans bought heavily in French loans during the 1770s, simultaneously with Jacques Necker's first ministry and presumably in part because of the appointment of a compatriot.

Terray's 1772 plan to broaden credit access in Amsterdam failed for reasons independent of its merits. With its failure passed an opportunity to reduce annuity rates. Both the Amsterdam loan and a *rente viagère* issue in Paris in 1771 opened below customary yields. But life-annuity loans floated later in the decade reinstated the higher yields of the Seven Years' War and its aftermath.[76] Necker displayed no reluctance to gratify Genevan interests, and his successors maintained and even slightly increased average yields in life-annuity loans. Therefore, although access to foreign capital was acquired during the 1770s and sharply expanded thereafter, continuing growth in the pool of resources on which France was drawing did not reduce credit costs.

The appearance of large-scale Dutch investment in the monarchy's loans cannot be traced to high returns alone, for those were a nearly constant feature of French borrowing. Nor is it possible to relate Dutch interest to any material improvement in French financial policy or in the monarchy's financial position, although investors may have been misled by Necker's assertion that significant reforms were underway. Instead the sharp increase of capital exports to France during the 1780s should be seen chiefly as the product of a reaction against Britain and against participation in British loans, and of a temporary decrease in demand from other foreign borrowers. The moment was distinctly propitious for French investments. Rentiers who directed their attention to France were able, so it must have seemed, to get in on the ground floor. Returns were far higher than those on the Amsterdam market, and Dutch rentiers may have reasoned that those excessive returns would be reduced in loans opened after the American war, when France would presumably regain financial equilibrium. Once committed in France to the extent that they were by 1787, Dutch investors found it difficult to withdraw without raising the prospect of a market collapse. Thus Dutch rentiers remained heavily committed even after 1788 when, once again, France suspended payments on part of its obligations.[77]

Nevertheless, the Dutch investor who added French rather than British securities to a portfolio was rejecting the caution that had traditionally characterized lending to foreign governments. Even if Dutch appraisals of the credit worthiness of debtor states appear, in retrospect, to have been inaccurate more often than accurate, investors and intermediaries had construed variations in risk among different borrowers within a narrow range. The returns offered by the French treasury stood at the upper edge of that range and more often wholly above it. There was a speculative feature in lending for yields that surpassed what Poland had been obliged to pay in the aftermath of the first partition, and what Sweden had paid in the early 1770s, when there was a strong possibility of partition of that state.

On the other hand there were also reasons why the French debt could be regarded with assurance. Rentiers may be expected to have been aware that the exchange between guilders and livres tournois had deviated very little (in fact by no more than four deniers de gros per écu of three livres) since early in the century.[78] That slight variation added a connotation of stability to both monies of account and obscured price movements. In addition, the investor who followed developments in France was aware that self-proclaimed reformist elements were at work. Necker, who proposed a reorganization of the administration of revenues, had declared a surplus of ordinary receipts over ordinary expenditures as of February 1781. His *Compte rendu au roi* was intended "to convince prospective creditors of the soundness of the royal finances,"[79] and implied that the debt itself was comparatively modest when in fact extraordinary expenditures had made it anything but modest. As a contemporary observer noted, Necker was able to inspire confidence and maintain the treasury's credit solely by frequent recourse to loans.[80] The next controller general to serve for a sustained period, Calonne, also professed support for economies and repeatedly reassured rentiers of his commitment to meet France's obligations. Such declarations and assurances were intended to convey an impression of soundness during a time in which the realities of the budget were not at all apparent.

In addition to higher returns there was also in French paper the attraction provided by the energy and enterprise of Dutch entrepreneurs who dominated substitution ventures for which French life annuities provided security, and who also marketed blocks of French securities directly. On their way up, such men were willing to take chances that were not acceptable to traditional and better-established elements in the market. Their apparent success led investors and other brokers to emulate them in exploiting placements in France.

Dutch willingness to invest in French securities was met by the French need to borrow. Jacques Necker, who gained an undeserved reputation for financial competence, found himself in his first ministry (1777–81) in a political situation that seemed to demand borrowing. Accordingly Necker met the extraordinary costs of the War of the American Revolution and some other minor expenditures as well through a series of loans,[81] loans continued by his successors, on ruinous terms, loans that magnified the French debt and led directly to the virtual bankruptcy of 1788. Still, it is less important that servicing the debt accumulated by 1788 (nearly 5 billion livres) cost about half of all expenditures than it is that credit costs were so much higher for France than for other states that they reduced severely the total debt that could be carried even by half of expenditures. French deficit financing was based on credit inflation but, to the extent that maintenance costs were absorbed early, France failed to seize the same benefit from inflationary price trends as other states.[82]

As numerous authorities have indicated, French fiscal arrangements had brought the government to the verge of insolvency by the 1780s. J. F. Bosher has taken issue with the widely accepted notion that the tax structure was basically responsible for this situation.[83] He suggests, to the contrary, that the problem could not have been resolved merely by an improvement in the revenue system, but required a thorough reorganization, which in his view was begun in 1771, halted with the conclusion of Necker's first ministry in 1781, and begun again with Calonne's fall from office in 1787. What both points of view tend to overlook is the decreasing time span during which more efficiency in assessing revenues or in administering collections and expenditures could have been brought to bear to save the monarchy from crisis. The burden of debt that already existed by 1771 was, despite Terray's reforms, substantial, and whether or not a formal budget existed (and Bosher has shown that even the term "budget" was foreign),[84] there was unquestionably a large and only partially comprehended imbalance between revenue and expenditure. Although administrative reforms produced some economies, both the debt itself and the cost of debt maintenance increased in the two decades after 1771. As a result a reformist program was difficult to afford, and a program that achieved substantial savings would have required years to take effect, a period of time that could have been available only if ignorance of the actual state of affairs had been more extensive even than it was. Necker himself was at least partially aware of the extent of royal indebtedness, and should have been well aware that borrowing during his first administration, totaling about 530 million l.t. according to G. Susane, had added substantially to an already burdensome debt.[85] His successors, even had they continued the reforms begun and proposed by Necker, could also have done no more than continue to borrow. Nevertheless, they too overlooked an opportunity to reduce yields, namely, that provided by a surge of capital imports from the Dutch Republic in the early 1780s.

As was the case also in Dutch investment in the British public debt, rentiers added French securities to their portfolios chiefly by investing through agents in the debtor state. No source has yet been developed that permits a satisfactory reconstruction of the amount of French paper in Dutch hands at any given point. Although it can be demonstrated that such holdings increased markedly during the 1780s, it is necessary to deal in estimated ranges. On the other hand, Dutch rentiers also participated during the 1780s in stock-substitution ventures in which subscriptions were employed to acquire one or more types of French securities. That method of investment, which tended to attract small- rather than large-scale investors, represented no more than a fraction of all capital exports into French government loans, but the available evidence about it is more comprehensive.

Contemporary observers acknowledged and commented upon the reversal of the trend around 1780 under which Dutch resources moved toward France rather than Britain. The most reliable of those commentators was L. P. van de Spiegel who, in 1782, when secretary to the states of Zeeland, appraised the total invested by the Dutch in foreign government loans at f. 335 million. Of that sum van de Spiegel thought some f. 25 million to be in French holdings.[86] Four years later the Prussian ambassador at The Hague, Thulemeyer, estimated that the Dutch received f. 12 million per annum in interest and annuities from France, indicating an investment, at an average return of 5 percent, of f. 240 million, or nearly a tenfold increase over van de Spiegel's figure.[87] If the average return is assumed to have been somewhat higher, 6.5 or 7 percent being the maximum possible, then the increase would have been to between f. 185 and about 171.5 million.[88] What weakens one's willingness to rely on Thulemeyer is the fact that he had some reason to exaggerate. As Prussian ambassador he was involved in an intricate and subtle effort to reassert Frederick William II's prestige at The Hague.[89] He could have forwarded that goal by seeking to convince anti-British but not necessarily pro-French elements in the States General and provincial states that the French commitments of Dutch rentiers were excessive. On the other hand, Thulemeyer had been ambassador in The Hague since 1763 and had observed foreign investment patterns with some care.

Van de Spiegel's estimate relates to the eve of substantial expansion in Dutch holdings in French securities. Because of that it can be used in conjunction with an analysis of Dutch investment patterns that includes a comparison of holdings in 1779–80 with 1789–90. On the basis of collateral-succession tax inventories in Amsterdam, Alice Carter has found that holdings in France increased from 4 to 18.6 percent of all investments abroad outside Britain within that decade.[90] Such inventories tend to understate foreign, and particularly French, holdings of Amsterdam rentiers because assessors were not required to specify the assets behind stock-substitution securities. But on the assumption that portfolio distribution patterns among Amsterdam rentiers were similar to those among Dutch rentiers in general, Carter's analysis suggests an increase from van de Spiegel's f. 25 million estimate to a minimum of slightly more than f. 115 million by 1789–90.

From general estimates by contemporary observers one must shift to the surviving papers of merchants, bankers, and rentiers, detailed and fragmentary records that give no more than a glimpse of all foreign investment from the Republic but transcend factional lines among investors. For that reason they may be taken as suggestive about capital movements among the many investors whose records have not survived.

Dutch interest in French loans began to grow at the end of the 1770s, but the takeoff seems to have been sparked by a French loan opened in Amsterdam in 1781 on behalf of the United States, and the appealing terms of the loan floated in Paris by Controller General Joly de Fleury in January 1782.[91] Joly de Fleury also tried to borrow directly in Amsterdam and Antwerp. Although that plan failed, succeeding controllers general renewed the effort to tap Dutch capital and, in 1786, Calonne appointed Henri Fizeaux & Co. and N. & J. van Staphorst as French bankers in Amsterdam, thus easing the collection of returns on French securities.[92] Nevertheless, by that point Dutch capital exports to France were slowing.

These trends are evident in documents detailing the French investments of the prominent Amsterdam rentier Jan Jacob Brants, whose correspondence with a French agent and a balance struck in 1773 indicate a holding of 25,000 l.t. in depreciated state paper. Brants's annuities paid a comparatively modest nominal return of 2.5 percent, and he resolved by 1782 to convert them into more lucrative securities.[93] In the meantime, in 1779 or early 1780, he added four life-annuity contracts of 4,000 l.t. each, returning 8.5 percent per annum.[94] From that point, as his portfolio management accounts show, Brants's French holdings expanded rapidly. In 1782 he had a total investment of f. 44,567,12 in life and perpetual annuities, but within three years that had expanded tof. 78,994,1, and by 1790 to f. 104,490,14,8. The expansion was accompanied by increasing diversification. At the beginning of the decade Brants held only annuities. By 1790 he had added shares in lottery loans of 1783, in loans extended to commercial houses in Lyons on the security of French annuities, in negotiations opened in Amsterdam on the security of French life annuities, and in a single-unit (French annuities) investment trust opened by Couderc & Brants in 1787. In addition, he had in at least one instance extended a private loan on hypothecated French annuities, and had amassed altogether a sizable portfolio of life-annuity contracts.

Among Brants's investments were 125 bills in the 125 million l.t. perpetual-annuity loan of December 1784 returning 5 percent per annum plus generous premiums at redemption. Evidently this was among the most sought after of French issues in the United Provinces. Brants's own investment, acquired between 1785 and 1792, totaled 128,500 l.t. at face value.[95] Receipts haphazardly preserved in the papers of Henri Fizeaux & Co. reveal that a further 779,000 l.t. was acquired by twenty-one rentiers, bankers, and brokers in seven Dutch cities in the early months of 1787.[96] Fizeaux's house was, of course, only one of the firms involved in the transfer of bills bought by French agents for Dutch investors and speculators. In the same year Couderc & Brants formed a single-unit investment trust on bills in this loan. They proposed to raise f. 1,035,000 to buy 2,300,000 l.t. in those bills, with redemption to occur over twenty-two years, during which the return of 5 percent per annum would be supplemented by premiums increasing from 15 percent per share in 1789 to 60 percent in 1810 as some shares were drawn for redemption each year.[97]

On occasion the demand from the United Provinces for certain French issues was sufficient to affect the speculative market in Paris. Such was the case with the loan of 80 million l.t. issued in December 1785. After opening at a premium, when most of the notes were taken up by a few bankers on short-term drafts, the notes were soon (February 1786) being sold at a 3-percent discount. The banker Etienne Clavière attempted to marshal Dutch support to restore the premium, but without immediate success, although early in March the issue recovered, advancing to a premium of 1.5 percent.[98] Clavière attributed this about-face in part to "des demandes considerables venues de Hollande."[99] In fact the original premium was rumored due in part to Dutch purchases as Clavière, whose own attempt to acquire a small lot had been blocked, indicated in asserting that another banker who had been allowed to cover his subscription with short-term drafts had taken no less than 10 million l.t. intended for Dutch buyers.[100]

What must have annoyed Clavière about being excluded from this issue was that for some time he had been deeply involved in efforts to develop Dutch support for his own speculative activities. An optimistic man with vast ambitions, Clavière had as early as 1782 attempted to induce Dutch rentiers to follow the Genevan example in corporate investments in French life annuities.[101] Although failing in this, he did succeed in building up contacts that would support his speculative activities later in the decade. Amsterdam was appealing as a source of capital because interest rates there for loans on adequate collateral were much lower than the inflated cost of secured credit in Paris, so that a canny manipulator like Clavière could profit on speculations using borrowed capital.[102] During 1784, 1785, and 1786 Clavière corresponded with one of his contacts in Amsterdam, Pieter Stadnitski, counseling Stadnitski on Calonne's new loan projects and arranging for himself a series of loans on the collateral of shares in the new French India Company.[103]

In the initial loan through Stadnitski, Clavière hypothecated 104 shares for f. 52,000 (approximately their par value) at 7.5 percent.[104] He expected Stadnitski to negotiate a loan on the security of those shares, but as no evidence of such a transaction has been found it may be assumed that Stadnitski raised this extensive advance privately among merchants, bankers, and investors. After opening this path to speculative support, Clavière called upon it again and again. By July 1786 he had at least 491 India Company shares mortgaged through Stadnitski.[105] Even that coverage was insufficient to satisfy Clavière's ambitions, for his correspondence reveals that he intended to enlist Stadnitski and Stadnitski's associates directly in Parisian speculations, all of course under his own direction.[106] By the spring of 1786, however, Stadnitski was disillusioned with the stock-mortgaging operations even though Clavière was by then paying 8 percent. Although the reasons for Stadnitski's change of attitude are not clear, we may assume that Clavière's repeated glib claims about the munificence of speculative opportunities in Paris both alarmed and appealed to Stadnitski. If Clavière could make a profit even on 7.5- and 8-percent loans, then what might direct investments yield? On the other hand, what effect would the dangerous inflation of credit and security prices in Paris in 1786 have on an overextended speculator like Clavière? Stadnitski's memory of the panic of 1772–73 in Amsterdam may have led him to wonder when the sustained bullish market in Paris would tumble.

Although Stadnitski arranged his own extensions to Clavière privately, a number of Amsterdam firms actively negotiated public loans for French banking and commercial houses on similar security. Those projects resemble the Clavière loans except that the public at large participated by purchasing shares. If the speculative boom was to be fed, annuity contracts, government paper, and shares in joint-stock ventures had to be mortgaged, and there was no better place to do that than Amsterdam. Efforts were made through public negotiations to raise at least f. 6,378,000 for Paris and Lyons houses between 1781 and 1786.[107] And this figure is no more than indicative of the total actually involved in such operations, as Clavière presumably was not unique in arranging private loans. Some of the more prominent Paris houses figured in the public negotiations. In March 1784 Vandenyver, Frères & Cie negotiated f. 1,100,000 at 5 percent on life-annuity contracts through Hope & Co.,[108] and two years later Doerner & Cie f. 500,000 on perpetual annuities from the loan of 125 million l.t.[109]

By then both Genevan and Parisian rentiers had discovered that it was possible to borrow in Amsterdam using as security French annuity contracts already bought on time. The method was this: An Amsterdam firm would be engaged to open a loan at 4 to 5 percent, with the principal to be amortized over fifteen years or so. The security for the operation would be provided by life annuities previously bought on time and rehypothecated to the negotiation floated in Amsterdam. Because those annuities paid 8 to 10 percent, the rentiers who had originally acquired them on time could expect to retire their indebtedness in Amsterdam by means of the annuity income, and eventually to come into possession of the *rentes* without any capital outlay.[110]

Nor were these the only efforts directed at attracting Dutch capital to Paris. In January 1785 the firm of J. & Th. van Marselis participated in opening a loan for f. 2,310,000 on behalf of the duc de Chartres,[111] and in the spring of 1791 A. & S. Boas of The Hague attempted to negotiate f. 470,000 for the account of an association of Parisian booksellers, but authorized and guaranteed by Louis XVI.[112] Members of the various French Companies of Finance also found the Amsterdam money market useful. In 1786 the snuff merchant Bolongaro Crevenna, well informed about the complicated maze of French financial administration, raised f. 1 million at 5 percent.[113] Appointments to the Companies of Finance, such as the General Farm, were secured by means of *fonds d'avance*, in the case of the Farm in the amount of 1,560,000 l.t. per appointee. This deposit was held during the lease of the particular company, generally a period of six years plus perhaps another six for liquidation, and itself paid a return of 5 percent. Although the financier could not reclaim his deposit until the expiration of his lease, he could alienate or mortgage the receipt that he was given, and the receipt holder had legal title to the *fonds d'avance*. Crevenna was aware that Amsterdam rentiers had for some time been buying into such receipts privately. He proposed simply to unite some of those purchases, thus reducing realization costs.

These examples taken together indicate not only a substantial increase in Dutch investment in France during the 1780s, but an increasing variation in the form of investment. Dutch rentiers, brokers, and bankers were carefully exploiting the many opportunities for profitable investment offered by the great bull market of the 1780s in Paris.

The same trends are evident in life-annuity-based negotiations launched in Amsterdam in 1782 and thereafter that enabled participants to seize directly the advantages of lucrative French life-annuity loans. At least fifteen such undertakings, involving approximately f. 5,824,000, were opened during the 1780s.[114] The corporate annuity-based negotiation was already a familiar form to Genevan investors, who, during the 1760s and 1770s, elaborated the technique of constituting French life annuities on Genevan demoiselles selected on the basis of the determinants of longevity as then understood. Properly managed, such an operation transformed an investment in self-amortizing assets thought by many contemporaries to encourage the disintegration of estates into an advantageous investment whose high earnings permitted quick recapitalization of principal. The banker opening such an operation often extended credit to his clients for the acquisition of a block of contracts. Clients then employed the annuity to retire their debt to the banker if they had bought on time, or, if they had bought outright, merely enjoyed the return. Dutch brokers generally did not adopt sales on time, preferring instead to market shares in a collective ownership of life-annuity contracts.

There was a substantial risk in assuming that France would not once again renege on financial obligations. That risk was reflected, inadequately as it turned out, in the high return paid by France. The French treasury suspended annuity payments in

1793, although from 1791 livre bills brought smaller yields than were customary in the 1780s.[115] Because of the high annuity the substitution undertakings formed from 1782 through 1785 managed to regain their capital outlay, but those launched in 1786 and thereafter (the last in 1788) incurred heavy losses.

Total Dutch investment in France during the 1780s remains difficult to estimate satisfactorily. The evidence presented here about individual investment enterprises and substitution ventures accounts for a cumulative total of something over 40 million l.t. during a period in which all French loans certainly exceeded 1.3 billion and may have reached 1.6 billion l.t.[116] It also suggests that direct investment was more extensive than the total of individual instances given here. Thulemeyer's estimate, if it is taken at the lower range of an average return of 6.5 or 7 percent, or at f. 171.5 to 185 million (373 to 403 million l.t. at current rates), provides what appears to be a maximum reasonable range. The minimum increase would appear, on the basis of a calculation from the Amsterdam collateral-succession inventories, to have been to some f. 115 million (at current rates about 250 million l.t.). Over the twenty-five years preceding 1788, Genevan investment in their favorite French life annuities reached some 130 million l.t., most of which was concentrated in the last decade of the period. Although there is some overlap in these figures because Genevan investors sometimes borrowed in Amsterdam to buy French life annuities, the total investment from the two centers probably amounted to a minimum of 380 million l.t., and may have totaled as much as 500 to 530 million l.t.[117] Those figures, which do not include credits acquired elsewhere abroad, account for some 24 to 41 percent of French borrowing in the period.

The United States

By the latter stages of the War of the American Revolution the United States had virtually exhausted its two principal nontaxation revenue sources, paper currency issues and domestic long-term loans.[118] Moreover, credit that France and Spain had extended to it became a tenuous source of future revenues because of their higher deficits owing to participation in the conflict with

Table 7-3. *Gross and net proceeds of Dutch loans to the United States*

	Gross proceeds	Net proceeds after commission charges
1782	f. 5,000,000	f. 4,775,000
1784	2,000,000	1,860,000
1787	1,000,000	915,000 (est.)
1788	1,000,000	920,000
1790	3,000,000	2,865,000
1791	8,500,000	8,160,000
1792	5,950,000	5,637,500
1793	1,000,000	965,000
1794	3,000,000	2,865,000
	f. 30,450,000	f. 28,962,500
1791 (Antwerp)	2,050,000	1,975,375,13
	f. 32,500,000	f. 30,937,875,13

Britain. Because Congress's efforts to persuade its primary fiscal agents, the states, to forward sufficient tax revenues were also unsuccessful, there was no alternative but to expand the search for credit. The attempt to borrow in Amsterdam may be traced to 1778, but little success was enjoyed before 1781, when France opened a loan in the Dutch Republic for f. 5 million earmarked for the United States.[119] That was the first occasion on which any significant sum was obtained from Dutch investors, but the 1781 loan succeeded because it was issued by France and because the States General of the Republic revived a policy long out of use by adding a collateral guarantee. There was little prospect that future advances might be obtained by the same route, however much goodwill toward the United States might prevail in France or the Dutch Republic. Still, the United States had been introduced to Dutch investors.

Although the United States offered a premium yield in 1782 in the first major loan opened independently, that issue, managed by a consortium of three Amsterdam banking houses, moved very slowly. Indeed the net sum remaining after costs, f. 4,775,000 out of f. 5 million (Table 7-3),[120] became available only gradually between 1782 and 1786. In subsequent loans during the 1780s commission charges and yield were adjusted to reduce the subscription period, but in these too subscriptions moved more slowly than was the case with other borrowers. Revenues from the issues of 1782–7, f. 7,550,000 (or slightly more than $3 million at forty cents to the current guilder[121]), were used chiefly to meet obligations abroad. Those expenses were otherwise difficult to cover because the states forwarded to Congress only about 25 percent of the quotas assessed them in that period, specie was scarce in the United States, and foreign currencies costly.

The initial issue of that series delivered resources vital to an impecunious government, but of course the organization of foreign credit carried with it the obligation to meet debt charges. Lacking domestic resources that might be used for that purpose, the United States serviced its debt in the Dutch Republic through new loans. In Amsterdam the bankers, W. & J. Willink and N. & J. van Staphorst, managed to conceal from the investing public the fact that American solvency rested on fresh advances and were compensated for the difficulties they faced in placing Congress's loans by generous commissions. Congress's agents professed distress at the slow rate at which the bankers managed to place notes, for increasingly those intermediaries seemed able to mount subscriptions only as service payments were falling due. Nonetheless, satisfaction could be taken in the fact that the loans eventually succeeded and that the annuity rate was held to no more than 5 percent in 1787 and 1788. It was, after all, preferable to pay higher commissions than a higher interest.

From the American perspective the replacement of the Articles of Confederation by the Constitution and the allocation to Congress of taxation authority far in excess of what had been available under the Articles could be expected to improve Congress's credit position in Amsterdam. That case was argued persuasively in 1790 and 1791, and those arguments, together with a threat that the United States might transfer its banking agency elsewhere, and growing familiarity among investors with the United States as a borrower, helped gain appreciably better terms for subsequent loans opened by the federal government. More than anything else, however, it was the anxiety of Dutch bankers about competition that established the terms under which federal government loans would be opened and set the precedent for lower costs.[122]

Table 7-4. *Foreign loans and central government revenues and expenditures of the United States, 1789–94 (in thousands of dollars)*

	4 Mar. 1789– 31 Dec. 1791	1792	1793	1794	totals
Revenues					
Ordinary revenues	4,419	3,670	4,653	5,432	18,174
Domestic and foreign loan revenues	5,791	5,071	1,068	4,609	16,539
Total revenues	10,210	8,741	5,721	10,041	34,713
Foreign loan revenues (by estimated date of availability for disbursement)	(4,410)	(3,042)	(386)	(1,146)	(8,984)
Expenditures					
Civil list, war, and miscellaneous	1,921	1,878	1,710	3,501	9,010
Interest on public debt	2,349	3,202	2,772	3,490	11,813
Redemptions of public debt	2,939	4,062	3,047	2,311	12,359
Total expenditures	7,209	9,142	7,529	9,302	33,182

Although the implementation of the Constitution strengthened American public finance, an evaluation of the position of the United States in 1790 shows that Dutch bankers acted hastily and prematurely. When Congress adopted a revenue program designed to meet central government demands and service domestic and foreign debts, the liabilities assumed from the Confederation and the states were estimated to amount to $77.8 million.[123] The magnitude of that assumption, even scaled down by nearly $7 million as it was by more extensive data about liabilities, can be grasped by projecting that sum and the actual total of the debt in succeeding years (1791: $75.4 million; 1792: $77.2 million; 1793: $80.3 million; 1794: $78.4 million) against tax revenues, given in Table 7-4.[124] In 1792, the first year for which figures are available on an annual basis for both revenues and expenditures, interest payments on the American debt amounted to $3.2 million, a figure equivalent to 87 percent of tax revenues totaling $3.67 million. Debt charges including redemptions equaled no less than $7.26 million, or 198 percent of tax revenues. Neither Dutch investors nor Dutch bankers employed any consistent measure to gauge solvency or compare the credit positions of different states outside that of the punctuality of service, but such ratios between tax revenues on the one hand and interest payments and total debt charges on the other exceeded current levels among even fiscally straitened European governments.

Recognizing the fragile character of public confidence within the United States in federal government credit, Alexander Hamilton, secretary of the treasury, devised a financial program that combined interest payments on the foreign and domestic debt with small-scale but nonetheless significant redemptions of domestic indebtedness (while prolonging the foreign debt already due or falling due through renegotiation in the Dutch Republic). For the United States debt service required both interest and redemption payments, whereas in other states debt-related spending devoted to amortization had been reduced over years of credit exploitation to much smaller relative levels and debt service was composed principally of interest payments. That is to say, the United States could not adopt the most efficient technique of credit exploitation available because, in the face of the need to establish its credit, there was no choice but to provide for redemptions that might bolster public confidence.

Whereas appropriations available for debt service were enlarged by smaller administrative and military spending, gains in that area were not great enough to pay debt charges or bring the federal government into approximate equality with European states in its overall public-credit position. From 1789 through 1795 American spending for current operations and interest payments alone regularly equaled or exceeded tax revenues. Through 1794 those two areas exceeded the cumulative total of tax revenues by $20.8 to $18.2 million, and all spending exceeded tax revenues by $33.2 to $18.2 million. Although the United States borrowed slightly more than was necessary to cover expenditures in that period, there was nevertheless, on an annual basis and in cumulative terms, a significant deficit in ordinary revenues through 1795.

It is true that the United States had other potential assets, such as a significant margin between the range of taxes then in use and the more extensive range employed by European states, and that such assets might have eased the financial position inherited from the Confederation. But neither that margin of taxable assets nor the vast tracts of unsettled land theoretically available for sale by the federal government could have generated the quick infusion of resources that the new government required. Tax revenues increased steadily during the early 1790s and beyond, but that was due to an expanding volume of trade goods subject to duties rather than to an increase in the rate or an expansion in the incidence of taxation. Hamilton properly discounted Congress's ability to raise taxes and devised a revenue program that, through 1795, was based chiefly on foreign and domestic loans rather than taxes.

A material improvement in the American position could be projected in 1790, when Congress adopted an initial program of taxation and approved with no more than minor alterations Hamilton's skillfully designed proposals for organizing the funding and assumption of state and Confederation debts and providing fresh credit. But not until 1796 were ordinary revenues sufficient to cover debt and nondebt spending. In the intervening years import duties and excise revenues increased simultaneously with foreign and domestic borrowing.

As long as debt service, although fluctuating from year to year, represented virtually a fixed level of expenditure,[125] any increase in revenues exceeding administrative and military spending would improve the financial condition of the United States. The excess of ordinary revenues over non-debt-related expenditures averaged $2.1 million from 1792 through 1795, but increased sharply in 1796 (from $1.8 million in 1795 to $5.8 million in 1796) and, although that figure fell in 1799 to a level reminiscent of the early years of the decade, it expanded again thereafter. In 1796 the position of the United States was superior to that of the major states of Europe and improving, whereas in Europe the Revolutionary wars were worsening an already serious situation. The share of tax revenues necessary for debt service in the United States in 1796 was only 38 percent, and the debt–revenue ratio had fallen from 21:1 in 1792 to less than 10:1.

When one strikes a balance on the liquid and potential assets and liabilities of the federal government in the years to 1796, one must acknowledge that the calculation points to insolvency. But the important fact is that such a balance was not struck then in Amsterdam, either in regard to the United States or other debtor states. As as result the United States acquired and retained an image of credit worthiness that was stronger than that held by France in the 1780s and, by the early 1790s, equivalent to that held by European states accepted by Dutch investors as the most secure risks. Not only was the effective return paid in 1792 on the combined foreign and domestic debt of the United States no more than 4.1 percent, but also the cost of fresh foreign credit had fallen in 1790 to a level equal to the minimum return acceptable to Dutch investors for long-term foreign loans of any type.[126]

There is more than a little irony in the observation that the favorable terms of the foreign loans of 1790 and thereafter were established before it was clear that the United States would emerge from the transition to a federal government with the sweeping revenue authority granted under the Constitution intact. And there is even more irony in the observation that the favorable credit image reflected by the 1790 loan in Amsterdam was in large measure the product of developments that were unconnected with the appropriateness and potential effectiveness of the fiscal program being unfolded at the same time by Hamilton. The success of the American loans in the Dutch Republic and their success on decidedly favorable terms were central ingredients in the triumph of Hamilton's program of national public finance, and in what E. James Ferguson has termed "the Nationalist effort to achieve political centralization by fiscal reform."[127]

From 1790 through 1794 Congress raised loans in Amsterdam and Antwerp totaling f. 23.5 million, of which some f. 22,460,000 (or $8,984,200 at par rates) was available after costs, and in addition the United States borrowed $7.56 million on the domestic market (see Table 7-4). The net additional credit acquired in those years after redemptions was $4.18 million, or 23 percent of tax revenues. Foreign loan proceeds were counterbalanced to a degree by the cost of servicing outstanding credits, by 1793 more than f. 1.3 million per annum. But through 1792 and again in 1794 there remained a significant surplus, and one that was available at the crucial point of transition to the expanded tax authority of the Constitution. The Dutch loans were employed not only to pay off most of the debt and debt arrears owed France, in effect transferring those obligations to the Dutch Republic, but also to settle smaller debts owed Spain and foreign military officers who had served in the American Revolution, to pay some diplomatic expenses, and to provide funds for purchases of American domestic debt certificates prior to the redemption program initiated in 1796.[128]

Hamilton grasped the importance of treating the domestic debt in a fashion that would enhance the stability of the new regime, and he designed a funding and assumption program that satisfied most creditors without alienating individuals and regions that could not expect to benefit from it. Hamilton also grasped the importance of providing for the settlement of the foreign debt as another measure that would contribute to the regime's stability. Moreover, he understood the extent to which the market price of domestic debt certificates reflected the public image of the financial and political integrity of government. At the same time that he prepared a program of funding and assumption, Hamilton began the settlement of arrears on the debt to France and established a sinking fund that could be used to manipulate the price of domestic debt certificates.

Beginning with the 1790 loan, proceeds were dispatched to Paris (f. 1.5 million) and bills were drawn by the treasury on Amsterdam (f. 800,000) to bring the sinking fund into operation to buy domestic debt.[129] That dual program was continued thereafter and, as Hamilton portrayed its results in 1793, to the benefit of the United States. Domestic debt purchases in particular were advantageous because they produced multiple gains. When paper could be bought in the United States or Europe below par, such purchases both reduced ultimate redemption costs and, since Dutch loans were raised at effective returns of 4.5 to 5.5 percent but could be used to buy notes costing the treasury 6 percent per annum, saved interest.[130] But those savings were not as important in the success of Hamilton's program as was the pressure that domestic debt purchases applied toward appreciation of prices.

Between 1790 and July 1792, as Hamilton reported in 1793, all or nearly all debt purchases were funded by foreign loans.[131] Through 1794 some $3 million was spent in that direction.[132] Although that was a significant aid toward driving prices toward their implied par values, coincidental developments outside the sphere of Hamilton's influence were of even more assistance. That part of the paper in question made up of loan-office and settlement certificates traded in the period from 1782 to 1788 at 20–25 and 10–15 percent, respectively. Both groups of paper appreciated sharply during 1789, as a result of the adoption and implementation of the Constitution, and by December the settlement certificates, generally the weaker of the two, were trading at 45–50 percent. Prices dipped in response to Hamilton's January 1790 report on public credit but rose again after midyear.[133] The 6-percent stocks of the funding program of 1790 reached par at the end of July 1791, and for the remainder of that year and through 1792 traded at or slightly above par.[134]

The appreciation of 1789, the fall of 1790, and the renewed appreciation of the second half of 1790 and thereafter were all influenced by foreign investment in the domestic debt, and the two upward trends appear to have been determined by foreign investment. Between 1785 and 1803 Dutch investors accumulated some $13.1 million of the total outstanding domestic debt of $60.9 million.[135] For the most part those purchases were concentrated between 1787 and 1793, when some twenty-eight stock-substitution ventures were organized to sell American securities to the Dutch public.

In forcing market prices toward implied par rates, European purchases of the domestic debt met an important requirement of Hamilton's program of simultaneous interest payments and redemptions, namely, the establishment of public confidence in the credit worthiness of the federal government. Moreover, European purchases expanded the domestic market for future loans by the mere transfer of capital to the United States and by absorbing part of the outstanding debt. As a further consequence of European demand, foreign-exchange costs fell between 1790 and 1792,[136] leaving American obligations abroad easier to meet and reversing the high cost of European currencies that had prevailed in the 1780s. Purchases in the domestic debt by European investors also transferred capital to an economy impoverished for that resource and, by forcing domestic debt paper toward par values, strengthened the monetary position of the United States.[137]

As Ferguson has pointed out, there was reason in 1790 to

doubt "whether federal revenues would support both [the Congress's and the states's] debts, or, if taxes were raised to an adequate level, whether they would be resisted."[138] Doubts about the adequacy of revenues faded with the simultaneous elaboration of two revenue sources, domestic taxes and foreign loans. From 1789 through 1792 foreign loan proceeds nearly matched domestic tax revenues. In the two years following the adoption of the Funding Act, those advances, totaling f. 16.5 million (some $6.6 million) in 1791 and 1792, probably exceeded domestic tax revenues.[139] They made it possible to transfer to the Dutch Republic most of the foreign debt dating from the Revolutionary era, and to transfer it under favorable costs and a redemption term that stretched to 1809. Because of that transfer and the subsequent increase of American tax revenues, there was not, after 1790, any further question about the integrity of the foreign debt, and thus no external threat to the program of national public finance pursued by Hamilton. The foreign loans also permitted profit taking on and manipulation of the domestic debt and, together with coincidental and massive purchases by Europeans, drove market prices up and held them there. Establishment of public confidence in the domestic debt, measured by market prices, lent an appearance of solvency and even reliability to American finances before that was justified by such indexes as the ratio of debt-service costs to revenues or of accumulated indebtedness to current revenues, and permitted a shift in the period from 1793 through 1795 to a credit system that increasingly emphasized domestic borrowing. With foreign assistance Hamilton's fiscal program succeeded, and in 1794 and 1795 domestic resources and British capital were used together to settle the remainder of the debt due France. Hamilton's was a sound program that dealt cleverly and fairly with conflicting views in the United States about the federal and state debts and about use of the revenue authority theoretically available to Congress under the Constitution. But it could not have succeeded on the strength of the resources available within the United States alone.

8

THE COLLAPSE OF SOLVENCY

Contraction in Amsterdam

The visible decline of the Amsterdam capital market began in 1793[1] when the expansion of the War of the First Coalition to include the Dutch Republic and the approach of French troops led to what was viewed at the time as a temporary languor in capital supply. As that image suggests, the market was prepared to withstand a short conflict whose consequences for international finance were roughly proportional to the effects of remembered wars. But the war that began in 1792 was not of brief duration and its financial consequences stood in no relation to prior experience.

Because Dutch governments heightened their borrowing, even unrestrained willingness on the part of investors to take up loans would not have permitted continued market expansion. Debt accumulation by domestic government and the annual addition to the outstanding total of foreign government loans together may be estimated at some f. 30 million per annum by the latter 1780s.[2] Under the Batavian regime and its successors the domestic debt grew by slightly more than f. 30 million per year between 1795 and 1802, and then by about f. 21 million during the remainder of the war. In the same period total investment in loans to foreign governments appears to have regained the prewar level after partial bankruptcies and the suspension of payments by some debtors, but on an annual basis new investment fell to less than half its prewar level. Thus the annual addition in both sectors together stood between f. 35 and 40 million from 1795 to the Peace of Amiens, and fell to less than f. 30 million thereafter. The part of the total absorbed by domestic government increased from some 33 percent (1787–95) to 80 percent (1795–1802), and then fell to about 75 percent. In the expanding demands of domestic government Dutch investors lost part of an already shrinking leverage that prewar lending levels had given them over foreign borrowers, and behind shrinking leverage there stood nothing but a forceful contraction of the market.

Whereas the long-run trend to 1793 had been an increasing conversion of assets from other sectors into foreign loans, the wartime trend was a conversion of all types of assets toward domestic borrowing and taxation. Between 1793 and 1815 the average annual growth in the nominal-value balance of foreign loans (some f. 4 to 5 million) declined to a quantity below estimated savings (at 25 to 37.5 percent) from annuity income on outstanding holdings (f. 6 to 12 million per annum).

Those realities were not immediately recognized, and in fact investors and intermediaries alike continued for several years after 1793 to expect a restoration of the prewar setting. Less frequent new loans in the second half of 1793 and thereafter were still floated under traditional modes of organization and types of security. Declining confidence in the credit worthiness of some borrowers was met by discounts that raised returns above nominal levels but not by better means of attaching debtors to their obligations or an increase in annuity rates sufficient to compensate for wartime risks. What at first escaped notice was that a fundamental transformation was underway in the magnitude of governments' financial requirements and in the volume of capital that would be necessary were an international credit structure to remain of significant use. The signs of that transformation might have been seen first in the increase of government spending and deficits without a countervailing increase in tax revenues. But wartime spending plateaus remained obscure except in Britain because budgetary data were still privileged.

Nonetheless, there were other signals to which more importance might have been attached, such as the French suspension of debt service in 1793 and, four years later, the confirmation of partial bankruptcy in a virtual annulment of two-thirds of the debt and of annuity arrears. Eighteenth-century governments dealt arbitrarily with foreign and domestic investors' interests when that was necessary, but the living memory of Dutch investors did not extend to any steps as harmful as the French actions. Occasional temporary service suspensions, Terray's suspension of payments on some short-term paper in 1770 and 1771, even the apparent abrogation of Austrian loans secured on Silesian revenues, all paled before France's display of disregard for its credit standing. Investors might also have attached more significance to the abrupt turnabout in the financial position of domestic government. Deterioration was noticed in the early 1780s and discussed openly by the late 1780s, but until 1795 the problem was left by government authorities to resolve itself. Then, in forced loans and levies, the Batavian regime signaled a revision in financial policy that was hardly in keeping with any expectation of an impending restoration of the prewar market setting. Ironically, the tax redistribution involved in the forced levies of the Batavian period and continued in subsequent reforms permitted the Dutch government to defer partial bankruptcy, but by transforming lenders into taxpayers.

There were also several less emphatic signals that might have claimed attention, among them the opening of negotiations by Austria in London in 1793 for a loan equivalent to about f. 36 million. That should have been construed as evidence that the traditional f. 3 million size of loans floated in Amsterdam was being reduced to insignificance. Hope & Co. had late in the 1780s foreseen a series of loans on behalf of Russia of comparable cumulative magnitude to the imperial loan in London, but the expansion of the Austrian issue to something over f. 55 million in 1794 and the opening of a fresh loan in 1797 should have provided thought-provoking background for the Dutch loan opened for Austria in 1794 at f. 2.5 million.

There was no shortage of general or specific laments about changing conditions in the years when these signs made their appearance. Both investors and intermediaries experienced and expressed disquietude, but the problem was one of alternatives. Investment options had not changed since the 1770s except within the field of lending to governments. Still there was some tardiness in responding to the defective structure of loan security and in adopting measures that would retard losses. The stock-substitution technique offered a method of consolidation and retrenchment that could reduce perception costs on holdings in the domestic loans of European states but which could also, by attracting large-scale participation, marshal demand and thereby apply pressure toward higher prices. These possibilities were not generally realized until 1802 and thereafter.[3] Sounder safeguards were also introduced in some loans issued after 1800, usually in the form of a reversion to tying service and redemption to commodity shipments, but those did not always prove effective in the long run.

Given the predominantly national, even regional, character of the area from which the market drew resources, and any secular expansion of deficit spending, the Amsterdam market's position would inevitably have deteriorated. The volume of resources to which it had access was insufficient to support a role greater than that of an arbiter on prewar margins between total expenditures and combined tax revenues and domestic borrowing. But the problem was not only that the pattern of expanding wartime followed by contracting postwar deficits characteristic of the second half of the eighteenth century had been altered in rhythm, but that all the major and many minor powers and borrowers were involved together in a European war for the first time since 1763. Neither Amsterdam nor all the capital markets of Europe could, in the antagonistic setting of the Revolutionary wars, marshal enough credit to meet demand.

Moreover, other changes that threatened the prewar international credit structure occurred in large measure in areas over which the Amsterdam market could exercise little or no control. After 1792 the market began to lose its independence from the political determination of investment objectives and gradually to become subservient to domestic and foreign pressures. Dutch government inaugurated that trend, first by manipulating capital flow in forced levies and loans, and then by regulating the issue of foreign loans. As the Dutch state's dependence on France was forcibly heightened under Napoleon, foreign influence on investment flows increased. The Napoleonic Empire was able to use Dutch credit to anticipate proceeds of some levies imposed on its satellites, and a substantial part of post-1795 activity in the market involved loans whose proceeds were earmarked for France although nominally intended for another state.

Such realities were not clear in the 1790s because even the

best-informed intermediaries lacked a trustworthy notion of the budgetary position of debtor states and of cumulative debts and credits outstanding. In other words, they lacked any precise understanding of the role that the market had come to fulfill in balancing deficits against the often contradictory implications of domestic borrowing, paper currency issues, deferred tax reform, and incremental spending. The financial structure that integrated foreign loans or foreign investments in domestic loans into a program intended to defer or replace tax reform and sometimes also to enhance prosperity and tax revenues had not developed simultaneously across Europe or out of explicit fiscal theory that explained the mechanism. Nor had the Amsterdam market begun large-scale foreign lending with an understanding of the consequences of such a step, or developed an understanding during the second half of the eighteenth century. Instead both debtors and creditors had come to fill their respective roles by modifying traditional usages. For debtors, foreign borrowing involved merely an adaptation from much older credit practices, one that had the additional advantage of permitting a stable expansion of domestic credit exploitation. For creditors, lending to governments arose out of customary usages in commerce and commercial finance. The transition through loans based on the security of commodity anticipations to those secured exclusively on a government's pledge to repay occurred in such a fashion that its negative implications remained obscure or unheeded.

The international credit structure faltered in 1793 but it did not fall wholly out of use during the Revolutionary and Napoleonic wars. Nevertheless, its relative significance, measured by the share of overall expenditures or deficit spending funded by any state through foreign borrowing, declined dramatically. During the Napoleonic wars Britain emerged as a source of subsidies to allies, and those transfers took over some of the functions filled previously by Dutch capital exports.[4] Outside the Iberian peninsula, however, British subsidies did not play a major role until 1813 and thereafter. By that point even massive transfers could not salvage financial programs, which, on the continent, had turned to domestic credit inflation to cope with wartime expenses. Lacking foreign loans the most common policy followed was monetary creation with exclusively financial rather than mixed financial and economic objectives. The resulting inflation varied in intensity from a rate identifiable as hyperinflation in France during the 1790s to more restrained trends in some states, which countered rapid inflation by devaluation and conversion operations or by slowing the rate of monetary creation.

Britain and the United States were able to withdraw from the international credit structure, the former beginning during the Fourth Anglo-Dutch War,[5] and the latter on the eve of the shift in Dutch investment activity toward domestic lending. Britain's withdrawal was possible both because economic growth was reflected in an unreformed tax structure and because that growth and the war with France were sufficient to make politically feasible the reorientation of assessment toward direct taxes (in the form of a levy on incomes). During the wars of 1793–1815 Britain reduced the share of expenditures financed by borrowing (Table 6-1) despite unprecedented subsidies to allies and military and naval spending. The United States, on the other hand, stood aloof for the time being from the conflict in Europe and avoided the crippling spending faced by continental states. Hamilton's program of public finance had already, by the summer of 1793, acquired the time and credit assistance necessary for its implementation. When Dutch loans ceased to be available, after 1794, they were no longer essential. In succeeding years tax revenues expanded to the point at which, from 1796, they regularly equaled or exceeded expenditures.

For other states foreign credit availability deteriorated at an inopportune time, in the early stages of a lengthy war and thus on the ascending side of spending requirements. Moreover, on the continent the economic growth reflected in British revenues and the commercial expansion evident in American revenues were largely absent between 1793 and 1815. To an important degree that was the case because the war forced those states to revive arbitrary techniques for expanding revenues that had been shelved in preceding decades. Their revival reintroduced financial instability that was felt in all sectors of economic activity. The measures adopted by continental states to deal with wartime financial demands will be surveyed simultaneously with the treatment those states accorded credit previously acquired from the Dutch Republic and some additional loans extended during the war.

The collapse of solvency

Pandemic of bankruptcy on the continent

France. The partial suspension of payments by France in August 1788 might be construed in retrospect as the harbinger of a general continental financial crisis. But it did not have a long-standing effect on the price of French annuities in Amsterdam,[6] and indeed it had no apparent effect on the attitude of investors participating in government loans negotiated by other powers. Although concern was sometimes voiced before 1793 about the financial stability of different governments, annuity-rate trends indicate that apprehension was not yet great. Although governments were accumulating staggering debt–revenue ratios, ignorance of budgetary data and a broad tolerance for government indebtedness left most states in financial positions that were, by the standards of Dutch investors, still supportable.

What is evident about the French position in 1788 is that a deficient rationalization of credit exploitation was no longer tolerable. Given the existing level of revenues, any further long-term borrowing could occur only to the degree that credit costs were reduced or that spending was pared in other areas. An alternative financial program was necessary. As Mathias and O'Brien have demonstrated, taxation incidence in France (as measured by taking tax revenues as a percentage of estimated commodity output) had declined after about 1735.[7] France therefore also possessed a large margin of resources that might have been taxed merely by reinstituting the ratio of taxation to commodity output prevailing earlier in the century.

In preference to a reorganization of its long-term credit system or an overt reform of old regime tax structure, revolutionary France adopted a program of requisition. Revenues would be provided through the issue of paper currency backed by confiscated land and the short-term element of a public credit structure relying on private enterprise would give way to instruments created by the government itself.[8] Monetary creation was not initially intended to occur at such a rate that assignats would depreciate against specie, but taxpayer resistance reduced ordinary revenues at the same time that the utilization of long-term credit was allowed to lapse.[9] In consequence the requisition of church and other properties was broadened to include the value sacrificed by holders of depreciating assignats, who lost the difference between the value given for notes and that subsequently received from them. That covert system of taxation affected all creditors, including Dutch and Genevan rentiers who held royal securities serviced in assignats. Nevertheless, redistribution of assessment through monetary inflation was no more than a short-term expedient. Because France had shifted to monetary creation at the same time that ordinary tax revenues, linked in 1789 to satisfaction with the regime, were interrupted, the new financial structure collapsed under wartime demands within less than a decade. There was no alternative but to abuse the authority of seigniorage, and the nominal value of assignat circulation eventually reached about 40 billion livres. The failure of an effort to achieve monetary and financial restabilization in 1796 by converting assignats into *mandats territoriaux* led in September 1797 to a formalization of the partial repudiation of liabilities inherited from the monarchy. Two-thirds of annuity debts remaining in 1793, when service had been suspended, were paid off in nearly worthless paper, and the remainder converted into 5-percent perpetual annuities.[10]

Commodity output levels projected for France by Mathias and O'Brien suggest expansion during the Revolutionary and Napoleonic period, and thus a continued position in which the share of output taken in taxation was significantly below the 1735 level. Nevertheless, an overt redistribution or increase of taxation was no more expedient politically in the latter 1790s than it had been earlier in that decade. In formalizing partial bankruptcy the Directory merely acknowledged appropriations made earlier from assignat holders and creditors in general. But at the same time that government devised an alternative financial policy, a program of supranational requisition that was subsequently taken over and refined under Napoleon. Satellite and dependent states were obliged to assist in meeting France's wartime expenses. In the Republic the Batavian Revolution of 1795, made possible by the approach of French forces, brought an opportunity for Dutch Patriots to put political theory into practice. It also brought a chance to back conviction with open purses. In the beginning additional levies and forced loans, necessitated for the most part by an indemnity of f. 100 million imposed by France in 1795, were welcomed by Patriot merchants and bankers. But their willingness to pay for what was at first construed as political liberty faded as it became clear that France was intent on squeezing the Patriot as well as the Orangist. Nevertheless, Dutch sensitivities were not permitted to intrude upon the supranational system of taxation, and indeed Dutch resources were brought into use to provide other satellite or dependent states with the means to meet French indemnities. The Batavian Republic and its successors introduced regulations on foreign loan issues that could be employed to manipulate capital movement to benefit France.[11]

Early in the war France therefore achieved the nullification of two-thirds of its outstanding liabilities; created, failed to sustain, and in 1797 allowed to collapse a paper currency credit structure; and turned then to indemnities extracted from allied and dependent states and slightly later to administrative reforms that appear to have reduced overhead in tax collection. By such means France met the costs of the Napoleonic wars and carried them without significant tax increases in the prewar territory of the state.

Austria. The covert system of assessment involved in monetary inflation was used widely during the Revolutionary and Napoleonic wars. Austria, Sweden, Denmark, Russia, and Spain all expanded money supply as a principal source of credit. But, unlike France, those states issued paper currency in tandem with uninterrupted tax revenues and often simultaneously with increased overt taxation. As a result they were able to prolong the usefulness of monetary inflation as a source of revenue supplements, but in no case was seigniorage ultimately sufficient to meet wartime expenses.

Confronted with growing pressure on ordinary revenues, Austria sought during the War of the First Coalition both to expand access to foreign credit and to increase the use of bank notes, first put into circulation in 1762. Because the Amsterdam market was unprepared to accommodate very large loans, the empire opened negotiations in London. There, with the assistance of parliamentary guarantees, Austria raised £4.6 million in an issue opened in May 1794 and subsequently enlarged further the balance outstanding. When payments were suspended on loans from Britain in 1797 the principal stood at £6.22 million.[12]

The shift of Austrian borrowing to Britain should not, however, be taken to signify that London had suddenly emerged as the leading European capital market. The London market of the 1790s was fundamentally unprepared for such a role for two reasons. An expanding public debt retained a nearly exclusive hold on government lending by British investors, and foreign loans could not be allowed to compete with the credit needs of a government at war. Secondly, British banking houses were inexperienced in the organization and management of loan transactions with foreign governments, and their rather halting steps in that direction during the 1790s proved disheartening for intermediaries and investors alike. As was evident in the Austrian loans, there was a long-standing prejudice in London against foreign loans and in organizing credit for Austria Walter Boyd, leading partner in Boyd, Benfield & Co., expected substantial investment from abroad.[13] Moreover, there was about that issue a definite awkwardness, and not only in difficulties encountered in getting investors to adhere to subscription pledges when Austrian military fortunes waned. Boyd, Benfield, established in London in 1793 after Boyd's departure from France, was new to the field and inadequately informed about British custom in major loans. In the first issue the method of transferring the annuity to subscribers remained vague, and no provision was made to pay the annuity with coupons or similar instruments.[14]

In 1797 proceeds of the last London loan were transferred to Vienna, and although a few minor foreign loans were raised thereafter, Austria had lost access to foreign credit in the necessary volume. Not only could the empire no longer rely on Dutch savings, but its credit in Amsterdam had also been damaged by service suspensions in 1795 and 1796, on the eve of a concentrated period of reimbursement terms stretching from 1798 through 1804.[15] In 1797 Austria suspended the convertibility of bank notes into specie and augmented the rate at which new notes were issued. By the end of 1799 fl. 141 million was outstanding and payments in bank notes required a 7-percent premium over payments in silver.[16] The failure of the foreign loan segment of the imperial financial program, and Austria's inability to cover that loss out of domestic taxation, led to withdrawal from the First Coalition and the signing of peace preliminaries with France on 18 April 1797.

Although the empire rejoined the European conflict in December 1798, it no longer possessed the means for sustained participation. The withdrawal of February 1801 was followed by more than four years of aloofness. In the meantime monetary deterioration was slowed but tax revenues remained insufficient for both peacetime demands and service on the accumulated debt. Payments on the Dutch loans were resumed in 1802 when lengthier redemption terms were established, stretching reimbursements from 1806 through 1825. At that point Austrian liabilities in the Batavian Republic, excluding annuity arrears, totaled fl. 30,420,800 due in Amsterdam and fl. 5,700,000 in Rotterdam, together about 5.25 percent of a rapidly expanding imperial debt.[17] Excluding the British loans, which Austria professed to believe had been a subsidy, the total foreign debt in 1802 appears to have been fl. 65.5 to 67 million, to which should be added some fl. 23.7 million in annuity arrears.[18] Austria was able to draw additional resources from voluntary and forced long-term domestic loans, coinage debasement, expanded direct taxation, and wartime subsidies from Britain, but the principal device used after the turn of the century was still the issue of paper currency. Expressed in specie values, tax revenues declined to an average of only fl. 50.8 million per annum between 1806 and 1810, against expenditures of fl. 87.4 million. Recurrent deficits were met by currency issues, and note circulation expanded from fl. 337.2 million at the end of 1802 to fl. 1,060.8 million in March 1811.[19] In terms of silver, the value of notes outstanding decreased after 1805 (at which point fl. 377.1 million in notes was trading at 68.5 percent of face value), but paper continued to be issued to the benefit of the imperial treasury.

Between 1793 and July 1811 the cost of gulden in Amsterdam plunged from an average of 35 stuivers banco against a rixdollar to 2 stuivers.[20] That had not been a matter of consequence to Dutch rentiers as long as Austrian loans were serviced in guilders, according to their terms, but in 1804 the empire announced that payments would henceforth be transferred to Vienna, where they would take place in bank notes. In 1805 the settlement of annuity arrears was begun, but at a discount, and *beurs* prices declined. Reacting without haste, Goll & Co. tried nonetheless to salvage something for investors by forming in 1808 an administrative office to handle the variety of Austrian securities in circulation.[21] Such a device, introduced in 1802 as a way of applying pressure toward a price recovery on French paper, could have the desired effect if it coincided with at least an absence of measures on the part of the debtor that creditors regarded as detrimental. But in the circumstances of 1808 Austria had no alternative to depredations against rentiers. In the treaty of 1805 with France, and again in 1809, the empire suffered severe losses in population and territory and was forced to accept a levy of Fr. 85 million.[22]

There was no comfort for Dutch rentiers in learning that Austria, even with the best will, could do nothing for them, and indeed in 1805 an attack was launched in Amsterdam on the bankers Goll and Osy for what was portrayed as their inadequate handling of investors' interests.[23] An anonymous pamphleteer, described only as the holder of a substantial quantity of notes and past-due annuity coupons, charged the bankers with negligence in permitting revision of the original conditions of Austria's foreign loans without the consent of lenders. Goll and Osy had, so it was argued, become surrogate lenders in undertaking the management of loans to Austria. Yet they had not fulfilled that charge, and indeed had cravenly submitted to the arbitrary alteration of terms without protest to the debtor, and without even commiseration for the creditors.[24]

The response, also anonymous but presumably commissioned by Goll, exploded the misconception about responsibilities of the banker to the lender, asserting without qualification that bankers were properly only the agents of borrowers in a contractual relationship between borrower and lender alone. The borrower's agent might, of his own, seek to serve the interests of the creditors, and Goll and Osy had done that, if, alas, in a fashion that could not at that point be revealed.

There is no doubt that the bankers had not assumed any obligation to cover deficiencies in service payments, and no charge could be brought on that basis. But from the perspective of 1805 at least one investor believed that concessions to Austria in 1796 and twice again thereafter had sacrificed investors' interests too readily. In reality, however, neither Goll nor the investors had retained any leverage over Austria, and the defects of Amsterdam practice in arranging security for loans were finally clear. That the pamphleteer chose to attack Goll and Osy rather than the empire reveals a misplaced hope that an unoffended Austria might in future be persuaded to compensate for damages. There was always some prospect of that, for it might be necessary to reach a settlement of claims if Austrian credit on the Amsterdam market were to be revived. But more serious issues confronted Austria. The increasing discount against paper currency, which reached 88 percent in March 1811, and the exhaustion of alternative sources of credit, led unavoidably to the bankruptcy of the empire in 1811.[25] Moreover, the measures adopted to deal with deficits in the Revolutionary and Napoleonic era had disrupted the economy and diminished the empire's trade. Food prices advanced ahead even of the devaluation of paper currency, a factor of benefit to certain segments of society but in general disruptive. In 1811 interest payments were reduced by 50 percent although the principal of the long-term debt was retained in full, and bank notes in circulation were converted to redemption notes at the ratio of 5:1. Still lacking other resources, Austria expanded the issue of redemption notes, which led to renewed depreciation and, by December 1815, to a discount of 72 percent.

In the face of monetary and economic disorder and a debt burden that the bankruptcy of 1811 had done too little to mitigate, Austria abrogated part of outstanding redemption-note liabilities in 1815 and revived the foreign loan alternative. Negotiations on settlement of the Dutch debt were begun in 1816 and completed two years later.[26] They resulted in fresh guarantees behind the principal of the debt and the rehabilitation of service. Settlement on more generous terms than those accorded by most other debtors, albeit still with losses arising out of annuity suspensions and payment in depreciated paper, restored Austria's ability to borrow in Amsterdam and assisted the empire's return to foreign capital markets in the postwar era.[27]

Sweden and Denmark. Between 1811 and 1815 Sweden and Denmark also adopted partial debt repudiations. For Sweden that move may be traced to the Russian seizure of Finland during the War of the Third Coalition, and therefore to the end of Sweden's neutrality. Despite British subsidies,[28] military expenditures could not be met without a renewed expansion of bank notes (following an 1803 conversion of National Debt Office paper at two-thirds its nominal value). As Bank of Sweden notes also depreciated, spending had to be pared and in 1808 both service and redemption payments on the Dutch debt were suspended. With the end of the Russian conflict Sweden concluded an alliance with France, but in 1812 the opportunistic Bernadotte, master of foreign policy since 1810, chose to side with Britain and Russia. The Estates took the occasion of finding Sweden at least nominally in conflict with the Netherlands, since 1810 a part of the French Empire, first to reduce the debt by two-thirds, and then to declare null all remaining unpaid obligations.[29]

In 1815 noteholders from the Swedish loans delegated an agent to present their case for reclamation to Charles XIII.[30] After some hestitation Charles agreed to a settlement based on the 1812 act nullifying two-thirds of the f. 10 million balance outstanding in 1808.[31] As a result a payment of f. 3,462,382,10 was arranged, together with the surrender of claims against the French Empire totaling nearly 3 million livres and designated for past-due interest. That left the agent, Willem Gerrit van de Poll, to turn to France in search of settlement of those claims.[32] In the Netherlands van de Poll, Hasselgreen, and Ketwich & Voombergh (successors to Hogguer & Co. in these matters) solicited claims from noteholders and, in 1816, began a division of the first draft received from Stockholm, paying 15 percent of claims.[33] Subsequent payments totaled 17.5 percent and stretched from 1816 into 1824.[34] Despite its default Sweden was able to turn in the postwar period to other capital markets, in particular Hamburg and London, to raise loans for subsequent deficits.[35]

For Denmark the monarchy's alliance with Napoleon led early in 1813 to a declaration of partial bankruptcy and the introduction of a new monetary system.[36] The principal effect of financial and monetary reorganization on the foreign debt was an extension to 1835 of the term over which reimbursements were scheduled. Although Danish annuities were trading at less than half of par in 1814, when the *Prijs-courant der effecten* resumed publication, prices moved gradually toward par in the postwar period. As a consequence Denmark could rehabilitate the balanced exploitation of credit that had become a part of royal policy in the 1760s, although the foreign capital markets approached for loans in 1818, 1819, 1821, 1825, and thereafter were Hamburg and London rather than Amsterdam.[37] There as in Austria it was chiefly the domestic debt that had been formally devalued.

Russia. Although for Russia fresh credit from the Dutch Republic was curtailed in 1793, substantial resources were still mobilized in Amsterdam during the Napoleonic wars. Rather than being managed by formal loan negotiations, however, credit was organized as part of a 1798 renegotiation of the combined Russian and Polish debt.[38] Each successive series of eighteenth-century Russian loans had served two purposes jointly, the provision of supplementary revenues and the prolongation of earlier credits. Advances raised between 1788 and 1793 began to fall due in 1797, when investors could no longer be drawn into the customary prolongation. In lieu of that Russia negotiated a conversion involving f. 88.3 million, including f. 53.5 million due from the loans of 1788–93, f. 15.9 million from credit extended to Poland and Polish magnates, f. 3 million from a loan negotiated in Antwerp in 1788 and transferred to Amsterdam, f. 4.5 million in commission, and f. 11.4 million to form a reserve fund.

The reserve fund was in reality a covert source of credit upon which Russia began to call in 1808 by selling notes representing the fund. The f. 11 million then available was supplemented by more than f. 6 million in notes that had been bought up in lieu of reimbursements since 1798.[39] Together those measures carried debt charges through 1812, but upon their exhaustion Russia had no recourse but to inform Hope & Co. that both annuity and redemption payments would be suspended. The liabilities not met in 1813 and 1814 were, however, included in a second conversion in 1815 involving f. 101.6 million.[40] For that reason the Russian settlement, although clearly a conversion rather than a redemption, might be regarded as especially handsome. Certainly it assists in explaining why Russia could return to the Amsterdam market for fresh loans and prolongations in the 1820s and 1830s. But it should not be forgotten that the eighteenth-century debt was settled only over the very long term. In 1855, when J. J. Weeveringh tried to strike a balance on the old loans as distinct from post-1815 credits, more than f. 60 million was still outstanding on the sum owed in 1815.[41]

If the foreign debt was treated with care, Russia's domestic debt was not. Lacking access to foreign credit sufficient for much more than debt charges thereon, and provided with large but still insufficient British subsidies, Russia financed participation in the Napoleonic wars chiefly by issuing assignats. By

1810 that recourse was near exhaustion. At that point an ambitious array of measures, including the prohibition of additional assignat issues, a large-scale domestic loan, spending economies, tax increases, a reorganization of the ministry of finance, and sales of state land, raised revenues.[42] But the domestic loan failed to raise as much as had been hoped and, because of continuing deficits, assignat issues could not be concluded (Table 7-1).

In 1812 assignats were declared legal tender at their market rate (25.8 percent of par) for all transactions, and for the remainder of the war taxes were collected only in paper currency that continued to depreciate.[43] There was no formal declaration of a devaluation until late in the 1830s, and subsequent to 1812 the government professed support for restoring that paper to equal value with silver. But the market rate never advanced to a higher level than that fixed for conversion in 1839, 350 to 100 silver rubles. Faced in the immediate postwar era with continued deficits, Russia concentrated on maintaining a stable dual monetary sytem rather than on raising the assignat to par, and on organizing fresh loans abroad. The measures of 1812 had thus formalized losses that assignat holders had suffered since the late 1780s in value sacrificed against specie. Those losses were not of course commonly realized in any single transaction, but were spread among transactions conducted in assignats over the period from the latter 1780s and were modified whenever assignats were accepted initially at a discount. There was nonetheless a cumulative tax shift of substantial proportions to successive holders.

In the postwar era Russia gradually retired assignats.[44] Circulation was reduced by 1823 from a high of 836 million rubles (1817) to the level of 595.8 million, which was maintained until 1840, when the empire restored a silver standard. But equivalent gains in market rates did not follow the reduction in currency supply, and in 1823–4 retirements were brought to a close. Any rapid rise of assignats toward par would in any case have been disruptive. After the war Russia also developed an internal market for interest-bearing notes, although the principal source of supplementary revenues remained foreign loans.

Spain. In contrast to other debtors, Spain does not appear ever to have come quite to the point of formalizing a repudiation of its foreign liabilities. Several schemes were advanced to provide funds to meet annuity payments in 1809 and thereafter, when Hope & Co. refused to continue paying those obligations out of its own resources, but the essential problem could not be resolved by such methods.[45] Both governments claiming power were bankrupt, and neither was more likely than the other to abide by liabilities in the Dutch Netherlands.

At the conclusion of the Napoleonic wars there was some hope in Amsterdam that payments might be resumed. Nineteenth-century Spanish governments were given to vacillation and, although service was not resumed in 1815, it was briefly in the early 1820s, at which point a new loan was floated. In 1830 and 1831 old notes were converted into perpetual annuities, which in fact they had long been because of Spain's failure to meet redemption terms. There was another conversion, for some notes the fourth since 1799, in 1834, when one-third of the debt ceased to bear interest. On the remaining two-thirds service continued only until 1836. The discounts on Spanish paper on the Amsterdam market indicate that by 1836 investors had for the most part written off those loans, recognizing that Spain had reneged on its commitments.[46]

The Netherlands. This reconstruction of the collapse of solvency on the continent cannot be closed without an examination of Dutch borrowing in wartime and the bankruptcy of the Dutch state. It has been established that the seventeenth-century Republic devised a public credit system that permitted it to play a great-power role out of line with taxable resources in the state, and that by the conclusion of the War of the Spanish Succession the Republic had no alternative but to withdraw from European conflicts. Between 1713 and 1780 public corporations made some progress in reducing debts but, in the absence of economic growth, tax reform and increases promised less than elsewhere because the per capita rate of assessment was already the highest in Europe. A margin of borrowing power regained between 1713 and 1780 was exhausted between 1780 and 1793, and the Republic entered the wars of the French Revolution in an insupportable position. Yet financial crisis was deferred for more than a decade and a half by two means: The first, a policy followed between 1788 and 1803, consisted of forced loans and levies, and the second, introduced in 1805, stressed both financial rationalization and an overt redistribution of taxes.

Forced loans and levies, occasional during the eighteenth century, were reintroduced in 1788 in the province of Holland, in the aftermath of the abortive Patriot Revolution of 1787. Because van de Speigel, the pensionary of the province, refused to accept a political accommodation with the Patriots, merchants and bankers identified with that group tried to depress the value of assets subject to assessment under the forced loan. Nonetheless f. 53 million was raised, and breathing space acquired for what was, in van de Spiegel's eyes, an imminent program of financial reform.[47] But a political accommodation over reform could not be reached, and not only Holland but also other public corporations continued competitive loan issues and in the process consumed the little that remained of revenues that might be spent for debt service.

Once in power in January 1795 the Patriots found both pragmatic and ideological reasons for introducing voluntary and forced loans and levies on property and income. The fiscal bequest of the regent–Orangist regime could not be carried without a program that required propertied segments of the public, both those in power before 1795 and those who came to power in 1795, to pay emergency assessments.[48] While the new regime launched an inquiry into the condition of public finances,[49] it also turned to a program that anticipated an emerging assumption of the new power elite – taxes should be proportional to wealth. Up to 1803 most assessments were loans rather than levies but, as market prices deteriorated on the paper issued in them, the taxation feature became evident. Although the Batavians tried to stabilize political conditions in the Republic, some among them at least recognized that it would not be possible both to sustain the international role of the Amsterdam capital market and build the new order.[50] They chose to sacrifice the market even though it had been the source of the wealth of some Patriot leaders.

Under the enthusiasm of coming to power, the Batavians misjudged the options open to them. Because they were obliged by their French allies to add the cost of liberating the Republic (in the form of an indemnity of f. 100 million) to inherited liabilities,[51] the Batavians were deprived of the grand opportunities that they had imagined lay before them in 1795 and were confronted instead with grave financial problems. France advised the new regime to repudiate part of its debt, but the Batavian Revolution had not changed attitudes about the sanctity of public credit.[52] Although the formulation of taxation proportional to wealth appeared to offer a resolution, awaiting only the introduction of such a program, in reality the tax base available to the new regime was not sufficient to support debt service and political reform.

Under the unitary constitution adopted in 1798, the Batavian Republic assumed the debts and fiscal responsibilities of the Generality, the provinces, the admiralties, and the East India Company.[53] At the same time the administrative system of tax assessment and collection was centralized, and a declaration made of intent to tax according to wealth.[54] Translating that formula into specific measures proved no easy task, and not until 1806 was a tax-reform program implemented. The national system introduced then paralleled the unitary government adopted in 1798 and went some way toward equalizing tax distribution among economic classes and political subdivisions.[55] But the principle of taxation according to wealth was never satisfactorily implemented. Revenues increased in response to measures introduced in 1806, rising from f. 35.8 million in 1805 to f. 42.7 million in 1806, but expenditures remained at nearly twice that level, rising from f. 72.2 to 77.3 million.[56] With a debt in excess of f. 1 billion, service required a sum equal to or greater than tax revenues. The Batavian regime was in an untenable position.

In the interim the enthusiasm with which Patriots and some heretofore apolitical elements had greeted the revolution of 1795 had changed to disquietude and then to disgust.[57] What had actually been won in 1795 was not even the liberty for a still rather select group to share power or displace the personnel of the regent oligarchy and the stadholderian regime, but subjection to a France shifting its own deficits to satellite states.[58] Successive forced impositions up to 1803 yielded proportionally smaller sums, suggesting public resistance and a declining tax base, and leading the regime to resume the issue of competitive loans.[59] Those included consolidation loans designed to reduce the complexity of debt management and, in 1807, the use of private entrepreneurs to devise acceptable terms and manage an issue of f. 40 million.[60] Even though the new regime restricted foreign lending,[61] and thereby bolstered demand for domestic government paper, that program ultimately benefited France more than it did the Dutch.

The 1806 tax-reform program might still have preserved solvency for a longer period had it coincided with political stabilization and economic recovery. But the war continued, and with it the disruption of commerce, industry, and international finance. As a consequence of deteriorating economic conditions, tax income stopped growing; in 1811 ordinary revenues amounted to no more than f. 33.4 million.[62] In 1808 and 1809 the kingdom of Holland fell into arrears in interest payments on its debt, and in 1810, after incorporation into the French empire, the long-deferred measure of arbitrary reduction of liabilities was enacted. Thenceforth interest was paid at one-third the level stated on any given note, although the nominal capital of the debt remained unchanged for the time being.

In the end the Batavian and French periods, as the Dutch label the era from 1795 to 1813, left the state bankrupt. Obligations inherited by the kingdom of the Netherlands totaled more than f. 1.25 billion, an increase of some 59 percent over the 1795 figure.[63] That debt was reorganized and divided into two types of paper, one-third in the so-called actual or real debt, paying 2.5-percent interest, and two-thirds in deferred debt, on which reimbursements were suspended while the real debt was being paid off.[64] Projections prepared in 1814 indicated that nearly three centuries would have to pass before the principal could be extinguished.[65] In fact the specification of part of the debt as deferred (and presumably not "real") was a confirmation of partial bankruptcy. In 1841 the deferred-debt notes still outstanding were converted at a fraction of their nominal value. Together with the renewed inflation of the second half of the nineteenth century, which eroded the value of pre-1815 debts still outstanding, the conversion of 1841 settled most of the debt of 1813 and simultaneously confirmed the former Republic's credit program as, ultimately, a progressive system of taxation.

There was therefore a pandemic of bankruptcy across Europe during the Revolutionary and Napoleonic wars, a pandemic that was not finally settled until decades later, but nonetheless one whose consequences were by and large suffered by creditors during the wars. An attempt will be made in the following chapter to assess Dutch losses in a more systematic fashion. The conclusion to be drawn here deals with general consequences of the collapse of solvency. At first glance widespread repudiation of domestic and foreign debts may appear to mark a watershed in political and financial history, but upon closer inspection the effect will be seen to have been economic.

In the same fashion that the wars of 1792-1815 were more closely associated with traditional rivalries within the European state system than with the ideological veneer given conflict by the French Revolution, the financial crisis was a product of old weaknesses in the financial practices of old-regime continental states. The erection of an international credit structure and a general shift in most states toward interest-only credit had been an expedient response to rather than a resolution of financial problems. More fundamental matters - agrarian economies in which productivity gains were modest at best and in which economic growth was insufficient to bear the burden of political and military ambitions, unproductive war spending, and inefficient revenue administration - were not thereby attacked. Sustained conflict, the indulgence of an inclination to compete when solvency depended on cooperation, inevitably depleted credit resources and reversed declining costs gained with the shift to international credit exploitation. But the repudiations were not the occasion of any general reformulation of public finance policy.

The crisis of solvency points to the degree to which European states moved, wittingly and unwittingly, to a covert system of taxation by using policies under which creditors delivered assets to the state by accepting and holding depreciating paper. In the short run, at least, wartime exigency forced European governments toward a partial correction of regressive taxation. But covert redistribution was not widely maintained in the aftermath of the Napoleonic wars.

On the continent the financial balance had been wiped sufficiently clean, and foreign debts treated with great enough care, that the international credit structure could be revived in 1815. In the nineteenth century, however, that structure no longer served chiefly as underpinning for an expedient system of government finance since sustained peace, economic growth, and eventual tax redistribution led to a long period of greater stability in European finance than had existed in the early modern era. Moreover, the primary allocation of credit to war spending and debt service gave way to lending and borrowing that explicitly pursued economic objectives. A desire to stimulate economic growth had not been the motivating force in the demand for or the supply of investment capital in the eighteenth century. But in the same fashion that institutions and techniques serviceable in commerce and commercial finance were modified in the eighteenth-century Dutch Republic to serve international government finance, so the market serving political requirements established precedents and procedures for an international credit structure serving economic as well as political objectives.

Where the pandemic had the greatest impact, however, was in eradicating substantial parts of government debts, releasing revenues for spending on other objectives than annuity payments, and freeing savings for uses other than lending to government. Had defaults been avoided without any change in revenue levels or debt–revenue ratios, many continental states would have emerged from the Napoleonic wars in positions that required them continually to refinance existing debts and borrow fresh sums, and therefore, as vigorous competitors for private savings. Defaults diminished the pool of eighteenth-century savings that had found employment in lending to government, but, in the sustained era of peace that followed the Congress of Vienna, governments borrowed less than would have been necessary without defaults, leaving wartime fortunes and new savings to find investment in industry and transportation.

9

ECONOMIC CONSEQUENCES OF LENDING TO FOREIGN GOVERNMENTS

Although economic objectives ultimately played a secondary role in the financial policies followed by eighteenth-century states, those policies included elements that, wittingly and unwittingly, affected economic trends. If it is generally appropriate to assume that, within certain limits, government expenditures financed by voluntary lending have a greater expansionary effect than those financed by taxation, then it would appear that mercantilist expedient programs tended until the 1790s to enhance economic activity wherever employed throughout Europe.[1] Those programs should therefore be linked with other stimuli in explaining the growth discernible in much of Europe. That states that combined foreign borrowing with paper currency issues were able, until the 1790s, both to enlarge revenues and to increase economic activity is suggested by the expansion of tax revenues in constant values ahead of tax reforms. In Austria and Russia, for example, paper currency issues appear until about 1790 to have filled lacunae between the previous money supply and the supply that could be supported by existing levels of economic activity or higher levels made possible by a larger supply. Where interest-bearing loans were the principal technique of credit inflation, the link between money supply and economic expansion is more imprecise. But there too credit took the place of taxation. Because, however, loans were not spent directly to enhance production for export markets, the assist toward monetary stability and economic growth given by capital imports tended, despite interim expansion of production encouraged by borrowing, to diminish as service payments surpassed new credits.

Except for France, which borrowed at unnecessarily generous yields, debtor states seem, on the testimony of domestic credit costs, also to have been able to mobilize long-term credit without coming into conflict with sectors of their economies in need of investment capital and able to employ credit profitably at the low yields that prevailed until the Revolutionary wars.[2]

It does not necessarily follow that capital available to Britain, Austria, and the Dutch Republic at rates ranging between 2.5 and 5 percent was also available to all sectors of their economies. The developing modern sector of industry in Britain did not employ the London capital market to finance ventures and relied instead on self-financing and the reinvestment of profits. But it is important to notice that the first phase of industrialization, the phase preceding that in which power-driven machinery and extensive social-overhead capital investments were emphasized, was significantly less capital-intensive than was the case from the 1830s. The portion of national income saved did not have to change dramatically to permit that first phase of development, nor was large-scale capital availability a necessary forerunner of industrialization in the eighteenth or early nineteenth century. The orientation of the London market toward government lending may therefore reflect not so much a defect in the structure of the market as demand dominated by government. By its very nature the modern sector of industry in the first phase of its development was disinclined to compete on that market to finance capital formation. Because of self-financing and borrowing from friends and relatives, such requirements were met on a scale that was far more modest than the customary size of loans negotiated by the government (although not more modest than the size of individual units of investment in the funds). In Britain, but not also in Austria and the Dutch Republic, credit costs remained low enough during the Revolutionary and Napoleonic wars to permit continued self-financing and borrowing from friends and relatives rather than reallocation of those assets toward lending to government or other areas. Whereas the portion of government spending financed by borrowing decreased in comparison to prior experience, neither wartime taxation nor wartime borrowing prevented capital formation in a developing modern sector of industry that continued to stress other inputs over capital.

Economic consequences

The increased but not disruptive government spending permitted by an international credit structure tended in the second half of the eighteenth century to expand economic activity. On the whole, however, capital available through that structure was neither specifically allocated to nor withheld from economic sectors susceptible to productivity gains. Governments spent additional resources chiefly for military and debt-service requirements. For that reason the impact of the credit structure on the output of goods and services is difficult to specify. But Dutch lending did not merely ease the pursuit of excessively combative diplomatic objectives. At other times governments had fought wars beyond their means without regard for disruptive financial and economic consequences, so that, presumably, dynastic aggressiveness was less affected than economic activities that would otherwise have been dampened. In other words, greater financial stability meant more economic growth or less contraction than would have occurred without Dutch capital exports and an international credit structure. In either hypothetical situation the Dutch economy would have benefited from higher-than-otherwise commercial services, if not also somewhat greater imports and exports, whereas other economies enjoyed higher-than-otherwise production and trade, both importing and exporting more. Paradoxically, some of the negative consequences of war were thereby avoided.

Financial flows and economic flows

Dutch foreign lending should not be taken in isolation from the flow of goods, services, and capital between the Republic and other states, but it is necessary to acknowledge that borrowers and lenders alike usually functioned as though Dutch capital exports and annuity imports were separate from economic flows. In approaching foreign borrowing in financial rather than economic terms, European governments overlooked the potential of capital imports to assist export-oriented economic policies. Credits obtained from the Dutch were not employed under government auspices to subsidize or underwrite industry, agriculture, or trade, although nongovernment foreign lending from the Republic financed commercial flows and was sometimes used in the private sector to expand production in mining, industry, and plantation agriculture.

Nor did Dutch banking intermediaries organize or lenders extend credit to foreign governments with the expectation that capital exports would increase foreign demand for Dutch goods and services. Indeed the increasing importance of lending to foreign governments should be interpreted as a reaction to the declining profitability of trade and industry in the Republic rather than as an attempt to revive waning sectors of the Dutch economy. On the other hand, nongovernment lending did serve certain economic objectives. There, however, the principal goal was to stimulate factorage and entrepôt services for merchant bankers dealing in or aspiring to deal in West Indian agricultural commodities, Swedish industrial products,[3] or other areas. Outside Britain, Dutch investors tended to extend credit under fixed terms rather than to acquire stock in foreign banks, joint-stock companies, or other enterprises susceptible to growth and thus to an increase in the value of their assets. Moreover, that characteristic grew stronger as the pace of inflation and thus of declining value in fixed-return assets gained momentum toward the end of the eighteenth century. In the long run nongovernment foreign lending was, outside the rather grand but ultimately unsuccessful speculation in plantation loans, an incidental feature of market activity.

The role of foreign lending in economic flows may be surveyed through an estimation of the principal entries in the Dutch balance of payments. Although in decline, Dutch fishing and shipping continued to the end of the eighteenth century to furnish more goods and services to foreign consumers than were supplied the Dutch by foreign fishing and shipping. Income on foreign investments was clearly growing, and was a second credit item on current account. On the other hand, contemporary observers claimed that foreign industrial products were becoming increasingly attractive to Dutch consumers over the second half of the eighteenth century. There can be no certainty that a growing preference for foreign goods led to an overall net debit on exchanges of manufactured goods, but in any case exports of manufactured goods were declining and imports increasing. European and colonial agricultural imports were, for the most part, reexported, but it is likely that exports of agricultural products originating in the Republic were not sufficient to balance imports of grain, wine, sugar, coffee, spices, and other goods that were not reexported. On balance, however, the Dutch current

Table 9-1. *Estimated totals of long-term foreign loans outstanding compared to balances attainable through 100% reinvestment of annuity earnings (in millions of guilders)*

	Estimated balances	Attainable balances projected at an average return of 4% to 1780 and 4.5% from 1780		
1763	200	(200)		
1770	250	263.2	(250)	
1780	350	389.6	370	(350)
1790	500–650	605	574.7	543.5

account contained a substantial credit surplus, provided chiefly by commercial and financial services and annuity receipts.

Under capital account there was indisputably a substantial debit. The import of foreign capital for private or government use was minimal whereas the Dutch were active in lending to foreign governments, private enterprise, and international trade. In government finance the debit created by each year's addition to the sum outstanding abroad was, however, approximately balanced by annuity receipts under current account, as is indicated by Table 9-1.[4] Foreign-exchange earnings from annuity receipts appear therefore to have been consumed by new foreign investments. Any judgment about the balance between other types of capital exports and annuity, dividend, and interest receipts on them is impossible because of the paucity of information.

The most plausible general hypothesis is that capital-account debits declined until they were in approximate balance with current-account credits under annuity, dividend, and interest receipts, leaving at least in the early part of the period after 1763 a credit surplus provided chiefly by commercial and financial services furnished foreign merchants, manufacturers, and other groups. That credit surplus, brought into balance by bullion imports, seems to have been diminishing in volume and, by about 1790, to have become a debit.[5] In the long run capital imports resulting from annuity payments received on foreign loans tended to depress the cost of foreign currencies in guilders, and therefore to expand the volume of exports from debtor states to the Republic. Because, as it appears, the Republic was shifting toward a debit on current account, the counter trend toward higher-cost foreign currencies produced by foreign investment was modified. According to this interpretation those contradictory paths prevented the specie flow adjustment that might have made Dutch goods and services more competitive.

During the Revolutionary and Napoleonic wars Dutch exports declined, commercial and financial services were disrupted, and annuity receipts were reduced by defaults. Continued voluntary and involuntary capital exports fell, in the long run, below annuity receipts, but it is not clear whether remaining annuity receipts were sufficient to balance other imports. In any case Dutch goods and services did not become significantly more attractive to foreign buyers, and there was no shift toward greater production for any subtantial segment of the Dutch economy.

With these trends in mind we may return to the impact of Dutch capital exports on the flow of goods and services between the Republic and its trading associates. Quite clearly the transfer of Dutch savings abroad was assisted by a persistent credit surplus on current account. But as Table 9-1 indicates, lending to foreign governments was, in terms of foreign-exchange earnings and entries on the Dutch balance of international payments, a self-sustaining item. The long-run approximate balance of capital exports with annuity receipts, indicated by that table, suggests also that the capital flow did not amount to the maximum sum permitted by current-account credit or debit surpluses. Between 1763 and 1780, when the Republic probably had a credit surplus, capital exports were less than all foreign-exchange earnings. Thereafter, during the apparent shift toward a debit on current and capital account, capital exports did not diminish until foreign lending was disrupted by war and increased taxation in the Republic.

The direction of attention in this study to the financial side of Dutch lending should not, of course, be taken to indicate that capital exports were incapable of an unintentional stimulation of foreign demand for Dutch goods and services. In the event, however, it is difficult to identify export or reexport sectors in the Republic that were directly assisted. In spending loan proceeds for military and naval armaments and supplies, European governments did little to encourage Dutch exports, for the Republic was not a major producer of military equipment. Gains realized in that area were therefore limited to rather modest earnings on the distribution of hardware and other supplies and on commercial and financial services rendered in that distribution. Although it must be acknowledged that Dutch lending deferred insolvency among some debtor states, it does not necessarily follow that the Republic thereby preserved existing export markets, for, solvent or insolvent, foreign governments were not important consumers of Dutch goods and commercial services. In the end the chief service that Dutch lenders provided themselves and their economy by successive foreign investments was to furnish debtors with the assets and foreign exchange necessary to service existing foreign debts.[6]

On the other hand, Dutch lending did influence trade flows among debtor states, for borrowers could either import more or export less. But the stimulus was short-lived in that, after an initial period of capital imports, debtors found that capital-account credits moved toward balance with current-account debits for service payments. Rather than increasing exports to pay loan charges borrowers preferred the capital-account credits of new loans. In the process they deferred having to reduce other imports or increase exports in order to settle debts. During the Revolutionary and Napoleonic wars, when Dutch capital exports became largely involuntary contributions to France and when most borrowers' current-account debits could no longer be balanced by new loans, several borrowers defaulted or deferred service payments. For the Dutch, voluntary and involuntary exports during the war probably equaled or fell slightly below declining annuity, dividend, and interest receipts. Ultimately few eighteenth-century borrowers ever fully repaid their obligations and even those benefited from interim price inflation.

Although there was a stimulus in each borrower's initial period of capital-account credits, it was chiefly squandered. Greater imports or fewer exports might either have improved the standard of living in a debtor state or increased its productive assets, or both. In fact Dutch loans were absorbed by war, and to a significant extent reexported to hire mercenary soldiers and sailors, to maintain foreign armies and navies, to subsidize allies, to pay indemnities, and to buy war matériel. In such circumstances who are the beneficiaries? Moreover, the sums lent by the Dutch are impressive but their grandeur would be diminished by comparing them to cumulative or annual European import and export values. Nor was the advent of foreign government lending a major discontinuity in economic flows, for Dutch investors were shifting assets that were already largely international. In the final analysis Dutch lending had a marginal rather than a central impact on trade flows except to the extent that it tended to foster wars disruptive of trade.

Capital abundance and a modern sector of industry in the Republic

Where the financial policies of old regime governments included long-term objectives the aim, however vaguely specified, was chiefly to increase taxable resources that could be exploited through traditional and unreformed revenue systems. But some observers in both creditor and debtor states thought they could identify certain consequences of lending and borrowing for economic development. British observers, who had longer experience with this issue than their counterparts in other debtor states, perceived foreign investment in the public debt either as harmful, as a threat to financial stability and a loss of authority to creditors possessed of a different set of political loyalties, or as beneficial, as a source of capital worth more because of the domestic resources that it released for other pursuits than the cost of service. The view that foreign credits were harmful was often proclaimed, but never forcefully enough to lead to the adoption of impediments to investment from abroad. In the Dutch Republic there were also contrary views, one portraying foreign lending as harmful because it deprived the state of resources needed by its own government, industry, and commerce, and the other arguing that investment opportunities at home were so inadequate that a foreign outlet was necessary. There opponents of foreign lending likewise failed to persuade authorities to intervene.

Proponents of foreign borrowing in Britain and opponents of lending in the Republic together furnished an image of the Dutch role in international finance as disadvantageous for the development of the Dutch economy, and it is that image that became dominant in nineteenth- and early-twentieth-century historical analyses. The conjuncture of those views with divergent patterns of development in the two states was too attractive to be taken as coincidental, so that a force seen as harmful to a stagnant or declining Dutch economy, although beneficial to Britain undergoing industrialization, was assumed to describe a causal link between the two divergent patterns. That analytical structure is no longer regarded as satisfactory, but it does not follow that Dutch capital accumulation had no significant impact on the subsequent presence or absence of capital formation in a modern sector of industry in the Republic or its rivals. A satisfactory resolution of the problem of Dutch economic retardation must await more extensive information about comparative factor costs in different branches of industry in the Republic and its rivals, the extent to which economic advantages derived by borrowers may have rebounded to influence the Dutch economy, and other issues. Nevertheless, it is possible to assess the degree to which capital accumulation in international finance should be cited to account for retardation.

The broad question at hand is this: Why did the Dutch Netherlands fail to create a significant modern industrial sector more or less simultaneously with Britain and Belgium? More specifically, what impact did extensive capital accumulation and sophisticated Dutch capital markets have on the failure of modern industry to develop? Because capital accumulation was oriented toward lending to governments, which was not productive in the same sense as investment in capital goods, did Dutch markets impede investment in productive areas? In other words, were Dutch capital markets incapable of providing or Dutch capitalists unwilling to provide a latent sector of modern industry with the low-cost credit that, because of equivalent or higher costs for other factors in industrial production in comparison to competitors, was necessary to make Dutch industrialization feasible?

The large scale and broad range of investment ventures pursued through the Amsterdam capital market make it appear that the Dutch Netherlands had a clear advantage in mobilizing capital for industrial development and economic modernization. During most of the second half of the eighteenth century high aggregate capital supply and conversion of assets from other sectors led to investments in such diverse areas as plantation agriculture, domestic and foreign trading companies, and foreign mining and manufacturing, and the volume of assets assigned to government lending continued to grow. Market intermediaries were flexible and attuned to the introduction of novel sectors of investment, and rentiers, although functioning in a biased situation that militated toward low returns on government loans, were willing and able to follow the lead of intermediaries.

Dutch proprietary wealth (or rentier capital) had traditionally accommodated degrees of venturesomeness reflected by the persistence of variations in yield among different types of investments. Capital was allotted to several areas, such as plantation loans, substitution ventures in the domestic debt of the United States, and foreign lending in general, which were acknowledged to carry significant risks. In theory, then, Dutch investment capital should have been available into the 1790s to all lenders able to pay returns of 4 to 6 percent, the range of the more risky sectors of lending activity, and able also to furnish security of equivalent attractiveness to that offered by planters, foreign governments, and other borrowers. Indeed the preference displayed by investors for domestic over foreign borrowers may be assumed to have made potential credit costs for Dutch industry able to offer equivalent security lower than those for foreign industry.

Joel Mokyr has pointed out that, in addition to having well-developed capital markets and substantial savings, the Dutch Netherlands at the end of the eighteenth century also enjoyed other advantages, including an urbanized labor force and an efficient agrarian sector, which might have made a conversion to modern industry more likely there than in other continental states.[7] But those same advantages should have made the traditional sector of industry in the Republic competitive in international markets in the period before mechanized techniques of production were an alternative. In fact most elements of Dutch industry were in decline in the eighteenth century.[8] If the reasons for that are complex and include comparative factor costs, changing tastes, and output quality as well as levies by other states on the import of Dutch goods and the export of raw materials, the Republic would seem still to have been able to duplicate protectionist legislation adopted elsewhere and thereby control domestic markets.

Protectionist measures would presumably have revived traditional industry insofar as its products could have been accommodated by the Dutch market and remaining foreign markets. In the hypothetical case of protective tariffs, industrial innovation would have been profitable because it would have been undertaken either in competition with high-priced foreign goods or with the products of less efficient, traditional modes of manufacturing in the Republic. The ultimate consequences of industrial innovation under those terms are difficult to predict, except under the assumption that home markets could have remained protected without other negative consequences until factor costs and product quality were approximately equivalent to those of foreign manufacturers. In that event a modern sector of Dutch industry would eventually have entered world markets.

Charles Wilson has suggested that a community of interest between international trade and international finance obstructed Dutch industrial development.[9] In his view antiprotectionism among staple market interests, directed particularly against segments of industry, such as textiles, that were not integrated into staple market functions, was seconded by allies in the financial community. The commercial-financial alliance prevented the flow of commercial capital into industry "so that Dutch economic development was postponed by a leakage of capital into international finance."[10] Compensation for restricted opportunities in trade was sought in finance.

This interpretation points up an important affinity, personified by merchants who remained active in the carrying trade yet broadened their interests to include large-scale transactions in commercial drafts and the organization and management of foreign loans. Taken by itself, however, that connection can be misleading. The movement of Dutch savings into international finance represented an exploitation of shifting opportunities rather than a denial of capital to a needy sector of the domestic economy. If investors were disinclined to extend long-term credit to existing industry, the explanation should be sought in the declining profitability of industry rather than in a selective bias against that sector. Moreover, the interests of commerce and those of finance were not always synonymous with the objectives of staple market merchants, as is indicated by the struggle over tariff reform surrounding the unsuccessful *Propositie* (plan) of 1751 for a limited porto-franco. Against the insistence of staple-goods merchants that tariff policy should continue to be designed principally to serve their objectives, the *Propositie* embodied a contrasting view that transcended the staple market and sought to foster the development of finance, insurance, and transit trade across the Republic.[11]

A merger of commercial and industrial interests was extremely complex, as is also illustrated by the *Propositie*. To manufacturers the chief attraction of that proposal was in its recommendation of reduced duties on raw-material imports rather than in the introduction of protective tariffs against foreign products competing with Dutch manufactures.[12] In other words, the industries that would have benefited from the *Propositie* were only those whose factor costs were otherwise approximately equivalent to the factor costs facing foreign competitors. But such a merger did exist in the form of tariff regulations beneficial to certain segments of Dutch industry, including some not associated with the staple market *trafieken* (refining and finishing industries dealing largely in export markets).[13] It should also be recognized that the ultimate interests of merchants and investors came into conflict in any activity that tended to restrict investment opportunities, such as resistance to tariffs that might have revived Dutch industry.

But the chief defect in the line of reasoning that relates economic retardation to a community of interest between merchants and bankers against industrial protection lies in its unrealistic portrayal of economic issues in terms of a choice between trade (and finance) and industry. A thriving industrial sector, able to innovate and perhaps eventually to have expanded into foreign markets, was in the long run an issue of great consequence, although it is not clear that industrialization beginning between 1770 and 1800, for instance, would ultimately have been more advantageous than industrialization beginning in some later period. But in the eighteenth-century Republic less importance was attached to the tariff policy that might have led toward industrial development than to other approaches related to contrasting visions of the interests of trade, and to the requirement to provide revenues for admiralties dependent on duty income. The protective tariff barriers that might have brought an industrial revival were not rejected because capital would thereby have been drained from commercial or government finance. The question of an allocation of scarce resources did not arise because capital resources were not scarce, as is demonstrated by interest rates. There was in fact no point during the eighteenth century at which the Dutch confronted a choice between the internationalism of commerce and finance and a reorientation toward the domestic market, such as would have served certain elements of industry. Put in those terms there was no choice at all, for even in relative decline international interests were far too important to have been forsaken for the benefit of a wholly problematic notion of economic revitalization concentrating on a home market of some two million consumers. That was true not only because the profitability of existing industry was generally in decline but also because the scale of turnover and profits in trade exceeded anything that could be forecast for industry or indeed for any other sector of the economy outside foreign lending itself.

However, Wilson's point draws attention to a fundamental problem that persisted well into the nineteenth century – the difficulty of devising an economic policy that would be of particular benefit to any substantial part of the Dutch economy. The *Propositie* of 1751 was not a resolution, for it involved significant losses for the staple market without providing equivalent gains for other areas. The triumph of staple-market interests over the *Propositie* and over any subsequent revision of tariff policies was maintained until 1816, when selective tariffs were erected to foster certain elements of Dutch (and Belgian) industry. Such sustained attachment to a program that proved incapable even of preserving the staple market does not indicate pigheadedness so much as it reflects the degree to which Dutch action by itself was inadequate to alter trends determined largely by exogenous forces.

In the absence of protective tariffs, Dutch industry was left to compete on unequal terms with foreign manufacturers in domestic and foreign markets. The uncompetitiveness of Dutch goods in foreign markets should occasion no surprise, if only because of import duties assessed by other states. But uncompetitiveness in Dutch markets suggests that within an economy marked by vast assets apparently appropriate to capital-intensive industrialization there were fundamental hindrances that stymied industrial entrepreneurship. In contrast, the Austrian Netherlands (Belgium), lacking in particular the advantages of an urban labor force and comparable aggregate savings, nonetheless possessed other assets that enabled entrepreneurs to form a sector of modern industry competitive in international markets in the first half of the nineteenth century. In considering Dutch retardation in the face of Belgian industrialization, Mokyr has related the absence of industrialization in the Dutch Republic and the pace at which industry developed in Belgium to capital markets. Before taking up that element of his argument, however, it will be necessary to summarize his comparative portrayal of development and retardation.

Although per capita income appears to have been substantially lower in Belgium than in the Dutch Netherlands, Dutch wages were high and remained high over the entire period to 1850 whereas wages were low in Belgium throughout. Moreover, Belgium had a large rural, or Z-good, industrial sector producing textiles and other goods that could be manufactured at lower cost by adopting British technology and reorganizing the method of production (from protoindustrial domestic manufacturing without significant fixed capital assets to enterprises with fixed capital assets in technology yielding higher productivity). That sector also provided a labor supply in proximity to urban areas, labor exploitable without an increase in wages that reduced the profitability of modern industry or endangered its ability to compete in an open market.[14]

Another factor of particular importance was the political divergence of the two states between 1794 and 1814. Annexation of the Austrian Netherlands to France in 1794 opened to Belgian manufacturing all the advantages of a market including greater France (the enlarged French Republic and to some degree the satellite states under French control), an area from which goods produced outside were prohibited or taxed. In contrast the Dutch Netherlands, although defeated by France in the campaign of 1794–5, was not incorporated into the French Empire until 1810, and French tariff barriers were not relaxed until 1812.[15] In the interim the Dutch tariff program designed to serve the staple market was retained despite the fact that Dutch access to raw materials and foreign markets was restricted by both British and French actions, and despite also the decline of carrying trade during the war.

Belgian entrepreneurs began to adopt the techniques of modern industry around 1798. Mokyr describes these entrepreneurs, who took advantage of a cheap labor supply, a broad market arena, and British technology, as having used their own assets to acquire the capital goods necessary to found a sector of modern industry. In following years they expanded the scale of their activities by reinvesting profits. The continuing but slow process of capital formation was managed principally by reinvestment, although in the 1830s lending among the subsectors of modern industry gained importance. The modern sector was profitable, but Mokyr maintains, in contrast to the view of Jan Dhondt and Marinette Bruvier, that Belgian rentiers disdained to invest in it throughout the period to 1850.[16] In his view Belgian industry developed slowly because capital supply was limited to the existing assets of industrial entrepreneurs and to the part of profits that entrepreneurs were willing to reinvest in industry as opposed to other areas, such as real estate and government securities.

A significant sector of modern industry did not appear in the Dutch Netherlands until the end of the nineteenth century, although between the 1770s and 1790s a small number of entrepreneurs formed mechanized industries, and although modern techniques of production were occasionally adopted in some areas after 1830.[17] The endeavors of the late eighteenth century were part of a larger movement tied closely to the Economic Branch of the Holland Society for Science. Although Economic Branch members generally encouraged a reinvigoration of industry and sometimes participated directly in projects in both the traditional and the potential modern sector, their efforts were directed principally toward the traditional sector. In the long run the movement they led came to nothing. Despite the fact that the Economic Branch was able to mobilize capital, often by drawing upon the willingness of compatriots to contribute to schemes designed to expand employment, the traditional sector of Dutch industry had not declined because of a want of capital but because it could not produce goods of competitive price and quality.[18] Modern enterprises formed within the same period also came to nothing although they were supplied with capital and although they employed British technology and British technicians.[19]

The available evidence on industrial experimentation in the late eighteenth century is sparse, but Johan de Vries has argued that an observation from *De Koopman* of 1776 explains the failure of the Dutch to form a modern sector of industry.[20] According to an anonymous commentator, high labor costs made much Dutch industry, and textiles in particular, uncompetitive with British manufacturing. The labor-cost argument has been a feature of most explanations of Dutch economic retardation, but it has often been joined with other factors, including entrepreneurial enervation, deficient technical expertise, insufficient raw materials, and inadequate aggregate capital demand. Mokyr has for the most part rejected those additional elements as they apply to the period from 1795 to 1850,[21] and argued not that rentiers were vile coupon clippers who disdained investment in industry regardless of its returns but that the Dutch Netherlands did not then have capital markets capable of developing links between investors and those entrepreneurs who might have initiated a sector of modern industry.[22] Thus he maintains that Belgian industry developed more slowly than would otherwise have been the case because links with capital markets were absent, and Dutch industry failed to develop at all, at least in part because such links were also absent in that state.

Mokyr's contention about capital markets is controversial enough in the case of Belgium, where industrial development occurred but left documentation on financing that has been interpreted differently by different observers. For the Dutch Netherlands, as applied at least to the earlier part of the period Mokyr treats, it is inevitably more controversial because Dutch capital markets are known to have been highly developed and because there the case is based on a hypothetical situation (absent links) that is plausible in economic theory but has not been tested rigorously in the historical setting. Furthermore, that argument ignores a substantial body of evidence suggesting that links were present without being supported by countervailing evidence suggesting that links were absent. In particular Mokyr discounted de Vries's evidence about investment capital in industrial startups in the 1770s and 1780s, and was not aware of loans floated on Dutch markets by foreign and Dutch industry.[23]

In Mokyr's framework links are held not to have existed either because investors were biased against industry or because of defects in Dutch capital markets. Although we must deal with probabilities rather than certainties, we can examine these two possible explanations to see whether they are more or less likely than an alternative proposition, that links existed but were not much exploited because of other problems faced by industry.

Given their general preference for domestic over foreign loans and their investment in a number of loans to foreign industry, lenders should have been more rather than less willing to invest in, or offer better terms to, loans to Dutch industry. Only three such loans have been cited in comparison to hundreds of government loans, which establishes that loans to Dutch industry were infrequent but not why. From what else we know (that investors bought into loans having a wide range of risk, that investors' interests were best served by any expansion of credit demand, and that the preferences of investors were determined by such considerations as the probable punctuality of service rather than by the purpose for which credit was to be employed), the argument of a bias against only Dutch industry looks less and less likely. What, however, of defects in Dutch capital markets, and of sectors of Dutch markets besides the government loan apparatus?

Both foreign and Dutch industry raised loans through the Amsterdam market, but it must be acknowledged that the government loan apparatus was not well suited to all forms of industrial borrowing. Borrowing to initiate an enterprise was not likely to find many lenders because lenders required that borrowers hypothecate the kind of assets that had demonstrated the ability to pay returns sufficient for service. Wholly new enterprises could not expect to borrow there except perhaps to the extent that credit would be used to acquire assets of generally accepted value and reliable earnings potential, such as real estate, rather than assets of hypothetical value and earning power, such as new industrial technology. But since existing enterprises, some in the Republic and some not, raised substantial loans, the conclusion is inescapable that industry could have financed expansion or retooling as long as existing assets with convincing earning power were available to be mortgaged. In short, it is more plausible to suppose that links existed between industry and the government loan apparatus than it is to suppose that they did not. Amsterdam's capital market was not "perfect," but the defects of it and other Dutch capital markets did not lie in the realm of leading investors away from investment opportunities.

Moreover, the government loan segment of Dutch capital markets was less likely than other segments to lend to industry because, as in Britain and Belgium, private financing outside the government loan apparatus was the customary technique of both short- and long-term lending to commerce and industry. When existing industry sought capital, it drew on short-term commercial credit and private loans negotiated among individuals. Such credit was sometimes arranged as sleeping partnerships, but in the Dutch Republic private loans in commerce and industry appear more frequently to have taken the form of promissory notes. Individual cases of lending to industry under such a format, including instances of loans for industrial innovation or initiation, have come to light.[24] Their number and evidence in general about lending to industry in the private loan sector of Dutch capital markets would undoubtedly be enlarged by a systematic search of estate inventories in the notarial archives or the collateral-succession tax records. There was probably not a thriving market in long-term industrial credit in the government loan apparatus, private lending via IOUs, or sleeping partnerships, but that can better be accounted for by the relative unattractiveness of industrial entrepreneurship than by positing absent links or a general bias among investors against investment in Dutch industry.

Why, since links existed, were they not much used for lending to modern industry? If industrialization was feasible in Belgium using self-financing and reinvested profits, then it should have been feasible by the same means in the Dutch Netherlands, with or without links with capital via capital markets, had factor costs and other elements been more or less equivalent. But were factor costs even approximately equivalent? De Vries has shown that labor-intensive industry suffered more severely than capital-intensive industry in the Dutch decline of the eighteenth century.[25] That trend was related to foreign competition in such labor-intensive sectors as textiles, but it demonstrates a continuing vitality where capital was a relatively more important resource and calls attention to the importance of labor costs. Since the few modern industrial enterprises organized between the 1770s and the 1790s generally failed despite having joined wealthy businessmen and entrepreneurs with access to modern technology, there is all the more reason to search for an explanation of the failure of a modern sector of industry to emerge in costs faced by Dutch industry.

Although Mokyr portrays "the absence of capital markets and the consequent reliance on self-finance for the accumulation of capital" as "an essential element" in his model of early European industrialization,[26] the fundamental distinction between the Belgian and Dutch economies revolves around labor cost differentials. In 1819, the only year for which reliable comparative data are available, "the average wage paid in the northern provinces [of the United Kingdom of the Netherlands] was 56.5 percent higher than in the southern provinces [Belgium]."[27] Having assumed the absence of links between active or incipient industrial entrepreneurs and capital markets, Mokyr does not explicitly deal with the possible significance of available low-cost credit to a different path of economic development than the one actually followed in the Dutch Netherlands. Presumably low-cost credit would be expected to have reduced factor costs in mechanized industry, particularly in the production of cotton cloth, to such levels that entrepreneurs would have emerged to form a significant sector of modern industry.

Table 9-2 portrays average realizable returns on some domestic government securities from 1796 through 1811 and in the first half of 1814, indicating that returns from new investment in outstanding paper (averaging 7.67 percent through 1811) systematically exceeded prewar levels (of 3 to 4 percent) by a substantial margin.[28] During the war new loan yields also increased as borrowers provided discounts, chiefly by accepting outstanding paper trading below par at its par value in operations that combined refunding with borrowing, or increased returns outright. Although some low-yield assets were retained by investors, either out of sluggishness or because those assets were believed to carry low risks, the dominant and most visible sector of long-term lending activity was marked by high returns.[29] Because prices were fairly stable from 1795–9 through 1805–9,[30] new lending was profitable although risky.

Increasing credit costs and an enlarged range of high realizable returns constitute an element of discontinuity that might account for the failure of entrepreneurs using either their own or borrowed capital to develop a modern sector of industry after 1795. Since, however, the few pre-1795 mechanized industries

Table 9-2. *Average realizable returns on selected domestic government annuities, 1796–1814 (first quotations available in each semiannual period)*

	Realizable return,%	Number of quotations
1796/2	4.84	1
1797/1	5.45	1
1797/2	6.57	2
1798/1	7.88	2
1798/2	7.75	2
1799/1	7.72	3
1799/2	8.54	3
1800/1	7.68	3
1800/2	7.97	3
1801/1	7.67	3
1801/2	6.75	2
1802/1	6.44	3
1802/2	6.43	3
1803/1	6.65	2
1803/2	8.39	2
1804/1	7.77	2
1804/2	8.43	2
1805/1	8.70	2
1805/2	7.29	2
1806/1	7.35	2
1806/2	7.74	2
1807/1	7.17	2
1807/2	7.43	2
1808/1	7.08	2
1808/2	7.22	2
1809/1	7.48	2
1809/2	7.77	2
1810/1	9.52	1
1810/2	5.84	2
1811/1	11.62	2
1811/2	12.78	2
1814/1	7.68	2

about which something is known were short-lived and industry in general was in decline, the key element would not appear to have been increasing credit costs (which heightened the return expected from investments in industry) but some element that was continuous throughout, such as high wages. In this counter hypothesis the discontinuity of increased credit costs would be interpreted as having made the development of modern industry even less likely after 1795 than it had been before that date. And in fact even the ambition to attempt innovation that is evident in industrial start-ups in prewar decades waned during the war.

There is also a second element of discontinuity that must be examined. Before 1795 foreign manufactured goods were imported into the Republic with little or no cost added in the form of duties, whereas Dutch products faced duties in most foreign ports. After that date access to raw materials and foreign markets was restricted by both British and French action whereas Dutch markets remained open to goods produced in the part of Europe under French control. As a result Dutch entrepreneurs had less desirable marketing opportunities than did counterparts in Belgium, where French annexation opened otherwise protected markets in France and some of its satellite states. On balance, however, the marketing possibilities available to Dutch entrepreneurs may have been slightly enhanced in comparison to the prewar period. Restrictions on the entry of British goods left Dutch markets open only to producers who, in the early stages of French control, used no more sophisticated techniques of production than did the Dutch. That was precisely the period during which Belgian entrepreneurs formed a modern sector of industry in goods that appear to have been susceptible to competitive production in the Dutch Netherlands using mechanized techniques. Nonetheless, Dutch manufacturers, although suddenly in a more favorable position with respect to Dutch markets, failed to shift from traditional methods of production, new mechanized industries failed to appear, and existing ones continued to fare poorly. Access to low-cost credit might have made industrial entrepreneurship more attractive after 1795, particularly if taken in conjunction with a shift toward protective tariffs. As events occurred, however, credit costs increased and industrial protectionism remained a matter of incidental concern in comparison to commercial tariff policy.

"Had there been good capital markets, the modern sector [of industry] would have been able to borrow large amounts from nonindustrial savings as long as there were high quasi rents to be earned."[31] Good capital markets are those markets that can furnish credit at interest rates attractive both to industrial entrepreneurs and lenders. No wholly reliable data are available on the rate of profit in the modern sector of Belgian industry or in those few cases where mechanized industry was adopted in the Dutch Netherlands. A sample figure, based on estimates for capital–labor ratios in the Verviers textile industry, indicates tha the gross profit rate "was virtually stable around 13 percent" over the period to 1850.[32] Whether or not that figure is representative of the return on entrepreneurial investment in Belgian industry as a whole, it can be employed as a point of departure for commenting on the potential profitability of mechanized industry in the Dutch Netherlands and for contrasting potential profits there with interest rates on the Amsterdam capital market.

During most of the period surveyed in Table 9-2, a substantial margin persisted between realizable returns in domestic government finance and a gross profit rate of 13 percent. However, the potential profitability of Dutch industry must be reduced to accommodate substantially higher wages, and it may also be necessary to allow for high costs in other areas such as real estate.[33] Moreover, in the absence of a significant sector of Z-good production in textiles, the potential profitability of mechanized production of textiles or other goods had to be gauged in comparison to prices for imported goods. That was true because the Dutch market remained open to imports. Except for a brief hiatus after 1795, when imports from Britain were restricted and mechanized industry had not yet appeared on the continent to any significant extent, the prices involved in any comparison of textiles were those of goods produced by mechanized industry. That hiatus passed without its opportunities being seized. Given the unpredictability of an extended war and therefore the possibility of a renewal of unrestricted British imports, and interim smuggling,[34] it may be that the profitability of Dutch textile production in that period was still perceived in terms of prices charged for British goods.

In considering the attractiveness of industry to rentier capital, the Belgian profit rate should be reduced further to account for the unwillingness of industrialists to sacrifice all profits earned or expected on fixed capital investments made with rentier capital and their demand that part of those profits be reserved to compensate them for participation in the hypothetical joint enterprise. Precise weights cannot be assigned to these various elements, but taken together they explain why some mechanized industries failed and why a significant sector of modern industry was not established during the war. Potential profits were not high enough either to attract rentier capital or to match returns available to potential and actual industrial entrepreneurs in other types of activity and investment. Absent links with capital markets are not a necessary element of Mokyr's model.[35] Indeed, withdrawal of that feature does not require a fundamental revision of the arguments built around wage differentials and is entirely consistent with Mokyr's partial or complete rejection of other factors to which historians have sometimes assigned particular weight.

The Dutch case – a case of capital abundance – was unique in its setting. There savings rates probably exceeded 10 percent of national income for two centuries without sparking capital formation in modern industry. The question about comparative retardation in that economy has been posed in terms of missed opportunities, a drain of capital away from productive areas, or absent links with capital. Such interpretations assume that capital was a sufficient generator of economic modernization in the eighteenth century, that a shift from nonproductive lending (to government) to productive lending (to industry) was a simple yet, incredibly, an overlooked opportunity. But was that missed opportunity so available? The evidence marshaled here indicates that, in the Dutch setting, a setting lacking central planning and information gathering, capital should be perceived as responsive to opportunities rather than as an initiative force in its own right. Its essential neutrality was corruptible, in that government policy could (and did from the 1790s) influence the flow of credit in the government- and personal-lending sectors of the market, and also in that risk calculations were biased by incomplete information. But neither government influence nor information defects accounts for the absence of capital-intensive industrialization in the Republic. In the light of other factor costs faced by potential Dutch industrial entrepreneurs, especially high labor costs, it is necessary instead to approach Dutch retardation in terms of the characteristics of industrial development elsewhere in the first phase, the phase of emphasis on other resources than long-term credit. In that period the capital–labor ratio warrants less importance than it is assigned in

Mokyr's model. Capital availability and low credit costs could not surmount advantages in labor costs, protection, and other areas enjoyed in Britain and Belgium as long as resource costs continued to stress other factors than credit. By the time capital abundance and low credit costs might have played a more significant role, a period identifiable with the advent of power-driven machinery and extensive social-overhead capital investments, the Dutch Netherlands had lost the relative advantage it had held in the eighteenth century. The problem, therefore, is not to explain Dutch retardation up to the 1830s, when modern sectors of industry elsewhere were still not capital-intensive, but to examine capital availability and cost, the accessibility of technology, labor costs, market size and tastes, and the propensity to invest in industrial entrepreneurship and social-overhead capital improvements between the 1830s and the latter part of the nineteenth century, when the Netherlands finally did undertake to industrialize.

Erosion of the Dutch capital stock

Even before the inflationary trend of the second half of the eighteenth century significantly reduced the purchasing power of receipts from long-term investments, Dutch rentiers drew very modest benefits from their participation in government finance. An energetic effort to expand outlets, led by entrepreneurs who displayed no enervation of spirit, failed to redress that situation despite the exploitation of European and transatlantic opportunities. Foreign investments generally paid higher returns than were available on the domestic front, but the demand associated with new foreign outlets was not sufficient in the long run to increase returns ahead of rising prices. By the second half of the 1780s wholesale commodity prices (Chart 1-1) appear to have been increasing at an annual rate approximately equivalent to returns in the foreign loan sector of the market and in advance of returns on domestic government loans. A correction of the imprecise image that investors had about inflationary trends might have assisted an adjustment of returns toward the point at which real profits continued to be extracted. As events took place, returns increased in response to the greater risk of government lending during the Revolutionary and Napoleonic wars but not in pace with price movements. During the war demand from abroad was more than sufficient to have forced annuity rates above prevailing levels, but expanded credit mobilization and taxation by domestic government sharply reduced assets available for foreign lending. In keeping with the antiinvestor bias of their relationship with foreign borrowers, bankers preferred, in the brief interim before government policy began to manipulate credit flows, to slow the pace of new loan projects rather than to attempt to expand returns to a level in keeping with the new relationship between supply and foreign demand.[36] During the war average realizable returns increased, but the paper of debtors who serviced debts regularly and whose credit standing appeared to be secure continued to trade close to or at par. From this perspective it is evident that even the expanding sector of the Dutch economy composed chiefly of lending to governments suffered an erosion in its position before as well as after 1793. A low-cost credit structure that was still too high in cost to render overall factor costs in Dutch commerce and industry competitive in European markets was at the same time too low to permit maintenance of the Dutch capital stock in terms of real value.

The partial abrogation of debts by European governments during the Revolutionary and Napoleonic wars has long been assumed to have significantly eroded the Dutch capital stock entrusted to government lending during the eighteenth century.[37] Buist has recently objected to this assumption, arguing that those losses were more modest and that accumulated savings in the government loan sector were still, in 1815, substantial.[38] This problem is important because of the possibility that assets converted to government finance in the eighteenth century formed a capital stock that might then or later have been applied to such other uses as capital formation in industry. It remains theoretically possible, if unlikely, that a high survival rate would have lowered credit costs sufficiently to counterbalance high labor costs, particularly after 1830. Together with the selective protectionism introduced in 1816, low-cost credit might have made industrial entrepreneurship profitable in the northern provinces of the United Kingdom of the Netherlands despite increasing start-up costs tied to the lag behind Britain and Belgium. For that reason it may be useful to conclude by trying to

Chart 9-1. A composite index of selected foreign investments, 1793–1815.

reconstruct the portion of the eighteenth-century capital stock in government loans that survived the wars.

The stock available after 1815, enhanced continually by new savings, was unquestionably substantial, but the issue here is only the survival of the prewar stock in loans to government and its relative significance in terms of nineteenth-century prices and levels of government spending. To reach an approximation it is necessary to proceed through a series of estimates and assumptions toward a measure of the wartime impact of unrecapitalized annulments and inflationary losses inadequately compensated for by postwar deflation. Interim annuity losses will also be considered, but no attempt will be made to relate them to any consumption of capital by investors because of declining income. There were, inevitably, some losses on wartime realization in a depressed market, but those also cannot be established beyond the impression conveyed by Chart 9-1.[39]

Economic consequences

The outstanding balance of foreign government loans in the early 1790s has been calculated here at f. 500 to 650 million. Sums owing by domestic government at the same time may be estimated at f. 600 to 700 million.[40] Although debts owed at that time cannot be isolated completely from those owed in subsequent years, these amounts can be put to the test of annulments and of a commodity-price series.

Among foreign government debtors there were two sectors, the good pay and the poor pay. Minor differences disregarded, Britain, the United States, and Russia (including Poland) maintained service payments during the war so that there were no significant outright losses for Dutch investors who retained paper representing debts owed by those states. That sector accounts for some f. 340 million in loans to foreign governments outstanding in the early 1790s, more than half the total. In the poor-pay sector, composed of all other major borrowers, outright losses ranged in severity from virtual abrogation (Spain) to annulment of two-thirds of face value combined with unreinstated annuity losses (France and Sweden) to annuity arrears that were not subsequently recapitalized in full (Austria). Annulments cost somewhere between about f. 90 and 120 million of the prewar total, or between 16 and 21 percent of the mean of the estimated sum outstanding (f. 575 million).[41]

The Dutch Republic and its successors maintained the nominal value of the domestic debt outstanding in 1790 throughout the war. In 1814 two-thirds of a much enlarged total was converted to the status of a deferred debt, a category on which the annuity would not be paid except as that part of the debt that could gradually be reconverted to interest-bearing notes. The bulk of that was later, in 1841, reconverted, but at 6.8 percent of its face value. It is difficult to reach and to place chronologically a precise estimate of consequent losses, but because postwar prices reflect pessimism about the value of the deferred debt, it is plausible to view these as fully anticipated losses. They may conservatively be estimated at 40 percent of the 1790 total. Outright losses appear then to have amounted to a minimum of f. 330 to 400 million on a total of f. 1,100 to 1,350 million, or 24 to 36 percent.

Something may also be hazarded about losses on returns. Average net annuity receipts may be estimated for 1790 at about

4.75 percent from loans to foreign governments, and at 3 to 4 percent from loans to domestic governments, or at a total of some f. 42 to 59 million. The heaviest wartime losses in this area came early on, in the French suspension of annuity payments in 1793 and the virtual annulment of arrears in 1797. But because post-1790 increases in the nominal level of debts outstanding complicate the picture, it is impossible to proceed in the fashion followed to estimate losses on capital stock. Subsequent investments are included in a carefully detailed calculation of sums outstanding and interest receipts compiled in 1811 by the minister of the interior, Montalivet. That memorandum puts annual interest receipts from loans to foreign governments at nearly f. 22 million, excluding, however, sums past due from all debtors and current receipts from France.[42]

Receipts deteriorated in 1811, but not sufficiently to counterbalance Montalivet's omission of annuities paid by France. If, in the confusion of conversions and reconversions, annuity proceeds on the outstanding domestic debt of 1790 are assumed to have remained at the average of 3 to 4 percent until 1810, the annual losses from unpaid annuities probably reached about f. 10 million on the 1790 sum, and that all in the foreign sector until 1810. Postwar settlements restored part of those losses, but did not compensate for the annuity reduction adopted by the kingdom of the Netherlands, amounting to some f. 12 to 19 million per annum on the 1790 figure. Overall, unpaid annuities may conservatively be estimated at an annual average of f. 10 to 15 million during and after the war.

Inflationary losses can be gauged only on the basis of Posthumus's index of selected wholesale commodity prices, and that must be adjusted to another base period than 1721–45. The capital stock outstanding in 1790 was not, however, accumulated with regularity in its two sectors. The debt owed by domestic government reflected credit extended in the seventeenth as well as the eighteenth century. On the other hand, the largest part of loans to foreign governments outstanding in 1790 was accumulated after 1740. Without a time series on accumulation in both sectors, it is necessary to select a median date by approximation. Using the year 1770 will tend to underestimate rather than overestimate the impact of subsequent price trends.[43] Table 9-3 converts Posthumus's price index to a 1765–74 base, and projects

Table 9-3. *Inflationary trends and the 1790 capital stock*

Period	Index	Purchasing power of adjusted capital stock (in millions of guilders)
1760–64	89.9	957.7
1765–69	99.6	863.5
1770–74	100.4	856.6
1775–79	104.2	825.3
1780–84	119.2	721.5
1785–89	120.0	716.7
1790–94	155.5	553.1
1795–99	200.8	428.3
1800–04	195.5	439.9
1805–09	201.5	426.8
1810–14	287.6	299.0
1815–19	174.3	493.4
1820–24	—	—
1825–29	114.0	754.4
1830–34	111.7	770.0
1835–39	111.7	770.0
1840–44	117.7	730.7
1845–49	126.0	682.5
1850–54	112.5	764.4
1855–59	120.8	711.9
1840–59	119.2	721.5

the estimated purchasing power of the adjusted capital stock of 1790 over the period from 1760–4 through 1855–9.[44] Figures for each five-year period represent the estimated purchasing power of the adjusted 1790 stock if it had been redeemed at face value and spent on the commodities assessed by Posthumus without affecting price trends. Such assumptions have, of course, no existence in reality. Redemptions were spread over the period from the 1790s throughout the nineteenth century, and some liabilities from the 1798 Russian conversion were probably still outstanding in 1917.

An estimate of the impact of inflation depends on the date selected as the median for redemptions and on annulments after 1815 not already taken into account. The postwar deflationary trend, during which some paper losses suffered earlier by investors were restored, was replaced by a gradual recovery from

1840–4.[45] Relative price stability between 1840–4 and 1855–9 and the trend of rising prices thereafter permit an averaging of adjusted prices of that period and an approximation of what would appear to have been minimum inflationary losses to the adjusted 1790 capital stock at some f. 139 million, or 16 percent (as of 1840–59). Combined losses from annulments and inflation between 1793 and 1840 would therefore be estimated at no less than f. 469 to 539 million, or 35 to 49 percent of the 1790 capital stock.

If this range is reasonably accurate, investment in hothouse industrialization might have lost investors less than foreign lending. And in the long run early losses on industrial production for a protected but overcapitalized home market or for an open market but on uncompetitive terms would presumably have been replaced by profits. In the meantime, however, capital equipment bought under such terms would have lost value to much the same extent as government securities, becoming outmoded and difficult to replace in the absence of profits. Neither the actual choice (government lending) nor the putative choice (a temporarily unprofitable modern industrial sector) would have preserved the Dutch capital stock, although losses on industrial investment might to some degree have been counterbalanced merely by earlier-than-otherwise industrialization. Certainly there was no balancing feature in government lending; even the prestige of it was lost when Amsterdam ceased to be able to furnish further loans.

What, in summary, could the Dutch, blessed with advantages so appropriate to industry suited to high capital–labor ratios, have usefully done before the 1830s to further industrial development? Until about 1795 (after which disinvestment would have found few buyers and diminishing prices for government securities) capital could have been diverted to temporarily unprofitable use in industry for the sake of eventual gains.[46] But it would be unreasonable to think the future so clear as to permit many individual investors more or less simultaneously to decide that ultimate gains would justify immediate losses. Protection might have made Dutch industry prosper in a closed market and provided the Dutch with useful experience for a subsequent entry into world markets. But that too could have occurred only if certain short-term losses were accepted in return for possible long-term profits. Only a cut in factor costs would have attacked the problem directly and, given the nature of modern industry between the 1770s and the 1830s, only wages could have been cut sufficiently to have made the difference. But there were social and economic costs in such action as well. In the event, none of these things was done. The absence of action is itself evidence of the difficulty of finding a policy whose short-term disadvantages were not excessive. We have seen the future so clearly that we have lost sight of the compelling social, political, and economic costs that kept the Dutch from duplicating British and Belgian industrialization and of the unavoidability of an erosion of the Dutch capital stock before the time arrived when unusually high aggregate savings constituted a singular asset for industrialization. The problem was neither a disinclination nor an inability to invest in industry, but the possession of only one abundant resource, and that one not yet capable of redressing deficiencies and higher costs in other pertinent resources.

Construed as an unintentional holding action, lending to governments preserved what was, by eighteenth-century standards, still a sizable sum. But in terms of government spending after 1815, the stock surviving from 1790 was distinctly in accordance with the second-rate position of the Amsterdam capital market after 1815. Even more important, however, is the observation that interim losses were suffered in the face of a transformation in the volume of savings that can be considered substantial. In the eighteenth century aggregate Dutch savings had been sufficient, despite an expansion of international linkages, to keep Dutch credit costs equal to or less than those prevailing abroad. Whether that position, potentially favorable for commercial, financial, and industrial entrepreneurship, could have been retained had there been no serious inroads into the volume or real value of the 1790 capital stock is doubtful. In light of losses actually suffered, the surviving stock was no longer enough to give Dutch entrepreneurs an advantage in credit cost.

Not only did war and inflation erode Dutch savings and diminish the importance of the Amsterdam market, but the war also gravely injured the business community. None of the grand banking and commercial houses of the prewar period survived with their former position intact, and no new firms arose during the war to take their place. There was, first of all, the turnover inevitable among small partnerships in any lengthy period. But in sustained war and more frequent commercial and financial crises it was difficult to survive or to build a business. Hope & Co. emerged in 1815 as the one Amsterdam house able in some measure to compete and cooperate in government finance with firms in London, Paris, and Frankfurt, but it had in the meantime experienced serious reverses and a turnover in its core of partners that resulted in 1813 in the sale of ownership to Alexander Baring of London.[47]

Among other firms that figure in this narrative, A. & S. Boas and Hogguer & Co. had earlier fallen into difficulties and been liquidated. Likewise R. & Th. de Smeth and the Widow E. Croese & Son failed during the European commercial and financial crisis of 1810 and 1811. N. & J. & R. van Staphorst outlasted the war but faded after 1815.[48] On the other hand, a few firms continued to thrive during much of the war. The balance sheets indicate that Goll & Co., for example, enjoyed high profits in several years.[49]

But the more substantial problem, and the more accurate characterization of the war's impact on the business community, lay in the failure of new houses to emerge. Firms that had obvious potential for moving into government finance or other areas, like those led before the war by Pieter Stadnitski and Abraham van Ketwich, did not pass to a second generation of directors capable of extending their activities. The entrepreneurial groups from which successors to the dominant bankers of the 1780s were likeliest to have emerged – the commission agents and brokers of foreign lending and commerce – contracted during the war and in particular between 1810 and 1813.[50] Neither junior members nor outsiders often succeeded in carving out for themselves positions equivalent to those their elders had held. Instead there was a decline both in the membership of the banking community and in its capacity to seize opportunities, and thus in its ability to rejuvenate itself after the war. Nonetheless, Dutch bankers declined to apply to the structure of the firm the refinements in capital access developed earlier in government finance. Nor was the apparent paradox of maintaining a partnership form of business enterprise beside joint-stock and limited-liability capital market techniques acknowledged.

Still, Amsterdam practice in mobilizing resources for foreign and domestic lending had demonstrated the power of joint-stock capital formation applied outside overseas commercial monopolies. Loans continued to be raised for governments on an international scale after the Napoleonic wars, and the techniques applied or evolved in Amsterdam remained in use elsewhere. When European industry reached the point at which such methods of capital formation were necessary for continued expansion, the banking techniques required were available in a form that had years of experience behind it. The Amsterdam market had not taken any significant step toward industrial capitalism, but it had preserved and added to the stock of financial practices that would later be applied to industrial capitalism.

"By the gracious dispositions of Divine Providence, we have the best prospect of recovering Liberty and Independence, so miserably lost during nineteen years."[51] Liberty and independence were regained, but by late 1813 the authors of this lament, associates in the Holland Land Company investing in unsettled land in the United States, and members of other surviving Amsterdam houses could recognize the consequences of secular war and seemingly endemic crisis. The war's conclusion was greeted with joy, of course, but it could not be expected that a complete revival of the Amsterdam market would follow. Annulments, uncompensated annuity arrears, higher taxes, and inflationary inroads had not destroyed the capital stock nor spoiled the savings imperative of Dutch society, but even in the enlarged kingdom of the Netherlands there were not sufficient resources to restore the role in commercial finance and lending to governments that Amsterdam had played in the previous century.

ABBREVIATIONS

Manuscript locations

A.N.	Archives nationales, Paris
A.R.	Algemeen Rijksarchief, The Hague
E.H.B.	Nederlandsch Economisch-Historische Bibliotheek, Amsterdam
G.A.A., G.A.R.	Gemeente Archief (Amsterdam or Rotterdam)
N.E.H.A.	Nederlandsch Economisch-Historisch Archief, formerly in The Hague
R.A.	Riksarkivet (Stockholm)
U.B.A.	Universiteit Bibliotheek, Amsterdam

Manuscript sources

HLC	Archief Holland Land Company
KV	Archief Ketwich en Voombergh
SvH	Archief Stadnitski en van Heukelom
Pros.	Plannen, prospecti, statuten, leningen, loterijen, en negotiatiën (in five dossiers)

Printed material

Journals

AHR	*American Historical Review*
AESC	*Annales: économies, sociétés, civilisations*
BMHG	*Bijdragen en mededelingen van het historisch genootschap*
EHJ	*Economisch-historisch jaarboek, from 1970 Economisch- en sociaal-historisch jaarboek*
EHR	*English Historical Review*
EcHR	*Economic History Review*
FHS	*French Historical Studies*

Abbreviations

JEEH	*Journal of European Economic History*
JEH	*Journal of Economic History*
JGA	*Jaarboek van het genootschap Amstelodamum*
JMH	*Journal of Modern History*
RHES	*Revue d'histoire économique et sociale*
SEHR	*Scandinavian Economic History Review*
TvG	*Tijdschrift voor geschiedenis*
TvR	*Tijdschrift voor rechtsgeschiedenis*
ZGWA	*Zeeuwsch genootschap der wetenschappen, Archief*

Other

A.H.	Harold C. Syrett, ed., *The Papers of Alexander Hamilton*
D.T.	Robert Fruin and H. T. Colenbrander, eds., *Dépêches van Thulemeyer, 1763–1788*
F.P.A.R.	*Finances publiques d'ancien régime; finances publiques contemporaines*
GS	H. T. Colenbrander, ed., *Gedenkstukken der algemeene geschiedenis van Nederland van 1795 tot 1840*
De Koopman	*De Koopman, of bijdragen ten opbouw van Neerlands koophandel en zeevaard*
Metelerkamp	Rutger Metelerkamp, *Tableau statistique de la Hollande en 1804*
MNM	*Staatkundige historie van Holland . . . benevens de maandelijksche nederlandsche mercurius*
NNJ	*Nieuwe nederlandsche jaarboeken*
[Oudermeulen]	[C. van den Oudermeulen], *Recherches sur le commerce, ou idées rélatives aux intérêts des différens peuples de l'Europe*
Posthumus	N. W. Posthumus, *Inquiry into the History of Prices in Holland*
Ricard	Samuel Ricard, *Traité général du commerce*
T.J.	Julian P. Boyd, ed., *The Papers of Thomas Jefferson*
Weeveringh	J. J. Weeveringh, *Handleiding tot de geschiedenis der staatsschulden*

NOTES

Chapter 1. Introduction

1 As is appropriate for the preindustrial era and for a book about a capital market, capital is taken here to mean assets of any type for which there were markets where those assets (land, trade commodities, commercial paper, urban real estate, securities, or other kinds of property) could reliably be transformed into specie or converted from one type to another. The phrase "Amsterdam capital market" refers to the sector of lending activity in which individuals, private and public companies, and governments raised long-term credit by issuing loans divided into shares and merchandised among the investing public at large, but here the focus will fall on government borrowing, which dominated the market apparatus. This characterization of the Amsterdam market excludes such important types of activity as commercial lending and short-term government borrowing. Foreign government loan proceeds were often transferred to debtor states by means of commercial drafts, and discounting such paper was always one of the options open to rentiers considering government lending. Moreover, all states used short-term credit instruments for day-to-day functions, although usually only Dutch governments circulated those instruments on Dutch capital markets. And of course Amsterdam provided circulating credit essential to manufacturing, commerce, and certain agricultural enterprises. This characterization also excludes the important but not yet explored sector of short- and long-term loans granted by Dutch entrepreneurs and rentiers to individuals, another alternative to lending to government. These types of credit will be taken up only where they influenced the long-term government loan apparatus of Dutch capital markets or where they figure in interpreting the economic effects of foreign government lending.

This description of capital and of the Amsterdam market is obviously broader and different in kind than the definitions applied by economic historians who seek to account for technological change and industrial growth, and who are concerned with capital formation in industry and specifically with formation in capital equipment that yields higher productivity. (See Phyllis Deane, "The Role of Capital in the Industrial Revolution," *Explorations in*

Economic History, X, no. 4 (Summer, 1973), 349–64, on the problem of defining the concept of capital in early industrial revolutions and on capital in the English industrial revolution; and Joel Mokyr, "Capital, Labor and the Delay of the Industrial Revolution in the Netherlands," *EHJ*, XXXVIII (1975), 280–99, and *idem*, *Industrialization in the Low Countries, 1795–1850* (New Haven, Conn., 1976), passim, on hindrances to capital formation in Dutch industry.) There were substantial fixed capital investments in the eighteenth-century Dutch economy, most notably in urban industry and among the assets of merchants and international trading companies. For the most part, however, Dutch industry and shipping employed traditional technologies and therefore the productivity of their fixed capital assets and labor would not appear to have increased significantly over the course of the century.

2 Data for reconstructing the distribution of assets across all sectors of the Dutch economy are unavailable, but it may be assumed that both the absolute and relative volume of savings in foreign goverment lending increased during the second half of the eighteenth century. Alice Carter's survey of the collateral-succession tax inventories, which tends to understate foreign investment, supports that assumption. Alice C. Carter, "Dutch Foreign Investment, 1738–1800," *Economica*, XX, n.s. (November, 1953), 322–40.

3 P. W. Klein, *Kapitaal en stagnatie tijdens het hollandse vroegkapitalisme* (Rotterdam, 1967), pp. 7–10. Also *De Koopman*,VI, 132, for a sarcastic expression of sympathy for the lack of investment outlets for the rich by "de Welmeenende" (the well-intentioned). Mokyr, *Industrialization*, pp. 212–15, has objected to Klein's use of a theoretical model appropriate for interpreting short-term shifts in investment demand to account for long-term trends in the Dutch economy. The inadequacies of the explanatory model aside, Klein's observation points to a long-term phenomenon of insufficiently profitable investment alternatives.

4 Herbert Lüthy, *La banque protestante en France de la révocation de l'édit de Nantes à la Révolution*, 2 vols. (Paris, 1959–61), II, 76, 488–545, and 555–6.

5 William Short to Alexander Hamilton, 18 Dec. 1790, in *A.H.*, VII, 357.

6 The chief source of foreign capital appears to have been Brabant. See Marten G. Buist, *At Spes Non Fracta: Hope & Co., 1770–1815* (The Hague, 1974), pp. 99–100.

7 Foreign-exchange earnings from annuity receipts appear to have accounted for additions to the sum of loans outstanding to foreign governments between 1763 and 1790 (see Table 9-1). However, individual investors undoubtedly spent most of their annuity income in other directions. If a reliable eighteenth-century estimate of savings ratios (see p. 12) is applied here, annuity earnings would have been reinvested at a rate between 25 and 37.5 percent. The remainder would then have been drawn from a continuing shift out of traditional investment sectors. See also Chap. 4.

8 Edward Heyvaert, *De ontwikkeling van de moderne bank- en krediettechniek tijdens de zestiende en zeventiende eeuw in Europa en te Amsterdam in het bijzonder* (n.p., 1975), p. 97.

9 Frustrations were vented in part in the Patriot movement of the 1780s. See

C. H. E. de Wit, *De strijd tussen aristocratie en democratie in Nederland, 1780–1848* (Heerlen, 1965), pp. 15–60 and 79–105; and E. H. Kossmann, "The Crisis of the Dutch State, 1780–1813: Nationalism, Federalism, and Unitarism," in J. S. Bromley and E. H. Kossmann, eds., *Britain and the Netherlands* (The Hague, 1971), IV, 157–75.

10 An attack launched in *De Koopman*, IV, 273–84, after the crisis of 1772–3 illustrates the tensions involved in that relaxation. In the view presented there the cashiers (*kassiers*), who handled payments on account, had ceased to fill their traditional and "proper" service function to merchants and, in undercutting the hierarchy of commercial roles, had unbalanced the structure and contributed to the crisis.

11 Klein, *Kapitaal en stagnatie*, p. 8. Mokyr, *Industrialization*, p. 213, argues that Klein's "claim that the distribution of income was becoming more skewed since the mid-seventeenth century is unsupported" and conflicts with evidence Mokyr has gathered about sustained high wage levels and highly developed poor relief in the Republic. Wages were high and poor relief comparatively generous, but such conditions are not inconsistent with an increasing maldistribution of income or wealth as long as income was not exclusively a factor of economic production within the Republic. International commercial and banking activities provided at least a wealthy elite with income immune to the decline of some sectors of the domestic economy. For a discussion of eighteenth-century views on the distribution of wealth see Joh. de Vries, *De economische achteruitgang der republiek in de achttiende eeuw* (2nd ed., Leiden, 1968), pp. 170–2.

The rate at which savings accumulated in all sectors and combined value and distribution of those savings cannot be estimated reliably. Theo P. M. de Jong, "Sociale verandering in de neergaande Republiek," *EHJ*, XXXV (1972), 3, n. 4, puts national resources at some f. 10 billion and foreign investments at 20 to 25 percent of that as of 1780. Both figures are tentative, and my own impression is that both are too high even if the latter is taken to include foreign commercial investment. See also Metelerkamp, pp. 28–9, for some steps toward a sector-by-sector reconstruction of resources as of 1804.

12 Violet Barbour, *Capitalism in Amsterdam in the 17th Century* (Ann Arbor, 1963 reprint), pp. 28–9.

13 Cited by ibid., p. 29, from Sir William Temple, *Observations upon the United Provinces of the Netherlands* (1673), reprinted in 1932, p. 102.

14 Simon Kuznets, *Economic Growth and Structure: Selected Essays* (New York, 1965), p. 263, dealing with developed economies; and Sebastien de Vauban, *Projet d'une dixme royale . . .* (new ed.; Brussels, 1708), pp. 3–4, dealing not with savings ratios but with the portion of the population with comfortable wealth and thus, by implication, able to accumulate assets.

15 Hope to Auckland, August 1791, in G. W. Vreede, *Mr. Laurens Pieter van de Spiegel en zijne tijdgenooten, 1737–1800*, 4 vols. (Middelburg, 1874–7), IV, 386.

16 Gouverneur Morris, *A Diary of the French Revolution*, ed. by B. C. Davenport, 2 vols. (London, 1939), I, 447–8.

17 B. E. de Muinck, *Een regentenhuishouding omstreeks 1700* (The Hague,

1965), pp. 50–2 and 79. Van Ellemeet's savings accumulated at the ratios shown in the table. Van Ellemeet retired as receiver general in 1707 and with the gradual liquidation of his affairs his income fell. Total savings over the period from 1685 through 1712 amounted to some f. 1,123,000.

1685–89	about half of an average income of some f. 20,000 per annum
1690–94	57% of f. 44,000
1695–99	64 of 66,000
1700–04	67 of 92,000
1705–09	67 of 105,000
1710–12	41 of 60,000

The monetary system in use in trade and finance in the Dutch Republic was based on the florin or guilder, divided into 20 stuivers (each of 2 deniers or groten), and each stuiver into 16 penningen. A sum including stuivers and penningen was written set off by commas, thus f. 121,17,3. Commercial handbooks from that period (for example, Ricard, II, 2–16) outline the types of coins in circulation as well as exchange usages. See also John J. McCusker, *Money and Exchange in Europe and America, 1600–1775* (Chapel Hill, N.C., 1978). Wherever guilder amounts appear herein they refer to current rather than bank money unless otherwise indicated.

18 Buist, *Hope & Co.*, app. G, pp. 520–5, covering 1762–1815.

19 Ibid., pp. 37, 42–3, 486–94, and 525.

20 G.A.R., notary Willem Boon, XXXVII, 33. 1763.

21 This figure includes securities but not personal property or real estate. For estate inventories (which do not value assets) and related documents see G.A.A., notaries A. van Beem, 15150/113b and 114, 15151/186 and 201, 15155/178, and 15164/181; J. Fabius, 19480/161; and T. M. de Man, 19995/977.

22 G.A.A., notary A. van Beem, 15137/228. In 1789 N. & J. van Staphorst & Hubbard, a major banking house that shared direction of loans to the United States with W. & J. Willink, was capitalized at only f. 200,000. P. J. van Winter, *Het aandeel van den amsterdamschen handel aan den opbouw van het amerikaansche gemeenebest*, 2 vols. (The Hague, 1927–33), I, 200, n. 4.

23 G.A.A., Archief van Eeghen, Ad/1, for partial information on Pieter and Christiaan van Eeghen; *idem*, Archief Brants, 641–2, on Couderc, Brants & Changuion, and Familiearchief ten Broeke, Willink, ten Broeke Willink en van Leuvenigh Willink, 494, 15–17, on Bernard Willink; and R. Mees, *Gedenkschrift over de firma R. Mees & Zoonen ter gelegenheid van haar tweehonderdjarig bestaan, 1720–1920* (n.p., n.d.), app. 14, giving Rudolf Mees's assets in 1796 at f. 709,239,11,8, of which 21 percent was invested in the firm and the remainder in real estate, promissory notes and loans to individuals, foreign and domestic government loans, and other areas. See also G.A.A., Archief Brants, 78 and 126–7 for current assets and 77 and 123–5 for a ledger and journals of Jan and Jan Jacob Brants, substantial rentiers who

combined active business with silent partnerships and portfolio and real estate management on a grand scale.

24 J. Rogge, *Het handelshuis van Eeghen: Proeve eener geschiedenis van een amsterdamsche handelshuis* (Amsterdam, 1949), p. 66.

25 Sir John Carr, *A Tour Through Holland Along the Right and Left Banks of the Rhine . . . in . . . 1806* (Philadelphia, 1807), pp. 16–17, noted the practice of passing apparel on from generation to generation and (p. 181) remarked on the "invincible industry, the caution, and frugality of the people."

26 The most thorough study of the plantation loans is Johannes Petrus van de Voort, *De westindische plantages van 1720 tot 1795: Financiën en handel* (Eindhoven, 1973); but see also J. Hudig, *De west-indische zaken van Ferrand Whaley Hudig, 1759–1797* (Amsterdam, 1922); W. W. van der Meulen, "Beschrijving van eenige westindische-plantageleeningen," *BMHG*, XXV (1904), 490–580; Charles H. Wilson, *Anglo-Dutch Commerce and Finance in the Eighteenth Century* (Cambridge, 1941), pp. 182–6; and A. J. A. Quintus Bosz, *Geld, credietbehoefte en negotiaties in Suriname voor 1865*, Address at the University of Surinam (1971), pp. 7–25.

27 On the defects of the plantation loans see, in addition to sources cited in the previous note, Elias Luzac, *Hollandsch rijkdom, of tafereel van nederlandsch koophandel en zeevaart*, 2nd ed., 4 vols. (Leiden, 1801), II, 316–20 and IV, 214–18; *De Koopman*, passim in the numbers for 1773; *D.T.*, p. 167, dispatch of 13 Sept. 1776; and Henry Brougham, *An Inquiry into the Colonial Policy of the European Powers*, 2 vols. (Edinburgh, 1803), I, 357.

28 European rulers and government officials sometimes acknowledged the role played by the Amsterdam market in government finance. For instance in 1774 Frederick the Great requested of his ambassador in The Hague information on loans to Austria and Russia and, late in 1781, when a renewal of the Russo-Turkish conflict threatened, inquired about Russia's credit standing. *D.T.*, pp. 132 and 294, dispatches of 22 July 1774 and 15 Jan. 1782 respectively. (The ambassador's reports were systematically opened and copied in The Hague (ibid., p. v).) On the same point see also ibid., p. 270, dispatch of 24 July 1781; and *NNJ*, 1793, 180ff.

29 P. J. Blok, *Geschiedenis van het nederlandsche volk*, 8 vols. (Groningen, 1892–1908), VI, 294, n. 4, refers to a list of foreign loans in the Steyn papers at the Rijksarchief giving Amsterdam issues in an unspecified period before 1772 at nearly f. 100 million excluding investment in the English funds but including plantation as well as government loans. Dutch investments in the English funds are assumed here to have reached about f. 200 million (78 percent of £25 million at current exchange rates) during the Seven Years' War and to have remained at that level until the War of the American Revolution. See below, pp. 123–4 for further information.

30 This figure, which excludes nongovernment foreign investment outside the English joint-stock companies, falls close to one of the more conservative estimates of 1795 putting the total at f. 700 to 800 million but perhaps excluding some sectors. *GS*, I, 669.

31 Estimates of the balance outstanding and net annual additions to it are based on a compilation from loans to foreign governments dealt with in subsequent

chapters. My estimate of new lending coincides with a figure offered by Henry Hope in August 1791 (Vreede, *Van de Spiegel*, IV, 386–7). Hope put the flow at f. 20 million per annum over the previous three years, and listed all loans to foreign governments and investment undertakings in foreign government annuities at f. 34 million from 1 July 1790 to 1 Aug. 1791. Of that f. 8 million (23.5 percent) was said to have been drawn from reimbursements of prior advances.

32 Such estimates went as high as f. 1.5 billion (for 1783). De Vries, *Economische achteruitgang*, p. 65, citing *Hollands rijkdom*, IV, 310. For other estimates from the period before 1790 see ibid., pp. 65–66; *Encyclopédie méthodique, économie politique et diplomatique*, 4 vols. (Paris, 1784–8), III, pt. 2, 780 (at 1.6 to 1.7 billion livres tournois, or some f. 750 to 800 million); Adriaan Kluit, *Iets over den laatsten engelschen oorlog met de republiek . . .* (Amsterdam, 1794), p. 271, citing the *Vaderlandsche historie*, III, 13 (as of 1781 more than f. 300 million in England and not less than that in France); and Eberhard August Wilhelm von Zimmermann, *A Political Survey of the Present State of Europe. . .* (London, 1787), p. 183 (loans outstanding in 1781 at f. 585 million, including f. 165 million in England, f. 170 million in France, and f. 250 million in Germany, Denmark, Sweden, and Russia together).

33 Joh. de Vries, ed., "Van de Spiegel's 'Schets tot een vertoog over de intrinsique en relative magt van de Republijk' (1782)," *EHJ*, XXVII (1958), 92–3. The plantation loans, totaling f. 60 to 80 million, are excluded from the estimates given in the text.

34 *NNJ*, 1789, 729, provides a calculation based on the prospectuses of loans to the effect that the Republic earned between f. 50 and 60 million annually in interest, excluding income from England and France. At an average return of 4.5 percent, that would have placed loans at more than f. 1 billion plus whatever was invested in England and France, an excessive figure. Also W. M. Keuchenius, *De inkomsten en uitgaven der Bataafsche Republiek voorgesteld in eene nationale balans* (Amsterdam, 1803), p. 11: a billion guilders in foreign loans at an unspecified earlier point, and some f. 800 million as of 1802 or 1803. Note that throughout "billion" is employed according to American usage (viz., 1,000,000,000).

35 Metelerkamp, pp. 28–9. Other estimates may be found in I. J. Brugmans, *Paardenkracht en mensenmacht* (The Hague, 1961), pp. 18–19; and Brougham, *Colonial Policy of the European Powers*, I, 299–300, as much as or more than £300 million (or about f. 3.3 billion), with two-thirds of that in foreign loans.

36 For an introduction to eighteenth-century taxation see Gabriel Ardant, "Financial Policy and Economic Infrastructure of Modern States and Nations," in Charles Tilly, ed., *The Formation of National States in Western Europe* (Princeton, N.J., 1975), pp. 174–214; *idem*, *Histoire de l'impôt*, 2 vols. (n.p., 1971–2), I, 587–99, and II, 13–130; and *idem*, *Théorie sociologique de l'impôt*, 2 vols. (Paris, 1965), I, 53ff. and passim.

37 P. G. M. Dickson, *The Financial Revolution in England: A Study in the Development of Public Credit, 1688–1756* (New York, 1967), p. 333, men-

tions a Dutch loan in England in 1749. No other references to foreign borrowing on the part of Dutch governments were uncovered. The available data do not permit assessment of the quantity of foreign capital invested in Dutch government loans, although the low yield must have discouraged such investment. Alfred Cobban, *Ambassadors and Secret Agents: The Diplomacy of the First Earl of Malmesbury at The Hague* (London, 1954), p. 81, mentions without details an English loan in the late 1780s to the Zeeland chamber of the Dutch East India Company, and there and on pp. 88–9 other cases where advances were considered but not made.

38 Quoted by Joseph Albert Ernst, "Currency in the Era of the American Revolution: A History of Colonial Paper Money Practices and British Monetary Policies, 1764–1781" (Ph.D. diss., Univ. of Wisconsin, 1962), p. 398, published with some omissions (Chapel Hill, N.C., 1973). Also Gouverneur Morris to the same effect in a letter to George Washington, 26 Oct. 1778, in Edmund C. Burnett, ed., *Letters of Members of the Continental Congress*, 8 vols. (Washington, 1921–36), cited by Ernst, p. 398.

39 De Vries, *Economische achteruitgang*, pp. 19–57, esp. p. 31; and Charles H. Wilson, "The Economic Decline of the Netherlands," *EcHR*, IX, no. 2 (May, 1939), 111–27. Stagnation in the carrying trade did not go unnoticed. In the middle of the eighteenth century a proposal was advanced to lower tariffs, but its introduction would have reduced tax revenues at a time when an unstable international situation required greater revenues for naval preparedness. Subsequent efforts in the same direction were also unsuccessful. See Johannes Hovy, *Het voorstel van 1751 tot instelling van een beperkt vrijhavenstelsel in de republiek* (Groningen, 1966); and Chap. 9.

40 De Vries, *Economische achteruitgang*, passim, esp. pp. 167–84.

41 On the commission trade and short-term credit and on marine insurance usages in Amsterdam see Ricard, I, 198–208.

42 De Vries, *Economische achteruitgang;* and Klein, *Kapitaal en stagnatie.* There were contemporary opponents of the transition and of lending to foreign governments, such as the editor of *De Koopman* (e.g., III, 3–4 and VI, 122–3); and Cornelis Zillezen, *Wijsgeerig onderzoek, wegens Neerlands opkomst, bloei, en welvaard. . .* (Amsterdam, 1796), pp. 198ff. The Prussian ambassador reported on that opposition in a dispatch of 11 Feb. 1777, in *D.T.*, p. 173. On opposition in the pages of *De Borger,* which appeared between September 1778 and August 1780, see Th. H. Nefkens, "De denkbeelden van De Borger omtrent de economische achteruitgang der Republiek in de achttiende eeuw," *Economie*, XXXVI, no. 10 (July, 1972), 489ff. But there were also a few outspoken proponents, e.g., NNJ, 1789, 725–9. See also L. G. J. Verberne, *Het sociale en economische motief in de bataafse tijd* (Tilburg, 1947), pp. 5ff.

43 The same observation may apply to country estates and artistic and literary works, in which several Amsterdam merchants, bankers, and rentiers bought extensively. See, for example, Thomas Jefferson's Memorandum on a Tour. . . , in *T.J.*, XIII, 8–12; Felix Faulcon, *Voyages et opuscules* (Paris, 1805), p. 59; and Sir John Sinclair, *The Correspondence of the Right Honourable John Sinclair. . .* , 2 vols. (London, 1831), II, 184.

44 Published commentary on the increasing cost of necessities appeared at least as early as 1769. *De Ondersoeker*, I, 25 (reference supplied by Johan de Vries).

45 Posthumus, I, ci. The commodities include agricultural and nonagricultural items (ibid., I, lxxxiii–lxxxiv).

46 Paper currency issues were resisted by the Dutch business community and were used on no more than a small scale and in the short term, such as in 1794.

Chapter 2. The Amsterdam capital market

1 Ricard, I, 74–80; J. G. van Dillen, *Van rijkdom en regenten* (The Hague, 1970), pp. 256–69, 439–41, 444–7, and 641–5; *idem*, "The Bank of Amsterdam," in *idem*, ed., *History of the Principal Public Banks* (The Hague, 1934), pp. 79–123; Z. W. Sneller, "De rotterdamsche wisselbank 1635–1812," pp. 107–84 (esp. pp. 128–49 on agio) in *Rotterdams bedrijfsleven in het verleden* (Amsterdam, 1940); Violet Barbour, *Capitalism in Amsterdam in the 17th Century* (Ann Arbor, 1963 reprint), pp. 43–9; Edward Heyvaert, *De ontwikkeling van de moderne bank- en krediettechniek tijdens de zestiende en zeventiende eeuw in Europa en te Amsterdam in het bijzonder* (n.p., 1975), pp. 108–30; and, for an eighteenth-century analysis based on information supplied by the banker Henry Hope, Adam Smith, *An Inquiry into the Nature and Causes of the Wealth of Nations*, ed. by Edwin Cannan (New York, 1937), pp. 446–55.

2 Ricard, I, 73, describes Amsterdam cashiers merely as "personnes d'une réputation bien établie & d'une probité reconnue, à qui les négocians & d'autres particuliers riches confient des sommes considérables d'argent comptant." For more extensive information see van Dillen, *Rijkdom*, pp. 451 and 600; *idem*, "Het bedrijfsleven van Amsterdam in de achttiende eeuw," in Antoine Everard d'Ailly, ed., *Zeven eeuwen Amsterdam*, 6 vols. (Amsterdam, 1945–51), IV, 87; W. F. H. Oldewelt, ed., *Kohier van de personeele quotisatie te Amsterdam over het jaar 1742*, 2 vols. (Amsterdam, 1945), I, 18–20; W. C. Mees, *Proeve eener geschiedenis van het bankwezen in Nederland gedurende den tijd der republiek* (Rotterdam, 1838), pp. 25–7 and 250–9; *De Koopman*, IV, 273–94; E. E. de Jong-Keesing, *De economische crisis van 1763 te Amsterdam* (n.p., 1939), pp. 94–5, 153–4, and 161–5; and M. G. Emeis, *Honderdzestigjaar kassierderij* (Amsterdam, 1966), pp. 5–10. Richard Hayes, *The Negociator's Magazine . . .* , 11th ed. rev. by Benjamin Webb (London, 1777), p. 263, deals with the division of current and bank-money drafts among Amsterdam's trading associates, although by 1777 that information was out of date.

3 M. F. J. Smith, *Tijd-affaires in effecten aan de amsterdamsche beurs* (The Hague, 1919), pp. 1–10 and 39–101; J. G. van Dillen, "Isaac le Maire en de handel der Oost-Indische Compagnie," *EHJ*, XVI (1930), 1–165; and Joseph de la Vega, *Confusion de confusiones (1688), Portions Descriptive of the Amsterdam Stock Exchange*, ed. and trans. by H. Kellenbenz (Boston, 1957).

4 The only eighteenth-century source comparable to de la Vega is [Isaac de Pinto], *Tableau, ou exposé de ce qu'on appelle le commerce, ou plutôt le jeu d'actions, en Hollande*, in *Traité de la circulation et du crédit* (Amsterdam, 1771), pp. 289–312. But see also Elias Luzac, *Hollandsch rijkdom, of tafereel van nederlandsch koophandel en zeevaart* . . . , 4 vols., 2nd ed. (Leiden, 1801), II, 304–20.

5 [De Pinto], *Le jeu d'actions*, pp. 291–9; and J. G. van Dillen, "Effectenkoersen aan de amsterdamsche beurs, 1723–1794," *EHJ*, XVII (1931), 1–46.

6 Smith, *Tijd-affaires*, p. 148; and Ricard, I, 210.

7 There were nonetheless *op naam* notes outstanding in 1798 when provincial debts were amalgamated into the national debt. Weeveringh, I, 17–20.

The term "*in blanco*" had earlier distinguished futures transactions not based on any actual exchange of securities from real exchanges. Joh. de Vries, *De economische achteruitgang der republiek in de achttiende eeuw*, 2nd ed. (Leiden, 1968), pp. 61–2.

8 At that time it was still customary to draw notarial accords for transfers (e.g., G.A.A., notary G. van der Groe, 6588/419–21), a practice that fell into disuse in the eighteenth century.

9 See, e.g., the management accounts of Jan and Jan Jacob Brants in G.A.A., Archief Brants, 78, 126, and 127. The Brants, father and son, bought and sold securities, but tended to hold paper until it was redeemed.

10 Substitution portfolios were often composed principally of high-yield securities, but even when annuity payments were suspended managers did not try to compensate by speculative trading. See, e.g., the case of a tontine organized in 1770 and based in part on plantation loans that collapsed in the crisis of 1772–3 in N.E.H.A., Kleine aanwinsten, 55, with records to 1847.

11 Similar institutions were organized in other municipalities. According to J. Melles, *Het huys van leeninge: Geschiedenis van de oude lombarden en de stedelijke bank van lening te Rotterdam, 1325–1950* (The Hague, 1950), p. 77, there were 84 municipal and provincial loan banks in the Republic in 1798. In addition to ibid., pp. 42–95 and passim, see G.A.A., Archief van het college van commissarissen van de Bank van Leening van 1614 tot 1863; L. Jansen, *Geschiedenis van de stads bank van lening te Amsterdam, 1614–1964* (Amsterdam, 1964), pp. 9–76; van Dillen, *Rijkdom*, p. 267; *idem*, "Bank of Amsterdam," pp. 96–100; and Philopolis (pseud.), *An Account of the Bank of Loan at Amsterdam Commonly Called the Lombard* (London, 1733).

12 Jansen, *Stads bank van lening te Amsterdam*, pp. 53–4; and Melles, *Het huys van leeninge*, pp. 122–38. Also the latter, p. 75, for figures on Rotterdam loan bank credits in 1794: 71,563 loans amounting to f. 508,039. Of those only 101 exceeded f. 500, and the average in that category was about f. 996.

Ricard, I, 80, found that the Amsterdam loan bank "n'a presque aucun rapport avec . . . le Commerce général," although in both Amsterdam and Rotterdam the banks extended credit to municipal treasuries and the West India Company.

13 The interest on loan-bank extensions of f. 500 or more declined in Amsterdam

from 9 percent in 1617 to 6 percent from the middle of the seventeenth century until after 1800 and, in Rotterdam, from 8 percent in 1635 to 4 percent in 1738 and thereafter. Jansen, *Stads bank van lening te Amsterdam*, pp. 23 and 59; and Melles, *Het huys van leeninge*, pp. 65–6, respectively.

14 Van Dillen, *Rijkdom*, pp. 265–8 and 641–3. Such credits remained well within the limits of the bank's assets and the ability of borrowers to repay until the latter part of the eighteenth century. Then the East India Company was unable to honor its obligations, but the city treasury, which had borrowed from the bank to lend to the company, assumed those liabilities.

15 For some indication of the scale of transactions by such firms as Clifford & Zoonen; Hope & Co.; R. & Th. de Smeth; Horneca, Hugguer & Co.; Muilman & Zoonen; and Andries Pels & Soonen see: de Jong-Keesing, *Economische crisis van 1763*, pp. 66–74 and 185–8; and Marten G. Buist, *At Spes Non Fracta: Hope & Co., 1770–1815* (The Hague, 1974), pp. 6 and 476–85. Both sources draw on bank records, which of course do not include all transactions. The prevailing commission in the early 1760s for the *grote banquiers*, who handled numerous transactions, was ¼ percent and, for houses only incidentally involved in transfers, ⅓ percent.

16 On the advent of discounting see van Dillen, *Rijkdom*, pp. 451–2; and Heyvaert, *Bank- en krediettechniek*, pp. 121–8.

17 Elias Luzac estimated total current acceptances for foreign accounts in 1778 at f. 200 million. A. M. de Jong, *Geschiedenis van de Nederlandsche Bank*, 4 vols. (Haarlem, 1967 reprint), I, 2 and n. 1, citing Luzac, *La richesse de la Hollande*, II, 127–8. See also Luzac, *Hollandsch rijkdom*, IV, 228–9; and Ricard, I, 204–7. André Houwink, *Acceptcrediet, economische en bankpolitieke beschouwingen over den in het bankaccept belichaamden credietvorm* (Amsterdam, 1929), p. 24, dates the appearance of acceptance credit in the Dutch Republic from about 1720.

18 On advances on commodities see Ricard, I, 207–8. According to this edition (1781), interest charges were 3 to 4 percent. The largest body of potential information on such advances exists in notarial accords between borrowers and lenders, but in the absence of general indexes the Amsterdam notarial records present virtually an impenetrable mélange of data.

19 G.A.A., Archief Brants, 126 and 127 on Jan Jacob Brants, 1773 to 1800; and de Jong-Keesing, *Economische crisis van 1763*, p. 84, citing Desolate Boedelskamer records on the insurance underwriter Adriaan Scharff from February until July 1763. Brants's extensions ranged from f. 80 to 50,000, with the larger advances presumably representing investment in commercial, industrial, and real estate enterprises as a silent partner. In six months Scharff granted 25 separate loans totaling f. 248,000 and ranging from f. 4,200 to 31,000.

20 Ibid., pp. 83–6.

21 See n. 13 on loan-bank rates, and van Dillen, "Bank of Amsterdam," p. 95, on the declining interest rate on short-term extensions from the Bank of Amsterdam to the East India Company (from 6.25 percent in 1615 to 2.5 percent between 1723 and 1746, and 3 percent from 1748 to 1782).

22 G.A.A., Archief Brants, 126 and 127, for data on over 50 advances from the

period mentioned or carried over from earlier extensions by Jan Brants. De Jong-Keesing, *Economische crisis van 1763*, p. 84, suggests that in 1763 private loans were usually granted at 4 percent and on 75 percent of the value of assets mortgaged. On the margin see also Ricard, I, 208.

23 Guy Antonetti, *Une maison de banque à Paris au XVIIIe siècle: Greffulhe Montz et Cie (1789–1793)* (Paris, [1963]), p. 145.

24 Ibid., pp. 198–9, citing rates for the early summer of 1789, a period of tight credit, at 5 to 6 percent, and 3.5 percent for August 6, after the critical point had passed. Ricard, I, 207, gives the Amsterdam discount rate at 2 to 3 percent for bills of two or three months, but that information may not have been revised for the 1781 edition.

25 De Vries, *Economische achteruitgang*, pp. 78–9.

26 The standard source on the crisis of 1763 is de Jong-Keesing, *Economische crisis van 1763*. See also W. P. Sautijn Kluit, *De amsterdamsche beurs in 1763 en 1773* (Amsterdam, 1865), pp. 1–63; J. G. van Dillen, "De beurs crisis te Amsterdam in 1763," *TvG*, XXXVII (1922), 241–53; W. M. F. Mansvelt and J. G. van Dillen, "De crisis van 1763 en de economische achteruitgang van Amsterdam (een discussie)," *TvG*, XXXVII (1922), 400–8; and W. M. F. Mansvelt, "Het amsterdamsche acceptbedrijf en credietwezen in de 18e eeuw," *Algemeen handelsblad*, 25 Oct. 1922.

27 De Jong-Keesing, *Economische crisis van 1763*, pp. 121 and 177–80.

28 Kluit, *Amsterdamsche beurs in 1763 en 1773*, pp. 65–128; *De Koopman*, IV, 294–6; and de Vries, *Economische achteruitgang*, pp. 77–9.

29 G.A.A., Archief Thesaurien ordinaris, Stads beleening kamer, 1, Notulenboek. See also J. C. Breen, "Eene amsterdamsche credit-instelling uit het laatst der achttiende eeuw," *TvG*, XV (1900), 138–43; G.A.A., N.11.247.12; and U.B.A., 565B14, plans d'emprunts, pt. 9. Loans were made at 3.5 percent on securities and 4 percent on commodities for three to six months, and for up to 75 percent of the value as determined by independent brokers. Altogether, credits totaling f. 522,000 were arranged between January and June. As a point of comparison, Clifford's liabilities were about f. 4.6 million. Van Dillen, *Rijkdom*, p. 612, n. 29.

30 N.E.H.A., Pros., III, 181; NNJ, 1781, 147–9; and Breen, "Eene amsterdamsche credit-instelling," 143–55. Using resources of the Bank of Amsterdam, the municipal treasury provided a drawing power of up to f. 2 million. See also Antonetti, *Greffulhe Montz & Cie*, pp. 198–9; and NNJ, 1789, 725–7, on a minor crisis in Amsterdam in the early summer of 1789 and a proposal for a discount bank.

31 De Jong, *Nederlandsche Bank*, I, 4–35, on the development toward a central credit institution in the Bank of the Netherlands.

32 Antonetti, *Greffulhe Montz & Cie*, pp. 230–2, discusses the crisis at Paris in 1792 in which 800,000 l.t. was subscribed in support from Amsterdam.

33 In eighteenth-century Dutch usage, advances to foreign governments, commercial, mining, and industrial enterprises, West Indian planters, and other borrowers were called loans or negotiations (*negotiatiën*). This term has no English equivalent, but it should be taken to signify an investment operation organized and managed by intermediaries who raised capital through the

sale of shares to the investing public. The organizational framework will be dealt with in this section. Dutch investors regularly obliged foreign borrowers using the market apparatus to pay service and redemptions in the United Provinces in current guilders.

34 J. E. D. Binney, *British Public Finance and Administration, 1774–92* (Oxford, 1958), pp. 90–116, for an interpretation of annuity and interest in English usage. An ultimate due date was established for perpetual redeemable annuities, but one removed from the time of issue by as much as a century. P. G. M. Dickson, *The Financial Revolution in England: A Study in the Development of Public Credit, 1688–1756* (New York, 1967), pp. 51–62. On French practices see [Robert Joseph Pothier], *Traité du contrat de constitution de rente* (Paris, 1774), especially pp. 4–5; and Herbert Lüthy, *La banque protestante en France de la révocation de l'édit de Nantes à la Révolution*, 2 vols. (Paris, 1959–61), II, 467–72.

Perpetual annuity (*eeuwigdurende rente*) loans not subject to redemption without the lender's consent had been issued in the seventeenth century by the province of Holland, but those were converted to redeemable paper in 1641. D. Houtzager, *Hollands lijf- en losrenteleningen vóór 1672* (Schiedam, [1950]), pp. 7 and 64.

35 In standard practice individual notes did not specify due dates because borrowers usually arranged to retire loans over several years. Notes to be retired in a given year were determined in lotteries usually held on the eve of successive due dates. Notice of the numbers drawn was given in leading periodicals, but the process of retiring notes or, in prolongations, exchanging them was seldom completed within the year.

On the necessity of specifying a due date see U.B.A., Handschriften IV, f, 18a, in the memorandum of 14 Jan. 1791 by Théophile Cazenove: "Il est impratiquable d'emprunter en Hollande une somme considérable d'argent sans fixer le terme & un terme raisonable pour la durée du pret. La proposition d'un engagement indéfini exiteroit la défiance."

36 Where fresh loans replaced older issues that had fallen due, the creditors, at least technically, could demand reimbursement from the new issue. But it is not clear that the holder of due notes was entirely free to withdraw an investment because the pressure to reinvest was often intense and apparently effective.

37 Luzac, *Hollandsch rijkdom*, II, 306, on the role of perceptions of solidity in price movements.

38 NNJ, 1789, 725, the discount rate "is considered to be the thermometer of the abundance or tightness of money."

39 *Staatkundige historie van Holland, behelzende eene staatkundige bespiegeling van de voornaamste gevallen der nederlandsche geschiedenissen benevens de maandelijksche nederlandsche mercurius*, 28 vols. (Amsterdam, 1780–1807) (with variations in the title). That was a successor to the *Maandelijkse nederlandsche mercurius* (1756–79), which itself succeeded earlier series of the same type.

40 Amsterdammers also had access to foreign publications, such as the *Journal de commerce* of Frankfurt, that included commercial and price information, and to the numerous periodicals of other cities in the Republic.

41 See van Dillen, "Effectenkoersen," 1.
42 From that point the MNM lists prices for most major foreign and domestic government loans and for the British funds.
43 For examples see van Dillen, "Effectenkoersen," 13–14; G.A.A., N.34.003, N.34.004, N.49.03, and N.41.008; and N.E.H.A., Archief SvH, "Diverse documenten, descharges, particuliere beschieden, enz." Those lists were seldom comprehensive and often failed to distinguish carefully among issues by the same borrower on different types of security.
44 N. J. Polak, "Het noteeringsvraagstuk aan de amsterdamsche effectenbeurs in de eerste helft der negentiende eeuw," *EHJ*, X (1924), 198–201, relates the appearance of the *Prijs-courant der effecten* to a growing need for price information and control over *beurs* intermediaries, both of which arose out of the sharper price fluctuations of foreign government securities in the wartime period.
45 See below, pp. 65–7.
46 E.g.: *De Koopman*, III, 212–16; Anton Friderich Büsching, *Erdbeschreibung*, 8th ed., 13 vols. (Hamburg, 1787–1816), I, 152–4 and passim; and Eberhard August Wilhelm von Zimmermann, *A Political Survey of the Present State of Europe* . . . (London, 1787), pp. 11, 40–1, and passim.
47 For example, Jakob Gottlieb Isaak Boetticher, *Statistical Tables; Exhibiting a View of All the States of Europe* . . . , with changes by William Playfair, trans. (London, 1800), p. 10, citing Danish revenues and expenditures as of about 1789 (when the first German edition appeared). Boetticher puts revenues at £1,520,000, expenditures at £1,050,000, and the debt at £2,600,000. In fact the state debt was substantially larger and revenues appear to have been much smaller. See Chart 6-1 and the discussion of Denmark in Chap. 6. Moreover, there was almost certainly a deficit during the Swedish war of 1788–90. The same source indicates surpluses for Russia and Sweden and a modest deficit for Poland, but gives only revenue estimates for other states.
48 Budgetary data were available from parliamentary votes on supplies (although that source was incomplete) and from political and financial commentaries. On the former see B. R. Mitchell and Phyllis Deane, *Abstract of British Historical Statistics* (Cambridge, 1971), p. 382.
49 See, for example, N. & J. van Staphorst & Hubbard et al. to T. Cazenove, 10 May 1791, in U.B.A., 565B14, plans d'emprunts, pt. 4: "l'Argent devient de plus en plus abondant" (in a letter dealing with a projected loan for the state of Pennsylvania); and Gouverneur Morris, *A Diary of the French Revolution*, ed. by Beatrix Cary Davenport, 2 vols. (London, 1939), I, 278, relating information passed on by J. van Staphorst: "Money is tolerably abundant in Holland" (that after a period of tight credit in the summer of 1789). Such vague references were also used to describe competition for investment capital when several loans were brought onto the market at the same time and on the occasion of political and economic developments which either did or were expected to leave rentiers more or less anxious to buy into loan issues.
50 *T.J.*, XIII, 10–11.
51 Morris, *Diary*, I, 451.
52 NNJ, 1789, 729.

53 For example, Morris, *Diary*, I, 438–9, reporting a conversation apparently with Nicolaas Hubbard of N. & J. van Staphorst & Hubbard on the prospects of a loan for the United States. Hubbard warned that what might be raised depended on international affairs and added "that the first Impression [of a conflict] would be to check all Loans." Morris had pointed out that war in Germany, which was the prospect in March 1790, should enhance American credit, but Hubbard responded that that would happen only in "a future Period."

54 P. J. van Winter, *Het aandeel van den amsterdamschen handel aan den opbouw van het amerikaansche gemeenebest*, 2 vols. (Amsterdam, 1927–33), I, 47; and Ricard, I, 210. See also U.B.A., 565B14, plans d'emprunts, pt. 1. In the Dutch Republic as elsewhere on the continent notaries recorded partnership and liquidation agreements, powers of attorney, bill protests, estate inventories and other accords arising out of inheritances, the variety of documents dealing with the organization and management of loans and negotiations, and other transactions. In the process the notary provided an outside control, attesting to observance of proper legal forms but not to the credibility of contents except when evidence was displayed to him. Among other functions performed was control over the issue of shares in loans, to assure borrower and lender alike that share numbers were not duplicated, and oversight over lottery drawings in which notes were selected for redemption.

Merchants and bankers sometimes used the same notary time and again, but more often they dispersed their business over many. Pieter Stadnitski, for example, employed no fewer than nineteen, some more often than others. On a family of notaries over several generations see H. K. de Raaf and H. M. A. Schadee, comp., *Tweehonderd jaar notariaat en zeezaken: Gedenkschrift van het kantoor der notarissen Schadee en hunnen associé's, Rotterdam, 1724–1924* (Rotterdam, 1924).

55 On the functions of banking and the range of interests of bankers see in particular George V. Taylor, "Types of Capitalism in Eighteenth-Century France," *EHR*, LXXIX (1964), 486–7; Antonetti, *Greffulhe Montz & Cie*, pp. 119–74, esp. 145ff., and p. 245; de Jong-Keesing, *Economische crisis van 1763*, pp. 55–86; Buist, *Hope & Co.*, pp. 3–69 with references therein to more detailed treatments of Hope's interests elsewhere in the text; and Lüthy, *La banque protestante*, passim, esp. II, 141ff., 243ff., and 265–6. *De Koopman*, I, 289ff., describes the organization and management of Dutch merchant houses.

56 Firms that opened and managed substitution ventures and small loans usually retained the label applied to them in other transactions and were not called bankers.

57 The tie between prominence in trade with a given state and an intermediary position in that state's loans was not subsequently lost. L. van den Berg, "Lijst der voornaamste handelshuizen te Amsterdam en Rotterdam in het jaar 1800," *EHJ*, VI (1920), 265–71, ranks houses by trade sector. Leading merchants in a sector were often leading bankers in that sector.

58 Firms could experience short-term difficulties, even a brief suspension of payments, yet continue to direct foreign loans. In 1763 Hasselgreen sus-

pended payments and reorganized, yet later served as one of Sweden's banking agents in Amsterdam. A distinction should be made between the house with a reputation for basic soundness, though perhaps caught up occasionally in the overextension of other firms, and the house that regularly took what were regarded as unreasonable risks. As was also the custom elsewhere, Amsterdam partnerships were ordinarily short term, but some houses remained active over generations with changes among the partners and with or without changes in the style.

59 U.B.A., 565B14, plans d'emprunts, pt. 5, by T. Cazenove, whose eccentricities in spelling and accenting have been preserved here and in other quotations.

60 In the language of the day commission agents were termed "*entrepreneurs*," or undertakers. Unless otherwise indicated, the term "broker" should be taken herein in the sense of a middleman who negotiates contracts of purchase and sale for other parties, and not merely in the sense of the banker's agent for evaluating the market in foreign loans. On the broker as general intermediary in commerce and finance see Jacques Le Moine de l'Espine, *De koophandel van Amsterdam naer alle gewesten der waereld* . . . , ed. by Isaac le Long, 9th ed. rev., 3 vols. (Rotterdam, 1780), I, 91–124; Ricard, I, 71; and, for legal definitions, Jan Floris de Jongh, *De nederlandsche makelaardij* (Haarlem, 1949), pp. 16–30.

61 Receipts and disbursements in loans could be handled by cashiers, but large firms sometimes maintained their own internal cashiers' department. On the latter point *De Koopman*, IV, 275.

62 U.B.A., 565B14, plans d'emprunts, pt. 1, a memoir by Cazenove indicating that commission agents were responsible for placing or accepting on their own account the blocks for which they contracted; and N.E.H.A., Archief KV, "Notten diversen," for samples.

63 Since payment dates were customarily spread over several months, subscribers could anticipate the redemption of other paper in their portfolio, arrange sales, or organize credit.

64 Buist, *Hope & Co.*, apps. D-II and D-III, pp. 498–501; and N.E.H.A., Archief KV, "Verschillende negotiaties ten behoeve van Zweden . . . 1772–1807."

65 Most agents signing contracts in the Russian, Swedish, Polish, and Spanish loans were based in Amsterdam, including 19 of the 23 (excluding bankers and brokers) that marketed notes in 10 or more issues. Paper was sold throughout the United Provinces and, on a limited scale, abroad. See notarial accords on transfers of Generality and provincial paper to various buyers by Pieter Stadnitski (in G.A.A., notaries P. C. Heidweiller, J. Croon, P. C. Nahuys, R. van Eibergen, J. Harmsen, and P. de Wilde) for an idea of the geographical range of one agent's contacts.

66 Having gained management of Russian loans in Amsterdam in 1787, Hope & Co. expanded the number of its agents from 23 in 1788 (the first issue of the series) to 33 in 1792. Buist, *Hope & Co.*, pp. 498–501. Henry Hope viewed the use of commission agents as the most desirable technique for mobilizing capital, and recommended such a system to Beerend Roosen in Hamburg when a Russian loan was proposed there. In Antwerp, where a Russian issue was floated in 1788, Hope believed that commission agents were not used

and that as a result investors were given a leverage lacking in Amsterdam (ibid., pp. 100–1). In fact Antwerp firms used a network of underwriters, the details of which remain obscure. Reference to this may be found in Jean Martin Smets to J. Liljencrantz, 17 Dec. 1786, R.A.S., Liljencrantz samling, E4661.

67 See U.B.A., Handschriften IV, f, 18a, and 565B14, plans d'emprunts, pt. 5, for draft memoirs describing the method of issue provided to the governor of Pennsylvania in 1790, when a loan was being considered to fund a settlement with the Penn family.

68 See chap. 6, n. 112.

69 By dispersing management of its Dutch loans among several houses Sweden was adopting a technique repugnant to Amsterdam bankers, who preferred monopolistic control over the loans of individual states. But Sweden pointedly wished to maintain competition. The principal firms directing loans for that state were Hope & Co. in association with Horneca, Hogguer & Co. and Jan & Carel Hasselgreen. On Horneca, Hogguer [whose successive styles were Horneca, Fizeaux & Co. (1773–9); Fizeaux, Grand & Co. (1779–84); Henri Fizeaux & Co. (1785–7); Hogguer, Grand & Co. (1788–94); and Hogguer & Co. (from 1795)] see Lüthy, *La banque protestante*, II, 330–8; and Buist, *Hope & Co.*, p. 85, n. 4. (Henri Fizeaux continued occasionally to use the style Fizeaux, Grand & Co. after 1 Jan. 1785.) The chief area of that firm's activities was Baltic trade, but it was also involved in marine insurance and colonial trade. Hasselgreen was active in trade with Sweden and in sugar refining. On Hope's commercial transactions with Sweden see ibid., pp. 87–9.

70 Adams's understanding of the Amsterdam market in the early years of his appointment was of course weak, but he devoted some effort to informing himself, and by 1787 had as good a grasp as an outsider could expect to gain. On the early years of stumbling see van Winter, *Amsterdamschen handel*, I, 46–7; and, for an example of Adams's later knowledgeability, J. Adams to T. Jefferson, 12 Feb. 1788, in *T.J.*, XII, 581–2. For a sample of the thoroughness of American representatives in exploring conditions on the Amsterdam market see W. Short to A. Hamilton, 2 Dec. 1790, in *A.H.*, VII, 175–87. Short occasionally forwarded incorrect data, but for the most part Adams's successor also had a firm grasp of market practices and current trends.

71 W. Short to T. Jefferson, 28 Jan. 1790, in *T.J.*, XVI, 134; and van Winter, *Amsterdamschen handel*, I, 193–4. Also ibid., II, 156–7 and 161 on a Russian ploy involving a loan in Antwerp that led to more attractive terms in Amsterdam issues.

72 Buist, who helped me by critically examining my analysis of market structure, has objected to some of my interpretations (such as that the structure favored high commission and low annuity rates) in an article that summarizes my analysis. See Marten G. Buist, "The Sinews of War: The Role of Dutch Finance in European Politics (c. 1750–1815)," in *Britain and the Netherlands*, ed. by A. D. Duke and C. A. Tamse (The Hague, 1977), VI, 124–40, esp. 130–7.

73 Borrowers technically could issue loans at par and the negotiated interest

rate or at a discount which transformed a lower nominal return into a higher real return. In Amsterdam such discounts were seldom employed, but borrowers sometimes used premiums (usually in the form of redemption bonuses) to retain lower nominal returns. A 1788 memorandum written, in my judgment, by Pieter Stadnitski, indicates a market bias in which discounted long-term paper offering the promise of regular service at the prevailing interest rate would move toward par more quickly than the note paying a higher yield would move toward the price at which its effective yield was equal to the current interest rate. U.B.A., 565B14, plans d'emprunts, pt. 1, "Consideratiën over het te formeerene plan der Negotiatie van 200000 Dollars Liquidated Debt. . . ." Small discounts could also be given via the percentage accorded commission agents who would rebate part of their commission to investors or to intermediary brokers.

74 This chart has been compiled from loan issue data mentioned or cited in subsequent chapters (and drawn chiefly from G.A.A., notarial archives; and N.E.H.A., Pros., dossiers I–V). Although loans included have been determined by the arbitrary standard of available information about annuity charges, the likelihood of error is not significant. Average annuity rates (weighted according to sums subscribed in loans opened at different rates) for the 1760s and early 1770s are less satisfactory than later averages in part because of a lower incidence in which the necessary information is available for all loans issued, and in part because of the lesser frequency of loans in that period. Fluctuations in that period may exaggerate actual shifts in annuity rates. Two life-annuity issues and annuities with imprecise premiums have been excluded. All annuity rates reflect the return to investors paying in the full face value of notes (rather than returns as a factor of *beurs* prices or returns calculated according to the combined annuity rate and commission charges paid by the borrower). It should also be noted that subscriptions were not always completed within the year of issue. Finally, the minimum rates given for 1778–80 (3.5 percent) are distorted by the forced prolongation of Spanish loans. Those aside, the minimum of those years would be 4 percent.

75 These rates are based on data in subsequent chapters. They are, in addition, in agreement with observations in Ricard, I, 210–11. See also U.B.A., 565B14, plans d'emprunts, pt. 1, which indicates that in cases where notes could be expected to sell at a premium the commission agent was not allotted a percentage but drew a profit from the premium.

Commission charges on the initial issue, which sometimes covered compensation for management of service and redemptions, were deducted from the proceeds of a loan. The borrower raising f. 3 million at 5 percent on a total commission of 6.5 percent therefore received f. 2,805,000, so that the nominal 5-percent yield was actually paid at about 5.35 percent by the borrower but of course received at 5 percent by the lender.

76 The word "prospectus" is not synonymous but it has been adopted to distinguish such printed notices from other sources of information about loans. Ricard, I, 210, also uses prospectus. An extensive collection of such documents in N.E.H.A., Pros., in five dossiers and in *idem*, Archief Loopuyt, has provided details on numerous loans opened in Amsterdam by foreign powers

and on other types of negotiations. In general it has been possible both to verify and to expand the data in those documents with other sources, particularly notarial accords.

77 E.g., the United States paid 8 percent in commission charges in 1788 but only 4 percent in its 1791 loans, in both cases issued with 5-percent yields. On the other hand, while maintaining the same level of commission charges, Russia was sometimes able to raise advances at as little as 4-percent interest.

78 Van Winter, *Amsterdamschen handel*, II, app. V, 476–7; Buist, *Hope & Co.*, pp. 100–10 and app. D-I, p. 497; Jan Gotlib de Bloch, *Les finances de la Russie au XIXe siècle*, 2 vols. (Paris, 1899), I, 74; and N.E.H.A., Archief KV, "Verschillende negotiaties ten behoeve van Zweden . . . 1772–1807." This chart omits the Swedish life-annuity loan of 1790 and the 1782 loan issued in Amsterdam by France but with the proceeds earmarked for the United States. The 1784 American loan paid premiums that increased the return above 4 percent. In 1788 the commission charges on the American loan of 1787 were increased to 9 percent. Commissions on the Swedish loans of 1782, 1783, and 1788 are uncertain.

79 *MNM*, 1792–6; and the *Prijs-courant der effecten* for the dates indicated. The Generality notes listed are *op naam;* from 1797 the province of Holland listing is for bearer notes issued at the Amsterdam revenue office (the *MNM* does not distinguish between bearer and *op naam* paper or among revenue offices); and the East India Company notes are from the lotteries of 1785 and 1786.

80 Buist, *Hope & Co.*, p. 104.

81 U.B.A., 565B14, plans d'emprunts, pt. 1, "Consideratiën over het te formeerene plan der Negotiatie van 200000 Dollars Liquidated Debt . . . ." Also *De Koopman*, VI, 177–8, on the inability of investors to recognize the defects of a 1775 Spanish life-annuity loan; and W. Short to A. Hamilton, 2 Dec. 1790, in *A.H.*, VII, 182–3: "the knowledge which the money lenders have of the powers to whom they lend" was "founded for the most part on conjectural basis" leaving "a wide field for their imagination & fears."

82 Van Winter, *Amsterdamschen handel*, I, 183.

83 W. Short to A. Hamilton, 18 Dec. 1790 in *A.H.*, VII, 349. The primary attachment to self-interest of firms involved in organizing and managing foreign loans did not go unrecognized in the literature available to investors [Th. H. Nefkens, "De denkbeelden van De Borger omtrent de economische achteruitgang der republiek in de achttiende eeuw," *Economie*, XXXVI, no. 10 (July, 1972), 493], but there was no effective reaction among investors.

84 *A.H.*, VII, 348–49. Short's view of the Amsterdam market, developed when he was one of the principal American agents in the negotiation of loans, was hostile because he thought the terms demanded by bankers too stiff. His commentary on investors is phrased with dramatic scorn, and probably overstates the attitude among commission agents. See also Cazenove's view, "The Dutch Capitalits [sic] are not fond of novelties," in U.B.A., 565B14, plans d'emprunts, pt. 1.

85 Van Winter, *Amsterdamschen handel*, I, 169–70, on Thomas Jefferson's realization of the importance of this standard; *De Koopman*, III, 172–5, on its

application in domestic government loans; Ricard, I, 210, on foreign loans; and U.B.A., Handschriften IV, f, 18a, the memorandum of 14 Jan. 1791: "L'èxpérience constate, que toutes les Puissances qui ont payé aux hollandois avec ponctualité les intérêts & les prémiers remboursemens promis, ont trouvé & trouvent constamment à emprunter en Hollande bien au dela du triple des sommes qu'ils ont remboursées: Même la simple publication de rembourser ou de continuer un Emprunt au choix des préteurs, á ordinairement pour èffet la continuation volontaire du pret, toutes les fois que la Puissance qui fait faire la proposition, á pris soin de remplir ses engagemens. C'est ainsi que les Cours de Petersbourg, Vienne, Stockholm, & Coppenhague tout en remboursant d'une main un million, ont toujours emprunté deux nouveaux millions de l'autre main . . ."

86 N.E.H.A., Archief SvH; *idem*, Archief KV; and G.A.A., Archief SvH. Both collections are fragmentary rather than comprehensive, most notably in the lack of correspondence and early ledgers. See also the articles on Stadnitski and van Ketwich in the *Nieuw nederlandsch biografisch woordenboek*, VIII, 1283–6, and II, 667–8, respectively.

87 Other firms that developed successful commission agencies and were able, at least partly because of that success, to expand their activities are mentioned on pp. 44–5.

88 N.E.H.A., Archief SvH, with dossiers on the period before Stadnitski's death in 1795; G.A.R., notary W. Boon, XXXVII/33, for the marriage contract of 1763; and G.A.A., notaries A. van Beem, J. Fabius, and T. M. de Man, for accords on the settlement of Stadnitski's estate. The *Naamregister van alle de heeren kooplieden der stad Amsterdam . . . voor het jaar MDCCLXVI* (Amsterdam, 1766), p. 94, lists Stadnitski as a merchant trading with Germany, but the editions of 1790 and 1792 no longer include him. He had by then withdrawn from commodity trade except through the subsidiary firm of Pieter Keer & Co.

89 Buist, *Hope & Co.*, pp. 100–10, and apps. D-II and D-III, pp. 498–501. See also N.E.H.A., Archief KV, "Notten diversen," and "Verschillende negotiaties ten behoeve van Zweden . . . 1772–1807."

90 Ibid., "Inhoud: diverse papieren betreffende de firma Hogguer"; N.E.H.A., Pros., III, 199; and Willem Hendrik Berghuis, *Ontstaan en ontwikkeling van de nederlandse beleggingsfondsen tot 1914* (Assen, 1967), pp. 51–74. The first multiple-unit investment trust without a tontine or life-annuity feature offered on the Amsterdam market appears to have been organized in 1773 by two bankers in The Hague. N.E.H.A., Pros., III, 24.

91 Ibid., I, 50, and V, 35 and 180; N.E.H.A., Archief KV, "Jaarlijkse rekeningen wegens de administratie van amerikaanse fondsen . . ."; and, on van Ketwich and the introduction of the administrative office, *idem*, Pros., III, 264; *idem*, Archief KV, "Rekeningen en documenten der administratie van franse leningen, 1803 tot ongeveer 1881"; G.A.A., N.12.17.09; and W. Goppel, "Ontwikkeling en beteekenis van de administratiekantoren," *De nederlandsche financier*, Jubileumsuitgave of the *Dagelijksche beurscourant*, 2 Feb. 1939, 31–4.

92 Loans secured on crown jewels had been common early in the eighteenth

century. Some of those advances, extended mostly to German princes, were organized by the Rotterdam Loan Bank, which, however, withdrew from the field in 1725. Melles, *Het huys van leeninge*, pp. 161–8.

93 In shifting from commodity to revenue anticipations, Austria acknowledged the fragility of goods that had become subject to interruptions in supply. Copper anticipations were first offered in 1700, but shortly thereafter production was disrupted by a revolt in Hungary. In 1705 the imperial mercury monopoly was undercut by entry into the European market of Far Eastern mercury. But commodity-based loans never wholly disappeared from the market, and in the Austrian case mineral shipments continued to furnish the means for service and redemptions. During the eighteenth century mercury prices were unstable (Posthumus, I, 478–81), which may explain the increasing frequency with which Austria used Bank of Vienna debentures to secure loans. Other states generally adopted the practice of securing loans on tax revenues during the 1760s and 1770s, slightly ahead of Austria's shift to debentures secured on a bank whose revenues were part of the tax revenues of the empire. To Hope & Co., participating in management of Swedish loans, the collateral offered by treasury-note debentures guaranteed by the Bank of Sweden "imparted the character of a secured loan." Buist, *Hope & Co.*, p. 75.

94 On receiver-general management and States General loan guarantees see B.E. de Muinck, *Een regentenhuishouding omstreeks 1700* (The Hague, 1965), pp. 21–2; N.E.H.A., Archief KV, "Verschillende negotiaties ten behoeve van Zweden . . . 1772–1807"; and van Dillen, *Rijkdom*, pp. 457–8.

95 Domestic government loans were also based on general revenue anticipations so that, in appearance, the use of debentures formalized for foreign borrowers an implicit feature of domestic loans. Dutch governments did not customarily specify the income sources on which loans were settled, so that the adoption of general rather than specific descriptions of the security behind advances had a precedent.

96 *De Koopman*, I, 44.

97 Ibid., II, 184, offers a breakdown of Amsterdam's population by profession as of about 1770. The total number of inhabitants (246,800) is too high, but the numbers assigned to the more carefully differentiated ranks may be more accurate. According to this list there were some 150 bankers and large-scale merchants of the first rank and 1,900 merchants, shipowners, rentiers, insurance underwriters, commission agents, factors, and smaller-scale merchants of the second and third ranks.

98 Van Winter, *Amsterdamschen handel*, II, 187, found artisans and domestic servants among investors in loans to the United States.

99 E.g., J. Hudig, *De west-indische zaken van Ferrand Whaley Hudig, 1759–1797* (Amsterdam, [1922]), p. 25, on participation by widows and guardians of minors in plantation loans.

100 For a survey of contemporary evidence on mortality by sex see J. A. Volgraff, ed., *Les oeuvres de Nicolas Struyck (1687–1769)*, trans. by J. A. Volgraff (Amsterdam, 1912), pp. 187–7, 216, and 230–3. Household management practices were sometimes highly formalized among business

classes, with the result that widows were often prepared to assume direction of affairs outside the family.

101 H. Hardenberg, *Het burgerweeshuis voor nederlands hervormden te 's-Gravenhage, 1564–1964* (The Hague, 1964), p. 199, on that orphanage's endowment in 1807 when it was concentrated principally in municipal and national government long-term paper; and Cornelis Wernard van Voorst van Beest, *De katholieke armenzorg te Rotterdam in de 17e en de 18e eeuw* (The Hague, 1955), pp. 86–120, on income and assets (including by 1770 domestic and foreign government notes) of Roman Catholic institutions in Rotterdam.

102 On stock substitution see Berghuis, *Nederlandse beleggingsfondsen*, passim; Herman Wagenvoort, *Tontines, een onderzoek naar de geschiedenis van de lijfrenten bij wijze van tontine en de contracten van overleving in de Republiek der Verenigde Nederlanden* (Utrecht, 1961), passim; *idem*, "Contracten van overleving en andere tontines," *TvR*, XXV (1967), 584–94; *Bouwstoffen voor de geschiedenis van de levensverzekeringen en lijfrenten in Nederland* (Amsterdam, 1897), passim; N.E.H.A., Pros., dossiers III and V; *idem*, Kleine aanwinsten, 55, 143, 264, 273, and 284; *idem*, Archief KV, "Papieren nopens enige vragen . . . over tontines en andere cassen . . . 1811"; E.H.B., P. Ned. 1780:8 and 1836:12; and U.B.A., 565B14, plans d'emprunts, pt. 7. See also H. G. Schuddebeurs, "Het nederlandsche verzekeringsbedrijf gedurende de laatste twee eeuwen . . . ," *EHJ*, XIV (1928), 62–4, on insurance companies.

103 George V. Taylor, "Noncapitalist Wealth and the Origins of the French Revolution," *AHR*, LXXII, no. 2 (January, 1967), 469–96. See also Ralph E. Giesey, "Rules of Inheritance and Strategies of Mobility in Prerevolutionary France," *AHR*, LXXXII, no. 2 (April, 1977), 271–89.

104 Ibid., p. 278.

105 Van Winter, *Amsterdamschen handel*, II, 124–7, gives an example of that in the substitution negotiations organized on the American domestic debt. See also U.B.A., Handschriften IV, f, 18a, the memorandum of 14 Jan. 1791 by T. Cazenove (*idem*, 565B14, plans d'emprunts, pt. 5, on authorship) concerning a projected loan for Pennsylvania. Cazenove described the issue of f. 1,000 bearer shares in foreign loans as a means of making "ce genre de proprieté convénable & facile pour toutes les classes de citoyens; éparpillés dans la Campagne & les petites villes," and continued: "une grande portion de ces proprietés se débite par petites parties dans la classe des bourgeois, & de tous ceux qui oeconomisent annuellement des sommes bornées, & qui n'ont ni la volonté, ni les moyens de corréspondre hors de leur patrie."

106 The collateral-succession inventories were drawn up in connection with a tax on estates passing out of the direct line of inheritance. Alice C. Carter, "Dutch Foreign Investment, 1738–1800, *Economica*, XX, n.s. (November, 1953), 322–40; and *idem*, "Dutch Foreign Investment, 1738–1800," in the Light of the Amsterdam 'Collateral Succession' Inventories," *TvG*, LXVI (1953), 27–38.

107 Prices in van Dillen, "Effectenkoersen," 19–46.

108 Carter, "Dutch Foreign Investment," *Economica*, 328, found Dutch investors in the English funds to have eschewed turnover.

109 William Fairman, *The Stocks Examined and Compared: or, A Guide to Purchasers in the Public Funds* (London, 1795), p. v, noticed a similar short-term trend in London and offered (pp. 58–65) tables for calculating the prices at which notes paying different nominal returns yielded equal interest.

Secular quotations are unavailable before 1792, but price disparities are evident on single days in 1783 and 1788 for which price currents are available. [Oudermeulen], II, pt. 2, 263–8; and G.A.A., N.41.088, respectively.

Chapter 3. Public credit in the Dutch Republic

1 Generality and provincial revenue systems are discussed in P. H. Engels, *De geschiedenis der belastingen in Nederland* (Rotterdam, 1848), pp. 81ff.; Folkert Nicolaas Sickenga, *Bijdrage tot de geschiedenis der belastingen in Nederland* (Leiden, 1864), passim; J. G. van Dillen, *Van rijkdom en regenten* (The Hague, 1970), pp. 270–83; Dirk Houtzager, *Hollands lijf- en losrenteleningen vóór 1672* (Schiedam, 1950), passim; B. E. de Muinck, *Een regentenhuishouding omstreeks 1700* (The Hague, 1965), pp. 104–60 and 224–96; and P. G. M. Dickson and John Sperling, "War Finance, 1689–1714," in *New Cambridge Modern History*, ed. by J. S. Bromley (Cambridge, 1970), VI, 294–8. See also Charles Wilson, "Taxation and the Decline of Empires, an Unfashionable Theme," *BMHG*, LXXVII (1963), 10–26; and, on division of taxation between direct and indirect levies in the latter years of the Republic, Simon Schama, "The Exigencies of War and the Politics of Taxation in the Netherlands, 1795–1810," in J. M. Winter, ed., *War and Economic Development* (London, 1975), pp. 107–9.

2 On the Amsterdam admiralty see J. R. Bruijn, *De admiraliteit van Amsterdam in rustige jaren, 1713–1751* (Amsterdam, 1970); and, for tables of the duties collected by the five admiralties over the period to 1795, J. Hovy, *Het voorstel van 1751 tot instelling van een beperkt vrijhavenstelsel in de republiek* (Groningen, 1966), pp. 5–22.

3 Available information on taxation and public finance in Dutch municipalities is even more fragmentary than for the Generality, the provinces, and the admiralties. Among useful sources are Herman Wagenvoort, *Tontines, een onderzoek naar de geschiedenis van de lijfrenten bij wijze van tontine en de contracten van overleving in de Republiek der Verenigde Nederlanden* (Utrecht, 1961); *idem*, "Contracten van overleving en andere tontines," *TvR*, XXV (1967), 584–94; H. M. Kesteloo, "De stadsrekeningen van Middelburg VII, 1650–1675," *ZGWA*, VIII, pt. 4 (1901), 1–82; *idem*, "De stadsrekeningen van Middelburg VIII, 1675–1700," *ZGWA*, VIII, pt. 4 (1901), 83–134; *idem*, "De stadsrekeningen van Middelburg IX, 1700–1810," *ZGWA*, VIII, pt. 5 (1902), 1–202; *Verzameling van authentique stukken, kunnende dienen tot bijlaagen voor de nieuwspapieren*, 5 vols. (Amsterdam, 1793–6), V, 106–

32, on Amsterdam, 1774–94; H. J. Koenen, *Voorlezingen over de geschiedenis der finantiën van Amsterdam* (Amsterdam, 1855); H. Rootlieb, "Bijdrage tot de kennis van Amsterdam's financiën in den franschen tijd," *JGA*, XII (1914), 131–78; N.E.H.A., Pros., passim; *idem*, Archief KV, "Obligatie en wisselbrieven der stad Middelburg . . . 1784" and "Lening voor de stad Hoorn, 1787. . ."; and *idem*, Kleine aanwinsten, 337.

4 Engels, *Belastingen*, pp. 81–3.

5 Contribution levels were altered slightly in wartime. The redistribution of 1792 may be traced to 1785 when a commission was appointed to study the quota system. The effort may be followed in tedious detail in *NNJ*, for example, 1790, 486–1506 and 1556–1640.

6 On Cornelis van de Jonge van Ellemeet, receiver general from 1674 to 1707, see de Muinck, *Een regentenhuishouding*.

7 Sickenga, *Belastingen*, pp. 284–5. On disparities between South Holland (south of the River IJ) and North Holland see Adrianus Maria van der Woude, *Het Noorderkwartier: Een regionaal historisch onderzoek in de demografische en economische geschiedenis van westelijk Nederland* . . . , 3 vols. (Wageningen, 1972), I, 164–5 and 193.

8 Despite the weakness of central fiscal authority, the States General sometimes guaranteed loans floated by other governments within the Republic and abroad. De Muinck, *Een regentenhuishouding*, pp. 86 and 91–2. The Generality's revenues overlapped with provincial income but that part which was distinct from revenues from the provinces was quite modest, no more than f. 750,000 in 1714 from the Generality lands. Dickens and Sperling, "War Finance," p. 294. Anton Friderich Büsching, *A New System of Geography* . . . , trans. by P. Murdoch, 6 vols. (London, 1762), III, 468–9, estimates Generality receipts in about 1755 at f. 21 million, including provincial quotas.

9 Gregory King estimated 1695 per capita income in England at £17 16s. and per capita taxes at £1 4s., and in the Republic at £8 2s. 9d. and £3 1s. 7d. respectively. See the *Natural and Political Observations* . . . , reprinted in *Two Tracts*, ed. by George E. Barnett (Baltimore, 1936), pp. 18–19 and 49–56. King's projections must be treated with caution, but they remain, as has often been remarked, the most reliable available evidence extending to national product and consumption. According to those figures 38 percent of per capita income was paid in taxes in the Republic and only 15 percent in England. (Peter Mathias and Patrick O'Brien, "Taxation in Britain and France, 1715–1810: A Comparison of the Social and Economic Incidence of Taxes Collected for the Central Governments," *JEEH*, V, no. 3 (Winter, 1976), 613, estimate the "share of per capita output collected as taxes" in Britain at 16 percent in 1715 and 24 percent in 1790.) Using more accurate data about population and net government revenues than that available to King, the proportions shown in the table appear for about 1700. In the 1780s per capita taxes in Holland remained far higher than in England and France. Net annual provincial tax revenues of f. 23 million represented a per capita payment of about f. 29,7 (population 783,000 as of 1795). An approximation suggests that the level in Great Britain was then some f. 17,4,8 (population estimated at 9.4 million; net revenues at an average of £14.6 million during the 1780s) and in France about f. 8,10 (population estimated at 26 million;

revenues at 474 million l.t. as of 1787). Sources: Bernard H. Slicher van Bath, "Historical Demography and the Social and Economic Development of the Netherlands," *Daedalus*, XCVIII, no. 2 (Spring, 1968), 609–10; B. R. Mitchell and Phyllis Deane, *Abstract of British Historical Statistics* (Cambridge, 1971), pp. 386–8; Dickens and Sperling, "War Finance," p. 296; J. F. Bosher, *French Finances, 1770–1795* (Cambridge, 1970), p. 90; and sources cited in n. 22. Exchange calculations have been made using averages from rates provided by Posthumus, I, 595, 607–10, 651, 654–5. All figures exclude municipal and other taxes, which may also have been heavier in the Republic than elsewhere.

	Population	Net revenues	Per capita distribution
Britain	6.8 million	£4.344 million	£ .639 (or about f. 7.03)
province of Holland	.885 million	f. 13 million (in 1689)	f. 14.69

10 Late in the Napoleonic wars, when foreign holdings in the British public debt had become insignificant, the relative per capita holdings were as shown in the table. But of course the British debt was growing more rapidly than the Dutch. Sources: B. R. Mitchell, *European Historical Statistics* (London, 1975), pp. 22–4; Mitchell and Deane, *British Historical Statistics*, p. 402; and W. Dirksen, "Openbare financiën in Nederland van 1790 tot 1820; veranderingen bij de overgang van republikeinse statenbond naar koninkrijk," in *F.P.A.R.*, p. 103.

	Population	Public debt	Per capita holdings
Britain	11.97 million (in 1811)	£609.6 million (in 1811)	£50.93 (or f. 556.15 at an exchange rate of 35 and an agio of 4%)
Kingdom of the Netherlands (excluding Belgium)	2.047 million (in 1816)	f. 1,254 million (in 1813)	f. 612.6

11 Van Dillen, *Rijkdom*, p. 283; Houtzager, *Hollands lijf- en losrenteleningen*, pp. 57–8 and 90–1; and Violet Barbour, *Capitalism in Amsterdam in the 17th Century* (Ann Arbor, 1963 reprint), pp. 82–3. See also the more or less random data given in Sidney Homer, *A History of Interest Rates* (New Brunswick, N.J., 1963), pp. 175–8. Nominal and effective yields based on price currents of 6 Nov. 1747, 30 Sept. 1788, and 3 May 1798 indicate some of the distinctions made by investors among public corporations (and even among revenue offices within the same province) and point out the late-century trend toward higher annuity rates (see table). G.A.A., N.41.088; J. G. van Dillen, "Effectenkoersen aan de Amsterdamsche beurs, 1723–1794," *EHJ*,

XVII (1931), 13; and Weeveringh, I, 17–20. No price currents listing government paper are available between 1747 and 1788. Quotations for all three dates reflect abnormal situations, the first because of Dutch entry into the War of the Austrian Succession in April 1747, the second as a result of the Patriot Revolution of 1787 and Patriot attempts to drive down the price on public debt notes, and the third because of the wars of the French Revolution and domestic political strife in the Republic. Nominal annuity rates sometimes included a tax ranging up to 1.5 percent of the face value of the note. See Sickenga, *Belastingen*, p. 444.

	1747		1788		1798	
Borrowing unit	nominal	effective	nominal	effective	nominal	effective
Holland–The Hague	2%	2.8%	2.5%	3.6%	2.5%	6.3%
Amsterdam	2	2.7	2.5	3.5	2.5	6.3
Enkhuizen	2	3	—	—	—	—
The Generality	3	4.1	3	3.7	3	7.6
Zeeland	2	4	2	4.4	2	11.4
	4	4.7	4	4.4	4	9.2
Gelderland	3	3.8	3	3.2	3	7.5
Utrecht	2.5	3.7	2.5	3.4	2.5	6.3
	3	3.8	3	3.5	3	6.8

12 This is based on estimates of total debt and debt service for 1761, 1787, and 1794, which are listed in Table 3-1. It is important to notice that public corporations in the Dutch Netherlands generally issued loans at par or with very slight discounts. Approximately equivalent service costs for the nominal sum of the British public debt disguise discounts customarily offered by the exchequer and make service costs appear to have been lower than in fact they were when compared to the actual sums raised in public loans.

13 A calculation will demonstrate the importance of low service costs. In 1761 Holland had an outstanding debt of some f. 350 million, on which service totaled f. 14.4 million (an average of 4.11 percent), or 72 percent of 1768 revenues, the closest date of available information. A 5-percent average return would have cost f. 17.5 million, or 87.5 percent of 1768 revenues, and a 6-percent return f. 21 million, or 105 percent of revenues.

14 The assertion that investors would have reacted negatively to revelations about the reality of the fiscal situation implies that there were investment alternatives able to absorb assets withheld from government lending. Entirely satisfactory alternatives were not available, but the risk of lending to government might still have been acknowledged by stabilized or increased annuity rates.

15 In 1782 L. P. van de Spiegel, secretary to the states of Zeeland (and from 1787 to 1795 pensionary to the province of Holland), prepared a memoir surveying the economic and financial position and outlook of the Republic. Although the memoir was circulated among high government officials, van

de Spiegel's plan to revise it for publication was never fulfilled. The memoir stands as evidence of the obscurity of public indebtedness, for van de Spiegel attempted not a survey of current liabilities of public corporations but merely an estimate of debts added since the Peace of Münster (1648), given as about f. 425 million. Joh. de Vries, "Van de Spiegel's 'Schets tot een vertoog over de intrinsique en relative magt van de republijk' (1782)," *EHJ*, XXVII (1958), 81–100.

16 W. A. E. A. van der Grinten, "Van lijfrenten in overouden tijd," *Haagsch maandblad* (1924), 576–7; *Bouwstoffen voor de geschiedenis van de levensverzekeringen en lijfrenten in Nederland* (Amsterdam, 1897), pp. 242–59; Jan de Vries, "On the Modernity of the Dutch Republic," *JEH*, XXXIII, no. 1 (March, 1973), 201 and n. 23, citing an inquiry of 1514 that "uncovered scores of simple villages which had issued *lijfrenten* . . . on their own authority"; Weeveringh, I, 4; and Houtzager, *Hollands lijf- en losrenteleningen*.

17 Early in the seventeenth century some public corporations also employed the *eeuwigdurende rente*, an unredeemable annuity (see chap. 2, n. 34), but redeemable annuities were preferred. Hendrik C. Diferee, *Studiën over de geschiedenis van den nederlandschen handel* (Amsterdam, 1908), pp. 53–7; and van Dillen, *Rijkdom*, pp. 282–3.

18 Johan de Witt, *Waerdije van lijfrenten naer proportie van losrenten* (The Hague, 1671). Translations may be found in *Le rapport de Johan de Witt sur le calcul des rentes viagères*, trans. by P. J. L. de Chateleux (The Hague, 1937); and Robert Gibbs Barnwell, *A Sketch of the Life and Times of Johan de Witt, Grand Pensionary of Holland* . . . (New York, 1856), pp. 81–108 (with omissions in the tables).

19 See the sources cited in n. 22.

20 Provincial loans were raised and administered by the revenue officials of the province but in Holland officials both sold notes themselves and through private brokers. Municipalities employed their own authorities to market notes, but in the eighteenth century increasingly used private brokers and bankers. See, for example, de Muinck, *Een regentenhuishouding*, p. 85, on the sale of notes by the Generality receiver general through Amsterdam brokers. Also, on the Amsterdam market in the 1670s, Julius Grossmann, *Die Amsterdamer Börse vor zwei hundert Jahren: Ein Beitrag zur Geschichte der Politik und des Börsenwesens im mittleren Europa (1672–1673)* (The Hague, 1876).

21 Deferred revision of the quota distribution left in distress those provinces whose relative economic position had deteriorated. The Prussian ambassador observed in 1767 that Gelderland's offer of a gift to the new princess of Orange had been declined because of that province's grave financial position. And in 1771 Thulemeyer also commented on the serious status of Zeeland's finances. *D.T.*, pp. 44 and 71–5, dispatches of 22 Dec. 1767 and 23 Aug. 1771 and thereafter. Moreover, the Generality was obliged to suspend debt service for brief periods in 1713 and 1757. De Muinck, *Een regentenhuishouding*, p. 19.

22 Van Dillen, *Rijkdom*, pp. 283 and 635; Houtzager, *Hollands lijf- en losrenteleningen*, pp. 78–9, 85–6, and 107–8; Wilson, "Taxation," 17; Sickenga, *Belastingen*, p. 312; Dickens and Sperling, "War Finance," pp. 296–8; Mete-

lerkamp, pp. 171–5 and 206–7, n. 3; Eberhard August Wilhelm von Zimmermann, *A Political Survey of the Present State of Europe . . .* (London, 1787), pp. 181–2 (which, however, exaggerates the debts of the Republic and the province of Holland); Ageus Jacobus van der Meulen, *Studies over het ministerie van Van de Spiegel* (Leiden, 1905), pp. 328 and 416; and W. M. Keuchenius, *De inkomsten en uitgaven der Bataafsche Republiek voorgesteld in eene nationaale balans* (Amsterdam, 1803), pp. 2–3 [whose estimate for 1748 (f. 404 million) appears to neglect interim redemptions]. An estimate of provincial indebtedness in 1714 by Dickens and Sperling, "War Finance," p. 298, of f. 250 million is undoubtedly too low. It conflicts with reliable estimates of debt service in 1721 and 1728, and also with that source's evidence about additions to the provincial debt between 1689 and 1714 (of f. 156 million). See also de Vries, ed., "Van de Spiegel's 'Schets,' " 93, about the increase of overall indebtedness in the Republic between 1648 and 1782; and Table 5-1. For details on some specific loan issues by Holland see G. A. Fokker, *Geschiedenis der loterijen in de Nederlanden* (Amsterdam, 1862), p. 127; N.E.H.A., Pros., III, 135, 150, 160, 292, and V, 37, 71, 107, 119a, 130, 153, 161; and van der Meulen, *Van de Spiegel*, pp. 332–4 and 343–415. Amounts in parenthesis under Outstanding debt have been projected from data on service costs (at 4 and 4.5 percent).

23 The Generality also reduced its debt from something in excess of f. 58 million to about f. 20 million between 1717 and 1786, and on the whole public indebtedness declined between 1713 and the Fourth Anglo-Dutch War. De Muinck, *Een regentenhuishouding*, p. 19; Weeveringh, I, 9; and J. T. Buijs, *De nederlandsche staatsschuld sedert 1814* (Haarlem, 1857), p. 10. The reduction was possible not only because the Generality benefited from a long era of peace but also because the Union turned to an alternative source of income. In 1726 a national lottery was inaugurated, and over the remainder of the eighteenth century it provided a regular and gradually increasing sum of revenues. Average net proceeds advanced from slightly less than f. 190,000 per annum in the 1730s to more than f. 340,000 in the 1780s. Fokker, *Loterijen*, pp. 121–56; and the table of proceeds in F. J. B. d'Alphonse, *Eenige hoofdstukken uit het "Apercu sur la Hollande"* (The Hague, 1900), pp. 523–6.

24 Extraordinary spending in the 1740s was met in part by a temporary graduated income tax, assessed from 1742 to 1753, and in 1747 by a *liberale gift*, or voluntary extraordinary property tax. See W. F. H. Oldewelt, ed., *Kohier van de personeele quotisatie te Amsterdam over het jaar 1742*, 2 vols. (Amsterdam, 1945); Isaac de Pinto, *An Essay on Circulation and Credit*, trans. by S. Baggs (London, 1774), p. 119, n. 2; Weeveringh, I, 6; and Houtzager, *Hollands lijf- en losrenteleningen*, p. 108.

25 J. Aalbers, "Holland's Financial Problems (1713–1733) and the Wars against Louis XIV," in *Britain and the Netherlands*, ed. by A. C. Duke and C. A. Tamse (The Hague, 1977), VI, 79–93, has reached the same conclusion.

26 However, taxes were farmed in some parts of the Republic (including Gelderland, Overijssel, and the Generality lands) until 1805. Engels, *Belastingen*, pp. 85–6, suggests that tax revenues were doubled in the areas affected by popular uprisings. Holland's revenues do not appear to have been expanded

to that degree, although in the absence of data for the 1730s and 1740s this matter must remain open. For 1788–94 Sickenga, *Belastingen*, p. 310, puts collection overhead in the two subdivisions of the province of Holland at no more than 7.7 and 10 percent of proceeds.

27 *De Koopman*, III, 180–190 and 215–16.

28 Van der Meulen, *Van de Spiegel*, gives a thorough reconstruction of the fiscal implications of political events in that period. On the revolutions of 1787 and 1795 see C. H. E. de Wit, *De strijd tussen aristocratie en democratie in Nederland, 1780–1848* (Heerlen, 1965), pp. 108–78; Simon Schama, *Patriots and Liberators: Revolution in the Netherlands, 1780–1813* (New York, 1977); Pieter Geyl, "The Batavian Revolution: 1795–1798," in *Encounters in History* (Cleveland, 1961), pp. 226–41; R. R. Palmer, "Much in Little: The Dutch Revolution of 1795," *JMH*, XXVI (March–December, 1954), 15–35; and, on the social renewal sought by the Batavians, H. F. J. M. van den Eerenbeemt, "Het huwelijk tussen filantropie en economie: Een Patriotse en Bataafse illusie," *EHJ*, XXXV (1972), 28–64.

29 Houtzager, *Hollands lijf- en losrenteleningen*, p. 108, on the lapse of life annuities between 1780 and 1794.

30 Sickenga, *Belastingen*, p. 327. Holland's position deteriorated during the 1780s because of deficits caused in part by aid to the East and West India companies, which faced what were regarded as short-term liquidity problems. See ibid., p. 250; and van der Meulen, *Van de Spiegel*, app. I, 5.

31 Van Stralen to Schimmelpenninck, 21 Nov. 1803, in *GS*, IV, ii, 473. Generality, admiralty, East India Company, and some other debts are estimated at an additional f. 150 million, and all liabilities, presumably including those of municipalities and other public corporations, at f. 787 million.

32 Public indebtedness could be increased while confidence in government credit worthiness was fostered, but such techniques as could be brought to bear for that purpose were soon exhausted. In a 1784 loan, for example, Holland offered subscribers the option of investing half in cash and half in outstanding paper dating back into the seventeenth century, intending to raise fresh advances while at least momentarily strengthening the provincial credit position by mobilizing demand for old notes. But the manipulative ability gained through consolidation and prolongation of old loans or, later, through trading in outstanding paper to force prices upward, could not arrest a trend toward higher annuity rates. As rates rose Dutch governments faced the twofold problem of having to offer higher returns in new loans while outstanding paper was being discounted toward effective yields matching those of new issues. (For illustrations of these points see N.E.H.A., Pros., III, 149 and V, 20 and 135; G.A.A., N.41.088; *MNM*, 28 Aug. 1794; and *Verzameling*, IV, 245.) To the degree to which retirements could be arranged through purchases at depreciated rates, public credit gained. But it lost in both the immediately higher cost of new loans and the anxiety of investors saddled with depreciating notes to redress their position by adding higher-yield paper to their portfolios.

33 See Chart 5-1.

34 Gabriel Ardant, *Histoire de l'impôt*, 2 vols. (n.p., 1971–2), II, 44. Total reve-

nues expanded from 161 to 366 million l.t. and indirect tax income from 60 to 192 million l.t. Mathias and O'Brien, "Taxation," 622, offer slightly different figures for the same period but appear to confirm the trend toward indirect taxation. Estimates that distinguish between indirect and direct tax revenues must be regarded as suggestive rather than authoritative because opinions vary about placing some taxes under one or the other type.

35 Ibid. There was not, however, a regular pattern of growth.

36 Compare Table 3-1 with the weighted averages of the relative prices of selected commodities in Chart 1-1. Apparently the Republic had already shifted emphasis to indirect levies in the seventeenth century and had, therefore, relatively less latitude to increase revenues in the area where resistance to new or increased assessments was lower than in the case of direct property or income levies. In the retrospective report of 1797 on pre-1795 revenues, the Republic's income was estimated at some f. 30 million per annum, of which f. 20 million was thought to have been raised on consumables. Sickenga, *Belastingen*, p. 327. It should also be recognized that the Republic suffered a relative loss of import and export duties as the volume of goods entering and leaving Dutch ports stagnated. Joh. de Vries, *De economische achteruitgang der republiek in de achttiende eeuw*, 2nd ed. (Leiden, 1968), pp. 20–4, 185–93, 221–3, and 228–9.

37 In foregoing a monetary role that went any further than providing a stable coinage and money of account, the Republic sacrificed potential income.

38 French taxation revenues were 127 percent greater in 1773 than in 1715, but in the province of Holland the increase between the 1720s and the 1780s was no more than about 21 percent.

Chapter 4. Supply and demand patterns

1 These figures are the mean of the range of nominal value assets estimated for given dates, as given in table. For 1770 and 1780 Dutch holdings in the British debt have been calculated at 12.5 to 16.5 percent of the end-of-year total of the funded debt using current exchange and agio rates. (See below, pp. 123–4 for further information. There is some arbitrariness in the use of end-of-1780 data because of uncertainty about the point at which decline in new Dutch investment around 1780 should be fixed. If the end-of-1779 funded-debt total were used, total Dutch assets in columns 1 and 2 would be reduced by f. 15 to 20 million.) The method of calculation involves a distortion since exchange and agio rates changed over time independently of the nominal or real value of Dutch holdings to debtors. Thus an amount believed to have been stable in sterling values after 1780 increased as the cost of sterling rose and agio declined. Of course the Dutch evaluation of those assets took current rates into account. For rates see Posthumus, I, 604–10 and 653–5. The greater variation in the 1790 range is otherwise chiefly the result of uncertainty about the sum of French liabilities.

	Estimated balance	Britain	Other states
1770	210–290	175–235	35–55
1780	310–290	220–290	90–100
1790	500–650	230–300	270–350

2 Sources for sums given for domestic government debts have been provided in chap. 3; those for foreign government liabilities will be furnished in chaps. 6 and 7. See Posthumus, I, ci, column E, for the deflator (1765–74=100).

3 Lending tended to be clustered rather than distributed evenly over time. The representations given here portray the span in which activity occurred, and in one case (the plantation loans of the 1780s) include gaps of as much as three years. The category "other" includes Portugal, Naples, and Sardinia, on which see chap. 7, no. 40. On loans to Swedish mining and industry see chap. 9, n. 23. Useful sources on loans raised by the lesser states of Germany, which will not otherwise be treated here, include N.E.H.A., Pros. I, 83 and 89, III, 1, 19, 59, 72, and 232, and V, 23 and 39; *idem*, Klein aanwinsten, 165; *idem*, Archief KV, "Acten van aanstellingen van directeuren, commissarissen en procuratiën . . . ," "Brieven aan den Heer D. J. Voombergh te Amsterdam," and "Papieren van Louise Brequet te Neufchatel, 1811" (at length on fraud in the 1771 Hesse-Darmstadt loan); E.H.B., 347 of the prospectuses in the L. Huizinga collection; G.A.A., notaries C. van Homrigh, 12383/648, 12396/279–80, 12410/511, and 12462/165–6, and P. Huntum, 14166/399 and 624; *idem*, Archief Wisselbank, 1359; *idem*, Archief Burgermeesteren, handel 2; *idem*, Archief Brants, 157; *idem*, N. 12.17.03 and the price currents in N. 49.03; U.B.A., 565B14, plans d'emprunts, pt. 6; W. W. van der Meulen, "Een en ander over Van der Capellen tot de Pol en zijn aanhang," in *Geschiedkundige opstellen uitgegeven ter eere van Dr. H. C. Rogge* (Leiden, n.d.), pp. 213, n. 2, and 219–24; and Weeveringh, II, 16–17. See also n. 10.

4 See G.A.A., notaries P. Schabaelje, 6145/723 and 6148/229, and G. van der Groe, 6586/496 and 514 [which indicates that the 1695 issue was marketed in notes (*obligaties*) in denominations of f. 1,000 to 4,000]; N.E.H.A., Archief KV, "Verschillende negotiaties ten behoeve van Zweden . . . 1772–1807"; Franz Mensi, *Die Finanzen Oesterreichs von 1701 bis 1740* (Vienna, 1890), pp. 342–3 and 369–90; H. von Srbik, *Der Staatliche Exporthandel Oesterreichs von Leopold I bis Maria Theresia* (Vienna, 1907), pp. 237–57; J. G. van Dillen, *Van rijkdom en regenten* (The Hague, 1970), pp. 314–21; and Johan E. Elias, *De vroedschap van Amsterdam*, 1578–1795, 2 vols. (Amsterdam, 1963 reprint), II, 1047. In 1695 Deutz called on the Generality receiver general, Cornelis de Jonge van Ellemeet, to assist when the managing house could not move notes rapidly enough. B. E. de Muinck, *Een regentenhuishouding omstreeks 1700* (The Hague, 1965), pp. 86–91. That link disappeared thereafter, although the timing of the withdrawal of receivers is uncertain.

5 J. A. Alting Bösken, *Over geldleeningen hier te lande door vreemde mogenheden aangegaan* (Utrecht, 1864), pp. 35–46; W. F. H. Oldewelt, "De Hoeffijserse schuld (1616–1681)," *JGA*, LI (1954), 37–52; and van Dillen, *Rijkdom*, pp. 457–8. A settlement was reached in 1681. The electoral heir had also negotiated advances from the Dutch Republic in 1610 and 1614. For the political background of the series see F. L. Carsten, *Princes and Parliaments in Germany* (Oxford, 1959), pp. 289ff.

6 See the formula in a 1703 loan on copper in N.E.H.A., Archief KV, "Verschillende negotiaties ten behoeve van Zweden . . . 1772–1807."

7 The commission on copper sales was later increased to 3 percent. Charges on the negotiation of loans seem to have amounted usually to ½ percent on the capital sum plus smaller percentages for brokerage and remittance, and from ¼ to 1 percent on annuity and redemption payments. Mensi, *Finanzen Oesterreichs*, pp. 365, 369, and 378–85; and von Srbik, *Der Staatliche Exporthandel Oesterreichs*, pp. 263–4 and 270. The commission charged by the Generality receiver general, ½ percent, was adopted here and may have served as a precedent. De Muinck, *Een regentenhuishouding*, p. 22. Elias, *Vroedschap*, II, 1051, gives the commission on a 1758 issue at 1 percent plus the equivalent of six months' annuity on the total negotiated (f. 756,650), or 3.5 percent. That pattern of increasing stress on the banking component evidently continued, for William Short to Alexander Hamilton, 2 Dec. 1790 (in *A.H.*, VII, 182), puts commission charges on later Austrian loans at 4 percent.

8 Mensi, *Finanzen Oesterreichs*, pp. 390–407 and 416–19. See also Jean Bérenger, "Public Loans and Austrian Policy in the Second Half of the Seventeenth Century," *JEEH*, II, no. 3 (Winter, 1973), 657–69, on borrowing patterns earlier in the seventeenth century; and Ernst Klein, *Geschichte der öffentlichen Finanzen in Deutschland (1500–1870)* (Wiesbaden, 1974), pp. 26–30, for a compact description of the dual imperial financial system in the early eighteenth century.

9 The only possible exception to this case seems to be credits extended to Spain during the 1770s for canal building. See the discussion of Spain in chap. 7. No expression of anticipated benefit for Dutch commerce or industry was encountered, but that interpretation cannot be ruled out.

10 The Dutch also invested directly in interest-bearing notes issued by the Electorate of Saxony. In the latter 1740s price current quotations indicate that such holdings were large enough to support a market in Amsterdam. J. G. van Dillen, "Effectenkoersen aan de amsterdamsche beurs, 1723–1794," *EHJ*, XVII (1931), 13, reproducing a price current of 6 Nov. 1747. Notarial accords (e.g., G.A.A., notary I. Pool, 12676/24) show extensive trading in this paper in the 1750s. On the *steuerschulden* see Walther Däbritz, *Die Staatsschulden Sachsens in der Zeit von 1763 bis 1837* (Leipzig, 1906), pp. 41 ff., 51ff., and 64ff.; and Jonas Hanway, *An Historical Account of the British Trade over the Caspian Sea . . .*, 3rd ed., 2 vols. (London, 1762), I, 443–4.

11 Von Srbik, *Der Staatliche Exporthandel Oesterreichs*, pp. 236–85, esp. p. 261, n. 2.

12 That total combines prolongations and fresh advances. Mensi, *Finanzen*

Oesterreichs, pp. 360–4 and 384–90; and N.E.H.A., Archief KV, an unlabeled bound volume of prospectuses and other papers.

13 G.A.A., Archief Wisselbank, 1359.

14 See pp. 122–3.

15 Charles H. Wilson, "The Economic Decline of the Netherlands," *EcHR*, IX, no. 2 (May, 1939), 111–13.

16 See the discussion of Austrian finance in chap. 6.

17 See the distribution records in N.E.H.A., Archief KV, "Notten diversen."

18 E.g., Hogguer, Grand, participating in the management of Swedish loans in Amsterdam, sent off small consignments in the latter stages of placements. *Ibid.*, folios 17–18 and 20. Notes in several of the Swedish loans circulated in Antwerp and probably on other capital markets as well. See Smets to Liljencrantz, 10 Feb. 1787, R.A.S., Johan Liljencrantz samling, E 4661.

19 Van Dillen, "Effectenkoersen," 33–6. The range on 4 percent paper was 3.7 to 4.2.

20 See the list of loans compiled by Johannes Petrus van de Voort, *De westindische plantages van 1720 tot 1795: Financiën en handel* (Eindhoven, 1973), pp. 269–323.

21 There was increasing activity in that period in lending to the lesser states of Germany, but those issues involved sums smaller than those customarily sought by major powers. A life-annuity loan floated by France in Amsterdam in 1772 could not be filled and was transferred to Paris. Until 1773 declining demand from foreign governments coincided with a continued increase in plantation loans.

22 Van Dillen, "Effectenkoersen," 37–9.

23 However, the effective return on Russian 5-percent securities during 1778–80 remained 4.9 percent, whereas that on Austrian 4 percent notes, regarded as the most secure of those of all borrowers using the market apparatus, was 4.08 percent. See price currents for single days in each of those three years in G.A.A., N.49.03.

24 Capital exports to France may have applied pressure toward higher yields in Amsterdam because of the premium returns offered in royal loans. But Chart 2-1 indicates that average annuity rates rose in 1782 and 1783 and then fell. There was no sustained higher level until after the flow to France had slowed (1789–91), and even then long-term credit costs in Amsterdam remained considerably below those in Paris in the mid-1780s. The massive capital export to Paris did not, therefore, fully integrate the great bull market in that city with the more restrained market in Amsterdam.

25 See the discussion of financial flows and economic flows in chap. 9.

26 That is, 25 percent of f. 10 million (4 percent of f. 250 million), or f. 2.5 million, in 1770, when the average annual addition to the balance was some f. 11.5 million, and 25 percent of f. 27.45 million (4.5 percent of f. 610 million), or f. 6.8625 million, in 1793, when the average annual addition was some f. 20 million.

27 Equivalent estimates using the higher savings ratio of three-eighths are 33 percent in 1770 and 51 percent in 1793. Under that ratio investments from other sources would have increased from some f. 7.75 million to f. 9.7 million.

28 New foreign government lending fell sharply with the decline of capital export to France in 1787 and 1788. Its average was below f. 20 million through 1790, but it then expanded.

29 Marten G. Buist, *At Spes Non Fracta: Hope & Co., 1770–1815* (The Hague, 1974), p. 107, has explained the availability of capital for Russian loans in 1791 by pointing to a massive withdrawal by Dutch investors from French securities depreciated by the declining value of the French assignat. That interpretation is based on Henry Hope's assertion that investors in French securities were by 1791 "doing penance," that since 1789 investments had been directed toward other borrowers, and that "what has been drawn from thence [France]" was being reinvested in other foreign loans. G. W. Vreede, *Mr. Laurens Pieter van de Spiegel en zijne tijdgenooten, 1737–1800*, 4 vols. (Middelburg, 1874–7), IV, 386–7, Henry Hope to Lord Auckland, August 1791. Capital flow had been directed elsewhere than France even earlier than 1789, but it does not follow that Hope's comments prove disinvestment. If Dutch rentiers had been selling off investments made directly in France then they should also have withdrawn from investments in undertakings opened in Amsterdam on the security of French annuities. But *beurs* quotations do not reflect such a move (see below, chap. 7, n. 77). And at least one rentier who displayed some talent in building a portfolio continued to buy French annuities in 1791 and 1792, when they were available at discounts created by the fall of the assignat. G.A.A., Archief Brants, 127, on Jan Jacob Brants. More probably Hope merely meant that capital that would earlier have been invested in France was being placed elsewhere.

30 On the replacement of R. & Th. de Smeth see Buist, *Hope & Co.*, pp. 93ff. and 143, n. 5, where the old story that Henry Hope traveled to St. Petersburg to persuade Catherine to change bankers is discredited.

31 Although Russian borrowing had encountered some difficulty in 1782, the date of the last issue, that does not appear to have influenced events in 1787. See *D.T.*, pp. 294–7, dispatches of 15 and 18 Jan. 1782. Thulemeyer had reported six months earlier (ibid., 270, dispatch of 24 July 1781) that the banker Boas had told Emperor Joseph II that Austria and Russia had the highest credit standing among states floating loans in Amsterdam.

32 On 30 Sept. 1788 a single point separated Russian and Austrian notes paying the same annuity rate. G.A.A., N.41.088.

33 Buist, *Hope & Co.*, pp. 94–6.

34 Ibid., pp. 95–8.

35 Ibid., app. D-1, p. 497, a table of those loans. Of seventeen issues of f. 3 million each, the sixteenth (opened in 1793) was subscribed only to f. 2.5 million and the last never brought onto the market.

36 Ibid., pp. 94–105.

37 For examples of this see ibid., pp. 95–6, on the first loans, and p. 104 on the sixth. Catherine was pleased enough with Hope's services to offer a title, but Hope declined.

In discussing ploys used by Dutch houses, the American envoy William Short observed that Hope "raised the price of the stock always before bringing a new loan on the market, so that it was desired & sought after, & by this means was enabled to make them more frequently & with more facility." Short to Alexander Hamilton, 18 Dec. 1790, in *A.H.*, VII, 351. The technique, of course, was to buy notes.

38 See the discussion of investor characteristics at the end of chap. 2.

39 One interesting but perhaps unrepresentative point of comparison may be suggested. Perceiving the French advance into Belgium as a threat to outspoken Orangists, Henry Hope chose in March 1793 to leave Amsterdam and, at least for the time being, to resettle in England. *Beurs* prices for Russian securities held steady through January 1793 but with the declaration of war in February plunged five points and more. By March, however, prices were recovering, and the resurgence continued through May. The source of quotations, the *Mercurius*, gives prices at semimonthly and monthly intervals, so that very short-term changes are not evident. Nonetheless those quotations suggest that Hope's departure, news of which was certainly available to commission agents and investors, either did not affect prices at all or stirred them for a period of less than two weeks. It should be recognized that Hope's departure did not mean that the firm was closed, but that it might have been construed as contrary to the interests of holders of Russian securities.

40 It is also true that Russia enjoyed a reputation for having substantial untapped resources, and that may have attracted investors. On that see, e.g., Buist, *Hope & Co.*, pp. 141 and 143.

41 See ibid., pp. 123–54, on negotiations between Hope and the Russian court through Hope's representative, Robert Voûte, and covering the period from August 1793 to June 1794.

Chapter 5. International government finance

1 Data, which include some nontax revenues, have been drawn from evidence presented in chaps. 3, 6, and 7, and from J. F. Bosher, *French Finances, 1770–1795* (Cambridge, 1970), pp. 89–90; Alain Guéry, "Les finances de la monarchie française sous l'Ancien Régime," *AESC*, XXXIII, no. 2 (March–April, 1978), 216–39; and Peter Mathias and Patrick O'Brien, "Taxation in Britain and France, 1715–1810: A Comparison of the Social and Economic Incidence of Taxes Collected for the Central Governments," *JEEH*, V, no. 3 (Winter, 1976), 604 and 642–3 (omitting averaged data and information for 1790–1, 1803–4, and 1807–8 because of the higher degree of probable error and the distortion of exchange rates). Whereas British data are net revenues paid into the exchequer, French revenue estimates are between net and gross taxes collected (ibid., 643–6). Otherwise, except for Sweden where data used are estimates of projected revenues, it is not clear whether figures represent net or gross receipts or something in between. The French and Russian revenue lines are less reliable than those for other states. By 1801, when exchange rates on London are once again available, British revenues exceeded f. 330 million.

Conversions have been made using average annual exchange and agio rates calculated from Posthumus, I, 600ff. and 652 ff.; Heinrich Friedrich von

Storch, *Supplementband zum fünften, sechsten und siebenten Theil des Historisch-statistischen Gemäldes des russischen Reichs* (Leipzig, 1803), pp. 5–7; and, for the Russian rate of 1809, from a single quotation for that year given in Marten G. Buist, *At Spes Non Fracta: Hope & Co., 1770–1815* (The Hague, 1974), p. 225, n. 1. Trends in exchange rates are discussed in appropriate sections of chaps. 6 and 7. Significant variations occurred in the rates for Russia, Sweden, and Denmark, in large measure because of an expansion in money supply, which is deflated here against a current-guilder index. For most of the period French, British, and Austrian currencies traded against guilders within a narrow range. Mathias and O'Brien have adopted wheat prices as a standard for comparing British and French revenues. There is no entirely satisfactory index, but guilder rates may be preferred for multilateral comparisons in certain periods if only because of wider availability. It should also be noted that substantial differences in tax systems and the entire incidence of taxation levied by other agencies than the central government are not taken into account here. Such problems are addressed for Britain and France in Mathias and O'Brien, "Taxation," passim. Finally, in this chart solid lines connect years for which consecutive annual data are available, and dashed lines indicate periods for which data are available at less frequent intervals.

2 In Great Britain, for example, net revenues increased by 56 percent between 1766–70 and 1786–90, but expenditures expanded by 66 percent. Most of that increase was accounted for by a 93-percent growth in the outlay for debt charges, which of course represented liabilities accumulated to permit wartime spending on the army and navy. Peacetime military spending increased by only 31 percent over the same period.

3 B. R. Mitchell, *European Historical Statistics, 1750–1970* (London, 1975), pp. 697 and 706–8; and, for exchange and agio rates, Posthumus, I, 602–14 and 653–5. Guéry, "Les finances de la monarchie française," 228, portrays the French deficit pattern from 1520 to 1780.

4 P. G. M. Dickson and John Sperling, "War Finance, 1689–1714," in *New Cambridge Modern History*, ed. by J. S. Bromley (Cambridge, 1970), VI, 313.

5 Charles Morazé, "Finance et despotisme," *AESC*, III, no. 3 (July–September,, 1948), 279–96, on the preoccupation of enlightened despots with postwar financial reform.

6 Mathias and O'Brien, "Taxation," 604–9 and 611–13.

7 Ibid., 635: "The French government could not–or did not–appropriate an increased share of a rising national income in the same way as the British government . . . did."

8 It is not yet possible to establish accurately the relative differences among states either in the distribution of taxation according to wealth or in the margin of assets that remained unseized because some individuals, groups, or corporations escaped the relative weight of taxes carried by others with similar assets and income but different social or political roles. Controversy over the relative regressivity of the British and French systems has failed to furnish the evidence necessary for a judgment. See Betty Behrens, "Nobles, Privileges and Taxes in France at the End of the *Ancien Régime*," *EcHR*, 2nd ser., XV, no. 3 (1963), 451–75; G. J. Cavanaugh, "Nobles, Privileges,

and Taxes in France: A Revision Reviewed," *FHS*, VIII, no. 4 (Fall, 1974), 681–92; Betty Behrens, "A Revision Defended: Nobles, Privileges, and Taxes in France," *FHS*, IX, no. 3 (Spring, 1976), 521–7; Cavanaugh's reply in *idem*, 528–31; Mathias and O'Brien, "Taxation," 629–40, Donald N. McCloskey, "A Mismeasurement of the Incidence of Taxation in Britain and France, 1715–1810," *JEEH*, VII, no. 1 (Spring, 1978), 209–10; and Peter Mathias and Patrick O'Brien, "The Incidence of Taxes and the Burden of Proof," in *idem*, 211–13.

9 On the Prussian system see Rudolf Braun, "Taxation, Sociopolitical Structure, and State-Building: Great Britain and Brandenburg-Prussia," in Charles Tilly, ed., *The Formation of National States in Western Europe* (Princeton, N.J., 1975), 243–327, esp. 278–81 and 294f.; and Emil Daniels, "Frederick the Great and His Successor," in *Cambridge Modern History*, ed. by A. W. Ward et al. (Cambridge, 1909), VI, 710–11 and 721. Conservative financial policies finally failed Prussia during the War of the First Coalition, and beginning in 1792 and 1793 loans were floated in both Frankfurt and Amsterdam. Prussia used foreign credit intermittently during the Revolutionary and Napoleonic wars, but was unable to develop dependable resources. As a result war expenses, and the indemnity levied by France after the Peace of Tilsit, were managed chiefly by tax increases and the sale of crown lands. On credit exploitation in 1792 and thereafter see NNJ, 1793, 1439–40; N.E.H.A., Pros., IV, 93, and V, 122 and 137; J. A. Alting Bösken, *Over geldleeningen hier te lande door vreemde mogendheden aangegaan* (Utrecht, 1864), pp. 52–6; Leopold Krug, *Geschichte der preussischen Staatsschulden*, in *Nachgelassene Schriften*, ed. by Carl Julius Bergius, I (Breslau, 1861), 32–8 and 131–3; Ernst Klein, *Geschichte der öffentlichen Finanzen in Deutschland (1500–1870)* (Wiesbaden, 1974), pp. 61–2 and 103–5; Barthold Georg Niebuhr, *Geschichte des Zeitalters der Revolution*, 2 vols. (Hamburg, 1845), II, 377–407; Jérôme Alexandre Sillem, *Het leven van Mr. Johan Valckenaer (1759–1821)*, new ed., 2 vols. (Amsterdam, 1883), II, 235–94; Charles Lesage, *Napoléon Ier, créancier de la Prusse (1807–1814)* (Paris, 1924), pp. 228–82; Montalivet to the emperor (Napoleon), 28 Oct. 1811, in *GS*, VI, 217; and, on postwar borrowing and tax reforms, Weeveringh, II, 633–70; and Ernst Klein, *Von der Reform zur Restauration: Finanzpolitik und Reformgesetzgebung des preussischen Staatskanzlers Karl August von Hardenberg* (Berlin, 1965), pp. 64–99.

10 Braun, "Taxation," 304.

11 Although French treasury officials sometimes identified elements of British policy that might be expected to improve the monarchy's financial position and flexibility [see Robert D. Harris, "French Finances and the American War, 1777–1783," *JMH*, XLVIII, no. 2 (June, 1976), 242–3], they failed to implement those methods on any significant scale. In fact Jacques Necker, who apparently can command only sharp antagonism or obsequious devotion, appears to have misunderstood the central elements of British superiority in building and exploiting public credit. From 1776 to 1781 Necker concentrated on introducing economies in ordinary (peacetime) expenditures sufficient to carry debt service added by wartime loans. Although he ex-

panded credit access, drawing on Genevan, Dutch, and Genoan resources, he did not use that access to reduce returns offered in subsequent French loans and maintained a borrowing format, the life-annuity loan, on terms that were highly disadvantageous. While Britain and other states reduced annuity rates in keeping with the secular trend of most of the eighteenth century toward lower credit costs and by expanding credit access, France continued to pay excessive yields.

12 The *rente viagère* issue of January 1782 made a primitive effort to vary returns according to age groups, but for the rest available knowledge was not brought to bear. The technique of applying mortality data to project life expectancy, and thus to evaluate life annuities, was explained in numerous handbooks published in the latter half of the century. See, for example, Emmanuel Etienne Duvillard de Durand, *Recherche sur les rentes, les emprunts et les remboursemens* (Paris, 1787), preceding p. 1; Antoine Deparcieux, *Essai sur les probabilités de la durée de la vie humaine* (Paris, 1746); *idem, Addition à l'essai sur les probabilités* . . . (Paris, 1760); and [Paul-Edme Crublier] de Saint-Cyran, *Calcul des rentes viagères sur une et sur plusieurs têtes* . . . (Paris, 1779). The last mentioned describes methods of investment in life-annuity loans, comments on grounds for selecting individuals as nominees, reproduces mortality tables, and in general offers a guide to the French loans of the 1770s. De Saint-Cyran also condemns the unnecessarily high returns of those loans: "C'est à cette cause en partie que l'on doit attribuer le désordre des finances dans quelques Etats de l'Europe. . ." (ibid., p. 28).

13 The return on *rentes viagères* was calculated on the basis of existing information on life expectancy in the population at large, and thus without regard for the fact that investors would select nominees. A. Bailly, *Histoire financière de la France, depuis l'origine de la monarchie jusqu'à la fin de 1786*, 2 vols. (Paris, 1830), II, 220.

14 Harris, "French Finances and the American War," 253, has calculated that the Genevan 30-contract formula (see chap. 7) was used in no more than 15 percent of the life-annuity contracts issued during Necker's first administration, implying that that method of constitution was less important than has been believed. But he overlooks the fact that that formula, which was merely a method of risk dispersal, was of no consequence to the French treasury. The issue is whether Genevan investors selected nominees with greater care than their counterparts elsewhere who employed the 30-contract formula or who constituted contracts singly or in groups of a different size. The availability of actuarial data indicates that all investors could have constituted contracts on nominees whose longevity prospects were much higher than the flat span projected by the treasury, and Dutch investors are known in general to have applied the same skill in selecting annuitants that was brought to bear in Geneva. Necker, who reintroduced the life-annuity issue after a lapse of six years, did not alter its terms to take actuarial realities into account or adjust returns in response to the expanding flow of investment from abroad.

15 One formula is

$$P = \frac{H}{i}\left(1 - \frac{1}{(1+i)^n}\right)$$

where P = price,
H = expected net average annual income,
n = number of years expected from purchase to extinction,
and i = rate of return on the investment.

16 This figure would increase if the estimated total of the French debt were scaled down. See n. 18.

17 Therefore Dutch investment in French loans during the 1780s may be explained by the twofold attraction of high returns and a credit structure more favorable to lenders.

18 Bosher, *French Finances*, pp. 89–90; Frédéric Braesch, *Finances et monnaie révolutionnaires*, 2 fascicules (Paris, 1934–6), fasc. II, 202; B. R. Mitchell and Phyllis Deane, *Abstract of British Historical Statistics* (Cambridge, 1971), pp. 388–402; and Posthumus, I, 609, for end-of-1787 exchange rates through Amsterdam. There is much uncertainty about the magnitude of the French debt on the eve of the Revolution or at any other point in the eighteenth century. Calculations made by Harris, "French Finances and the American War," 235–6, indicate that the costs of the American war may have been exaggerated by previous scholars. Moreover, the same source (248–9) estimates the French debt as of the end of 1782 at only 3.315 billion livres. Those arguments point to the conclusion that French indebtedness as of 1788 may have been significantly less than 5 billion livres, although the difficulty of reconstructing accounts leaves all estimates uncertain. However, Harris's figures on the 1782 debt (249) suggest an average annuity rate of only 4.99 percent (165.4 million on 3.3151 billion), an unaccountably low level. His approximation of the life-annuity portion of the debt (248, n. 44) is clearly suspect, for his cumulative total is less than the estimated total of subscriptions in life-annuity loans issued from 1771 through 1782 alone (Marcel Marion, *Histoire financière de la France depuis 1715*, 6 vols. (Paris, 1927–8), I, 472–3). In some cases loans were enlarged by treasury officials after 1782, but life-annuity debts outstanding in 1782 stretched back at least to 1702.

Within certain boundaries the size of the debt is less important than its cost as a portion of ordinary revenues (defined by Harris, "French Finances and the American War," 237, as those revenues "which could reasonably be expected to come in during the fiscal year from the existing tax structure"). Calculations offered here attempt to measure the relative cost of borrowing to the French treasury and the relative ability of the treasury to meet service payments out of ordinary revenues.

19 That is, a French debt of 8.6 billion l.t. would have cost, at the service rate paid by Britain on the funded debt, about 318 million l.t.

20 Lennart Jörberg, *A History of Prices in Sweden, 1732–1914*, 2 vols. (Lund, 1972), I, 78–9.

21 Ibid., I, 79; and Robert V. Eagly, "Monetary Policy and Politics in Mid-Eighteenth Century Sweden," *JEH*, XXIX, no. 4 (December, 1969), 749–50.

22 In contrast political authorities in some other states, e.g., L. P. van de Spiegel in the Dutch Republic, viewed the general inflationary trend of the latter part of the century as a product of an expanding money supply. Joh. de Vries,

ed., "Van de Spiegel's 'Schets tot een vertoog over de intrinsique en relative magt van de republijk' (1782)," *EHJ*, XXVII (1958), 90 and n. 5.

23 Spanish and Austrian note issues included interest-bearing paper currency. The United States issued paper currency during the American Revolution but by the period of borrowing in the Netherlands issues had been suspended except for indents used to service the domestic debt.

24 Mitchell and Deane, *British Historical Statistics*, pp. 386–8, 392, and 401–2; Josef van Hauer, *Beiträge zur Geschichte der österr. Finanzen* (Vienna, 1848), pp. 161–4 and 209–11; Herbert Hassinger, "Politische Kräft und Wirtschaft 1350–1800," in *Handbuch der deutschen Wirtschaft- und Sozialgeschichte*, ed.by Hermann Aubin and Wolfgang Zorn (Stuttgart, 1971), I, 652; Mitchell, *European Historical Statistics*, pp. 697 and 706–7; Karl Åmark, *Sveriges statsfinanser, 1719–1809* (Stockholm, 1961), pp. 406–14, 622–3, 626, and 648–9; V. Falbe-Hansen and Will. Scharling, *Danmarks statistik*, 6 vols. (Copenhagen, 1878–91), IV, 174–7 and 379–80; Dickens and Sperling, "War Finance," pp. 299–300; Gabriel Ardant, *Histoire de l'impôt*, 2 vols. (n.p., 1971–2), II, 44; and sources cited herein, chap. 3, n. 22; chap. 7, nn. 1, 5, and 41.

The debt sums used in these comparisons include the short-term liabilities of the United Kingdom. In other states short- and long-term debts are not distinguished in the available data, but the sums cited here appear generally to cover only long-term indebtedness. Through 1801 net receipts of Great Britain are compared with the nominal sum of the public debt of the United Kingdom; from 1802 gross revenues of the United Kingdom are compared with the nominal sum of the public debt of the United Kingdom. For Austria the ratio for 1768 is indebtedness to expenditures. The two columns for Austria and Denmark give, respectively, the ratio of the long-term interest-bearing debt to current revenues and the ratio of the interest-bearing debt plus outstanding paper currency to current revenues. For Denmark 1769 indebtedness has been extrapolated from data relating to 1766 and 1771, and the 1807 debt has been compared to 1806 revenues. Swedish figures all represent anticipated income compared to actual indebtedness composed of interest-bearing loans and paper currency in circulation. Data on bank note volume in Sweden are unavailable for 1801–15. Except for 1784 (where the domestic and foreign long-term debt and assignats in circulation are compared to revenues taken at the mean of 1783 and 1785 levels), cumulative Russian indebtedness cannot be reconstructed from available sources. Figures in that column represent the ratio of Russia's outstanding debt in the Dutch Republic plus assignats outstanding to current revenues. For France the 1713 debt (consisting of long-term liabilities only) has been related to 1714 revenues. All amounts are given in nominal sums, a distinction that is of some importance in regard to the British debt (which was greater than the amount actually raised in public loans because of discounts from par at issue) and to the sum of interest-bearing and paper currency indebtedness in all states where such paper depreciated. Changes in the ratio of debts to revenues result in some cases from manipulation of currency values, which will be discussed below.

In a more common method of projecting debt-repayment periods the average debt outstanding in a year (the average between first-of-year and end-of-year indebtedness) is divided by the amount of amortization payments during the year. Such a method requires more precise data about amortization than are available for the eighteenth century, where term and life annuities further complicate the problem. However, such an amortization-based ratio would clearly yield much higher figures than are presented in this chart and, where service included little or no reimbursement, would approach or reach infinity.

25 Credit policies were not formulated to take into account the capacity of an economy to acquire foreign exchange with which to redeem foreign debts. Because multilateral trade balances are usually obscure, no attempt can be made here to measure relative solidity in terms of foreign-exchange earnings.

Chapter 6. The debtor states: I

1 P. G. M. Dickson, *The Financial Revolution in England: A Study in the Development of Public Credit, 1688–1756* (New York, 1967), pp. 46 and 50ff. On the eighteenth-century public debt see also Alice C. Carter, "Analyses of Public Indebtedness in Eighteenth-century England," *Bulletin of the Institute of Historical Research*, XXIV, no. 70 (September, 1951), 173–81; J. E. D. Binney, *British Public Finance and Administration, 1774–92* (Oxford, 1958); J. J. Grellier, *The History of the National Debt from the Revolution in 1688 to . . . 1800* (London, 1810); *idem, The Terms of All the Loans Which Have Been Raised for the Public Service . . .*, 3rd ed. (London, 1805); Sir John Sinclair, *The History of the Public Revenue of the British Empire*, 3rd ed. reprinted, 3 vols. (New York, 1966); and B. R. Mitchell and Phyllis Deane, *Abstract of British Historical Statistics* (Cambridge, 1971), pp. 381ff.

2 Dickson, *Financial Revolution*, p. 227 and n. 4, citing the Archief Brants on the British view of the impact on British loans of issues opened by the Dutch.

3 Robert V. Eagly and V. Kerry Smith, "Domestic and International Integration of the London Money Market, 1731–1789," *JEH*, XXXVI, no. 1 (March, 1976), 198–212, maintain that London and Amsterdam short-term interest rates were closely integrated during the period surveyed. There is good, if largely impressionistic, reason to believe that case. But the figures they analyze, the "discount rate of the Bank of Amsterdam" (p. 199), appear to be the percentage premium or discount at which bank money traded in relation to current money. The Bank of Amsterdam did not set a discount rate because it was not involved on any significant scale in discounting bills or (outside cases cited above, dealing with loans to some public and semipublic bodies) in extending long or short-term credit.

4 Joh. de Vries, *De economische achteruitgang der republiek in de achttiende eeuw*, 2nd ed. (Leiden, 1968), p. 64.

5 Adapted from Dickson, *Financial Revolution*, p. 10.

6 Ibid., pp. 470–5.

7 See ibid., pp. 199–215.
8 See ibid., pp. 229ff. on reaction to the Pelham conversion.
9 Although some British observers professed concern at the end of the seventeenth century about the volume of Dutch investment in the public debt, overall foreign holdings in the funds (as government annuities and bank and company stock were collectively known) remained of modest significance until the early 1720s. By 1723–4, however, foreign holdings accounted for slightly over 9 percent of that part of the national debt composed of stock of the Bank of England and the South Sea and East India companies. Ibid., pp. 304 and 312.

The British view of investment in the funds from abroad had always been divided, with some commentators arguing that foreign capital was desirable because it released domestic resources for other uses, and others that it drained resources and threatened Britain's economic and fiscal stability. In its more extreme forms, the latter view was part of one of the more pervasive political myths current in eighteenth-century England. In the 1740s foreigners were widely believed to hold a quarter of the public debt. Similar and even higher figures were bandied about later in the century, but the myth distorted reality. See ibid., p. 305; John Hope, *Letters on Credit*, 2nd ed. (London, 1784), pp. 26–31; and, for the Dutch side, [Isaac de Pinto], *Traité de la circulation et du crédit* (Amsterdam, 1771), pp. 42ff.

10 Dickson, *Financial Revolution*, pp. 218–19; and Mitchell and Deane, *British Historical Statistics*, p. 401. All funded-debt data are for the end of the financial year (see Mitchell and Deane, p. 403, n. b), and are in nominal values.
11 Dickson, *Financial Revolution*, pp. 321–2.
12 During the 1720s and 1730s Sir Robert Walpole managed a net reduction of the debt of more than £6 million. Ibid., pp. 209–10.
13 That is, from 9 percent of £43.3 million, the funded debt at the end of the financial year 1739, to about 15 percent of £71.8 million, the total at the end of 1749. Mitchell and Deane, *British Historical Statistics*, p. 401. See also Dickson, *Financial Revolution*, pp. 228–32, on the long-term debt in 1749.
14 Mitchell and Deane, *British Historical Statistics*, p. 390, on expenditures, 1740 through 1749, totaling £95,123,000.
15 See chap. 3, n. 11.
16 As of 6 Nov. 1747 the effective return on province of Holland notes administered in The Hague and Amsterdam was 2.7 to 2.76 percent, whereas new English loans were offering 4 percent. The effective return on 4-percent British annuities in Amsterdam moved from 3.64 percent at the beginning of 1740 to 4 percent at the beginning of 1748. J. G. van Dillen, "Effectenkoersen aan de Amsterdamsche beurs, 1723–1794," *EHJ*, XVII (1931), 25–8.
17 Dickson, *Financial Revolution*, p. 322; and Alice C. Carter, "Dutch Foreign Investment, 1738–1800," *Economica*, XX, n.s. (November, 1953), 330–9. Carter's estimate relates to Dutch holdings alone and must be increased to account for all foreign holdings. The Dutch led among foreign investors but Swiss, Irish, German, and other nationals were also involved. See also *idem*, "Dutch Foreign Investment, 1738–1800, in the Light of the Amsterdam 'Col-

lateral Succession' Inventories," *TvG*, LXVI (1953), 29–31, for a discussion of movement by Dutch capital among the various British securities.

18 Mitchell and Deane, *British Historical Statistics*, p. 402. At an exchange of 35 schellingen (or deniers de gros) banco to the pound sterling, and with agio at 4 percent, those sums represented f. 186 to 328 million, but not all foreign ownership was Dutch ownership. On Dutch investment during the Seven Years' War see also E. E. de Jong-Keesing, *De economische crisis van 1763 te Amsterdam* (n.p., 1939), pp. 43–4 and, for the exchange-rate quotation, app. B.

19 Alice C. Carter, "The Dutch and the English Public Debt in 1777," *Economica*, XX, n.s. (May, 1953), 161; and Mitchell and Deane, *British Historical Statistics*, p. 402. Carter finds unreliable an estimate by the anti-Orangist L. T. van Nassau La Leck, whose exaggerated appraisal at three-sevenths was motivated by a desire that Dutch investors withdraw from England.

Dutch and Genevan rentiers also bought into the Irish tontines of the 1770s. See N.E.H.A., Pros., III, 25, for a prospectus issued on the 1773 tontine by an Amsterdam broker; and Charles Gautier, "Un investissement genevois: la tontine d'Irlande de 1777," *Bulletin de la société d'histoire et d'archéologie de Genève*, X (1951), 53–68.

20 Dickson, *Financial Revolution*, pp. 323–4. Contemporary estimates of foreign holdings varied widely. For examples relating only to 1781 and 1782 see Eberhard August Wilhelm von Zimmermann, *A Political Survey of the Present State of Europe* . . . (London, 1787), pp. 182–3, citing the *Political Journal* without further reference and estimating f. 165 million; NNJ, 1781, 38–9, giving two estimates, one of f. 300 million and another of f. 690 million; and, from L. P. van de Spiegel [in Joh. de Vries, ed., "Van de Spiegel's 'Schets tot een vertoog over de intrinsique en relative magt van de republijk' (1782)," *EHJ*, XXVII (1958), 92] f. 280 million.

21 Mitchell and Deane, *British Historical Statistics*, pp. 386ff. for data on revenues and expenditures.

22 Carter, "Dutch Foreign Investment," *Economica*, 339, suggests that Dutch investment held roughly at prewar levels through the war but that thereafter "there was clearly a flight from the English funds, going on until the end of the century." On Dutch withdrawal see also Charles H. Wilson, *Anglo-Dutch Commerce and Finance in the Eighteenth Century* (Cambridge, 1941), pp. 189ff.; Hope, *Letters on Credit*, pp. 24 and 63; and n. 30.

23 Even before the middle of the century some commentators had compared Britain unfavorably to France in regard to the former's ability to liquidate its debt. Dickson, *Financial Revolution*, pp. 21–3. Such sentiments were stronger during the 1770s and early 1780s.

24 *D.T.*, p. 279, dispatch of 23 Oct. 1781.

25 On the transition to French investments see the discussion in chap. 7.

26 Van Dillen, "Effectenkoersen," 33 ff. These data are based on first-of-year prices. The average for the 1780s as a whole was 4.6 percent.

27 Binney, *British Public Finance*, pp. 111 and 283 (app. 1).

28 Mitchell and Deane, *British Historical Statistics*, p. 402.

29 Dickson, *Financial Revolution*, pp. 322–3. For the view that Britain was

near failure during the Revolutionary and Napoleonic wars see Audrey Cunningham, *British Credit in the Last Napoleonic War* (Cambridge, 1910), pp. 14–15, 17–19, and 21–5.

30 Dutch earnings from the British funds were estimated in 1811 to be f. 12 million annually. Montalivet to the emperor (Napoleon), 28 Oct. 1811, in *GS*, VI, 219. At average returns of 3.5 to 4.5 percent, that would indicate a nominal value of f. 267 to 343 million, but this source quite correctly stresses the difficulty of estimating the value of investments. Dickson puts all foreign ownership at about £20 million, less than 4 percent of the long-term debt, between 1807 and 1810. At current exchange and agio rates that would represent about f. 220 million.

Dutch refugee capital was of some importance on the London capital market during the Revolutionary and Napoleonic wars, but the totals involved cannot yet be estimated.

31 As that chart indicates, Austrian revenues climbed between 1781 and 1794 to a level equivalent to British revenues 20 to 30 years earlier (1765–76). Even so Austrian gains were slower than British and, after 1794, Austria's revenues fell while Britain's continued to grow. The expansion through 1794 might be taken to suggest that tax income represented a high portion of those revenues that could be raised principally through indirect taxes in a society where significant economic growth does not appear to have prevailed. However, in the absence of comparative information about price trends and about the degree to which Austrian revenues may have increased as prices inflated rather than because the incidence or rate of taxation was increased, the question must remain open.

32 See Robert Horvàth, "Monetary Inflation in Hungary During the Napoleonic Wars," *JEEH*, V, no. 3 (Winter, 1976), 652–3; and Josef von Hauer, *Beiträge zur Geschichte der österr. Finanzen* (Vienna, 1848), p. 209.

33 Data in Chart 6-1 are from von Hauer, *Oesterr. Finanzen*, pp. 162–4. On the subsequent period see ibid., p. 164; and Adolf Beer, *Die Finanzen Oesterreichs im XIX. Jahrhundert* (Prague, 1877), pp. 391–2, although those two sources do not always give the same data. Exchange and agio rates for converting gulden into current guilders may be found in Posthumus, I, 601–18 and 653–6. Data in this table are in gulden but in Chart 6-3 revenues, expenditures, and British loans have been converted to current guilders using annual average exchange and agio rates. On the method of calculating the exchange see Joseph-René Ruelle, *Opérations des changes des principales places d'Europe* (Lyon, An VII), p. 13.

34 Hajo Holborn, *A History of Modern Germany, 1648–1840* (New York, 1964), p. 230.

35 Herbert Hassinger, "Politische Kräft und Wirtschaft 1350–1800," in *Handbuch der deutschen Wirtschaft- und Sozialgeschichte*, ed. by Hermann Aubin and Wolfgang Zorn (Stuttgart, 1971), I, 652.

36 Paul Stiassny, *Der österreichische Staatsbankerott von 1811* (Vienna, 1912), p. 19. Fl.11 million had been raised in Italy, fl.9 million in the Dutch Republic, and the remainder in Switzerland.

37 Von Hauer, *Oesterr. Finanzen*, p. 163.

38 G.A.A., notaries J. de Bruijn, 14087/3565, 14089/3914, 14090/3944, 14093/4470 and 4473, 14094/4557, 14107/5836, 14112/6322, and 14118/7098, and C. van Homrigh, 12372/114 and 121, 12380/150, 12381/224, 12389/1057 and 1130, 12394/801, 12442/505-7, 12445/4-6, 12446/153-6, and 12456/192; *idem*, N. 49.03, containing a price current for 8 Oct. 1778; *idem*, Archief Burgermeesteren, "Bankierszaken in negotiatiën met het buitenland"; N.E.H.A., Pros., III, 55, 71, and 74; *idem*, Kleine aanwinsten, 194; *idem*, Archief KV, "Acten van aanstellingen van directeuren, commissarissen en procuratiën. . ."; and J. Dinger, *Overzicht van alle ter beurze van Amsterdam verhandeld wordende binnen- en buitenlandsche effecten*, 5th ed. (Amsterdam, 1873), p. 362. Most Austrian issues were managed by Verbrugge & Goll, although the Amsterdam house of Caesar Sardi & Co. organized some loans in the 1760s, and the Rotterdam firm of Joan Osy & Zoon managed one of the 1779 advances. A. & S. Boas of The Hague also opened a loan in 1778 or 1779. *D.T.*, p. 213, dispatch of 11 June 1779. On Osy see H. Hardenburg, "Het handelshuis Osy," *Rotterdams jaarboekje*, 6th ser., II (1954), 154–76. The Sardi loans were taken over by Verbrugge & Goll in 1773. Rates in Chart 6-2 are averaged for years in which loans were issued at different returns.

39 Von Hauer, *Oesterr. Finanzen*, pp. 158–60. Only a fragmentary account is given of the sums involved.

40 Clifford continued to handle service transfers on loans managed by that house until 1773, when the firm failed. *D.T.*, p. 102, dispatch of 22 Jan. 1773.

41 G.A.A., notary J. de Bruijn, 14064/157, 169, and 180. Also 14113/6415 on an issue of 1747 and 14064/147 and 14119/7189 on one of 1754. Verbrugge & Goll opened a new loan in 1758 and assumed management of earlier advances negotiated through the Utrecht house.

42 On Johann Goll and a charge of swindling against him in 1750 in relation to business activities in Brussels between 1744 and 1746 see Johan E. Elias, *De vroedschap van Amsterdam, 1578–1795*, 2 vols. (Amsterdam, 1963 reprint), II, 1051. Goll was granted a patent of nobility by Maria Theresa in 1766, and in 1781, when he was aged and blind, Joseph II called on him during a state visit to the United Provinces. *NNJ*, 1781, 1352. Goll's partner was Gijsbert Antwerpen Verbrugge. On the associates in the firm after 1778 see Elias, *Vroedschap*, II, 1052. The papers of the house have not survived, but balance sheets from 1779–1824 may be found in N.E.H.A., Kleine aanwinsten, 22, "Balansen en kontrakten van associatie van de Firma Goll & Compagnie, bankiers te Amsterdam, 1779–(c. 1915)."

43 *D.T.*, p. 132, dispatch from Renfner, 22 July 1774.

44 Ibid., p. 213, dispatch of 11 June 1779. Thulemeyer puts the return on the part still outstanding at 6 percent. Available notarial accords do not suggest that so high a rate was ever charged in this period.

45 The notarial accords give a total of slightly more than f. 12 million in loans in 1778 and 1779.

46 Von Hauer, *Oesterr. Finanzen*, p. 209.

47 Ibid., pp. 155–88 and 209. See also Jean Bouchary, *Les manieurs d'argent à Paris à la fin du XVIIIe siècle*, 3 vols. (Paris, 1939–1943), III, 263; Herbert

Lüthy, *La banque protestante en France de la révocation de l'édit de Nantes à la Révolution*, 2 vols. (Paris, 1959–1961), II, 75–6; and, on an issue in Brussels in 1771, U.B.A., 565B14, plans d'emprunts, pt. 6.

48 G.A.A., notary C. van Homrigh, 12434/207, 12438/754, and 12485/139; and N.E.H.A., Pros., III, 68 and 69. The prospectuses suggest that Dutch investors wished to reinvest redemptions being received on Austrian loans. On direct foreign investment in Viennese loans see also Dickson, *Financial Revolution*, p. 333.

49 D.T., p. 132, dispatch from Renfner of 22 July 1774.

50 Ibid., p. 191. See also the dispatches of 26 June and 14 Aug. 1778 on pp. 192–4.

51 Ibid., p. 194, dispatch of 14 Aug. 1778.

52 The price lists may be found in G.A.A., N.49.03. They relate to trading on 8 Oct. 1778, 30 Mar. 1779, and 8 July 1780.

53 *D.T.*, p. 213, dispatch of 11 June 1779.

54 Ibid., p. 270, dispatch of 24 July 1781.

55 See the price current in [Oudermeulen], II, pt. 2, 263–8. Despite the recent fall in mercury prices, 3.5-percent notes secured on mercury consignments were trading slightly in advance of paper backed by bank debentures paying the same return.

56 Short to Hamilton, 2 Dec. 1790, *A.H.*, VII, 180, put Austria in a rank by itself, followed at a second level by Russia, the United States, and Denmark, and at a third by Sweden.

57 Into the 1770s both debtor and creditors preferred to establish due dates and renegotiate the debt as that might be necessary. But between 1778 and 1784 loan terms were set at ten years, after which either party could specify repayment with two years' notice. The notarial accords consulted do not include repayment calls so that it is necessary to estimate most redemptions and prolongations from 1790 to 1796. As long as creditors did not issue a call, a loan was prolonged under the original terms without renegotiation and thus without fresh commissions on the principal, an arrangement beneficial to the debtor since it favored retention of lower annuity rates. Perhaps for that reason most of the issues of 1788 and thereafter again specified due dates, usually twelve years.

58 G.A.A., notary C. van Homrigh, 12470/734–8; and N.E.H.A., Pros., III, 132 and 157. The 1784 issue was opened for subscriptions late in 1783, a year before the dispute between Austria and the United Provinces over reopening the Scheldt.

59 G.A.A., notary C. van Homrigh, 12488/653, 12490/249, 12494/99, 12497/476, 12499/796, and 12502/479; and N.E.H.A., Pros., III, 167, 194, 195, and V, 60, 68, 73, 112, and 114. On f. 6,250,000 raised in 1793 and 1794, see ibid., V, 120 and 134; *idem*, Kleine aanwinsten, 55, 24th account; and E. H. B., no. 239 of the collection of prospectuses gathered by L. Huizinga.

60 According to an estimate of 1796, Austria had borrowed f. 37,150,000 in the Republic since 1765, and f. 12 to 14 million more in the Austrian Netherlands (*GS*, I, lxvii and n. 1). The former figure is close to the current balance in 1796, but it falls far below the total subscribed over the period. Beer, *Die*

Finanzen Oesterreichs, p. 399, gives all loans through Goll, 1765–93, at f. 41,906,000, and through Osy, 1790–2, at f. 7,125,000. Those figures agree closely with data in the Amsterdam notarial archives, but of course they exclude loans of the 1760s through other houses.

61 B. R. Mitchell, *European Historical Statistics, 1750–1970* (London, 1975), pp. 697 and 706; Posthumus, I, 608–13 for exchange rates and 654–5 for agio; and the sources cited in nn. 38, 59, and 66 on Dutch and British loans. Mitchell's data on revenues and expenditures, and thus deficits, do not correspond closely with von Hauer's debt totals, suggesting a continuing process of retirement and new borrowing (probably because of large short-term liabilities) rather than a simple annual addition to the debt balance. Here Austrian revenues and expenditures and British loans are converted into current guilders. The Dutch loans are entered after the deduction of a commission of 4 percent. In British loans commission charges were included in the discount from par. For them, however, exchange-rate data after 1794 are fragmentary so that totals given in current guilders are approximate for 1795–7. Lacking information on transfer dates, the 1794–5 British loan is divided evenly between those two years. Probable prolongations are also deducted from the Dutch loan totals, which may tentatively be estimated to have raised a net sum of f. 29.5 to 30.7 million from 1788 through 1794. Redemptions scheduled for years in which no loans were raised in the Republic have not been deducted.

62 Between 1788 and 1792 Austria also raised advances in Leipzig, Trier, Regensburg, Köln, Zurich, Bern, and probably Frankfurt. The sums involved are not clear. Von Hauer, *Oesterr. Finanzen*, pp. 155–8; and Stiassny, *Oesterreichische Staatsbankerott*, p. 19.

63 Von Hauer, *Oesterr. Finanzen*, pp. 209–10.

64 Compare *bancozettel* trading rates from Beer, *Die Finanzen Oesterreichs*, p. 392, with revenue data from Mitchell, *European Historical Statistics*, p. 706.

65 *MNM*, December 1793.

66 On Austrian loans in London see Karl F. Helleiner, *The Imperial Loans: A Study in Financial and Diplomatic History* (Oxford, 1965); S. R. Cope, "The History of Boyd, Benfield & Co.: A Study in Merchant Banking in the Last Decade of the Eighteenth Century" (Ph.D. diss., Univ. of London, 1947); and G.A.A., Archief van Eeghen, P_2/c.

Helleiner suggests (p. 11) that Boyd, Benfield & Co., which negotiated the terms of the Austrian loan, was "guilty of deliberate misrepresentation" in permitting Austria to employ "bonds of one of its own departments [the Bank of Vienna] as a 'collateral.' " In fact Boyd, who was the active partner in the firm, was merely following practice that had been customary in Amsterdam. The defect in the London loans, as in the Dutch, was in the inevitable failure of the intermediaries to acquire for investors any effective claim on Austrian revenues. Except for the parliamentary guarantee, the only actual security behind the imperial loans was Austria's good faith. (In the 1795 issue investors claimed the right of suing the receivers of revenues on imperial domains, primary security for the issue. It is not clear whether Austria agreed to that provision, which, in any case, would have offered no real addition to the integrity of the security. Cope, "Boyd, Benfield & Co.," pp. 105–6.)

67 N.E.H.A., Pros., III, 77, and V, 134. The original London issue was also merchandised in the Dutch Republic through the Widow E. Croese & Co., but it is not known with what success. E.H.B., no. 257 of the collection of prospectuses gathered by L. Huizinga.

68 Robert V. Eagly, "Monetary Policy and Politics in Mid-Eighteenth Century Sweden," *JEH*, XXIX, no. 4 (December, 1969), 739–41; and B. J. Hovde, *The Scandinavian Countries, 1720–1865: The Rise of the Middle Classes* (Boston, 1943), p. 47. On Danish mercantilist policy see Hans Chr. Johansen, *Dansk økonomisk politik i årene efter 1784*, 1 vol, to date (Aarhus, 1968), I, 365–73 (the English summary).

69 Astrid Friis and Kristof Glamann, *A History of Prices and Wages in Denmark, 1660–1800* (Copenhagen, 1958), 7. Up to half the payment could be made in notes. On Danish finances around the turn into the eighteenth century see H. Kellenbenz, "Die öffentlichen Finanzen im Reich von der Mitte des 17. Jahrhunderts bis ins 19. Jahrhundert," *F.P.A.R.*, pp. 145–6.

70 Friis and Glamann, *Prices in Denmark*, I, 7–12. See also Axel Nielsen, *Dänische Wirtschaftsgeschichte* (Jena, 1933), pp. 293–301.

71 V. Falbe-Hansen and Will. Scharling, *Danmarks statistik*, 6 vols. (Copenhagen, 1878–91), IV, 378–9, indicate an increase in the combined foreign and domestic debt from 1,055,000 rdl. cour. in 1754 to some 20 million (not including the note debt) in 1766. Interest-bearing loans had also been used in the first half of the century, but the highest level of such indebtedness given in *Danmarks statistik* was 3,161,000 rdl. cour. in 1730.

72 The Amsterdam rate moved from 15.5 percent (that is, 115.5 Danish rdl. cour. for 100 rixdollars HCG) at the beginning of 1760 to a high of 35 percent at the end of July 1762. Friis and Glamann, *Prices in Denmark*, I, 83–4.

73 Weeveringh, II, 78; and Kristof Glamann, "The Danish Asiatic Company, 1732–1772," *SEHR*, VIII, no. 2 (1960), 121–4 and 143.

These advances were in addition to a loan of 500,000 écus (some f. 1,180,000) opened in Geneva in 1760. According to Lüthy, *La banque protestante*, II, 74–5, that advance was for colonial acquisitions and to equip a naval squadron in cooperation with Sweden to enforce the free-trade rights of neutrals. On this and other occasions Denmark also borrowed abroad in Hanover, Hamburg, Bern, Genoa, Frankfurt, and Antwerp, and raised domestic loans in Copenhagen and Altona. Johansen, *Dansk økonomisk politik*, I, 108 and 296. On earlier Dutch loans see Ernst Baasch, *Holländische Wirtschaftsgeschichte* (Jena, 1927), pp. 196–7; and Elias, *Vroedschap*, II, 875, n. h.

74 Respectively, J. G. van Dillen, *Van rijkdom en regenten* (The Hague, 1970), p. 607; and Weeveringh, II, 78. Weeveringh's figure appears altogether excessive.

75 Details on the 1764 loan, secured on toll revenues, are wanting, but it is mentioned in papers relating to an 1811 proposal to consolidate the Danish debt in the United Provinces. N.E.H.A., Archief KV, "Negotiatie groot twaalf millioen gulden tbv ZKM van Danemarken & Noorwegen, 1805–1811."

Holden Furber, *John Company at Work* (New York, 1970 reprint), p. 125, mentions 1764 issues without detail.

There were two loans in 1765. One, of uncertain amount, was issued by Clifford, the house that failed in 1772 and carried with it annuity and redemption funds forwarded to it by Denmark. *D.T.*, p. 102, dispatch of 22 Jan. 1773. Van Dillen, *Rijkdom*, p. 607, gives the total as f. 10 million, but his source is apparently the sometimes unreliable Elias, *Vroedschap*, II, 1046. By January 1773, when that loan was prolonged (N.E.H.A., Pros., III, 23), Jacob Dull & Zoonen were in charge. The second was for f. 400,000 at 4 percent and was arranged through van Orsoy. Glamann, "Danish Asiatic Company," 124. According to Glamann it was repaid in 1767, but part of the sums extended through van Orsoy remained unredeemed as late as 1783. See the listing in the price current for 6 Oct. 1783 in [Oudermeulen], II, pt. 2, 263. The same price current cites a loan to the bank managed by Boas, indicating that the 1763 advances had not been repaid either. Nielsen, *Dänische Wirtschaftsgeschichte*, p. 300, puts the foreign debt in 1766 at 8 million rdl. cour., and the total state debt at 20,250,000 rdl. cour. See Anton Friderich Büsching, *Erdbeschreibung*, 8th ed., 13 vols. (Hamburg, 1787–1816), I, 153–4; and *idem*, *Magazin für die neue Historie und Geographie*, XIV (1780), 87–92, for more extensive data on the state debt.

76 From 24.25 to 17.5 percent, 14 Jan. to 16 Dec. Friis and Glamann, *Prices in Denmark*, I, 86.

77 First-of-year quotations: 18.5 in 1766 and 23.5 in 1772. Ibid., I, 86–9.

78 Ibid., I, 69–74 and 78–103; Johansen, *Dansk økonomisk politik*, I, 108 and 296; Falbe-Hansen and Scharling, *Danmarks statistik*, IV, 378–80; and Nielsen, *Dänische Wirtschaftsgeschichte*, pp. 300 and 351–3. Table 6-2, for which exchange rates are wanting after 1800, excludes the sum outstanding in paper currency.

79 The sum given in parentheses is uncertain (see chap. 6, n. 91). For the sources: N.E.H.A., Pros., III, 23, 26, 53, 60, 73, 78, 136, 227, and V, 63; *idem*, Archief KV, "Negotiatie groot twaalf millioen . . . ," and "Contract tussen de heren J. Dull . . ."; and *idem*, Kleine aanwinsten, 55.

80 By 1784, according to budgetary estimates, proceeds from the Sound tolls totaled slightly less than the cost of servicing the foreign debt. K. D. Tönnerson, "Les finances publiques en Norvège à la fin de l'union dano-norvégienne et les réformes au lendemain de la rupture de l'union en 1814," in *F.P.A.R.*, pp. 189 and 193. There was also a collateral security on the general revenues of the kingdom. N.E.H.A., Pros., III, 26, 53, and 60. On the 1779 issue by the Danish Asiatic Company see *idem*, III, 73; and *Brief van een koopman uyt Rotterdam, aan zijnen vriend, te Amsterdam . . . Deensche Asiatische Compagnie te Coppenhagen* . . . (Amsterdam, 1779), an attack on foreign loans in general, pointing out that the security, the assets and revenues of the Danish company, had already been mortgaged and, moreover, that their value and other claims on them remained obscure. Dutch ownership of Asiatic Company stock was extensive in the early 1770s but declined after the company lost its monopoly. Ole Feldbaek, *India Trade Under the Danish Flag* (Odense, 1969), p. 13.

81 See the price currents for 1778, 1779, and 1780 in G.A.A., N.49.03. Prices were slightly below par in October 1783. [Oudermeulen], II, pt. 2, 263–8.

82 Falbe-Hansen and Scharling, *Danmarks statistik,* IV, 174–6, on tax revenues, which doubled between 1769 and 1806 (reaching some 5.2 million rdl. cour.). This movement, especially marked during the heaviest inflationary period at the turn of the nineteenth century, was chiefly the product of an increase in indirect tax revenues, but was also assisted by new levies and by the appearance in state balances of taxes formerly paid in kind but converted to money payments.

83 Friis and Glamann, *Prices in Denmark,* I, 11–13. See also W. F. Reddaway, "Denmark Under the Bernstorffs and Struensee," in *Cambridge Modern History,* ed. by A. W. Ward et al. (Cambridge, 1909), VI, 742–52; Weeveringh, II, 78; and Carl-Ferdinand Allen, *Histoire de Danemark,* trans. from the 7th ed., 2 vols. (Copenhagen, 1878), II, 212.

84 Johansen, *Dansk økonomisk politik,* I, 368.

85 Friis and Glamann, *Prices in Denmark,* I, 81–103; and n. 72.

86 Johansen, *Dansk økonomisk politik,* I, 369; Knud Erik Svendsen, "Monetary Policy and Theory in Denmark, 1784–1800," (pt. 1), SEHR, X, no. 1 (1962), 40–8; and, on the debate, ibid., 50–64. For further detail on the 1780s see Tönnerson, "Les finances publiques en Norvège," pp. 185–97; and William Coxe, *Travels in Poland, Russia, Sweden and Denmark,* 6th ed., 3 vols. (London, 1803), III, 227 and 254–5.

87 Johansen, *Dansk økonomisk politik,* I, 369–71; and Svendsen, "Monetary Policy," 50–64.

88 At the end of the 1760s and during the 1770s several Dutch merchants had negotiated loans for Danish planters. As in the case of advances to the Dutch West Indies, the security behind some issues was inadequate and, with the downturn in commodity prices, planters suspended payments. N.E.H.A., Pros., III, 136; and Johannes Petrus van de Voort, *De westindische plantages van 1720 tot 1795, financiën en handel* (Eindhoven, 1973), p. 107, and apps. xix and xx, pp. 265–6.

89 Svendsen, "Monetary Policy," 48. Foreign loans were thought expensive expedients because of service costs when exchange rates were unfavorable to Denmark, as they were from 1783 until 1794. Ibid., 39 and 64–5.

90 For example, a price current of 1788 lists Danish notes secured on Holstein, referring presumably to issues of 1774 and 1777 that fell due in 1778 and 1783, respectively. G.A.A., N.41.088. On the new loans see Johansen, *Dansk økonomisk politik,* I, 296. On Danish practice in prolongations see papers concerning the conversion proposal of 1811 in N.E.H.A., Archief KV, "Negotiatie groot twaalf millioen . . ."; and Weeveringh, II, 77.

91 The sum of the bank's loan is difficult to fix but may have been f. 2 million, an amount suggested in N.E.H.A., Archief KV, "Negotiatie groot twaalf millioen . . . ," and "Contract tussen de heren J. Dull. . . ." For the date of issue and managing house see the accounts of the private tontine known under the motto "Uit Voorzorg," in *idem,* Kleine aanwinsten, 55. On the Asiatic Company loan see N.E.H.A., Pros., V., 63; *idem,* Archief KV, "Negotiatie groot twaalf millioen . . ." and, on Dull's custom in dealing with commission

agents, "Verschillende negotiaties ten behoeve van Zweden . . . 1772–1807," papers of 1789 and 1791 on the Swedish debt in the Dutch Republic.

92 Working through Arnoldus Finmann, the monarchy exchanged f. 800 crown obligations for f. 1,000 notes. The total involved is unknown but probably did not exceed f. 2 million. Ibid., "Contract tussen de heren J. Dull . . . ," and a 14 Aug. 1811 accounting in "Negotiatie groot twaalf millioen . . ."; and N.E.H.A., Kleine aanwinsten, 55.

93 The extraordinary levy of 1789 revived a measure last employed in 1743 (details in Falbe-Hansen and Scharling, *Danmarks statistik,* IV, 262–3). According to Svendsen, "Monetary Policy," 65, the Swedish war cost some 5 million rdl. over ordinary expenditures.

94 Ibid., 62–72; and Friis and Glamann, *Prices in Denmark,* I, 12–13.

95 Svendsen, "Monetary Policy," 73; and Friis and Glamann, *Prices in Denmark,* I, 14.

96 A Danish loan of September 1790 is mentioned in U.B.A., Handschriften IV, f, 18a, but that probably refers to a prolongation of toll notes. See G.A.A., Archief Brants, 156, revealing the acquisition of prolonged notes by a private tontine.

On Dansk-Norsk Speciebank difficulties see Svendsen, "Monetary Policy," 73. In 1796 Denmark opened a loan in Altona. Christian Ulrich Detlev von Eggers, *Memoiren über die dänischen Finanzen,* 2 vols. (Hamburg, 1800–1), I, 49.

97 Falbe-Hansen and Scharling, *Danmarks statistik,* IV, 380, give interest on the state debt in 1805 at 1.73 million rdl. cour., one-third of 1806 revenues of about 5.2 million (ibid., IV, 174, converted from kr.).

98 N.E.H.A., Archief KV, "Negotiatie groot twaalf millioen . . ."; and *idem,* Pros., III, 227.

99 Johansen, *Dansk økonomisk politik,* I, 373. Weeveringh, II, 79, gives the trading rate of bank notes to specie in 1812 at 14:1.

100 Falbe-Hansen and Scharling, *Danmarks statistik,* IV, 264–5. The new levy was suspended in 1815.

101 N.E.H.A., Archief KV, "Contract tussen de heren J. Dull . . . ."

102 Weeveringh, II, 846–7.

103 Details may be found in draft proposals in N.E.H.A., Archief KV, "Negotiatie groot twaalf millioen . . . ." Dull and Breitenfeld & Gregory, which got involved in Danish loans sometime after 1802, were to manage the conversion, with Dull having the larger share. For reasons that are not clear, D. J. Voombergh of Ketwich & Voombergh received some proposals on the conversion, hence the material in the Archief KV.

104 Annuity payments were to be continued. Some notes outstanding in 1811 stretched back to 1764.

105 Available data suggest that the minimum sum raised in the Dutch Republic by the crown, the Kurantbank, and the Asiatic Company between 1762 and 1805 was f. 22.7 million, and the maximum (including less reliable figures on the loans of 1763–5) some f. 31 to 32 million. The crown treated the Asiatic Company loans, which totaled f. 2.7 million, separately and may not have intended to include them in the claim that two-thirds of Denmark's

total indebtedness had been settled. See also Montalivet to the emperor (Napoleon), 28 Oct. 1811, in *GS*, VI, 217, for an 1811 balance giving total Danish loans of all types at f. 26,192,000, with f. 8,867,000 outstanding.

106 Lennart Jörberg, *A History of Prices in Sweden, 1732–1914*, 2 vols. (Lund, 1972), I, 80 (for note supply), and II, 183 (for cost of living); and Karl Åmark, *Sveriges statsfinanser, 1719–1809* (Stockholm, 1961), pp. 400ff. (for domestic tax revenues). Budgetary data are derived from proposals and not from subsequent accounts. Sven and Helle Jensen were kind enough to translate parts of this work and of Falbe-Hansen and Scharling, *Danmarks statistik*.

107 Jörberg, *Prices in Sweden*, I, 78–9; and Eagly, "Monetary Policy," 740–56.

108 Marten G. Buist, *At Spes Non Fracta: Hope & Co., 1770–1815* (The Hague, 1974), p. 74; and Åmark, *Sveriges statsfinanser*, pp. 609–10 and 619.

109 Carl Hallendorff and Adolf Schück, *History of Sweden* (New York, 1970), pp. 335–6; and Robert Nisbet Bain, "The Hats and Caps and Gustavus III (1721–92)," in *Cambridge Modern History*, ed. by A. W. Ward et al. (Cambridge, 1909), VI, 764. Unlike the Hats, the Caps saw the excessive note issues of the war years as the cause of inflation. Eagly, "Monetary Policy," 752.

110 Åmark, *Sveriges statsfinanser*, p. 628.

111 G.A.A., notary C. van Homrigh, 12380/100 and 155, and 12439/25. There had earlier been some direct investment by Dutch capitalists in Swedish domestic loans. See, e.g., *idem*, Archief Brants, 78.

112 Tables of Swedish foreign loans may be found in Åmark, *Sveriges statsfinanser*, pp. 628–32 and 651–3. The data therein should be supplemented by accords from G.A.A., notary C. van Homrigh, 12380–478, passim; N.E.H.A., Archief KV, "Notten diversen," "Een pak met bewijzen van afgedane zaken . . . 1776, 1777, 1797, 1801, 1775," "Verschillende negotiaties ten behoeve van Zweden . . . 1772–1807," and an unlabeled dossier containing shares in loans; *idem*, Pros., dossiers III and V; *idem*, Kleine aanwinsten, 388; U.B.A., 565B14, plans d'emprunts, pt. 2; Folke Ludwigs, "Stats-obligationer från Gustaf III:s dagar," *Ekonomisk Revy*, no. 6 (1968), 373–8 (furnished through the courtesy of the author); Buist, *Hope & Co.*, pp. 73–92 and apps. C-I and C-II, pp. 495–6; and Elias, *Vroedschap*, II, 1057–9. Dr. Simon Hart, formerly director of the Municipal Archives, Amsterdam, generously furnished references to accords by the notary van Homrigh, and Kenneth E. Carpenter, director of the Kress Library of Business and Economics, Boston, translated Ludwigs's article.

113 Jörberg, *Prices in Sweden*, I, 84. For Sweden the principal foreign currency of exchange was the Hamburg rixdollar banco, which should be distinguished from Swedish, Danish, Dutch, and other rixdollars.

114 Bain, "The Hats and Caps," p. 773; Hovde, *Rise of the Middle Classes*, p. 48; William Coxe, *Travels into Poland, Russia, Sweden, and Denmark*, 3 vols. (Dublin, 1784), III, 169; and Eli F. Heckscher, *An Economic History of Sweden*, trans. by G. Ohlin (Cambridge, Mass., 1954), pp. 198–9. With Gustavus's assumption of the throne in 1771, continued French subsidies assisted his reassertion of royal prerogatives. On foreign subsidies over the period 1719–1809 see Åmark, *Sveriges statsfinanser*, pp. 589–94.

115 Jörberg, *Prices in Sweden*, I, 79–81, and II, 129–30. The ratio of the new silver rixdollar to the old daler (or dollar) was 6:1. Note circulation (in millions) followed this pattern (see table).

	Pre-1776 value	Post-1779 value
1763	44	7.3
1765	38.6	6.4
1770	35.1	5.8
1775	44.5	7.4
1780		5.7
1785		5.1

116 Parts of these loans also prolonged earlier issues. Liljencrantz's program was assisted not only by French subsidies but also by the proceeds of a state lottery begun in 1773. Claude Nordmann, *Grandeur et liberté de la Suède (1660–1792)* (Paris, 1971), p. 342. The dependence of the currency reform program on Dutch loans was acknowledged by [Johann Georg Canzler], *Mémoires pour servir à la connoissance des affaires politiques et économiques du royaume de Suède* . . . , 2 vols. (London, 1776), II, 421–2 and 426.

According to the Prussian ambassador in The Hague, Dutch merchants were apprehensive about the effect of the royal coup on commerce and loans, and were at first uncertain about the degree of control exercised by Gustavus over finances. *D.T.*, p. 92, dispatch of 2 Oct. 1772.

117 Jörberg, *Prices in Sweden*, II, 130 and n. 4.

118 Ibid., II, 131.

119 Ibid., II, 183–5.

120 Åmark, *Sveriges statsfinanser*, p. 630.

121 Ibid., pp. 631–2.

122 Swedish and Dutch practices in negotiating loans may be followed in N.E.H.A., Archief KV, "Notten diversen," 7–12 and 22–34, "Verschillende negotiaties ten behoeve van Zweden . . . 1772–1807," "Een pak met bewijzen van afgedane zaken . . . 1776, 1777, 1797, 1801, 1775," and "Brieven aan den Heer D. J. Voombergh te Amsterdam"; *idem*, Pros., III, 137 and V, 186; G.A.A., notary C. van Homrigh, 12476/83 and 84 and 12481/9; the Hope and Fizeaux, Grand–Liljencrantz correspondence, 1784–7, in R.A.S., Liljencrantz samling, E 4661; the Smets–Liljencrantz correspondence in *idem;* Buist, *Hope & Co.*, pp. 84–92; and Elias, *Vroedschap*, II, 1057 and 1059. Part of the Hope and Fizeaux, Grand (from 1 Jan. 1785, H. Fizeaux)–Liljencrantz correspondence is reproduced in Sandor Baumgarten, "Emprunts de Suède à Amsterdam," *TvG*, LXXVII (1964), 439–43.

123 Åmark, *Sveriges statsfinanser*, pp. 622–3, 626, and 648–9. From 1789 foreign claims are deducted from the foreign debt. The exchange here is fixed at 43.5 shillings specie per rixdollar HCG to 1789, and at 44 shillings from 1789. Devaluation is not taken into account until 1803, when the domestic debt was reduced by a combination of currency conversion and redemptions.

124 Ibid., pp. 137–42 and 406–12.

125 Bank note supply was reduced from 5.9 million rdr at the end of 1783 to 4.9 million at the end of 1786. Jörberg, *Prices in Sweden*, II, 131–2.

126 Created in 1789 to manage the state debt, the National Debt Office also issued notes that were originally interest-bearing but in 1791 were made non-interest-bearing and thenceforth circulated as paper currency.

127 Ibid., I, 81, and II, 128–9 and 132–7.

128 Notes issued by the National Debt Office, called riksdaler riksgälds, were not convertible into silver, whereas notes of the Bank of Sweden, the riksdaler banko, were convertible. Because of resistance to further issues by the bank, the war and postwar period saw an expansion of Debt Office paper.

129 N.E.H.A., Archief KV, "Verschillende negotiaties ten behoeve van Zweden . . . 1772–1807." Available documents concerning reformulation are rough drafts. Internal evidence indicates they were composed in two series, the first in the latter months of 1789 (dated by references to impending redemptions) and the second in the last part of 1791. The proposals are not signed but are sometimes labeled with the name of one or another commission agent or banker, and for this reason it is possible to suggest authorship for unlabeled drafts similar in content to those that are labeled. Most of the material dealing with reformulation takes the form of a justification that might be adopted by the Swedish committee of finances. The drafts are in French, the language of the Swedish court.

130 Stadnitski and van Ketwich are termed "brokers" in drafts dating from late 1791. Both were customarily commission agents in the Swedish loans, although Ketwich & Voombergh served as brokers as well as commission agents in the issue of August 1789.

131 Stadnitski proposed a funding operation to retire Swedish debts over 26 to 27 years while permitting new loans totaling up to f. 10 million, with cash and old notes acceptable in subscriptions. Van Ketwich preferred a 30-year term and new loans of f. 15 million, of which two-thirds would be subscribed in old notes.

132 Ibid., a draft labeled No. 2 Ketwich.

133 On Ruuth's disgrace see Nordmann, *Grandeur et liberté*, p. 401. Nordmann (p. 402) estimates the cost of the war at 20 million rdr Swedish, or more than f. 50 million.

134 N.E.H.A., Pros., V, 167; *idem*, Archief KV, "Verschillende negotiaties ten behoeve van Zweden . . . 1772–1807"; and Ludwigs, "Stats-obligationer," 375. The Boas life-annuity loan was excluded. The 1798 reformulation, stretching redemptions over 30 years, activated the funding and redemption term elements of the proposals advanced from Amsterdam in 1789 and 1791, although without a tie to new loans.

135 Jörberg, *Prices in Sweden*, II, 133–40.

Chapter 7. The debtor states: II

1 Jan Gotlib de Bloch, *Les finances de la Russie au XIXe siècle*, 2 vols. (Paris, 1899), I, 50–78, 113, 154–5, and 162–3; Marc Raeff, *Michael Speransky:*

Statesman of Imperial Russia, 1772–1839, 2nd ed. (The Hague, 1969), p. 83; and Paul Dukes, *Catherine the Great and the Russian Nobility: A Study Based on the Materials of the Legislative Commission of 1767* (Cambridge, 1967), p. 236. De Bloch (I, 58–67 and 77–8) cautions about defects in the account-keeping system used in Russia and the resulting distortion of data. By 1788 revenues and expenditures were generally recorded under a central system but there was still no comprehensive picture of the budget. Particularly before 1788 the data assembled here must be treated as the best estimates available rather than as satisfactorily accurate statements. (Dashed lines indicate gaps in data.)

2 De Bloch, *Les finances de la Russie*, I, 55–9 and 65–70; and James A. Duran, Jr., "The Reform of Financial Administration in Russia During the Reign of Catherine II," *Canadian Slavic Studies*, IV, no. 3 (Fall, 1970), 485–96.

3 Ernst Baasch, *Höllandische Wirtschaftsgeschichte* (Jena, 1927), pp. 197–8; and Dominique Maroger, ed., *The Memoirs of Catherine the Great*, trans. by Moura Budberg (New York, n.d.), p. 370. In an undated memorandum listing the achievements of her reign, Catherine mentioned that Elizabeth had tried to borrow 2 million rubles. Oddly enough this memorandum, written sometime after 1781, does not mention Catherine's successful loans. An attempt to borrow in Amsterdam early in the eighteenth century had been rebuffed.

4 De Bloch, *Les finances de la Russie*, I, 69.

5 Ibid., pp. 71 and 91; Walter McKenzie Pintner, *Russian Economic Policy Under Nicolas I* (Ithaca, N.Y., 1967), p. 186; and Heinrich Friedrich von Storch, *Supplementband zum fünften, sechsten und siebenten Theil des Historisch-statistischen Gemäldes des russischen Reichs* (Leipzig, 1803), p. 9. Assignat rates to 1797 have been drawn from von Storch in preference to de Bloch because the former offers the annual range as well as an annual average. See also de Bloch (I, 70) on the problem of conflicting information about the amount of assignats issued in 1790 and 1794. Table 7-1 takes into account occasional retirements. Circulation figures are, however, more or less official estimates, and there is reason to question their accuracy in some years. Attempts in 1809 and 1810 to reconstruct totals reveal uncertainty about prior estimates. A German expert, invited by Speransky to assist in the reform of Russia's finances, claimed that "trustworthy and knowledgeable sources" indicated that the circulation in 1788 may have been 140 to 150 million rubles rather than the 100 million of the official estimate. See David Griffiths and Karin Griffiths, eds., "M. M. Speranski as Viewed in L. H. Jacob's Unpublished Autobiography," *Canadian-American Slavic Studies*, IX, no. 4 (Winter, 1975), 517.

6 Von Storch, *Supplementband*, p. 9, for the range of market rates in each year from 1769 through 1797.

7 Ibid., pp. 5–8. Von Storch does not indicate whether the stuiver rate should be taken in terms of bank or current guilders, and all exchanges are calculated here as though the rate reflected current guilders. Until 1788 the ruble regularly traded in advance of the intrinsic value of silver rubles (36.5 stuivers). By the late 1780s, however, Russian officials believed that the ruble was trading below its proper level and that consequently Russia was paying

too dearly for imported commodities and loan service. Marten G. Buist, *At Spes Non Fracta: Hope & Co., 1770–1815* (The Hague, 1974), pp. 100–1 and 141. When the question was raised in 1788, Henry Hope took the view that par in the exchange was 34 stuivers to the ruble. According to von Storch, the average rate for that year was 35.

8 The cheap ruble rate of 1792 encouraged the formation in Amsterdam of substitution negotiations that, hoping for a rise in ruble values and windfall profits, acquired interest-paying notes issued in Russia. N.E.H.A., Pros., V, 101 and 128. The subsequent increase did not meet expectations.

9 As Buist (*Hope & Co.*, pp. 13 and 22) points out, de Smeth had lost heavily in the 1762 failure of de Neufville, and in general found the 1760s to be difficult years. Nonetheless, the house remained one of the foremost firms in Amsterdam. In 1781 the Prussian ambassador characterized de Smeth's resources, somewhat obliquely, as "très étendu." (The context clearly indicates that de Smeth's resources were thought to be very extensive.) *D.T.*, p. 244, dispatch of 23 Mar. 1781.

10 Ibid., p. 132, dispatch of 22 July 1774; de Bloch, *Les finances de la Russie*, I, 73–74; Baasch, *Holländische Wirtschaftsgeschichte*, p. 198; and P. Katzenelsohn, *Zur Entwicklungsgeschichte der Finanzen Russlands* (Berlin, 1913), pp. 104–5. Two segmented issues, floated in 1769 and 1770 through de Smeth at 5 percent, totaled f. 7.5 million. See also G.A.A., notaries P. Huntum, 14147/388 and 519, 14148/869, 14149/246, and 14170/887, and C. van Homrigh, 12395/14, 12399/843, and 12404/466; *idem*, N.12.16.04; and N.E.H.A., Archief KV, "Acten van aanstellingen van directeuren, commissarissen en procuratiën . . . ." De Bloch (I, 58 and 71) gives the cost of the first Turkish war at some 47.5 million rubles, of which 20 million was covered by higher taxes and perhaps as much as 14 million by assignat issues. There was a Turkish indemnity after the war [M. S. Anderson, *The Eastern Question, 1774–1923* (New York, 1966), p. xi], and that may have been used in part to retire advances from Genoa. Katzenelsohn, *Finanzen Russlands*, p. 105.

11 There was also at least one loan raised in Amsterdam on behalf of a private individual. See G.A.A., notary C. van Homrigh, 12439/122 and 12440/240, on the f. 2 million issue opened in 1777 or 1778 for Count Orlov (presumably Gregorie Orlov), and guaranteed by Catherine.

12 Thulemeyer informed Frederick II in January 1782 that the Russian debt in the Republic then totaled f. 13.5 million. (*D.T.*, p. 296, dispatch of 18 Jan. 1782.) Two loans were floated that year for f. 5.5 million, but the second fell somewhat short and it is not clear what part of those was accounted for by prolongations. Katzenelsohn, *Finanzen Russlands*, p. 105, gives total Russian foreign indebtedness in 1784 at 9.7 million rubles, or slightly over f. 19 million at current exchange rates. On this series of Russian loans see G.A.A., notary P. Huntum, 14174/94, 14176/766, 14180/189, 14183/294, 14187/293, and 14189/1227; and on commission charges Katzenelsohn (p. 105) and de Bloch, *Les finances de la Russie*, I, 74.

13 Russia also sometimes went to other markets. A 1788 proposal to open a loan in The Hague through A. & S. Boas fell through, but Russia successfully raised loans outside the Republic. Use of the Antwerp market is discussed by

Buist, *Hope & Co.*, pp. 99–101. There were advances from Genoa and Venice, and perhaps also from Lucca and Leghorn. Louis Philippe de Ségur, *Politique de tous les cabinets de l'Europe pendant les règnes de Louis XV et de Louis XVI*, 3rd ed., 3 vols. (Paris, 1802), I, 392; [William Tooke], *The Life of Catherine II, Empress of Russia*, 4th ed., 3 vols. (London, 1800), III, 208 and 395; Katzenelsohn, *Finanzen Russlands*, p. 106; and de Bloch, *Les finances de la Russie*, I, 75.

14 A loan was negotiated in 1764 by the elector of Saxony (see chap. 4, n. 3), who was also king of Poland. That advance was secured on crown jewels, but whether those were Polish or Saxon is not clear nor is it apparent where the loan was spent. On the 1764 reforms, which subordinated local treasury authorities to central management, see Jan Rutkowski, *Histoire économique de la Pologne avant les partages* (Paris, 1927), pp. 229–30.

15 William Coxe, *Travels in Poland, Russia, Sweden and Denmark*, 6th ed., 3 vols. (London, 1803), I, 50–1; and Rutkowski, *Histoire économique de la Pologne*, p. 237.

16 Ibid., pp. 208 and 236.

17 N.E.H.A., Pros., III, 2; and Buist, *Hope & Co.*, p. 112. In 1777 the Polish debt was some 23 million złotys (about f. 6.7 million). Daniel Z. Stone, "Polish Politics and National Reform, 1775–1788" (Ph.D. diss., Indiana Univ., 1972), p. 116, published in abridged form (New York, 1976). Various projects intended to reformulate Polish taxation along physiocratic lines came to nothing. Ambroise Jobert, *Magnats polonais et physiocrates français (1767–1774)* (Paris, 1941), pp. 15–57.

18 The specification may be found in the prospectus. The Polish guilder or złoty is calculated here at 3.43 to the Dutch guilder (Buist, *Hope & Co.*, p. 112).

19 Those loans, all paying 5 percent, were directed by Quirijn Willem van Hoorn. The first, opened in 1780, was due in 5 years, the second (1781) in 10, and the third (1782) in 8. In the 1782 loan Piotr Tepper & Co., earlier the king's agent in contacts with Amsterdam bankers, and Piotr Blanc & Co., royal bankers in Warsaw, were first designated to receive hypothecated revenues and make annuity and redemption payments to Amsterdam. N.E.H.A., Pros., III, 7, 9, 10, and 291.

20 An entry in N.E.H.A., Archief KV, "Notten diversen," folio 6, indicates that Fizeaux, Grand & Co. bought 30 annuities from the 1782 loan from van Hoorn in August 1784 at 94. That suggests either that sales had gone slowly or that van Hoorn had covered part of the issue, or both. In any case, the price was near par. Fizeaux, Grand sold half those securities at par in 1786, and held the others until redemption. Quotations for 6 Oct. 1783 (for the Hope loan only) and 30 Sept. 1788 put the Polish 5 percents at 100 to 102 and 99, respectively. [Oudermeulen], II, pt. 2, 264; and G.A.A., N. 41.088.

21 N.E.H.A., Pros., III, 3, 4, 5, and 6, and V, 81 and 88; Archief KV, "Notten diversen," folios 35–44 and 46–8; and Buist, *Hope & Co.*, pp. 114–17 and app. D-V, pp. 503–4. A proposal advanced late in 1793 for a loan of f. 10.5 million with Russian guarantee, to be used to cover King Stanislas's debts, fell through. Ibid., p. 142 and n. 3.

22 Buist does not deal with the standards or method employed in evaluating

Poland's financial position in 1777. In all likelihood the procedure was informal rather than rigorous.

23 Robert Nisbet Bain, *The Last King of Poland* (London, 1909), p. 121. Also Rutkowski, *Histoire économique de la Pologne*, pp. 214, 222, and 226–31, on the inadequacies of public (as distinct from royal) revenues, and pp. 231–2 on budgetary estimates after the 1775 reforms.

24 Bain, *Last King*, pp. 121ff. and 213–14; Rutkowski, *Histoire économique de la Pologne*, pp. 232–4; and Justine Klotz, *L'oeuvre législative de la diète de 4 ans* (Paris, 1913), pp. 226–31. Also Coxe, *Travels in Poland*, I, 52, n., on 1790 revenues and expenditures according to a report to the sejm; and Stone, *Polish Politics*, pp. 77–8, on shortcomings in the 1789 tax-reform measures.

25 *MNM*, September 1792 through December 1795. The quotations are sometimes monthly, sometimes semimonthly. For later prices Weeveringh, II, 846. During 1797, because of anticipation of a Russian takeover, Polish securities regained favor, trading in the 90s. Weeveringh's data show a substantial differentiation between securities in loans issued by de Smeth and Hogguer, Grand and the 1792 loan managed by de Haan, with the latter quoted at significantly lower prices. The *Mercurius* does not distinguish the de Haan loan from the others until January 1796, when that issue was more than 40 points below other Polish issues, but *Mercurius* quotations show a widening range beginning in September 1794. The divergence of the de Haan issue had appeared by April 1793. See the price list of 3 Apr. 1793 in N.E.H.A., Archief SvH, "Diverse documenten, descharges, particuliere beschieden, enz." Since the number of securities in the de Haan loan was smaller than that of other loans, Chart 7-3 exaggerates the decline at least from September 1794. In an effort to modify the distortion, high and low prices are charted separately from the third quarter of 1794.

26 Aside from the de Haan loan, the first annuity payment not met by Poland was due on 1 Mar. 1794 on the 1791 loan by van Hoorn and Gülcher & Mulder. Buist, *Hope & Co.*, app. D-V, p. 503. According to the *Mercurius*, the decline may be dated to between late May and late June 1794, when Polish securities fell nearly 20 points. That drop may also have reflected expansion of the Polish insurrection led by Kościuszko and a Russo-Prussian victory over Polish insurgents in June. The insurrection continued but Russo-Prussian strength increased, and in October Kościuszko was defeated and captured. By that point a third partition could be anticipated. M. Kukiel, "Kosciuszko and the Third Partition," in *Cambridge History of Poland*, ed. by W. F. Reddaway et al. (New York, 1971 reprint), II, 161–74.

27 *NNJ* reported in August 1793 (p. 1444) that Russia and Prussia might assume part of the Polish debt and that Russia would take over delinquent annuities, using tax revenues from that part of Poland under Russian control. On radical internal measures introduced in 1794 see J. Senkowski, "Aenderungen in der öffentlichen Finanzwirtschaft in Polen zu Ende des alten Reiches und während des Aufstandes vom Jahre 1794," in *F.P.A.R.*, pp. 204–9.

28 Stone, "Polish Politics," pp. 102–8. In the absence of any evidence on the motive behind raising credit in Amsterdam, three interpretations appear

plausible: (1) that the loans financed estate industries, (2) that foreign credit assisted the magnates' attempts at political aggrandizement in internal rivalries after the first partition, and (3) that by borrowing the magnates sought to expand agricultural production and take advantage of price trends.

29 Buist, *Hope & Co.*, app. D-V, pp. 503–4, lists loans to landowners included in the Russian conversion of 1798. Prospectuses and other information may be found in N.E.H.A., Pros., III, 8, 12, 14, 15, 93, 154, 155, 171, and V, 8 and 100; Archief KV, "Notten diversen," folios 45 and 49–50, and "Brieven aan den Heer D. J. Voombergh te Amsterdam"; and Buist, *Hope & Co.*, pp. 155–6. The loan of f. 535,000 opened for Adam Czartoryski may have begun on 1 Jan. 1792 rather than in 1793, as Buist indicates. There is some confusion about the f. 525,000 issue that Buist lists for Prince Jabłonowski for 1 Oct. 1787. A loan for the same amount and on behalf of the same borrower was floated in 1784. N.E.H.A., Pros., III, 13; and U.B.A., 565B14, plans d'emprunts, pt. 6.

The following loans not included in the 1798 conversion may be added to Buist's list: one of f. 250,000 to 300,000 projected (although perhaps not successfully completed) in 1782 for Count Ogiński; and another of f. 400,000 opened in 1792 for Anna, dowager of Prince Jabłonowski. N.E.H.A., Archief KV, "Een pak met bewijzen van afgedane zaken"; and Pros., V, 102; and Buist, *Hope & Co.*, pp. 165–66 and p. 166, n. 1. Loans were floated in 1786 and 1794 on behalf of the Count of Courland for, respectively, f. 1,000,000 and f. 600,000. N.E.H.A., Pros., III, 97, and V, 143. It is unlikely that issues listed by Buist and those added here form a complete catalogue.

30 The houses were Piotr Tepper, Piotr Blanc, Fryderyk Cabrit, and Count Prot Potocki.

31 See, for example, specifications of Ogiński's Lithuanian estates in N.E.H.A., Archief KV, "Een pak met bewijzen van afgedane zaken . . . ."

32 On this and other problems see Buist, *Hope & Co.*, pp. 156–9 and 166.

33 Blanc had offered supplementary guarantees as recently as the preceding year. N.E.H.A., Pros., III, 15, and V, 100. On the banking crisis in Poland in 1793 see Rutkowski, *Histoire économique de la Pologne*, p. 210.

34 Buist, *Hope & Co.*, pp. 118–19. Prot Potocki suspended payments sometime between 1792 and 1797. Ibid., p. 164. The close financial ties of landowners to bankers in Warsaw are mentioned briefly in Michał Kleofas Ogiński, *Mémoires de Michel Oginski sur la Pologne et les polonais depuis 1788 jusqu'à la fin de 1815*, 4 vols. (Paris, 1826–7), I, 235–8.

35 Buist, *Hope & Co.*, appendix D-V, pp. 503–4, gives dates on which annuity payments were suspended.

36 Buist, *Hope & Co.*, pp. 159–60. Voûte had earlier (in 1793) unsuccessfully sought to negotiate a Russian takeover of the royal loan directed by Hope. Ibid., pp. 136–7.

37 Ibid., pp. 162 and 166. Stanislas Poniatowski was evidently among those who raised private advances in Amsterdam. See J. Korzencowski, ed., "Souvenirs du Prince Stanislas Poniatowski," *Revue d'histoire diplomatique*, IX (1895), 492. There is no evidence to suggest that his debts formed part of the total assumed by Russia.

38 On Spanish economic revival in the second half of the eighteenth century see

Richard Herr, *The Eighteenth-Century Revolution in Spain* (Princeton, N.J., 1958), pp. 145–47; and on the canals Jaime Vicens Vives, *An Economic History of Spain*, trans. by Frances M. López-Morillas (Princeton, N.J., 1969), pp. 515 and 586. Spanish borrowing during the War of the League of Augsburg is discussed by B. E. de Muinck, *Een regentenhuishouding omstreeks 1700* (The Hague, 1965), pp. 86–7.

39 N.E.H.A., Pros., III, 203. There was also a loan in 1770. Buist, *Hope & Co.*, p. 280, n. 3; N.E.H.A., Pros., III, 81; and *idem*, Archief KV, "Acten van aanstellingen van directeuren, commissarissen en procuratiën . . . ," which indicates an issue of f. 1.3 million at 6 percent for the imperial canal in Aragon. See also N.E.H.A., Pros., III, 80, on a 1780 loan for f. 500,000 at 5 percent floated on behalf of the Royal Guipúzcoa Company of Caracas with the aim of commercial expansion.

40 Sardinia, Portugal, and Naples all raised credit in the Dutch Republic during the Revolutionary and Napoleonic wars. Useful MS. sources on those transactions include N.E.H.A., Pros., I, 88, III, 266, and V, 145; G.A.A., Archief Wisselbank, 1359; and *idem*, Archief SvH, "Stukken betreffende de diverse negotiaties, 1793–1858" (on an administrative office organized in 1812 for investment in the internal debt of the kingdom of Naples). See also Buist, *Hope & Co.*, pp. 339–45, 376–9, and 383–27; and Herbert Lüthy, *La banque protestante en France de la révocation de l'édit de Nantes à la Révolution*, 2 vols. (Paris, 1959–61), II, 69–73.

41 The canal project and lending capital to support it were parodied in heavy-handed fashion in *De Koopman*, IV, 465–69. That periodical favored investment in domestic industry and commerce and, in a letter supposedly from Seville, likened the Spanish loans to the Mississippi bubble. Subscriptions in that loan and the one of 1770 may have amounted to f. 3,208,000, or half the total asked in loans of 1778–80. See pp. 166–7.

42 N.E.H.A., Pros., III, 65–7, and V, 11.

43 *De Koopman*, VI, 126.

44 Ibid., VI, 119–46, and no. 23, 177–8. "De Welmeenende," expressing opposition, claimed in *De Koopman* (VI, 135) that two-thirds of the Spanish life-annuity loan would be subscribed by Dutch investors.

45 According to available quotations, shares in a Heshuysen-Boas loan listed as originating in 1770 were trading at 25 to 30 percent of par in 1778 and declined to 20 to 24 by 1780. See price currents for 8 Oct. 1778, 30 Mar. 1779, and 8 July 1780 in G.A.A., N.49.03. If these were the notes acceptable in lieu of cash for half of subscription, the nominal return of 3.5 percent would have amounted to an annuity of over 5.5 percent. Further funding was organized in 1785 and 1788 through the issue of 6 million pesos in *vales reales*. Earl J. Hamilton, *War and Prices in Spain, 1651–1800* (Cambridge, Mass., 1947), p. 81.

Although according to Buist the royal patents did not provide for redemption, the prospectus issued in Amsterdam for the 1780 loan, the only one available, did specify redemption terms, to begin in 1796 and conclude in 1800. Buist, *Hope & Co.*, p. 280; and N.E.H.A., Pros., III, 81.

46 The loans were 1 Apr. 1778 for f. 2 million; 1 Jan. 1779 for f. 2 million; and 1

Nov. 1780 for f. 2,416,000. The 1780 issue, and perhaps the earlier ones as well, was secured specifically on revenues from the Spanish postal service and otherwise on royal revenues in general.

In early trading the new 3.5-percent notes were exchanged at levels reflecting the discount implied in the conversion of old notes trading far below par, apparently confirming the estimate of n. 45. Quotations for 1779 and 1780 place new notes at 61–63 and 62½–63½, respectively. G.A.A., N.29.03.

47 N.E.H.A., Pros., III, 81.

48 Buist, *Hope & Co.*, p. 280.

49 The peso vellon was a money of account equal to 512 maravedis vellon or 272 maravedis de plata. The ducat (or ducado de cambio), another money of account that will be cited below, was equal to 375 maravedis de plata. Here f. 3,149,000 equaled slighly more than 1,310,000 ducats and about 960,000 pesos de cambio. (This and subsequent peso sums are given in pesos vellon because Spain's paper currency was issued in pesos vellon.) The clearest explanation of the Spanish money maze is provided by John J. McCusker, *Money and Exchange in Europe and America, 1600–1775* (Chapel Hill, N.C., 1978), pp. 98–107, using information on Cadiz. Current exchange and agio rates used in this and subsequent calculations have been drawn from Posthumus, I, 607–14 and 654–5.

50 Hamilton, *War and Prices*, pp. 78–80; and Herr, *Revolution in Spain*, p. 146.

51 N.E.H.A., Archief KV, "Notten diversen," folios 3–5, for placements by Fizeaux, Grand. Sales went slowly and were not completed until October 1785. See also Buist, *Hope & Co.*, p. 280 and n. 4; and U.B.A., 565B14, plans d'emprunts, pt. 1, the later of which indicates "that the court of Spain . . . had lost its credit in Holland [and] allowed heavy premiums to succeed." A f. 5 million loan planned by Echenique Sanchez & Co. for 1 Apr. 1782 had been withdrawn in October of the same year. G.A.A., notary C. van Homrigh, 12461/162–3.

52 Buist, *Hope & Co.*, pp. 78–80. Posthumus, I, 607–8, records a drop from the 1778 exchange average of 92.3 groten per ducat to a 1781 average of 84.9. Data for 1782 and 1783 are incomplete, but indicate a return toward prewar exchange levels followed by another fall in 1783.

53 Buist, *Hope & Co.*, pp. 280–1, and p. 280, n. 4.

54 See a price current for 30 Sept. 1788 in G.A.A., N.41.088; quotations from September 1792 in the *Mercurius;* and, on internal stabilization, Pierre Vilar, *A History of Gold and Money, 1450–1920*, trans. by Judith White (London, 1976), p. 287.

55 Herr, *Revolution in Spain*, p. 380.

56 N.E.H.A., Pros., V, 116; and Buist, *Hope & Co.*, p. 281.

57 Ibid., pp. 281–2.

58 Hamilton, *War and Prices*, pp. 81–4; and Herr, *Revolution in Spain*, pp. 381–4, on tax increases, a levy on church income, domestic borrowing, and other measures adopted between 1793 and 1795.

59 *Beurs* quotations began to rise in May 1795, presumably in anticipation of the treaty.

60 Ibid., pp. 391–7; and Hamilton, *War and Prices*, pp. 84–5.

61 N.E.H.A., Pros., V, 164; and Buist, *Hope & Co.*, pp. 283–4. Shares from the conversion loans of 1778–80 and from the Hope issue of 1792 were acceptable toward subscription. As security Spain offered the general revenues of the crown, the revenues of the Caisse d'amortissement, and, collaterally, drafts on the Mexican treasury.

62 The conclusion of the war and the resumption of bullion shipments from Mexico led to a recovery of the exchange at the end of 1801. The cost of a ducat had fallen from 85 groten in early 1798 to a low of 36 in December 1800, but was back to 74½ at the end of 1801.

The managing house, the firm of the Widow E. Croese & Co., gained the account by direct appeal in Madrid. The Batavian envoy, Johan Valckenaer, who served as an intermediary with Spanish officials, assisted Croese in the second and third loans (but not in the first, for Valckenaer was not in Spain in 1798). He also pressed Spain to meet annuity and redemption payments due on earlier loans. Jérôme Alexandre Sillem, *Het Leven van Mr. Johan Valckenaer*, 2 vols., new ed. (Amsterdam, 1883), II, 143–4. In 1805 Croese, caught up in Ouvrard's overextension, was forced to suspend payments. Buist, *Hope & Co.*, p. 303.

63 Hamilton, *War and Prices*, pp. 84–5, for information on the *vales*.

64 Buist, *Hope & Co.*, p. 283.

65 Ibid., pp. 284–380. Buist's reconstruction of the Mexican silver deal supersedes earlier versions based on the sometimes faulty memoirs of Ouvrard and Vincent Nolte, Hope's agent in New Orleans. On these see ibid., pp. 285, n. 1, and 292, n. 1. For the memoirs themselves, still exciting reading, see Gabriel Julien Ouvrard, *Mémoires de G.-J. Ouvrard sur sa vie et ses diverses opérations financières*, 3 vols., 3rd ed. (Paris, 1826–7); and Vincent Otto Nolte, *Fifty Years in Both Hemispheres*, trans. (New York, 1854), esp. pp. 48–99.

66 N.E.H.A., Pros., III, 235; and Buist, *Hope & Co.*, pp. 297–309 and 333.

67 Ouvrard suspended payments at the end of 1807, but had been pushed to the wall as early as 1805 as a result of inquiries into his affairs initiated by Napoleon. See also G.A.A., Archief Jan Dominicus Croese, 147.

68 Hope objected in particular to the Spanish practice of reissuing notes taken in under conversion loans [Buist, *Hope & Co.*, pp. 333ff.] and insisted that drafts drawn earlier by Croese on Spain be honored, permitting that house to resume business.

69 N.E.H.A., Pros., I, 100; and Buist, *Hope & Co.*, pp. 334–5.

70 Ibid., p. 357.

71 Ibid., p. 359, citing Labouchère correspondence.

72 Weeveringh, II, 848–9, for semiannual average prices in Amsterdam, as follows:

Loan	1808		1809		1810		1811	
1805	94	89	76	78	63	39	20	13
1807	89	81	71	68	55	38	21	16

73 Such measures were adopted in 1715, 1721, 1726, 1759, 1764–71, 1788, and 1793–7. In 1770 and 1771, for example, the abbé Terray suspended payment on the bills of the farmers general and the rescriptions of the receivers general. P. Coquelle, *L'alliance franco-hollandaise contre l'Angleterre, 1735–1788* (Paris, 1902), p. 209. His suspension of payments on short-term paper followed a series of arbitrary annuity reductions, beginning in 1764, that dangerously undermined French credit. Terray also reduced the return on part of the long-term French debt to accord with its market value. Marcel Marion, *Histoire financière de la France depuis 1715*, 6 vols. (Paris, 1927–8), I, 238–40 and 252. See also J. F. Bosher, *French Finances, 1770–1795* (Cambridge, 1970), p. 98.

74 See pp. 110–12.

75 The French treasury sought 26,785,715 l.t. (f. 12,723,214,12,8) at an annuity of 2,000,000 l.t. (8 percent on single-nominee and 7 percent on double-nominee contracts), and entrusted the issue to the Amsterdam house of Horneca, Hogguer & Co. Although the terms offered exceeded the going rate in Amsterdam, Horneca, Hogguer placed less than a quarter of the total, and most of that outside Amsterdam. G.A.A., notary C. van Homrigh, 12402/130; and Lüthy, *La banque protestante*, II, 487ff.

76 Marion, *Histoire financière*, I, 472–73. The life annuities created under the edict of November 1778 offered, after taxes, 9 percent on one nominee and 7.5 percent on two. That rate was raised once again in February 1781 to 10 and 9 percent net. Lüthy, *La banque protestante*, II, 504. Since these loans, in which subscriptions were often extended beyond their initial limits, met a willing and sometimes avid response, caution about lending to France was not the only force militating toward higher annuity rates.

77 As late as the spring of 1793 securities in two French issues were quoted at and above 90 on the 100 in Amsterdam. *MNM*, 27 May 1793. Between 1 May 1793 and 21 Oct. 1795 prices on shares in annuity-based substitution negotiations fell by as much as 55 points. E.H.B., Amsterdam, Pf. Ned. 1793:2; and G.A.A., N.34.003. For quotations on some domestic French loans in Amsterdam and Paris see *NNJ*, 1792, 133 and 1022, and 1793, 89, 305, and 1041. These fragmentary price data indicate that the depreciation of the assignat covered most of the devaluation of French securities and shares in the annuity-based negotiations into 1793, but that in that year prices fell in advance of exchange rates.

78 Lüthy, *La banque protestante*, II, 31. The calculation of the exchange between guilders and livres was based on monies of account, the French écu of three livres and the Dutch denier de gros. Par was $53^2/_7$ deniers to the écu.

79 Robert D. Harris, "Necker's *Compte Rendu* of 1781: A Reconsideration," *JMH*, XLII, no. 2 (1970), 172. Harris maintains that Necker distinguished between ordinary revenues and expenditures and extraordinary revenues and expenditures, and that the balance of ordinary revenues with expenditures was the crucial point in determining solvency. Creditors felt secure when "the ordinary revenues could support the carrying charges on the debt" (Harris, p. 165). Nonetheless any temporary surplus of ordinary receipts over ordinary expenditures could not in the long run obscure an imbalance be-

tween ordinary receipts and ordinary and extraordinary expenditures, and it is in this latter area that the massive additions to the debt of the 1770s and 1780s were accumulated.

80 [Antoine Jean Baptiste Auget de Montyon], *Particularités et observations sur les ministres des finances de France les plus célèbres, depuis 1660 jusqu'en 1791* (Paris, 1812), pp. 245–6 and 265.

81 Robert D. Harris, "French Finances and the American War, 1777–1783," *JMH*, XLVIII (June, 1976), 233–58, has come once again to Necker's defense. His calculations, based chiefly on data compiled from sources produced by Necker, indicate that extraordinary expenditures during the American war were slightly over 1 billion livres rather than the 1.8 to 2 billion customarily cited. Necker's administration opened with rather small deficits between ordinary receipts and expenditures but he managed in 1778 to balance that segment of entries. Thereafter he is credited with having introduced economies in ordinary expenses that may have been sufficient to absorb servicing of wartime loans.

82 France issued comparatively small amounts of non-interest-bearing paper through the Caisse d'escompte and military and naval departments during the 1780s. According to mercantilist fiscal theory, a larger money supply would reduce interest rates, and in those terms it would appear that French money supply was too low. On the other hand the monarchy relied heavily on short-term credit instruments that added to the supply of money, cost more than paper currency or long-term borrowing, and exposed the treasury to the capital demand pressures of the Parisian market in the 1780s.

83 See, for example, Bosher, *French Finances*, p. xi.

84 Ibid., pp. 42 and 303. This should not be taken to mean that there was no concept of adjusting expenses to income (which is what the word "budget" means). Turgot, for example, informed Louis XVI upon his own appointment as controller general in 1774 that he would reduce expenditures to the point that they were 20 million l.t. less than receipts. Douglas Dakin, *Turgot and the "Ancien Régime" in France* (New York, 1965 reprint), p. 131. See also Alain Guéry, "Les finances de la monarchie française sous l'Ancien Régime," *AESC*, XXXIII, no. 2 (March–April, 1978), 216–17.

85 G. Susane, *La tactique financière de Calonne* (Paris, 1901), p. 79 and nn. 1 and 2. Harris, "French Finances and the American War," 240, prefers the estimate of 520 million.

86 Joh. de Vries, ed., "Van de Spiegel's 'Schets tot een vertoog over de intrinsique en relative magt van de Republijk' (1782)," *EHJ*, XXVII (1958), 92–3.

87 H. T. Colenbrander, *De patriottentijd*, 3 vols. (The Hague, 1897–9), II, 80, n. 3.

88 Another estimate from NNJ, 1781, 38–9, suggests a total of f. 280 million in France in 1781. The source for this is not given and the amount so exaggerated as not to be credible.

89 Coquelle, *L'alliance franco-hollandaise*, passim, esp. pp. 341–2. Alfred Cobban [*Ambassadors and Secret Agents: The Diplomacy of the First Earl of Malmesbury at the Hague* (London, 1954), p. 58] disputes Coquelle's estimate of Thulemeyer's role, maintaining that the Prussian ambassador did

not pursue a consistent policy against alliance between the United Provinces and France. Rather, Cobban found that Thulemeyer was so inconsistent that the British ambassador, Harris, thought him pro-French, whereas the marquis de Verac, French ambassador, thought him pro-English.

90 Alice C. Carter, "Dutch Foreign Investment, 1738–1800," *Economica*, XX, n.s. (November, 1953), passim, esp. 337; *idem*, "Dutch Foreign Investment, 1738–1800, in the Light of the Amsterdam 'Collateral Succession' Inventories," *TvG*, LXVI (1953), 27–38; Charles H. Wilson, "Dutch Investment in Eighteenth-Century England: A Note on Yardsticks," *EcHR*, XII, ser. 2 (1959–60), 434–9; and Carter's response in *idem*, 440–4.

91 Lüthy, *La banque protestante*, II, 506, n. 49, on the loan of November 1779 and II, 521; and J.-B. Manger, *Recherches sur les relations économiques entre la France et la Hollande pendant la Révolution française (1785–1795)* (Paris, 1923), p. 16, on 1781 and 1782 issues.

92 Ibid., p. 61. Dutch investors preferred to collect through Paris agents, and the extent of business done by Fizeaux and van Staphorst was never great.

93 G.A.A., Archief Brants, 94, J. H. Hautot to J. J. Brants, 19 Mar. 1773. See also in the same collection 97, 123, and 124.

94 Ibid., 130. The partners in P. & C. van Eeghen, a firm involved in investments in the United States, expanded holdings in French *rentes* in much the same manner as Brants. G.A.A., Archief van Eeghen, P_3/a and N.E.H.A., Archief SvH, loose bundles of lists of shareholders.

95 G.A.A., Archief Brants, 127 and 130. Thirty thousand guilders of this total was held through shares in the Couderc & Brants negotiation.

96 N.E.H.A., Archief KV, "Een pak met bewijzen van afgedane zaken, over de jaren 1776, 1777 . . . ." A list in the same dossier indicates holdings of 1,303,848 l.t. in the loan of January 1782 transferred by Fizeaux, Grand & Co. of Amsterdam to its sister house in Paris to be held for the former.

97 N.E.H.A., Pros., III, 182; and G.A.A., Archief Brants, 127.

98 E. Clavière to P. Stadnitski, 15 Jan. 1786, and *idem* to *idem*, 27 Jan. and 6 Feb. 1786, A.N., T*646[3]. See also Lüthy, *La banque protestante*, II, 521–4, on Dutch investment in the January 1782 issue.

99 Jean Bouchary, *Les manieurs d'argent à Paris à la fin du XVIIIe siècle*, 3 vols. (Paris, 1939–43), I, 86–7, E. Clavière to P. Stadnitski, 6 Mar. 1786. Part of the Clavière–Stadnitski and Clavière–Cazenove correspondence is reproduced by Bouchary.

100 Ibid., I, 85, E. Clavière to T. Cazenove, 5 Jan. 1786. See also Clavière to Stadnitski, 6 Jan. 1786, A.N., T*646[3], in which Clavière wrote: "M. Haller [the banker in question] a offert, à ce qu'on assure, de plus longs termes aux Hollandais." Some confusion shortly developed over the extent to which those bankers actually covered such an enormous part of the loan. See Clavière to Stadnitski, 9 and 13 Jan. 1786, in ibid. Also Guy Antonetti, *Une maison de banque à Paris au XVIIIe siècle: Greffulhe Montz et Cie (1789–1793)* (Paris, [1963]), p. 171 and n. 134. Between May 1791 and May 1793 Greffulhe Montz collected about 5 million l.t. in *rentes* on behalf of Dutch clients.

101 Clavière's first contact with Stadnitski appears to have occurred through the

agency of Théophile Cazenove, a small-time broker and merchant with extensive family connections in London, Paris, and Geneva. In 1782 Clavière tried unsuccessfully to induce Cazenove to sponsor a negotiation based on the model of Genevan projects on French life annuities. A.N., T*646[1–3] and T*646[5]. A similar effort by Genevan bankers in 1779 also failed. Lüthy, *La banque protestante*, II, 516.

102 George V. Taylor, "The Paris Bourse on the Eve of the Revolution, 1781–1789," *AHR*, LXVII (1962), 963–4.

103 A.N., T*646[2–3] and T*646[5].

104 Clavière to Stadnitski, 7 Oct. 1785, and *idem* to *idem*, 9 Dec. 1785, in ibid., T*646[2]. The prospect of a 20,000 l.t. loan on life annuities was broached late in 1784, but nothing survives of any agreement. Clavière to Stadnitski, 26 Nov. 1784, *ibid.*, T*646[1]. As early as 1778, while still in Geneva, Clavière had borrowed f. 30,000 on shares in the Caisse d'escompte from a Haarlem rentier. Bouchary, *Les manieurs d'argent*, I, 13–14.

105 A.N., T*646[5]. The total borrowed on those stocks was f. 245,034, which was spread among 21 creditors. At other times, beginning in December 1785, Clavière had varying numbers of these stocks on loan through Stadnitski. Furthermore, Clavière had 43,000 l.t. from the December 1785 loan of 80 million hypothecated with Stadnitski, and when Stadnitski's agency dried up as a source of credit, in the spring of 1786, Clavière turned to Cazenove to arrange loans on the security of various types of paper.

106 Clavière to Stadnitski, 13 Jan. and 31 Mar. 1786, ibid., T*646[3].

107 N.E.H.A., Pros., III, 83–85, 87, 88, 92, 139, 140, and 145; U.B.A., 565B14, plans d'emprunts; and Lüthy, *La banque protestante*, II, 525–6 and 545–6.

108 Ibid., II, 546; and N.E.H.A., Pros., III, 87.

109 N.E.H.A., Pros., III, 139; and *idem*, Archief KV, "Notten diversen," folios 13–14.

110 Lüthy, *La banque protestante*, II, 516–17.

111 N.E.H.A., Pros., III, 134. Secured by a mortgage on the Palais Royal and other real estate, this loan was opened in cooperation with Girardot, Haller & Cie of Paris, and was apparently distinct from the tontine that the duc d'Orléans launched in November 1785. Jean Bouchary, *Les compagnies financières à Paris à la fin du XVIIIe siècle*, 3 vols. (Paris, 1940–2), I, 9–10 and n. 10; and Lüthy, *La banque protestante*, II, 530–2. See also Antonetti, *Greffulhe Montz et Cie*, pp. 157–58; and S. R. Cope, "The History of Boyd, Benfield & Co.: A Study in Merchant Banking in the Last Decade of the Eighteenth Century" (Ph.D. diss., Univ. of London, 1947), pp. 11–13, 21, and 46, on a 1789 loan for the duc d'Orléans directed by van Orsoy for f. 2 million.

112 N.E.H.A., Pros., V, 32.

113 Ibid., III, 94 and 95, and IV, 103. Also Yves Durand, *Les fermiers généraux au XVIIIe siècle* (Paris, 1971), pp. 163–6. On Crevenna see the article in the *Nieuw nederlandsch biografisch woordenboek*, X, 222.

114 At least f. 5,589,000 of this amount was actually subscribed and more may have been. Information is wanting on three of the fifteen. A table of these, sources, and additional detail on several aspects of Dutch investment may

be found in my "Dutch Investment in France, 1781–1787," *JEH*, XXXIII, no. 4 (December, 1973), 732–60; and "Life Annuity-Based Loans on the Amsterdam Capital Market Toward the End of the 18th Century," *EHJ*, XXXVI (1973), 102–30.

115 The average exchange rate between Dutch and French monies of account in the 1780s was about 54 deniers de gros to the écu; by January 1793 the rate was 17⅜.

116 Taylor, "Paris Bourse," 963, n. 38; and Lüthy, *La banque protestante*, II, 520 and 554. The addition of issues arranged by Loménie de Brienne would increase the estimated total of French loans from 1776 to more than 1.6 billion livres.

117 That is, the Genevan total added to the minimum and maximum estimates for the Dutch total.

118 This section summarizes my "Foreign Credit and Fiscal Stability: Dutch Investment in the United States, 1781–1794," *Journal of American History*, LXV, no. 3 (December, 1978), 654–78.

119 On earlier loans in France, Spain, and the United Provinces and on the 1781 issue see P. J. van Winter, *Het aandeel van den amsterdamschen handel aan den opbouw van het amerikaansche gemeenebest*, 2 vols. (The Hague, 1927–33), I, 29–58 [available in a trans. and rev. ed., *American Public Finance and Dutch Investment, 1780–1805*, 2 vols. (New York, 1977)]; Rafael A. Bayley, *The National Loans of the United States*, 2nd ed. (Washington, 1882), pp. 13–27; and E. James Ferguson, *The Power of the Purse* (Chapel Hill, N.C., 1961), pp. 40–4, 127–9, and passim.

120 For details on this and subsequent loans see van Winter, *Amsterdamschen handel*, I, 59–87 and 133–92, and II, 147–89 and 476–7. On the loan opened in Antwerp on 1 Dec. 1791 commission charges totaled 4 percent. Net receipts, however, were slightly more than 96 percent of the loan sum.

121 Hamilton calculated par (via bullion content) at 35.89 ninetieths of a dollar to one current guilder, or $.3988 (f. 2.51 to the dollar). Hamilton to the House of Representatives, 5 Feb. 1793, in Jonathan Elliot, *The Funding System of the United States and of Great Britain* (New York, 1968 reprint), p. 192. That has been rounded off to 40 cents. The dollar rate at the time of those loans was probably closer to f. 2.35, at which the yield would be calculated at more than $3.2 million. Because loan proceeds were not transferred in their entirety to the United States, such calculations have only a hypothetical applicability.

122 Van Winter, *Amsterdamschen handel*, I, 201–3.

123 See Bayley, *National Loans*, p. 31, for an itemized list.

124 *Report of the Secretary of the Treasury on the State of the Finances for the Year 1867* (Washington, 1868), pp. 356–9; van Winter, *Amsterdamschen handel*, II, 476–7; and, for debt totals, Davis Rich Dewey, *Financial History of the United States*, 12th ed. (New York, 1939), p. 113. Proceeds of loans raised in Amsterdam and Antwerp have been calculated after deduction of commissions. Budgetary data in reports of the secretary of the treasury are more comprehensive than those in Walter Lowrie and Matthew St. Clair Clarke, comps., *American State Papers, Finance* (Washington,

1832), I, 661–3, which offers a variation on format and omits service on the foreign debt and expenditures toward redemption of the public debt. That latter source is to be preferred, however, for a more detailed itemization of ordinary revenues and expenditures. Neither report distinguishes foreign loan from all loan proceeds. The sums given here as foreign loan proceeds represent value to the United States at par rates of exchange, but the chronology of actual availability for disbursement is uncertain enough to warrant qualification of those entries as estimates. Moreover, the largest part was transferred to Paris, which means that there were two rhythms of receipt and disbursement, one operating slowly via Philadelphia and the other with more speed directly from Amsterdam to Paris. Of the f. 19.55 million raised in the loans of 1790–2, f. 5,649,621,2,8 was remitted to the United States through bills drawn by the treasury. The exchange rates on those bills, including discount, averaged nearly 41 cents to the guilder. Elliot, *Funding System*, pp. 160–3.

125 Interest payments averaged $3.2 million per annum from 1792 through 1800, whereas tax revenues increased from $3.7 to 10.8 million.

126 To the degree that Hamilton's funding and assumption program reduced or deferred the 6-percent return that had been established on all federal securities, average service on the American debt in 1792 reflected a partial default. But that was not the view that American or European investors took. In the United States Hamilton's program was regarded favorably because it provided that paper long depreciated in trading was to be redeemed at par. At the same time, Dutch investors could take pleasure in what appeared to be a confirmation of the sagacity of their purchases of domestic debt. Ferguson, *Purse*, pp. 292–305, discusses Hamilton's program and responses to it.

127 Ibid., p. 292.

128 At the rates employed to transfer livre tournois values into dollars in Bayley, *National Loans*, p. 31, the debt to France and arrears on it, and the debt to military officers who served in the American Revolution and arrears on it, totaled as of 1790 45.77 million l.t., or $8.3 million. Of that sum and subsequent service, $5.39 million (29.72 million l.t.) was paid out of the Amsterdam and Antwerp loans between December 1790 and September 1792, and on terms highly beneficial to the United States. At exchange and agio rates prevailing when the French loans were raised (Posthumus, I, 607–608 and 654), the sum involved in those payments, f. 10.08 million in current money, would have brought about 21.8 million l.t. Although the United States did not take full advantage of the depreciation of the French assignat and evaluated the total of remittances at 24.19 million l.t., it nonetheless profited from the fall of the écu against the guilder. Elliot, *Funding System*, pp. 211–12, reproduces details on those transfers to Paris. See also ibid., pp. 427–8; Bayley, *National Loans*, pp. 40–1; and van Winter, *Amsterdamschen handel*, II, 164–7, on settlement of the remainder of the debt to France.

129 Hamilton to the House of Representatives, 13 Feb. 1793, in Elliot, *Funding System*, pp. 184–5.

130 Ibid., p. 190.

131 Ibid., p. 195.
132 Bayley, *National Loans*, pp. 26–7.
133 Ferguson, *Purse*, pp. 252–3 and 327–9.
134 Prices reported in the *Gazette of the United States*, reproduced by Elliot, *Funding System*, pp. 231–2.
135 Bayley, *National Loans*, p. 34. The combined foreign and domestic debt, including other categories of internal obligations, amounted in 1803 to $77 million. The part in foreign hands exceeded 50 percent. Pieter Stadnitski, who had participated as a commission agent in earlier loans for the United States, was the leading figure in developing this sector of enterprise. He not only introduced the first stock-substitution negotiation on domestic debt, but also brought two ventures on unsettled land in New York state onto the market in 1793.
136 On grain sales to Europe, which assisted the trend, see Ferguson, *Purse*, pp. 268–9. At the exchange rate employed by Stadnitski in calculations on his 1787 venture on the domestic debt, f. 1 million would have fetched some $425,000. At the rates that prevailed in 1792 the yield of f. 1 million would have been only about $404,000 (both excluding discount). There was a loss on receipts insofar as the Dutch loans of 1790 and thereafter were transferred to the United States, but there was a gain with respect to all drafts on European currencies for the government and the private sector and also, ultimately, on redemption of the Dutch debt. Available data on pre-1790 loans always reflect the par rate of 40 cents rather than the market rate.
137 Hamilton acknowledged the benefits of the federal securities issued in the funding program as "an engine of business, an instrument of industry and commerce" [quoted by John C. Miller, *The Federalist Era, 1789–1801* (New York, 1960), p. 50]. Because the Dutch pattern of investment eschewed turnover, assets once placed in domestic debt tended to remain there until redeemed. Moreover, a substantial part of the speculative profits gained by Dutch firms in transactions in the domestic debt was plowed back into unsettled land and other investment areas.
138 Ferguson, *Purse*, p. 326.
139 In a 1793 report to Congress, Hamilton put 1791 revenues at $3,553,195.18, which would indicate that Dutch loan proceeds exceeded domestic taxation revenues by nearly $230,000. Elliot, *Funding System*, p. 196.

Chapter 8. The collapse of solvency

1 That year was also marked by the French suspension of annuity payments and a general European banking crisis that affected Amsterdam in the spring. On the banking crisis, during which, of major banking houses, Pye Rich & Wilkieson and Christiaan van Orsoy & Zoonen failed, see Guy Antonetti, *Une maison de banque à Paris au XVIIIe siècle: Greffulhe Montz et Cie (1789–1793)* (Paris, [1963]), pp. 209–10 and 221–38.
2 The average annual addition to the combined debts of domestic governments

between 1782, when van de Spiegel's estimates suggest a total in excess of f. 545 million, and early 1795, when the debt was about f. 787 million, was no more than f. 18.6 million and probably closer to f. 7 million. But the bulk of that was incurred in 1787 and thereafter, so that the annual rate was probably no more than f. 2 to 3 million between 1782 and 1787 and a correspondingly higher amount, about f. 10 million, between 1787 and 1795. Since the annual rate of fresh investment in foreign loans between 1780 and 1793 was some f. 20 million, total new investment would appear to have peaked at about f. 30 million p.a. In both areas the addition of prolongation reinvestments would increase amounts given here. (Figures cited are in nominal values that do not reflect discounts offered by some borrowers after 1793 on new loans or the lesser real sum actually lent by the investor who acquired discounted paper on the market in order to participate in issues accepting outstanding paper in subscription.)

3 In 1802 Ketwich & Voombergh, van Halmael & Hagedoorn, and Willem Borski opened the first substitution negotiation specifically designed as an office for the administration or management of outstanding paper. Shares in the management trust were exchanged for French securities held in the name of the buyer, thus replacing paper that was tedious to negotiate with paper that could be transferred more readily. Within four years the *rentes* being handled totaled more than Fr. 58 million in face value. See N.E.H.A., Pros., III, 264; *idem*, Archief KV, "Rekeningen en documenten der administratie van Franse leningen, 1803 tot ongeveer 1881"; and G.A.A., N.12.17.09. Single- and multiple-unit trusts were subsequently formed on a variety of securities, but only the 1802 office appears to have enjoyed much success.

4 On the subsidies see John M. Sherwig, *Guineas and Gunpowder: British Foreign Aid in the Wars with France, 1793–1815* (Cambridge, Mass., 1969), passim, esp. pp. 362–9; and Ch. Wilson, *De l'influence des capitaux anglais sur l'industrie européenne . . .* (Brussels, 1847), p. 52–5.

5 Britain's withdrawal around 1780 was eased by the fact that foreign investors did not relieve themselves of existing holdings in the public debt at the same time that fresh capital imports from the Dutch Republic were curtailed.

6 If it is correct to estimate overall royal liabilities in 1788 at nearly 5 billion l.t., then only 2.3 percent of the debt was involved in the suspension of redemption payments on 16 August. In Amsterdam (and by 1792 in Paris) prices appear to have deteriorated only as the assignats lost value. Even in 1793 it was not clear that the suspension of annuity payments adopted in January would be sustained, or that the unfavorable exchange situation would linger.

7 Peter Mathias and Patrick O'Brien, "Taxation in Britain and France, 1715–1810: A Comparison of the Social and Economic Incidence of Taxes Collected for the Central Governments," *JEEH*, V, no. 3 (Winter, 1976), 608–9.

8 J. F. Bosher, *French Finances, 1770–1795* (Cambridge, 1970), pp. 273–5.

9 It is noteworthy that France did not attempt to maintain the value of assignats by borrowing abroad to fund specie imports (while reducing assignat creation) and apply pressure toward higher exchange rates on the French money of account.

10 In the interim France had paid no returns since 1792, except for a rather feeble effort in 1796 in paper that could be sold only with heavy losses. On the effect of French policy on substitution negotiations opened in Amsterdam in the 1780s on French life annuities see N.E.H.A., Archief SvH, the ledgers and the dossiers "Diverse documenten, descharges, particuliere beschieden, enz. I," *idem*, II, and "Rekening van de negotiatie van 1 January 1785, groot f. 228,000" (or accounts of other negotiations).

11 Despite the bankruptcy of 1793–7, Dutch investment in France revived around 1800. W. M. Keuchenius, *De inkomsten en uitgaven der Bataafsche Republiek voorgesteld in eene nationaale balans* (Amsterdam, 1803), p. 11, suggests that acquisitions of French securities after 1797 had restored the level of Dutch investment to that prevailing before the French debt reduction. Some part of the flow was the product of Dutch purchases of Bank of France stock. See N.E.H.A., Pros., III, 249; and, on an administrative office formed on bank shares, G.A.A., N.12.17.09. On the other hand, an early effort by Napoleon to tap Dutch savings through a loan was disappointing. On an attempt in March 1800 to raise Fr. 12 million in Amsterdam see Auguste Viesse de Marmont, *Mémoires du maréchal duc de Raguse de 1792 à 1832*, 9 vols. (Paris, 1857), II, 107–8; N.E.H.A., Pros., V, 172; H. T. Colenbrander, "Napoleon en Nederland van 1799 tot 1806," *De gids*, 4th ser., III (1908), 103–6; Marmont to Talleyrand, 21 Mar. 1800, in *GS*, III, 148–50 and also 606–9; and Guy Antonetti, "Les relations franco-bataves et l'échec de l'emprunt français de l'an VIII," *RHES*, LIII, no. 1 (1975), 61–72. See also W. M. Zappey, *De economische en politieke werkzaamheid van Johannes Goldberg (1763–1828)* (Alphen aan den Rijn, 1967), p. 39. Napoleon was miffed by the failure of that project and moved to suggest that those who would do nothing for him should expect nothing in return.

12 For sources see chap. 6, n. 66. Also, for a contemporary estimate of the interest (as distinct from the reimbursement) portion of the 1794 loan's annuity, see S. Worontzow to André Razoumowski, 23 Feb./6 Mar. 1795, in Alexandre Wassiltchikow, *Les Razoumowski*, ed. and trans. by A. Brückner, 3 vols. (Halle, 1893–4), II, pt. 4, 226–7. (Semyon Vorontsov was Russian ambassador in London.)

13 S. R. Cope, "The History of Boyd, Benfield & Co.: A Study in Merchant Banking in the Last Decade of the Eighteenth Century" (Ph.D. diss., Univ. of London, 1947), pp. 52–4, 93, and 98; and N.E.H.A., Pros., V, 144 (a prospectus issued in Amsterdam by Croese). See also Marten G. Buist, *At Spes Non Fracta: Hope & Co., 1770–1815* (The Hague, 1974), p. 142, n. 3, on reaction to a 1794 proposal involving a f. 12 million flotation to be managed by Hope & Co. in Amsterdam in association with Thomas Christie in London. The plan, advanced by a Polish adventurer, was to take advantage of depressed prices on loans outstanding in Amsterdam to Polish magnates. Christie rejected the plan not on grounds that it was speculative but on the basis "that loans to foreign countries were not very popular in England."

14 Other points, such as who was to pay the cost of remittances from Vienna, were also left unsettled. Cope, "Boyd, Benfield & Co.," pp. 58–9; and Karl F. Helleiner, *The Imperial Loans: A Study in Financial and Diplomatic His-*

tory (Oxford, 1965), pp. 170ff. The Austrian treatment of its liabilities in England confirmed misgivings about lending to foreign governments. A settlement was not reached until 1824. It is also true that the yields paid by Austria in the British loans were far higher than those paid in Amsterdam, and that therefore the London market was less attractive to borrowers.

15 Joseph von Hauer, *Beiträge zur Geschichte der österr. Finanzen* (Vienna, 1848), p. 160; and Weeveringh, II, 496. For quotations see ibid., II, 846–7 and 861–71; and *MNM*, September 1792 through August 1796.

16 Von Hauer, *Oesterr. Finanzen*, p. 210; and Robert Horvàth, "Monetary Inflation in Hungary During the Napoleonic Wars," *JEEH*, V, no. 3 (Winter, 1976), 656.

17 Von Hauer, *Oesterr. Finanzen*, p. 157; and Adolf Beer, *Die Finanzen Oesterreichs im XIX. Jahrhundert* (Prague, 1877), p. 392.

18 Von Hauer, *Oesterr. Finanzen*, pp. 156–9, for cumulative totals found due in 1802; and Paul Stiassny, *Der österreichische Staatsbankerott von 1811* (Vienna, 1912), p. 20.

19 Von Hauer, *Oesterr. Finanzen*, p. 210.

20 Weeveringh, II, 846–7; and Posthumus, I, 611 and 617.

21 N.E.H.A., Pros., I, 95 and IV, 76. That office continued to function at least as late as 1855 (Weeveringh, II, 505–7), but there is no evidence to indicate that it assisted in a recovery of prices. See also N.E.H.A., Pros., II, 3, an appeal of the transfer of service to Vienna because of the heavy losses involved. In that document the debt is put at nearly f. 45 million. A balance struck in 1811 gives the total of Austrian loans at f. 45,151,000, of which f. 3,151,000 had been repaid, leaving f. 42 million. There was also at that point a balance of some f. 6 million in annuity arrears. Montalivet to the emperor (Napoleon), 28 Oct. 1811, in *GS*, VI, 219.

22 Austria turned also to domestic lottery loans and tried to market notes abroad. E.H.B., nos. 287 and 300 of the prospectuses collected by L. Huizinga.

23 G.A.A., N.12.17.08, for *Brief, door een houder van eene aanzienlijke quantiteit obligatien* . . . (Amsterdam, 1805); and *Nadere aanmerkingen, over het gedrag, door de Heeren Goll en Comp.* . . . (Amsterdam, 1805). On related matters, specifically Hope & Co.'s efforts on behalf of investors in the Austrian loans, see also the letter of 9 Jan. 1812 in N.E.H.A., Archief KV, "Plan van negotiatie op 30 jarige renten, 1789"; and in *idem*, "Berekening van zes maanden interest van Amerikaansche fondsen . . . ," some correspondence of 1811 concerning settlement efforts.

24 *Brief, door een houder*, pp. 7–8 and 12–13, claims also that news of both the 1802 and 1805 measures was leaked to inside parties in advance of the formal announcement. For the response on that point, *Nadere aanmerkingen*, pp. 10ff.

25 See Stiassny, *Oesterreichische Staatsbankerott*, passim; K. Benda, "Situation financière et dévaluation de la monnaie en Hongrie en 1811," in *F.P.A.R.*, pp. 213–25; and Horvàth, "Monetary Inflation," 656.

26 J. Dinger, *Overzicht van alle ter beurze van Amsterdam verhandeld wordende binnen- en buitenlandsche effecten*, 5th ed. (Amsterdam, 1873), pp. 362–3; and Weeveringh, II, 501 and, for *beurs* averages from 1816, 861ff.

On the Austrian debt in the first half of the nineteenth century see ibid., II, 497–607; and Beer, *Die Finanzen Oesterreichs*.

27 Von Hauer, *Oesterr. Finanzen*, pp. 209–10; and, on postwar measures, Weeveringh, II, 508f.; and Horvàth, "Monetary Inflation," 658–9.

28 Sherwig, *British Foreign Aid*, passim, esp. pp. 161–4 and 366–8.

29 Weeveringh, II, 781. This source puts the total foreign debt in 1811 in excess of f. 30 million.

30 Public notices on this effort may be found in N.E.H.A., Archief KV, "Verschillende negotiaties ten behoeve van Zweden . . . 1772–1807." See also Johan E. Elias, *De vroedschap van Amsterdam*, 2 vols. (Amsterdam, 1963 reprint), II, 753–4; and Weeveringh, II, 781–3.

31 N.E.H.A., Archief KV, "Verschillende negotiaties ten behoeve van Zweden . . . 1772–1807." In 1814 Dutch claims totaled f. 14.7 million, past-due interest included. Buist, *Hope & Co.*, p. 91, n. 3. Because some claims remained outstanding, settlement dragged on into the 1840s when Ketwich & Voombergh, then in charge, returned the debentures on which the loans had been secured to Stockholm. Folke Ludwigs, "Stats-obligationer från Gustaf:s dagar," *Ekonomisk Revy*, no. 6 (1968), 378.

32 According to Weeveringh, II, 783, no settlement was ever received from France. The interest coupons continued to trade in Amsterdam as late as the middle of the nineteenth century, fetching less than ½ percent. Funds for the settlement of all foreign debts were provided by the sale of Guadeloupe. Karl Åmark, *Sveriges statsfinanser, 1719–1809* (Stockholm, 1961), p. 660. I wish also to thank J. Römelingh for information on the 1816 settlement.

33 Payments began in May 1816, some months before the due date for the presentation of claims, 31 Dec. 1816.

34 As follows:

1816	15 %
	10
1817	7
1824	.5
	32.5%

N.E.H.A., Archief KV, "Coupons van Zweedsche obligaties en certificaties."

35 Weeveringh, II, 783.

36 V. Falbe-Hansen and Will. Scharling, *Danmarks statistik*, 6 vols. (Copenhagen, 1878–91), IV, 380–1, on devaluation of the domestic debt. The state debt amounted to some 126 million rdl. cour. in 1814, and note issues to 142 million.

37 Weeveringh, II, 79. On postwar prices see also ibid., II, 850ff., and on the course of the eighteenth-century loans to the 1850s, II, 77–8. Also Falbe-Hansen and Scharling, *Danmarks statistik*, IV, 381ff., on the postwar era.

38 Buist, *Hope & Co.*, pp. 166–85; N.E.H.A., Pros., III, 313; and *idem*, Archief

KV, "Notten diversen." As compensation to investors for lengthening the term of redemption to 1810–30, the yield was established at 5 percent on all notes. Of course the assumption of the Polish debts gave investors more creditable assurances than they had previously had.

39 Buist, *Hope & Co.*, pp. 204ff. The reserve fund (whose notes fell outside the restrictions in force in the Republic on foreign loans) was initially set at f. 12 million, but after negotiations on commission charges were completed in 1798 additional charges were deducted from it. There is some confusion about its ultimate size (ibid., p. 204).

40 The actual total, f. 101,736,600, was reduced slightly by Russian payment of f. 136,600. Components were as shown in table. Ibid., pp. 270–4; Weeveringh, II, 672–3; and G.A.A., N.12.16.04. Britain assumed one-fourth of the debt in the postwar settlement and discharged that (£2,272,727) between 1815 and 1906.

f. 83,600,000	outstanding from the 1798 conversion;
17,886,600	past due annuities and interest thereon; and
250,000	as a bonus for overdue notes
f. 101,736,600	

41 Weeveringh, II, 673. See also Buist, *Hope & Co.*, p. 272, n. 2, for a correction of Weeveringh's figure for the middle of the nineteenth century. Dinger, *Overzicht*, p. 212, found that a balance of f. 43.6 million remained in 1873; and J. C. Loman, *Supplement op den vijfden druk van J. Dinger's overzicht van alle ter beurze van Amsterdam* (Amsterdam, 1880), p. 74, one of f. 37.6 million in 1880. J. J. Weeveringh, *Onze fondsenmarkt: Schetsen der financieele geschiedenis van staten . . .* (Amsterdam, 1885), pp. 190–213, follows the Russian debt to 1885.

42 Marc Raeff, *Michael Speransky: Statesman of Imperial Russia, 1772–1839*, 2nd ed. (The Hague, 1969), pp. 101–5.

43 Walter McKenzie Pintner, *Russian Economic Policy Under Nicolas I* (Ithaca, N.Y., 1967), pp. 185–7.

44 Ibid., pp. 32 and 184–220, dealing with Russian monetary policy into the 1840s. In 1820 the imperial debt totaled slightly over 159 million silver rubles, of which 75 percent had been drawn from foreign loans.

45 On those schemes, which included a project to transfer the Spanish debt to the United States in connection with the American acquisition of Florida, see Buist, *Hope & Co., pp. 366–71*.

46 Ibid., p. 380; Weeveringh, II, 872–82; and Johannes Apollonius Alting Bösken, *Over geldleeningen hier te lande door vreemde mogendheden aangegaan* (Utrecht, 1864), pp. 81–8. Albert Broder, "Les investissements étrangers en Espagne au XIXe siècle: méthodologie et quantification," *RHES*, LIV, no. 1 (1976), 45, gives the net total transferred to Spain from the Republic between 1768 and 1815 at 53,272,000 francs. This exploratory article does not include

references on this point or any indication about the method of calculating the exchange or net receipts on loans. Of course Spain was liable for the gross sums raised from Dutch investors, including those transferred to France.

47 A commission had begun work on tax reform in 1785, and some minor measures were adopted in 1791 and 1792 at the provincial and Generality levels. Although the forced loan raised f. 53 million, it added some f. 57 million to the provincial debt. A. J. van der Meulen, *Studies over het ministerie van Van de Spiegel* (Leiden, 1905), pp. 349–53, 370–1, 387–8, and 404; and Cornelis Zillezen, *Wijsgeerig onderzoek, wegens Neerlands opkomst, bloei, en welvaard . . .* (Amsterdam, 1796), p. 318. Van der Meulen, *Van de Spiegel,* p. 381, indicates that no one had a clear conception of the province's financial position. Other public corporations in the Republic were also in bad straits. From November 1792 through 1794 only 71 percent of quota impositions were paid by the provinces. C. H. E. de Wit, *De strijd tussen aristocratie en democratie in Nederland, 1780–1848* (Heerlen, 1965), p. 50. Holland fell behind in its quota payments in 1794.

On van de Spiegel's negotiations with the Patriots (through Pieter Stadnitski) see van der Meulen, *Van de Spiegel,* pp. 332–45; the van de Spiegel–Stadnitski correspondence in Archief L. P. van de Spiegel, A. R., Letterbook C, 51; *Brieven en negotiatiën van Mr. L. P. van de Spiegel, als raadpensionaris van Holland,* 3 vols. (Amsterdam, 1803), I, 125–6; and Noël to Lebrun, 24 Jan. 1793 in *GS*, I, 261–2.

48 On those forced and voluntary loans and levies see U.B.A., 565B14, plans d'emprunts, pt. 10; N.E.H.A., Pros., III, 307 and V, 161; Metelerkamp, pp. 24–5; E.H.B., 90C40 (a volume of decrees on loans and levies); N.E.H.A., Archief van de familie Sillem, IV, 207; R. Fell, *A Tour Through the Batavian Republic During the Latter Part of the Year 1800 . . .* (London, 1801), pp. 351–2; P. H. Engels, *De geschiedenis der belastingen in Nederland* (Rotterdam, 1848), pp. 160–1; and Weeveringh, I, 23–4. For those individuals with assets and income substantial enough to include them in the levies and loans, a total of 15.5 percent of property (10.5 percent with compensation in interest-bearing notes and 5 percent without) and an annual average of 6.47 percent of income (chiefly without compensation) was required between 1795 and 1802. There were also additional levies and loans in Amsterdam and in the province of Holland. See also N.E.H.A., Archief KV, "Qualificatien v. d. gecomm. commissie d. d. provisionele representanten . . ."; G.A.A., Archief van Eeghen, P_1/d; and *GS*, II, 16–17 and 486. These sources deal with short-term credit mobilized for the Batavian regime by the Amsterdam business community in 1795 and 1796.

49 The 1797 report on Holland's finances revealed that between 1788 and 1794 ordinary tax revenues totaled f. 169.7 million and expenditures f. 228.3 million. Of the latter figure more than f. 112.7 million, over 66 percent of revenues, had gone to debt service. A similar inquiry was made into Amsterdam's finances and there too voluntary and forced loans were necessary. *Verzameling van authentique stukken, kunnende dienen tot bijlaagen voor de nieuwspapieren*, 5 vols. (Amsterdam, 1793–6), V, 106–32; Metelerkamp, pp. 171–5; van der Meulen, *Van de Spiegel,* app. V, 4; and Zappey, *Johannes*

Goldberg, pp. 22–3. The Batavians did not follow through with a plan to open financial matters to public scrutiny and in fact continued the obscurantism of the previous regime.

50 On the views of Nicolaas van Staphorst, leader among the Patriots and partner in one of the two banking houses directing loans negotiated in Amsterdam by the United States, see Pieter J. van Winter, *American Finance and Dutch Investment, 1780–1805,* trans. by Mrs. C. M. Geyl and Irene Clephane, 2 vols. (New York, 1977), I, 528–9.

51 French officials charged with settling on an indemnity figure were impressed by the magnitude of Dutch wealth, and in particular by the reputed volume of Dutch foreign investments. See P. J. Blok, *Geschiedenis van het nederlandsche volk*, 8 vols. (Groningen, 1892–1908), VII, 11; and, on arrangements to meet the indemnity and additional impositions, J.-B. Manger, *Recherches sur les relations économiques entre la France et la Hollande pendant la Révolution française (1785–1795)* (Paris, 1923), pp. 110–42.

52 Nonetheless the new regime was unable to sustain public confidence in its financial position. Although the flight of the stadholder does not appear to have affected market quotations (*MNM*, price currents for 27 Dec. 1794 and 25 Feb. 1795), prices waned later in 1795.

53 On the variety of outstanding paper that had to be converted into national debentures see Weeveringh, I, 17–20.

54 W. Dirksen, "Openbare financiën in Nederland van 1790 tot 1820; veranderingen bij de overgang van republikeinse statenbond naar koninkrijk," *F.P.A.R.*, p. 115 and n. 88.

55 Ibid., pp. 115–17; F. N. Sickenga, *Bijdrage tot de geschiedenis der belastingen in Nederland* (Leiden, 1864), pp. 314–20; and H. J. Hofstra, "De belastingunificatie van 1805," in *Smeetsbundel: opstellen aangeboden aan Prof. dr. M. J. H. Smeets . . .* (Deventer, 1967), pp. 227–44. See also Simon Schama, *Patriots and Liberators: Revolution in the Netherlands, 1780–1813* (New York, 1977), pp. 384–9, 445–8, and 494–524, for a thorough and attractively written reconstruction of the period.

56 Simon Schama, "The Exigencies of War and the Politics of Taxation in the Netherlands, 1795–1810," in *War and Economic Development*, ed. by J. M. Winter (London, 1975), p. 124.

57 Those changes of outlook may be followed in the correspondence and taxation accounts of Pieter and Christiaan van Eeghen, partners in the firm of P. & C. van Eeghen, who appear to have been politically aloof before 1795. See G.A.A., Archief HLC, 73; and *idem*, Archief van Eeghen, P_1/a–b, P_1/CI–III, P_1/d, and P_1/f–t.

58 In 1804 nine years of French impositions were calculated to have cost f. 229 million, yet that burden had to be carried for another nine years. I. J. Brugmans, *Paardenkracht en mensenmacht* (The Hague, 1961), p. 17. An 1803 estimate relating to 1802 put the Batavian debt at f. 1 billion and service at f. 29.46 million, or 87 percent of ordinary revenues. Keuchenius, *Inkomsten en uitgaven*, pp. 1–2. See also van Stralen to Schimmelpenninck, 21 Nov. 1803, in *GS*, IV, ii, 472; and the memorandum by Gogel to Marmont, 8 Sept. 1804, in ibid., IV, ii, 514–17. In 1799, the first year of operation under the

centralized revenue system, ordinary revenues totaled about f. 36.35 million and expenditures f. 79.67 million. Blok, *Nederlandsch volk,* VII, 97. See also Schama, "Exigencies of War," p. 118.

59 Metelerkamp, p. 26; and van Stralen to Schimmelpenninck, 21 Nov. 1803, in *GS,* IV, ii, 472.

60 On the loans of 1800 and thereafter see G. A. Fokker, *Geschiedenis der loterijen in de Nederlanden* (Amsterdam, 1862), pp. 152–3; N.E.H.A., Pros., I, 10, 77, 81, and 99; *idem,* Archief KV, "Contract tussen de heren J. Dull . . ."; G.A.A., 25C21; *idem,* N.12.15.05; *idem,* Archief Wisselbank, 1359; Weeveringh, I, 149; and Jérôme Alexandre Sillem, *Het leven van Mr. Johan Valckenaer (1759–1821),* 2 vols. (Amsterdam, 1883), II, 246. Also, on the consolidation of the national debt in 1809, Dinger, *Overzicht,* p. 7; and J. F. Neeb, *De grootboeken der nationale schuld,* 3rd ed. (Nijkerk, 1889).

61 R. V. Heyliger, *De nederlandsche wetgeving op de vreemde geldligtingen* (Leiden, 1854), pp. 6–14 and 43. First introduced in 1802, those measures were renewed in 1808, expanded in 1809, suspended in 1810–13, and revived under the kingdom of the Netherlands.

62 Brugmans, *Paardenkracht,* p. 9. Revenues had risen over the period to 1810 (to f. 48 million) at a rate slightly greater than expenditures. The 1811 decrease continued in 1812, when the French revenue system was imposed on Dutch departments of the empire.

63 Neeb, *De grootboeken der nationale schuld,* p. 5, gives a total of f. 1,251,551,563, to which should be added the capital behind f. 700,000 per annum in life annuities. Service was f. 38,402,450 per annum.

64 Dinger, *Overzicht,* pp. 8–11.

65 Brugmans, *Paardenkracht,* p. 178, and, on the postwar financial situation, pp. 177–88.

Chapter 9. Economic consequences of lending to foreign governments

1 Since tax systems were designed to tap the turnover of commodities of common consumption, a higher level of economic activity fostered by mercantilist expedient programs might not have been fully reflected in revenues. Disproportionate gains by wealthier economic groups would not have appeared proportionally in tax revenues.

2 P. G. M. Dickson, *The Financial Revolution in England: A Study in the Development of Public Credit, 1688–1756* (New York, 1967), p. 12, indicates that up to the 1760s the British government "was able to borrow up to a third of its overall requirements in war time without competing with the capital requirements of the private sector, and without any significant effect on prices." The element of that observation concerning competition with the private sector would appear to apply in general to Britain, the Dutch Republic, and Austria into the early 1790s, from which point credit costs increased and, in Austria's case, domestic revenues were severely strained. On the

other hand, the United States managed to reduce effective returns and the cost of new credit during the 1790s.

3 See n. 23.

4 In terms of foreign-exchange earnings, the sum of foreign government loans outstanding in 1763, invested almost exclusively in the British public debt, may be explained as the result of transfers of current account surpluses on service and commodity exports with other trading associates to London, and of a shift in foreign commercial investments into government finance.

5 The most long-standing capital-export relationship existed between the Republic and Britain, but successive wartime purchases in the British public debt do not appear to have been accompanied by increased exports of goods to that state or reduced imports from it. Charles H. Wilson, *Anglo-Dutch Commerce and Finance in the Eighteenth Century* (Cambridge, 1966 reprint), pp. 198–9. London's increasing importance as an international payments center, together with a persistent Dutch deficit on the flow of commodities with Britain, eased the movement of Dutch credit surpluses with other areas to London. From the British perspective, wartime capital imports from the Republic were balanced at least in part by the export of subsidies to allies and transfers for naval and military expenses abroad. After about 1780 the bilateral balance between the Republic and Britain shifted, as new investments were suspended but annuity payments on existing Dutch holdings in the public debt continued. That development coincided with increasing Dutch capital exports to other European states, but the suspension of new investments may not have created an overall surplus on Dutch current account with Britain. If the Dutch balance of payments moved to a deficit around 1790, increased investments in loans to European states, financed still out of annuity receipts, would ultimately have meant bullion shipments abroad.

A secular shift of significant amounts of bullion toward or away from the Republic should be reflected in exchange rates. After having fluctuated for the most part between 34 and 37 from 1735 to 1783, the cost of sterling moved from 1784 to 1795 to a range between 36 and 44 schellingen per pound. (Posthumus, I, 597–612. Part but not all of the higher cost of sterling may be accounted for by the declining premium of bank money, in which sterling drafts were drawn.) That shift occurred despite the fact that during the 1780s there was little or no new Dutch investment in the public debt to balance against annuity receipts on existing holdings. Annuity receipts aside, the Republic had a persistent deficit on current account in trade with England, a deficit that had been countered by a credit surplus in trade with other areas. On the assumption that money supply was approximately proportional in the two states during the period in question, the shift in sterling costs can be interpreted to support the hypothesis of change to an overall debit surplus in international payments, the result of declining exports to or rising imports from other areas.

6 The Republic might have demanded that foreign governments alter their tariff policies in fashions beneficial to Dutch shipping and entrepôt functions in return for continued access to Dutch savings, but such a step was not taken and apparently not considered.

7 Joel Mokyr, *Industrialization in the Low Countries, 1795–1850* (New Haven, Conn., 1976), p. 24.

8 Joh. de Vries, *De economische achteruitgang der republiek in de achttiende eeuw*, 2nd ed. (Leiden, 1968), pp. 83–98.

9 Wilson, *Anglo-Dutch Commerce and Finance*, pp. 197–201.

10 Ibid., p. 201.

11 De Vries, *Economische achteruitgang*, p. 52. See also Johannes Hovy, *Het voorstel van 1751 tot instelling van een beperkt vrijhavenstelsel in de republiek* (Groningen, 1966).

12 De Vries, *Economische achteruitgang*, p. 52. Also ibid., pp. 118–24 on efforts to enhance industrial enterprise within the context of staple market interests and within limits imposed by government revenues.

13 Ibid., p. 120.

14 Mokyr, *Industrialization*, pp. 176–7 and 180–9. The wage differential between the two states seems also to extend backward in time from 1795. See also Joel Mokyr, "Capital, Labor and the Delay of the Industrial Revolution in the Netherlands," *EHJ*, XXXVIII (1975), 280–99; and *idem*, "The Industrial Revolution in the Low Countries in the First Half of the Nineteenth Century: A Comparative Case Study," *JEH*, XXXIV, no. 2 (June, 1974), 365–91.

15 Mokyr, *Industrialization*, pp. 26–82, 85–8, and 208.

16 Jan Dhondt and Marinette Bruwier ["The Industrial Revolution in the Low Countries, 1700–1914," in *Fontana Economic History of Europe*, ed. by Carlo M. Cipolla, 6 vols. (London, 1972–4), IV, pt. 1, 354–5] hold that the nobility, large landowners and rentiers investing through banks, and old commercial and industrial dynasties supplied funds to industrial entrepreneurs in both the early and later stages of Belgian development.

17 De Vries, *Economische achteruitgang*, pp. 121–36 and 180–4; and Mokyr, *Industrialization*, pp. 85–125. The Prussian envoy Thulemeyer reported on an effort at industrial and commercial reinvigoration as early as 1776, commenting specifically on a loan for f. 300,000 raised for a textile manufactory at Amersfoort. *D.T.*, p. 162, dispatch of 12 Apr. 1776. But he also recognized the continuing attraction of foreign loans. Ibid., and p. 173, dispatch of 11 Feb. 1777. Two other examples of long-term loans organized on behalf of Dutch industry through Dutch capital markets have come to light. See N.E.H.A., Pros., III, 304, about a pre-1780 issue for f. 200,000 for a porcelain manufactory; and *idem*, Archief KV, "Neg. voor een papierfabriek. . ." regarding an 1809 loan of f. 20,000 raised to set up a paper manufacturing establishment in The Hague.

18 De Vries, *Economische achteruitgang*, p. 111.

19 Ibid., pp. 128–34, develops two cases, one of a spinning mill set up in Kralingen, near Rotterdam, in 1776, and the other of a mill established in Utrecht in 1779. In both cases the associates included British entrepreneurs domiciled in the Republic (who appear to have been knowledgeable about recent advances in spinning technology) and Dutch capitalists. The Kralingen experiment folded by 1779, apparently because resources provided by the Rotterdam butcher Pieter Hodenpijl were exhausted. But John Thompson, one of Hodenpijl's associates at Kralingen, moved to Utrecht in 1779 and there

joined with a syndicate led by the financier Jan van Heukelom to form a second mill that remained in operation until 1799. More fragmentary information on other examples of the application of British technology to Dutch industrial production also indicates links with capitalists. Ibid., pp. 134–6.

20 Cited by ibid., p. 135.

21 Mokyr, *Industrialization*, pp. 203–30. Mokyr leaves unresolved the problem of the relative quality of Dutch entrepreneurs as profit maximizers and thus leaves some latitude for a revision of the traditional argument about entrepreneurial enervation. See ibid., pp. 215–21.

22 "The market in which the Dutch industrialist and the Dutch financier could conclude financial transactions did not exist. Therefore the entire connection between the 'capital' owned by the Amsterdam banking houses and the 'capital' accumulated (or not) in industry breaks down." Ibid., pp. 219–20, and see also p. 134.

It is, of course, incorrect to limit available capital to the assets of Amsterdam banking houses. Bankers were perhaps the last group of wealthy individuals who should be expected to have invested in industry, for they were already active entrepreneurs in a sometimes lucrative sector of enterprise and therefore inclined to invest surplus profits that could not be accommodated by the firm in more secure areas. The group in question should be broadened to include those people labeled "capitalists" by their contemporaries, that is, individuals with capital to lend.

Mokyr's evidence for the assumption that links were absent consists of the following: in Belgium only one incident was discovered in which a *société en commandite* was formed between a banker and an industrialist (p. 40); the presence of entrepreneurs' own capital appeared to account for the initial investment in recorded cases (p. 29 and passim); the nobility and old-time financiers were unwilling to invest in something they regarded as a reckless adventure (p. 39); and in the case of the Dutch Netherlands there is "virtual unanimity" among Dutch historians "that capital markets were inaccessible to Dutch manufacturers in the period under discussion" (p. 220). More accurately, many Dutch historians agree that little capital was invested in industry, which is not the same as Mokyr's claim that demand for capital among manufacturers could not be satisfied because of defective capital markets. Mokyr fails to deal with the specific imperfections of Belgian and Dutch capital markets except in terms of a possibly greater aversion to risk on the part of Dutch than Belgian manufacturers (p. 219 and n. 47). The factors behind the presumed incapacities of those markets are unexplained (Mokyr refers (p. 291, n. 47) to a theoretical study of imperfect capital markets creating risk aversion, but that study is hardly applicable in the case at issue), and Mokyr does not raise the question of credit acquired through other channels than sleeping partnerships except in discussing circulating credit (pp. 48–9). Finally, his reading of the evidence on investment by wealthy Belgians, which conflicts with that of Dhondt and Bruwier (n. 16 above), seems much too narrow.

23 Evidence that links existed, which will be summarized here, refers to types of lending that have been deemphasized because of concentration of atten-

tion on lending to governments. Pertinent segments of the present study, which refer to more detailed sources of information, include chap. 2, n. 26; chap. 7, discussion of Spain; chap. 7, n. 118; chap. 9, n. 17. The most extensive contacts developed between the Amsterdam market and industry existed in a series of advances organized between 1769 and 1785 for the Swedish iron industry and alum and brass works. The series extended to at least 12 loans totaling something in excess of f. 3,339,500, thus averaging more than f. 275,000. (All loans for which such information is available paid 5-percent returns and were based on a maximum of five-eighths of the assessed value of property offered for mortgage.) Swedish iron manufacturers and merchants specializing in iron exports had long relied on Amsterdam for short-term credit, and had in the process established the contacts necessary for exploiting a different credit structure. The reasons behind the transition to long-term advances are, however, unclear. Russian competition from about 1760 in the principal export area, Britain, may conceivably have encouraged an expansion of the scale of production beyond the traditionally small unit. On the other hand, the initial loans may have been tied to the disruption of domestic credit facilities resulting from policies introduced by the Cap faction. In any case the series taken as a whole suggests a broad but ultimately unsuccessful attempt at industrial and commercial expansion based on low-cost Dutch credit and on marketing through Amsterdam intermediaries. Sources: N.E.H.A., Pros., III, 16 and 207; *idem*, Kleine aanwinsten, 362; *idem*, Archief KV, "Verschillende negotiaties ten behoeve van Zweden . . . 1772–1807," "Lijsten van de uitlotingen van zweedsche obligaties," "Brieven aan den Heer D. J. Voombergh te Amsterdam," and "Berekening van zes maanden interest van Amerikaansche fondsen . . ."; G.A.A., N.12.16.02; *idem*, notaries C. van Homrigh, 12397/436, 12403/366, 12406/800, 12408/16, 12412/887, 12434/98, 12443/653, 12453/471, 12454/543, 12455/707, 12458/595, 12461/132, 12463/378, 12464/461, 12467/183 and 198, 12468/492, and 12478/469 and 533; P. Huntum, 14150/502 and 14156/410–11; and P. de Wilde, 14364/93; Johan E. Elias, *De vroedschap van Amsterdam*, 2 vols. (Amsterdam, 1963 reprint), II, 1057–8; and W. W. van der Meulen, "Beschrijving van eenige westindische-plantageleeningen," *BMHG*, XXV (1904), 505. These citations also include information on a loan organized for a Swedish merchant house and two other parties on landed estates without any evident tie to industry or mining. It should be noted that this is probably no more than a partial list and that further exploration in notarial archives would yield other cases.

See also *D.T.*, pp. 92–3, dispatch of 20 Oct. 1772; Kurt Samuelsson, "International Payments and Credit Movements by the Swedish Merchant-Houses, 1730–1815," *SEHR*, III, no. 2 (1955), 174–6, 186, and 193–5; Rolf Adamson, "Finance and Marketing in the Swedish Iron Industry, 1800–1860," *SEHR*, XVI, no. 1 (1968), 48–55; and G.A.A., notary H. van Heel, 12865/268 (on a 1759 loan for f. 45,000 at 5 percent floated for a sugar refinery at Bergen, Norway).

24 Instances of individual merchants and rentiers with significant assets in domestic and foreign industry may be found in P. J. van Winter, *Het aandeel*

van den amsterdamschen handel aan den opbouw van het amerikaansche gemeenebest, 2 vols. (The Hague, 1927–33), II, 194ff. and 230ff.; and G.A.A., Archief Brants, 126 and 127. Also n. 19 above.

25 De Vries, *Economische achteruitgang*, pp. 83–118.

26 Mokyr, *Industrialization*, p. 134.

27 *Ibid.*, pp. 168–89, esp. p. 176. See also pp. 166–8, where Mokyr deals with problems associated with the assumption that high wages will necessarily act as an incentive to introduction of more capital-intensive techniques of production.

28 Calculations have been made from data in Weeveringh, I, 50–1 and 55. The sample securities employed are Generality 3- and 4-percent annuities and Batavian 4 percent annuities due after the peace (i.e., after 1815). Debt reformulation by Dutch governments during the period complicates the selection of securities that are representative of the complex and changing assortment of paper in circulation. These three have been chosen because quotations on at least two of them are available for most of the period and because they appear to achieve a balance among prices that, in the fragmentary data available, ranged over a wide spectrum. Realizable returns have been adjusted from the second half of 1810 to account for the reduction of service to one-third of the level stated on any given note. Prices provided by Weeveringh are the first quotations available in each semiannual period. For that reason the July 1810 quotations do not reflect the actual returns earned in the second half of that year, for the annuity reduction was not decreed until 9 July. Rentiers appear, however, to have anticipated Napoleon's action. The realizable returns given here are the average of available quotations. For 1814 returns have been calculated using equivalent paper with the same nominal yield.

29 It should be remembered that the risks of lending to government in wartime were not always appreciated by Dutch investors before the suspension of payments obliged a revision of attitudes. Weeveringh, II, 846–9, offers semiannual averages on the major paper outstanding in foreign government lending from 1796 to 1811. These data reveal that paper was not bid up above realizable returns available on domestic government securities except when states suspended service or renounced part or all of their liabilities.

30 See Table 9-3.

31 Mokyr, *Industrialization*, pp. 147–8.

32 Ibid., p. 184.

33 Ibid., pp. 224–5.

34 For instance, Simon Schama, *Patriots and Liberators: Revolution in the Netherlands, 1780–1813* (New York, 1977), p. 577, refers to smuggling of British manufactures into the Dutch Netherlands by Dutch merchants.

35 It would also appear plausible to reject Mokyr's argument that links between capital markets and industrial entrepreneurs were absent in Belgium and to replace that with the hypothesis that mechanized industry was not sufficiently profitable to attract large infusions of long-term credit from outside that sector of the Belgian economy. Evidence cited by Mokyr (*Industrialization*, pp. 43 and 184) indicates that capital stock in the Verviers woolen

industry grew at only some 2.4 percent per annum between 1780 and 1850. Although such a low rate might be explained by other factors, it may indicate that the profitability of mechanized woolen manufacturing was not sufficiently greater than earnings in other areas to attract a higher level of reinvestment. The general validity of that observation is also suggested by the very slowness of the development process in Belgium. According to this line of reasoning, Belgian industrial entrepreneurs would not generally have been willing to sacrifice all profits drawn from hypothetical fixed capital investments made with outside credit. Because they would have demanded that part of those profits accrue to them, rentiers would have been disinclined to invest unless what remained available was equal to or higher than returns from government securities, real estate, or other areas. For Belgium, then, the problem might be posed around this question: What returns were Belgian industrial entrepreneurs willing or able to offer to raise rentier capital? Returns that were too low would not, of course, reflect imperfect capital markets. Furthermore, this revised hypothesis disposes of the awkward problem arising from Mokyr's contention that industrial entrepreneurs could invest in government securities and real estate but that rentiers, presumably encountered in that step if not otherwise, could not make the reverse step of expanding their portfolios to include long-term loans to industry.

In estimating alternative returns available to Belgian industrialists and rentiers it should be remembered that inhabitants of the Austrian Netherlands sometimes invested through the Amsterdam capital market. Moreover, some Antwerp houses tried during the 1780s and 1790s to compete with Amsterdam bankers for commissions on the management of foreign government loans. Their failure to establish an important sector of foreign lending in Antwerp can suggest either that returns were higher in Amsterdam and that consequently Belgian rentiers preferred to lend through foreign markets or that returns were lower in Amsterdam but that the volume of capital available in Belgium was simply inadequate to support major foreign lending. It is more plausible to assume that returns in Belgium were virtually identical to those in Amsterdam (save perhaps some minor difference reflecting the higher costs of perceiving returns on loans made on a foreign but proximate market) but that confidence in established Amsterdam banking houses drew capital there. In that case returns in Antwerp should also have advanced more or less with Dutch returns during the war, and more so since even the few foreign loans organized there during the 1780s and 1790s were not repeated. Lower annuity rates than those charged in Amsterdam would have encouraged such borrowers as Russia and Sweden to return to Antwerp. This interpretation would account for any reluctance of Belgian rentiers to invest in industry because they were already earning high returns that industrial entrepreneurs could not match or exceed. Belgian industrialization would then emerge in terms of the profitability of given enterprises as a rather fragile process, at least to about 1815, whereas the potential for duplication would seem to have been quite remote in the Dutch Netherlands.

36 In 1793, for example, Hope & Co. insisted on a deferral of new issues for Russia, although that state was eager to expand credit mobilization in Am-

sterdam. Marten G. Buist, *At Spes Non Fracta: Hope & Co., 1770–1815* (The Hague, 1974), pp. 123–54, on negotiations between Hope & Co. and the Russian court from August 1793 to June 1794.

37 Those analyses have overestimated losses because they have been based on a comparison of exaggerated sums outstanding before the wars with more realistic postwar figures.

38 Ibid., pp. 63 and 273–4.

39 Quotations from *MNM*, 1793–6; and Weeveringh, II, 846–50, 861, and 872. Through July 1796 the chart gives total average prices of selected securities from the first listing of each half year. Beginning with 1797 prices are averages for each half year. Quotations are not available for 28 Nov. 1811–1 Jan. 1814. The selected securities are Danish toll notes at 4 percent; Austrian, Russian, and Swedish 5 percents; Spanish 3.5 percents; Austrian 4 percents negotiated on Bank of Vienna debentures through Goll & Co.; and, for England, 3-percent consolidated annuities and bank stock at Amsterdam prices.

40 See above, p. 80, and chap. 3, n. 31. No effort will be made to trace losses in nongovernment domestic or foreign lending, an area that includes loans to West Indian planters, Swedish mining and manufacturing, domestic and foreign commercial ventures, negotiations organized on domestic securities and on unsettled land in the United States, and other investments.

41 That is, the total of approximately f. 7.5 million owed by Spain; plus slightly less than two-thirds of the sum outstanding from France, or f. 70 to 110 million of the f. 115 to 180 million owed in 1786 (reduced to reflect interim repayments of principal); plus two-thirds of the amount outstanding from Sweden in 1790, or f. 12 million. Unrecapitalized annuity suspensions are disregarded here but figure in the estimate of overall annuity losses that follows.

42 Montalivet to the emperor (Napoleon), 28 Oct. 1811, in *GS*, VI, 219. Of that Montalivet put income from Britain at f. 12 million and from all other sources at just below f. 10 million, reflecting a redistribution back toward Britain but no new lending to that state.

See also the rough draft list of sums outstanding and returns from government loans dating from about 1810 in N.E.H.A., Archief KV, "Contract tussen de heren J. Dull. . . ." Putting annual receipts from Britain at f. 8 million and from France at f. 3 million, that list gives total income from major debtors at just over f. 20 million. Other estimates may be found in Metelerkamp, p. 12; I. J. Brugmans, *Paardenkracht en mensenmacht* (The Hague, 1961), pp. 18–19; and E. H. Kossmann, "The Crisis of the Dutch State 1780–1813: Nationalism, Federalism, Unitarism," in J. S. Bromley and E. H. Kossmann, eds., *Britain and the Netherlands* (The Hague, 1971), IV, 173.

43 The median date for foreign government loans may have fallen a few years later than 1770, but not later than 1775. The median for domestic government loans was probably several decades earlier. See Table 3-1 for estimates of the province of Holland's debts from 1689 to 1794.

44 Posthumus, I, ci. Purchasing preferences changed over the period surveyed, but the mixture of agricultural and nonagricultural commodities used by Posthumus all remain appropriate to a preindustrial economy. There is no

reason to suppose that Posthumus's index is well suited to consumption patterns among the wealthy, but it can be used for purposes of comparison as long as wartime fluctuations in the price of consumables are acknowledged as a distortion. For that reason the comparison here is between the prewar period and 1840–59. Projections beyond 1855–9 have not been attempted because of presumably more radical changes in purchasing preferences coinciding with industrialization in the Netherlands, and because Posthumus's index stops with 1860–4.

The adjusted capital-stock figure represents total loans to foreign governments estimated to have been outstanding in 1790 less annulments recognized or fully anticipated by 1815 and not subsequently recapitalized plus loans to domestic governments outstanding less fully anticipated losses as of 1815. The base figure, f. 860 million, is the mean between the absolute minimum sum outstanding and not subsequently written off (f. 1,100 million less 400 million, or f. 700 million) and the absolute maximum sum (f. 1,350 million less 330 million, or f. 1,020 million).

45 Ibid., I, cii.

46 To consider another counterfactual possibility, lending to foreign governments might have been regulated earlier than it was with the aim of diminishing capital exports. While long-term credit remained cheap, up to the latter 1780s, such a measure would have been pointless because any reduction in credit costs would have been outweighed by losses by rentiers. Between the latter 1780s and 1802, when such regulation was reintroduced, curtailed capital exports would presumably have slowed or reversed rising credit costs. But would that effect have been sufficient to outweigh high labor costs as a factor hindering industrial development? And, given the mixed success of attempts at regulating capital exports early in the eighteenth century and in 1802 and thereafter, would regulation before 1802 have been effective enough to have had any significance? The most plausible conclusion is that earlier-than-actual regulation of foreign government lending would have harmed rentiers without helping industrial development to an equivalent degree.

47 Buist, *Hope & Co.*, pp. 65–9 and app. G, pp. 520–5.

48 N. W. Posthumus, "Nota over den toestand van de amsterdamsche handelshuizen in het jaar 1854," *EHJ*, VII (1921), 196–209, indicating also that W. & J. Willink, Dull & Co., and other banking houses had been liquidated between 1815 and 1854.

49 N.E.H.A., Kleine aanwinsten, 22. Posthumus, "Nota," 203, suggests a subsequent decline in Goll & Co.'s position.

50 Among cashiers, for example, the war was particularly devastating. The number operating in Amsterdam declined from about 36 in 1800 to 22–6 in 1810–13, largely as a result of bankruptcies. M. G. Emeis, *Honderdzestigjaar kassierderij* (Amsterdam, 1966), pp. 5–10.

51 Holland Land Company to LeRoy, Bayard, & McEvers, 2 Dec. 1813, in G.A.A., Archief HLC, 74.

LIST OF SOURCES AND WORKS CITED

Manuscript sources

Algemeen Rijksarchief, The Hague

Archief L. P. van de Spiegel, 51 Letterbook C

Archives Nationales, Paris

Etienne Clavière, T*646^1-646^5 and T 646^{2,3}

Gemeente Archief, Amsterdam

Archief Brants

Archief Burgermeesteren

Archief van het college van commissarissen van de Bank van Leening van 1614 tot 1863

Archief Holland Land Company

Archief Jan Dominicus Croese

Archief Thesaurieren ordinaris, Stads beleening kamer

Archief Wisselbank

Familiearchief ten Broeke, Willink, ten Broeke Willink en van Leuvenigh Willink

Kantoor-archief der firma van Eeghen & Co., te Amsterdam

Notarial archives, including accords drawn by the notaries A. van Beem, E. C. Bondt, G. Bouman, J. de Bruijn, J. Croon, R. van Eibergen, J. Fabius, G. van der Groe, J. Harmsen, E. Haverkamp, H. van Heel, P. C. Heidweiller, C. van Homrigh, P. Huntum, T. M. de Man, P. C. Nahuys, H. Outgers, I. Pool, P. Schabaelje, P. de Wilde, and J. H. Zilver

Brochures and price currents in the N series

Gemeente Archief, Rotterdam

Notarial archives, including accords drawn by the notary W. Boon

Nederlandsch Economisch-Historisch Archief, The Hague

Since I consulted papers therein, the collections in The Hague have been decentralized and transferred to provincial and municipal archives according to the principal geographical locale of contents. New locations for the major collections may be found in the *Jaarverslag* of the N.E.H.A., beginning with 1972. Two of the principal collections consulted for this work have been moved to the Municipal Archives, Amsterdam. But because the location of one collection employed extensively (N.E.H.A., Pros.) is now uncertain, and because, for the most part, the collections remain uninventoried beyond their status at the N.E.H.A., this designation of location has been retained here. Citation forms give the title of individual dossiers as those appeared when dossiers were consulted.

Administratiekantoor Ketwich en Voombergh en Wed. W. Borski, van af 1772 (now at G.A.A.)

Archief Loopuyt (now at the Municipal Archives, Schiedam)

Archief Stadnitski en van Heukelom, handelshuis te Amsterdam, 1780–1901 (now at G.A.A.)

Archief van de familie Sillem (now at G.A.A.)

Kleine aanwinsten, 1, 22, 55, 143, 165, 171, 194, 264, 273, 284, 328, 337, 355, 362, and 388 (now at E.H.B.)

Plannen, prospecti, statuten, leningen, loterijen, en negotiatiën, in five dossiers, numbered in sequence (N.E.H.A., Pros.)

Nederlandsch Economisch-Historische Bibliotheek, Amsterdam

The untitled collection of prospectuses gathered by the broker L. Huizinga and relating to the period from 1790 to 1846, numbered in sequence

Brochures and prospectuses in the series P. Ned.

Riksarkivet, Stockholm (copies of material supplied through the courtesy of Mr. Leif Gidlöf)

Joh. Liljencrantz samling, E4661

Universiteit Bibliotheek, Amsterdam

Copie du mémoire remis au Gouverneur de la Pennsylvanie sur la possibilité d'un emprunt en Hollande, 29 Dec. 1790, Handschriften IV, f, 18a

Plans d'emprunts fait à Amsterdam sur les fonds et terreins des Etats-Unis d'Amerique, formes de pleines pouvoirs, tontines, emprunts par lotterie, empr. forces en Hollande, etc. (1794–8) (in eleven parts, compiled by T. Cazenove), 565B14

Printed works

Aalbers, J., "Holland's Financial Problems (1713–1733) and the Wars against Louis XIV," in *Britain and the Netherlands*, vol. 6, ed. by A. C. Duke and C. A. Tamse, The Hague, 1977.

Adamson, Rolf, "Finance and Marketing in the Swedish Iron Industry, 1800–1860," *Scandinavian Economic History Review*, XVI, no. 1 (1968), 47–101.

Allen, Carl-Ferdinand, *Histoire de Danemark*, trans. from the 7th ed., 2 vols., Copenhagen, 1878.

Alphonse, F. J. B. d', *Eenige hoofdstukken uit het "Apercu sur la Hollande,"* Bijdragen tot de statistiek van Nederland, n.s., 1, The Hague, 1900.

List of sources and works cited

Alting Bösken, Johannes Apollonius, *Over geldleeningen hier te lande door vreemde mogendheden aangegaan*, Utrecht, 1864.

Anderson, M. S., *The Eastern Question, 1774–1923*, New York, 1966.

Antonetti, Guy, *Une maison de banque à Paris au XVIIIe siècle: Greffulhe Montz et Cie (1789–1793)*, Paris [1963].

"Les relations franco-bataves et l'échec de l'emprunt français de l'an VIII," *Révue d'histoire économique et sociale*, LIII, no. 1 (1975), 61–72.

Ardant, Gabriel, "Financial Policy and Economic Infrastructure of Modern States and Nations," in *The Formation of National States in Western Europe*, ed. by Charles Tilly, Princeton, N.J., 1975.

Histoire de l'impôt, 2 vols., n.p., 1971–2.

Théorie sociologique de l'impôt, 2 vols., Paris, 1965.

[Auget de Montyon, Antoine Jean Baptiste], *Particularités et observations sur les ministres des finances de France les plus célèbres, depuis 1660 jusqu'en 1791*, Paris, 1812.

Baasch, Ernst, *Holländische Wirtschaftsgeschichte*, Jena, 1927.

Bailly, Antoine, *Histoire financière de la France, depuis l'origine de la monarchie jusqu'à la fin de 1786*, 2 vols., Paris, 1830.

Bain, Robert Nisbet, "The Hats and Caps and Gustavus III (1721–92)," in *Cambridge Modern History*, vol. 6, ed. by A. W. Ward et al., Cambridge, 1909.

The Last King of Poland, London, 1909.

Barbour, Violet, *Capitalism in Amsterdam in the 17th Century*, Ann Arbor, Mich., 1963 reprint.

Barnett, George E., ed., *Two Tracts by Gregory King*, Baltimore, 1936.

Barnwell, Robert Gibbs, *A Sketch of the Life and Times of Johan de Witt, Grand Pensionary of Holland . . .*, New York, 1856.

Baumgarten, Sandor, "Emprunts de Suède à Amsterdam," *Tijdschrift voor geschiedenis*, LXXVII (1964), 439–43.

Bayley, Rafael A., *The National Loans of the United States from July 4, 1776, to June 30, 1880*, 2nd ed., Washington, 1882.

Beer, Adolf, *Die Finanzen Oesterreichs im XIX. Jahrhundert*, Prague, 1877.

Behrens, Betty, "Nobles, Privileges and Taxes in France at the End of the *Ancien Régime*," *Economic History Review*, 2nd ser., XV, no. 3 (1963), 451–75.

"A Revision Defended: Nobles, Privileges, and Taxes in France," *French Historical Studies*, IX, no. 3 (Spring, 1976), 521–7.

Benda, K., "Situation financière et dévaluation de la monnaie en Hongrie en 1811," in *Finances publiques d'ancien régime; finances publiques contemporaines*, [Brussels], 1972.

Bérenger, Jean, "Public Loans and Austrian Policy in the Second Half of the Seventeenth Century," *Journal of European Economic History*, II, no. 3 (Winter, 1973), 657–69.

Berg, L. van den, "Lijst der voornaamste handelshuizen te Amsterdam en Rotterdam in het jaar 1800," *Economisch-historisch jaarboek*, VI (1920), 265–71.

Berghuis, Willem Hendrik, *Ontstaan en ontwikkeling van de nederlandse beleggingsfondsen tot 1914*, Assen, 1967.

List of sources and works cited

Binney, J. E. D., *British Public Finance and Administration, 1774–92*, Oxford, 1958.

Bloch, Jan Gotlib de, *Les finances de la Russie au XIXe siècle*, 2 vols., Paris, 1899.

Blok, P. J., *Geschiedenis van het nederlandsche volk*, 8 vols., Groningen, 1892–1908.

Boetticher, Jakob Gottlieb Isaak, *Statistical Tables; Exhibiting a View of All the States of Europe . . .*, with changes by William Playfair, trans., London, 1800.

Bosher, J. F., *French Finances, 1770–1795: From Business to Bureaucracy*, Cambridge Studies in Early Modern History, Cambridge, 1970.

Bouchary, Jean, *Les manieurs d'argent à Paris à la fin du XVIIIe siècle*, 3 vols., Paris, 1939–43.

Les compagnies financières à Paris à la fin du XVIIIe siècle, 3 vols., Paris, 1940–2.

Bouwstoffen voor de geschiedenis van de levensverzekeringen en lijfrenten in Nederland, Directie van de Algemeene Maatschappij van Levensverzekering en Lijfrente, Amsterdam, 1897.

Boyd, Julian P., ed., *The Papers of Thomas Jefferson*, 19 vols. to date, Princeton, N.J., 1950–74.

Braesch, Frédéric, *Finances et monnaie révolutionnaires*, 3 fascicules; Paris, 1934–6.

Braun, Rudolf, "Taxation, Sociopolitical Structure, and State-Building: Great Britain and Brandenburg-Prussia," in *The Formation of National States in Western Europe*, ed. by Charles Tilly, Princeton, N.J., 1975.

Breen, Joh. C., "Eene amsterdamsche credit-instelling uit het laatst der achttiende eeuw," *Tijdschrift voor geschiedenis*, XV (1900), 137–55.

Brief, door een houder van eene aanzienlijke quantiteit obligatien en agterstallige coupons, ten lasten zijne Keizerlijke, Koninglijke en Apostolische Majesteit aan zijnen vriend en mede-geinteresseerden, Amsterdam, 1805.

Brief van een koopman uyt Rotterdam, aan zijnen vriend, te Amsterdam . . . Deensche Asiatische Compagnie te Coppenhagen . . ., Amsterdam, 1779.

Brieven en negotiatiën van Mr. L. P. van de Spiegel, als raadpensionaris van Holland, 3 vols., Amsterdam, 1803.

Broder, Albert, "Les investissements étrangers en Espagne au XIXe siècle: méthodologie et quantification," *Revue d'histoire économique et sociale*, LIV, no. 1 (1976), 29–63.

Brougham, Henry, *An Inquiry into the Colonial Policy of the European Powers*, 2 vols., Edinburgh, 1803.

Brugmans, I. J., *Paardenkracht en mensenmacht: Sociaal-economische geschiedenis van Nederland, 1795–1940*, The Hague, 1961.

Bruijn, J. R., *De admiraliteit van Amsterdam in rustige jaren, 1713–1751*, Amsterdam, 1970.

Buijs, J. T., *De nederlandsche staatsschuld sedert 1814*, Haarlem, 1857.

Buist, Marten G., *At Spes Non Fracta: Hope & Co., 1770–1815*, The Hague, 1974.

List of sources and works cited

"The Sinews of War: The Role of Dutch Finance in European Politics (c. 1750–1815)," in *Britain and the Netherlands*, vol. 6, ed. by A. C. Duke and C. A. Tamse, The Hague, 1977.

Burnett, Edmund C., ed., *Letters of Members of the Continental Congress*, 8 vols., Washington, 1921–36.

Büsching, Anton Friderich, *Erdbeschreibung*, 8th ed., 13 vols., Hamburg, 1787–1816.

Magazin für die neue Historie und Geographie, XIV (1780), 87–92.

A New System of Geography . . ., trans. by P. Murdoch, 6 vols., London, 1762.

[Canzler, Johann Georg], *Mémoires pour servir à la connoissance des affaires politiques et économiques du royaume de Suède jusqu'à la fin de la 1775me année*, 2 vols., London, 1776.

Carr, Sir John, *A Tour Through Holland Along the Right and Left Banks of the Rhine . . . in . . . 1806*, Philadelphia, 1807.

Carsten, F. L., *Princes and Parliaments in Germany*, Oxford, 1959.

Carter, Alice C., "Analyses of Public Indebtedness in Eighteenth-Century England," *Bulletin of the Institute of Historical Research*, XXIV, no. 70 (November, 1951), 173–81.

"The Dutch and the English Public Debt in 1777," *Economica*, XX, n.s. (May, 1953), 159–61.

Dutch Foreign Investment, 1738–1800," *Economica*, XX, n.s. (November, 1953), 322–40.

"Dutch Foreign Investment 1738–1800, in the Light of the Amsterdam 'Collateral Succession' Inventories," *Tijdschrift voor geschiedenis*, LXVI (1953), 27–38.

"Note on 'A Note on Yardsticks,' " *Economic History Review*, XII, ser. 2, no. 2 (1959–60), 440–4.

Cavanaugh, G. J., "Nobles, Privileges, and Taxes in France: A Revision Reviewed," *French Historial Studies*, VIII, no. 4 (Fall, 1974), 681–92.

"Reply to Behrens," *French Historical Studies*, IX, no. 3 (Spring, 1976), 528–31.

Cobban, Alfred, *Ambassadors and Secret Agents: The Diplomacy of the First Earl of Malmesbury at The Hague*, London, 1954.

Colenbrander, H. T., ed., *Gedenkstukken der algemeene geschiedenis van Nederland van 1795 tot 1840*, 10 vols., The Hague, 1905–22.

"Napoleon en Nederland van 1799 tot 1806," *De gids*, III, ser. 4 (1908), 100–25.

De patriottentijd, 3 vols., The Hague, 1897–9.

Cope, S. R., "The History of Boyd, Benfield & Co.: A Study in Merchant Banking in the Last Decade of the Eighteenth Century," Ph.D. diss., Univ. of London, 1947.

Coquelle, P., *L'alliance franco-hollandaise contre l'Angleterre, 1735–1788*, Paris, 1902.

Coxe, William, *Travels into Poland, Russia, Sweden, and Denmark*, 3 vols., Dublin, 1784.

Travels in Poland, Russia, Sweden, and Denmark, 3 vols., 6th ed., London, 1803.

List of sources and works cited

Cunningham, Audrey, *British Credit in the Last Napoleonic War*, Girton College Studies, 2, Cambridge, 1910.

Däbritz, Walther, *Die Staatsschulden Sachsens in der Zeit von 1763 bis 1837*, Leipzig, 1906.

Dakin, Douglas, *Turgot and the "Ancien Régime" in France*, New York, 1965 reprint.

Daniels, Emil, "Frederick the Great and His Successor," in *Cambridge Modern History*, vol. 6, ed. by A. W. Ward et al., Cambridge, 1909.

Deane, Phyllis, "The Role of Capital in the Industrial Revolution," *Explorations in Economic History*, X, no. 4 (Summer, 1973), 349–64.

Deparcieux, Antoine, *Addition à l'essai sur les probabilités de la durée de la vie humaine*, Paris, 1760.

Essai sur les probabilités de la durée de la vie humaine, Paris, 1746.

Dewey, Davis Rich, *Financial History of the United States*, 12th ed., New York, 1939.

Dhondt, Jan, and Marinette Bruwier, "The Industrial Revolution in the Low Countries, 1700–1914," in *Fontana Economic History of Europe*, ed. by Carlo M. Cipolla, 6 vols., London, 1972–4.

Dickson, P. G. M., *The Financial Revolution in England: A Study in the Development of Public Credit, 1688–1756*, New York, 1967.

and John Sperling, "War Finance, 1698–1714," in *New Cambridge Modern History*, vol. 6, ed. by J. S. Bromley, Cambridge, 1970.

Diferee, Hendrik C., *Studiën over de geschiedenis van den nederlandschen handel*, Amsterdam, 1908.

Dillen, J. G. van, "Het bedrijfsleven van Amsterdam in de achttiende eeuw," in *Zeven eeuwen Amsterdam*, ed. by Antoine E. D'Ailly et al., 6 vols., Amsterdam, 1946–51.

"De beurscrisis te Amsterdam in 1763," *Tijdschrift voor geschiedenis*, XXXVII (1922), 241–53.

"Effectenkoersen aan de amsterdamsche beurs, 1723–1794," *Economisch-historisch jaarboek*, XVII (1931), 1–46.

ed., *History of the Principal Public Banks*, The Hague, 1934.

"Isaac le Maire en de handel der Oost-Indische Compagnie," *Economisch-historisch jaarboek*, XVI (1930), 1–165.

Van rijkdom en regenten: Handboek tot de economische en sociale geschiedenis van Nederland tijdens de Republiek, The Hague, 1970.

Dinger, J., *Overzicht van alle ter beurze van Amsterdam verhandeld wordende binnen- en buitenlandsche effecten*, 5th ed., Amsterdam, 1873.

Dirksen, W., "Openbare financiën in Nederland van 1790 tot 1820; veranderingen bij de overgang van republikeinse statenbond naar koninkrijk," in *Finances publiques d'ancien régime; finances publiques contemporaines*, [Brussels], 1972.

Dukes, Paul, *Catherine the Great and the Russian Nobility: A Study Based on the Materials of the Legislative Commission of 1767*, Cambridge, 1967.

Duran, James A., Jr., "The Reform of Financial Administration in Russia During the Reign of Catherine II," *Canadian Slavic Studies*, IV, no. 3 (Fall, 1970), 485–96.

List of sources and works cited

Durand, Yves, *Les fermiers généraux au XVIIIe siècle*, Publications de la faculté des lettres et sciences humaines de Paris-Sorbonne, Série "Recherches," 70, Paris, 1971.

Duvillard de Durand, Emanuel Etienne, *Recherches sur les rentes, les emprunts et les remboursemens*, Paris, 1787.

Eagly, Robert V., "Monetary Policy and Politics in Mid-Eighteenth Century Sweden," *Journal of Economic History*, XXIX, no. 4 (December, 1969), 739–57.

and V. Kerry Smith, "Domestic and International Integration of the London Money Market, 1731–1789," *Journal of Economic History*, XXXVI, no. 1 (March, 1976), 198–212.

Eerenbeemt, H. F. J. M. van den, "Het huwelijk tusen filantropie en economie: Een Patriotse en Bataafse illusie," *Economisch- en sociaal-historisch jaarboek*, XXXV (1972), 28–64.

Eggers, Christian Ulrich Detlev von, *Memoiren über die dänischen Finanzen*, 2 vols., Hamburg, 1800–1.

Elias, Johan E., *De vroedschap van Amsterdam, 1578–1795*, 2 vols., Amsterdam, 1963 reprint.

Elliot, Jonathan, *The Funding System of the United States and of Great Britain*, New York, 1968 reprint.

Emeis, M. G., *Honderdzestigjaar kassierderij*, Amsterdam, 1966.

Encyclopédie méthodique, économie politique et diplomatique, 4 vols, Paris, 1784–8.

Engels, P. H., *De geschiedenis der belastingen in Nederland*, Rotterdam, 1848.

Ernst, Joseph Albert, "Currency in the Era of the American Revolution: A History of Colonial Paper Money Practices and British Monetary Policies, 1764–1781," Ph.D. diss. Univ. of Wisconsin, 1962.

Fairman, William, *The Stocks Examined and Compared: or, A Guide to Purchasers in the Public Funds*, London, 1795.

Falbe-Hansen, V., and Will. Scharling, *Danmarks statistik*, 6 vols., Copenhagen, 1878–91.

Faulcon, Felix, *Voyages et opuscules*, Paris, 1805.

Feldbaek, Ole, *India Trade Under the Danish Flag, 1772–1808*, Scandinavian Institute of Asian Studies Monograph Series, 2, Odense, 1969.

Fell, R., *A Tour Through the Batavian Republic During the Latter Part of the Year 1800 . . .* , London, 1801.

Ferguson, E. James, *The Power of the Purse*, Chapel Hill, N.C., 1961.

Fokker, G. A., *Geschiedenis der loterijen in de Nederlanden*, Amsterdam, 1862.

Friis, Astrid, and Kristof Glamann, *A History of Prices and Wages in Denmark, 1660–1800*, Copenhagen, 1958.

Fruin, Robert, and H. T. Colenbrander, eds., *Dépêches van Thulemeyer, 1763–1788*, Werken uitgegeven door het Historisch Genootschap, 3rd ser., 30, Amsterdam, 1912.

Furber, Holden, *John Company at Work*, Harvard Historical Studies, 55, New York, 1970 reprint.

Gautier, Charles, "Un investissement genevois: la tontine d'Irlande de 1777," *Bulletin de la société d'histoire et d'archéologie de Genève*, X (1951), 53–68.

List of sources and works cited

Geyl, Pieter, *Encounters in History*, Cleveland, 1961.

De patriottenbeweging, 1780-1787, Amsterdam, 1947.

Giesey, Ralph E., "Rules of Inheritance and Strategies of Mobility in Prerevolutionary France," *American Historical Review*, LXXXII, no. 2 (April, 1977), 271-89.

Glamann, Kristof, "The Danish Asiatic Company, 1732-1772," *Scandinavian Economic History Review*, VIII, no. 2 (1960), 109-49.

Goppel, W., "Ontwikkeling en beteekenis van de administratiekantoren," *De nederlandsche financier*, Jubileumsuitgave of the *Dagelijkse beurscourant*, 2 Feb. 1939, 31-4.

Grellier, J. J., *The History of the National Debt from the Revolution in 1688 to the Beginning of the Year 1800 . . .*, London, 1810.

The Terms of all the Loans Which Have Been Raised for the Public Service . . ., 3rd eds., London, 1805.

Griffiths, David, and Karin Griffiths, ed., "M. M. Speranski as Viewed in L. H. Jacob's Unpublished Autobiography," *Canadian-American Slavic Studies*, IX, no. 4 (Winter, 1975), 481-541.

Grinten, W. A. E. A. van der, "Van lijfrenten in overouden tijd," *Haagsch maandblad* (1924), 575-86.

Grossmann, Julius, *Die Amsterdamer Börse vor zwei hundert Jahren: Ein Beitrag zur Geschichte der Politik und des Börsenwesens im mittleren Europa (1672-1673)*, The Hague, 1876.

Guéry, Alain, "Les finances de la monarchie française sous l'Ancien Régime," *Annales: économies, sociétés, civilisations*, XXXIII, no. 2, (March-April, 1978), 216-39.

Hallendorff, Carl, and Adolf Schück, *History of Sweden*, New York, 1970 reprint.

Hamilton, Earl J., *War and Prices in Spain, 1651-1800*, Harvard Economic Studies, 81, Cambridge, Mass., 1947.

Hanway, Jonas, *An Historical Account of the British Trade over the Caspian Sea: with the Author's Journal of Travels from England Through . . . Holland . . .*, 3rd ed., 2 vols, London, 1762.

Hardenberg, H., *Het burgerweeshuis voor nederlands hervormden te 's-Gravenhage, 1564-1964*, The Hague, 1964.

"Het handelshuis Osy," *Rotterdams jaarboekje*, II, 6th ser. (1954), 154-76.

Harris, Robert D., "French Finances and the American War, 1777-1783," *Journal of Modern History*, XLVIII, no. 2 (June, 1976), 233-58.

"Necker's *Compte Rendu* of 1781: A Reconsideration," *Journal of Modern History*, XLII, no. 2 (June, 1970), 161-83.

Hassinger, Herbert, "Politische Kräft und Wirtschaft 1350-1800," in *Handbuch der deutschen Wirtschafts- und Sozialgeschichte*, ed. by Hermann Aubin and Wolfgang Zorn, 1, Stuttgart, 1971.

Hauer, Joseph von, *Beiträge zur Geschichte der österr. Finanzen*, Vienna, 1848.

Hayes, Richard, *The Negociator's Magazine . . .*, 11th ed. rev. by Benjamin Webb, London, 1777.

Heckscher, Eli F., *An Economic History of Sweden*, trans. by Göran Ohlin, Harvard Economic Studies, 95, Cambridge, Mass., 1954.

Helleiner, Karl F., *The Imperial Loans: A Study in Financial and Diplomatic History*, Oxford, 1965.
Herr, Richard, *The Eighteenth-Century Revolution in Spain*, Princeton, N.J., 1958.
Heyliger, R. V., *De nederlandsche wetgeving op de vreemde geldligtingen*, Leiden, 1854.
Heyvaert, Edward, *De ontwikkeling van de moderne bank- en krediettechniek tijdens de zestiende en zeventiende eeuw in Europa en te Amsterdam in het bijzonder*, n.p., 1975.
Hofstra, H. J., "De belastingunificatie van 1805," in *Smeetsbundel: Opstellen aangeboden aan Prof. dr. M. J. H. Smeets . . .* , Deventer, 1967.
Holborn, Hajo, *A History of Modern Germany, 1648–1840*, New York, 1964.
Homer, Sidney, *A History of Interest Rates*, New Brunswick, N.J., 1963.
Hope, John, *Letters on Credit*, 2nd ed., London, 1784.
Horvàth, Robert, "Monetary Inflation in Hungary During the Napoleonic Wars," *Journal of European Economic History*, V, no. 3 (Winter, 1976), 651–62.
Houtzager, Dirk, *Hollands lijf- en losrenteleningen vóór 1672*, Schiedam, 1950.
Houwink, André, *Acceptcrediet, economische en bankpolitieke beschouwingen over den in het bankaccept belichaamden credietvorm*, Amsterdam, 1929.
Hovde, B. J., *The Scandinavian Countries, 1720–1865: The Rise of the Middle Classes*, Boston, 1943.
Hovy, J., *Het voorstel van 1751 tot instelling van een beperkt vrijhavenstelsel in de republiek*, Historische studies uitgegeven vanwege het instituut voor geschiedenis der Rijksuniversiteit te Utrecht, 21, Groningen, 1966.
Hudig, J., *De west-indische zaken van Ferrand Whaley Hudig, 1759–1797*, Amsterdam, [1922].
Jansen, L., *Geschiedenis van de stads bank van lening te Amsterdam, 1614–1964*, Amsterdam, 1964.
Jobert, Ambroise, *Magnats polonais et physiocrates français (1767–1774)*, Paris, 1941.
Johansen, Hans Chr., *Dansk økonomisk politik i årene efter 1784*, Aarhus, 1968.
Jong, A. M. de, Geschiedenis van de Nederlandsche Bank, 4 vols., Haarlem, 1967 reprint.
Jong, Th. P. M. de, "Sociale verandering in de neergaande Republiek," *Economisch- en sociaal-historisch jaarboek*, XXXV (1972), 1–27.
Jong-Keesing, E. E. de, *De economische crisis van 1763 te Amsterdam*, n.p., 1939.
Jongh, Jan Floris de, *De nederlandsche makelaardij*, Haarlem, 1949.
Jörberg, Lennart, *A History of Prices in Sweden, 1732–1914*, 2 vols, Lund, 1972.
Katzenelsohn, P., *Zur Entwicklungsgeschichte der Finanzen Russlands*, Berlin, 1913.
Kellenbenz, H., "Die öffentlichen Finanzen im Reich von der Mitte des 17. Jahrhunderts bis ins 19. Jahrhundert," in *Finances publiques d'ancien régime; finances publiques contemporaines*, [Brussels], 1972.
Kesteloo, H. M., "De stadsrekeningen van Middelburg VII, 1650–1675,"

Zeeuwsch genootschap der wetenschappen, *Archief*, VIII, pt. 4 (1901), 1–82.

"De stadsrekeningen van Middelburg VIII, 1675–1700," *Zeeuwsch genootschap der wetenschappen*, *Archief*, VIII, pt. 4 (1901), 83–134.

"De stadsrekeningen van Middelburg IX, 1700–1810," *Zeeuwsch genootschap der wetenschappen*, *Archief*, VIII, pt. 5 (1902), 1–202.

Keuchenius, W. M., *De inkomsten en uitgaven der Bataafsche Republiek voorgesteld in eene nationaale balans*, Amsterdam, 1803.

Klein, Ernst, *Geschichte der öffentlichen Finanzen in Deutschland (1500–1870)*, Sozial- und Wirtschaftsgeschichte, 6, Wiesbaden, 1974.

Von der Reform zur Restauration: Finanzpolitik und Reformgesetzgebung des preussischen Staatskanzlers Karl August von Hardenberg, Veröffentlichungen der Historischen Kommission zu Berlin, 16, Berlin, 1965.

Klein, P. W., *Kapitaal en stagnatie tijdens het hollandse vroegkapitalisme*, Rotterdam, 1967.

"Stagnation économique et emploi du capital dans la Hollande des XIIIe [sic] et XIXe siècles," *Revue du Nord*, LII (1970), 33–41.

Klotz, Justine, *L'oeuvre législative de la diète de 4 ans*, Paris, 1913.

Kluit, Adriaan, *Iets over den laatsten engelschen oorlog met de republiek, en over Nederlands koophandel, deszelfs bloei, verval, en middelen van herstel*, Amsterdam, 1794.

Kluit, W. P. Sautijn, *De amsterdamsche beurs in 1763 en 1773*, Amsterdam, 1865.

Koenen, H. J., *Voorlezingen over de geschiedenis der finantiën van Amsterdam*, Amsterdam, 1855.

Koopman, De, of bijdragen ten opbouw van Neerlands koophandel en zeevaard, 6 vols., Amsterdam, 1768–76 [published by Gerrit Bom].

Korzencowski, J., ed., "Souvenirs du Prince Stanislas Poniatowski," *Revue d'histoire diplomatique*, IX (1895), 481–535.

Kossmann, E. H., "The Crisis of the Dutch State 1780–1813: Nationalism, Federalism, Unitarism," in *Britain and the Netherlands*, vol. 4, ed. by J. S. Bromley and E. H. Kossmann, The Hague, 1971.

Krug, Leopold, *Geschichte der preussischen Staatsschulden*, in *Nachgelassene Schriften . . .*, vol. 1, ed. by Carl Julius Bergius, Breslau, 1861.

Kukiel, M., "Kosciuszko and the Third Partition," in *Cambridge History of Poland*, vol. 2, ed. by W. F. Reddaway et al., New York, 1971 reprint.

Kuznets, Simon, *Economic Growth and Structure: Selected Essays*, New York, 1965.

Le Moine de l'Espine, Jacques, *De koophandel van Amsterdam naer alle gewesten der waereld . . .*, ed. and enlarged by Isaac le Long and subsequently re-ed., 9th ed., 3 vols., Rotterdam, 1780.

Lesage, Charles, *Napoléon Ier, créancier de la Prusse (1807–1814)*, Paris, 1924.

Loman, J. C., *Supplement op den vijfden druk van J. Dinger's overzicht van alle ter beurze van Amsterdam*, Amsterdam, 1880.

Lowrie, Walter, and Matthew St. Clair Clarke, comps., *American State Papers, Finance*, I, 3rd ser., Documents, Legislative and Executive of the United States, Washington, 1832.

Ludwigs, Folke, "Stats-obligationer från Gustaf III:s dagar," *Ekonomisk Revy*, no. 6 (1968), 373–8.

Lüthy, Herbert, *La banque protestante en France de la révocation de l'édit de Nantes à la Révolution*, 2 vols., Paris, 1959–61.

Luzac, Elias, *Hollandsch rijkdom, of tafereel van nederlandsch koophandel en zeevaart . . .* , 2nd ed., 4 vols, Leiden, 1801.

Manger, J.-B., *Recherches sur les relations économiques entre la France et la Hollande pendant la Révolution française (1785–1795)*, Paris, 1923.

Mansvelt, W. M. F., "Het amsterdamsche acceptbedrijf en credietwezen in de 18e eeuw," *Algemeen handelsblad*, 25 October 1922.

and J. G. van dillen, "De crisis van 1763 en de economische achteruitgang van Amsterdam (een discussie)," *Tijdschrift voor geschiedenis*, XXXVII (1922), 400–8.

Marion, Marcel, *Histoire financière de la France depuis 1715*, 6 vols., Paris, 1927–8.

Marmont, Auguste Viesse de, *Mémoires du maréchal duc de Raguse de 1792 à 1832*, 9 vols., Paris, 1857.

Maroger, Dominique, ed., *The Memoirs of Catherine the Great*, trans. by Moura Budberg, New York, n.d.

Mathias, Peter, and Patrick O'Brien, "Taxation in Britain and France, 1715–1810: A Comparison of the Social and Economic Incidence of Taxes Collected for the Central Governments," *Journal of European Economic History*, V, no. 3 (Winter, 1976), 601–50.

"The Incidence of Taxes and the Burden of Proof," *Journal of European Economic History*, VII, no. 1 (Spring, 1978), 211–13.

McCloskey, Donald N., "A Mismeasurement of the Incidence of Taxation in Britain and France, 1715–1810," *Journal of European Economic History*, VII, no. 1 (Spring, 1978), 209–10.

McCusker, John J., *Money and Exchange in Europe and America, 1600–1775*, Chapel Hill, N.C., 1978.

Mees, R., *Gedenkschrift van de firma R. Mees & Zoonen ter gelegenheid van haar tweehonderd-jarig bestaan, 1702–1920*, n.p., n.d.

Mees, W. C., *Proeve eener geschiedenis van het bankwezen in Nederland gedurende den tijd der Republiek*, Rotterdam, 1838.

Melles, J., *Het huys van leeninge: Geschiedenis van de oude lombarden en de stedelijke bank van lening te Rotterdam, 1325–1950*, The Hague, 1950.

Mensi, Franz, *Die Finanzen Oesterreichs von 1701 bis 1740*, Vienna, 1890.

Metelerkamp, Rutger, *Tableau statistique de la Hollande en 1804*, trans., Paris, 1807.

Meulen, Ageus Jacobus van der, *Studies over het ministerie van Van de Spiegel*, Leiden, 1905.

Meulen, W. W. van der, "Beschrijving van eenige westindische-plantageleeningen," *Bijdragen en mededeelingen van het historisch genootschap*, XXV (1904), 490–580.

"Een en ander over Van der Capellen tot de Pol en zijn aanhang," in *Geschiedkundige opstellen uitgegeven ter eere van Dr. H. C. Rogge*, Leiden, n.d.

List of sources and works cited

Miller, John C., *The Federalist Era, 1789–1801*, New American Nation Series, New York, 1960.

Mitchell, B. R., *European Historical Statistics*, London, 1975.

and Phyllis Deane, *Abstract of British Historical Statistics*, University of Cambridge Department of Applied Economics Monographs, 17, Cambridge, 1971.

Mokyr, Joel, "Capital, Labor and the Delay of the Industrial Revolution in the Netherlands," *Economisch- en sociaal-historisch jaarboek*, XXXVIII (1975), 280–99.

Industrialization in the Low Countries, 1795–1850, New Haven, Conn., 1976.

"The Industrial Revolution in the Low Countries in the First Half of the Nineteenth Century: A Comparative Case Study," *Journal of Economic History*, XXXIV, no. 2 (June, 1974), 365–91.

Morazé, Charles, "Finance et despotisme," *Annales: économies, sociétés, civilisations*, III, no. 3 (July–September, 1948), 279–96.

Morris, Gouverneur, *A Diary of the French Revolution*, ed. by Beatrix Cary Davenport, 2 vols., London, 1939.

Muinck, B. E. de, *Een regentenhuishouding omstreeks 1700*, Economisch- en sociaal-historische onderzoekingen, N.S., 3, The Hague, 1965.

Naamregister van alle de heeren kooplieden der stad Amsterdam . . ., Amsterdam, 1766, 1790, and 1792 (title varies).

Nadere aanmerkingen, over het gedrag, door de Heeren Goll en Comp. en Osy en Zoon, als banquiers van Zijne Keyzerlijke, Koninglijke en Apostolische Majesteit, gehouden, Amsterdam, 1805.

Neeb, J. F., *De grootboeken der nationale schuld*, 3rd ed., Nijkerk, 1889.

Nefkens, Th. H., "De denkbeelden van De Borger omtrent de economische achteruitgang der republiek in de achttiende eeuw," *Economie*, XXXVI, no. 10 (July, 1972), 485–506.

Niebuhr, Barthold Georg, *Geschichte des Zeitalters der Revolution*, 2 vols., Hamburg, 1845.

Nielsen, Axel, *Dänische Wirtschaftsgeschichte*, Jena, 1933.

Nieuw nederlandsch biografisch woordenboek, ed. by P. C. Molhuysen et al., 10 vols., Leiden, 1911–37.

Nieuwe nederlandsche jaarboeken, 79 vols., 1765–98.

Nolte, Vincent Otto, *Fifty Years in Both Hemispheres or, Reminiscences of the Life of a Former Merchant*, trans., New York, 1854.

Nordmann, Claude, *Grandeur et liberté de la Suède (1660–1792)*, Publications de la faculté des lettres et sciences humaines de Paris-Sorbonne, Série "Recherches," 63, Paris, 1971.

Ogiński, Michał Kleofas, *Mémoires de Michel Oginski sur la Pologne et les polonais depuis 1788 jusqu'à la fin de 1815*, 4 vols., Paris, 1826–7.

Oldewelt, W. F. H., "De Hoeffijserse schuld (1616–1681)," *Jaarboek van het genootschap Amstelodamum*, LI (1954), 37–52.

ed., *Kohier van de personeele quotisatie te Amsterdam over het jaar 1742*, 2 vols., Amsterdam, 1945.

[Oudermeulen, C. van den], *Recherches sur le commerce, ou idées rélatives aux intérêts des différens peuples de l'Europe*, 2 vols., Amsterdam, 1778–84.

Palmer, R. R., "Much in Little: The Dutch Revolution of 1795," *Journal of Modern History*, XXVI (March–December, 1954), 15–35.

Philopolis (pseud.), *An Account of the Bank of Loan at Amsterdam, Commonly Called the Lombard*, London, 1733.

Pieterse, Wilhelmina C., *Inventory of the Archives of the Holland Land Company . . .*, Amsterdam, 1976.

Pintner, Walter McKenzie, *Russian Economic Policy Under Nicolas I*, Ithaca, N.Y., 1967.

[Pinto, Isaac de], *Traité de la circulation et du crédit*, Amsterdam, 1771.

An Essay on Circulation and Credit . . ., trans. by S. Baggs (pseud. of Philip Francis), London, 1774.

Polak, N. J., "Het noteeringsvraagstuk aan de amsterdamsche effectenbeurs in de eerste helft der negentiende eeuw," *Economisch-historisch jaarboek*, X (1924), 198–220.

Posthumus, N. W., *Inquiry into the History of Prices in Holland*, 2 vols., Leiden, 1946–64.

"Nota over den toestand van de amsterdamsche handelshuizen in het jaar 1854," *Economisch-historisch jaarboek*, VII (1921), 196–209.

[Pothier, Robert Joseph], *Traité du contrat de constitution de rente*, Paris, 1774.

Quintus Bosz, A. J. A., *Geld, credietbehoefte en negotiaties in Suriname voor 1865*, Address at the University of Surinam, 1971.

Raaf, H. K. de, and H. M. A. Schadee, comps., *Tweehonderd jaar notariaat en zeezaken: Gedenkschrift van het kantoor der notarissen Schadee en hunnen associé's, Rotterdam, 1724–1924*, Rotterdam, 1924.

Raeff, Marc, *Michael Speransky: Statesman of Imperial Russia, 1772–1839*, 2nd ed., The Hague, 1969.

Reddaway, W. F., "Denmark Under the Bernstorffs and Struensee," in *Cambridge Modern History*, vol. 6, ed. by A. W. Ward et al., Cambridge, 1909.

Report of the Secretary of the Treasury on the State of the Finances for the Year 1867, Washington, 1868.

Resolutiën van de heeren Staaten van Hollandt ende Westvrieslandt, 1723.

Ricard, Samuel, *Traité général du commerce . . .*, ed. rev. by Mr. de M[orien], 2 vols., Amsterdam, 1781.

Riley, James C., "Dutch Investment in France, 1781–1787," *Journal of Economic History*, XXXIII, no. 4 (December, 1973), 732–60.

"Foreign Credit and Fiscal Stability: Dutch Investment in the United States, 1781–1794," *Journal of American History*, LXV, no. 3 (December, 1978), 654–78.

"Life Annuity-Based Loans on the Amsterdam Capital Market Toward the End of the 18th Century," *Economisch-historisch jaarboek*, XXXVI (1973), 102–30.

Rogge, J., *Het handelshuis van Eeghen: Proeve eener geschiedenis van een amsterdamsch handelshuis*, Amsterdam, 1949.

Rootlieb, H., "Bijdrage tot de kennis van Amsterdam's financiën in den franschen tijd," *Jaarboek van het genootschap Amstelodamum*, XII (1914), 131–78.

Ruelle, J. R., *Opérations des changes des principales places d'Europe*, Lyons and Paris, eds. of 1765 and An VII.

Rutkowski, Jan, *Histoire économique de la Pologne avant les partages*, Paris, 1927.

Saint-Cyran, [Paul-Edme Crublier] de, *Calcul des rentes viagères sur une et sur plusieurs têtes . . .* , Paris, 1779.

Samuelsson, Kurt, "International Payments and Credit Movements by the Swedish Merchant-Houses, 1730–1815," *Scandinavian Economic History Review*, III, no. 2 (1955), 163–202.

Schama, Simon, "The Exigencies of War and the Politics of Taxation in the Netherlands, 1795–1810," in *War and Economic Development*, ed. by J. M. Winter, London, 1975.

Patriots and Liberators: Revolution in the Netherlands, 1780–1813, New York, 1977.

Schuddebeurs, H. G., "Het nederlandsche verzekeringsbedrijf gedurende de laatste twee eeuwen, voor zoover dit werd uitgeoefend door naamlooze vennootschappen," *Economisch-historisch jaarboek*, XIV (1928), 1–178.

Ségur, Louis Philippe de, *Politique de tous les cabinets de l'Europe pendant les règnes de Louis XV et de Louis XVI*, 3rd ed., 3 vols., Paris, 1802.

Senkowski, J., "Aenderungen in der öffentlichen Finanzwirtschaft in Polen zu Ende des alten Reiches und während des Aufstandes vom Jahre 1794," in *Finances publiques d'ancien régime; finances publiques contemporaines*, [Brussels], 1972.

Sherwig, John M., *Guineas and Gunpowder: British Foreign Aid in the Wars with France*, 1793–1815, Cambridge, Mass., 1969.

Sickenga, Folkert Nicolaas, *Bijdrage tot de geschiedenis der belastingen in Nederland*, Leiden, 1864.

Sillem, Jérôme Alexandre, *Het Leven van Mr. Johan Valckenaer (1759–1821)*, new ed., 2 vols., Amsterdam, 1883.

Sinclair, John, *The Correspondence of the Right Honourable John Sinclair . . .* , 2 vols., London, 1831.

The History of the Public Revenue of the British Empire, 3rd ed., 3 vols., London, 1803–4.

Slicher van Bath, Bernard H., "Historical Demography and the Social and Economic Development of the Netherlands," *Daedalus*, XCVII, no. 2 (Spring, 1968), 604–21.

Smith, Adam, *An Inquiry into the Nature and Causes of the Wealth of Nations*, ed. by Edwin Cannan, New York, 1937.

Smith, M. F. J., *Tijd-affaires in effecten aan de amsterdamsche beurs*, The Hague, 1919.

Sneller, Z. W., "De rotterdamsche wisselbank 1635–1812," in *Rotterdams bedrijfsleven in het verleden*, Amsterdam, 1940.

Srbik, H. von, *Der staatliche Exporthandel Oesterreichs von Leopold I. bis Maria Theresia*, Vienna, 1907.

List of sources and works cited

Staatkundige historie van Holland, behelzende eene staatkundige bespiegeling van de voornaamste gevallen der nederlandsche geschiedenissen benevens de maandelijksche nederlandsche mercurius (with variations in the title), 28 vols., 1780–1807.

Stiassny, Paul, *Der österreichische Staatsbankerott von 1811*, Vienna, 1912.

Stone, Daniel Z., "Polish Politics and National Reforms, 1775–1788," Ph.D. diss., Indiana Univ., 1972.

Storch, Heinrich Friedrich von, *Supplementband zum fünften, sechsten und siebenten Theil des Historisch-statistischen Gemäldes des russischen Reichs*, Leipzig, 1803.

Susane, G., *La tactique financière de Calonne*, Paris, 1901.

Svendsen, Knud Erik, "Monetary Policy and Theory in Denmark, 1784–1800," *Scandinavian Economic History Review*, X, no. 1 (1962), 38–77; and XI, no. 1 (1963), 1–26.

Syrett, Harold C. ed., *The Papers of Alexander Hamilton*, 25 vols. to date, New York, 1961–77.

Taylor, George V., "The Paris Bourse on the Eve of the Revolution, 1781–1789," *American Historical Review*, LXVII, no. 4 (July, 1962), 951–77.

"Noncapitalist Wealth and the Origins of the French Revolution," *American Historical Review*, LXXII, no. 2 (January, 1967), 469–96.

"Types of Capitalism in Eighteenth-Century France," *English Historical Review*, LXXIX, no. 312 (1964), 478–97.

[Tooke, William], *The Life of Catharine II, Empress of Russia*, 4th ed., 3 vols., London, 1800.

Tönnesson, K. D., "Les finances publiques en Norvège à la fin de l'union dano-norvégienne et les réformes au lendemain de la rupture de l'union en 1814," in *Finances publiques d'ancien régime; finances publiques contemporaines*, [Brussels], 1972.

Vauban, Sebastien de, *Projet d'une dixme royale . . .*, new ed., Brussels, 1708.

Vega, Joseph de la, *Confusion de confusiones (1688), Portions Descriptive of the Amsterdam Stock Exchange*, ed. and trans. by Hermann Kellenbenz, Kress Library of Business and Economics, 13, Boston, 1957.

Verberne, L. G. J., *Het sociale en economische motief in de bataafse tijd*, Tilburg, 1947.

Verzameling van authentique stukken, kunnende dienen tot bijlaagen voor de nieuwspapieren, 5 vols., Amsterdam, 1793–6.

Vicens Vives, Jaime, *An Economic History of Spain*, trans. by Frances M. López-Morillas, Princeton, N.J., 1969.

Vilar, Pierre, *A History of Gold and Money, 1450–1920*, trans. by Judith White, London, 1976.

Volgraff, J. A., ed., *Les oeuvres de Nicolas Struyck*, trans. by J. A. Volgraff, Amsterdam, 1912.

Voorst van Beest, Cornelis Wernard van, *De katholieke armenzorg te Rotterdam in de 17e en de 18e eeuw*, The Hague, 1955.

Voort, Johannes Petrus van de, *De westindische plantages van 1720 tot 1795: Financiën en handel*, Eindhoven, 1973.

List of sources and works cited

Vreede, G. W., *Mr. Laurens Pieter van de Spiegel en zijne tijdgenooten, 1737–1800,* 4 vols., Middelburg, 1874–7.

Vries, Jan de, "On the Modernity of the Dutch Republic," *Journal of Economic History,* XXXIII, no. 1 (March, 1973), 191–202.

Vries, Joh. de, *De economische achteruitgang der republiek in de achttiende eeuw,* 2nd ed., Leiden, 1968.

ed., "Van de Spiegel's 'Schets tot een vertoog over de intrinsique en relative magt van de republijk' (1782)," *Economisch-historisch jaarboek,* XXVII (1958), 81–100.

Wagenvoort, Herman, "Contracten van overleving en andere tontines," *Tijdschrift voor rechtsgeschiedenis,* XXXV (1967), 584–94.

Tontines, een onderzoek naar de geschiedenis van de lijfrenten bij wijze van tontine en de contracten van overleving in de Republiek der Verenigde Nederlanden, Utrecht, 1961.

Wassiltchikow, Alexandre, *Les Razoumowski,* ed. by A. Brückner, 3 vols., Halle, 1893–4.

Weeveringh, J. J., *Handleiding tot de geschiedenis der staatsschulden,* 2 vols, Haarlem, 1852–5.

Onze fondsenmarkt: Schetsen der financieele geschiedenis van staten . . . , Amsterdam, 1885.

Wilson, Ch., *De l'influence des capitaux anglais sur l'industrie européenne depuis la Révolution de 1688 jusqu'en 1846,* Brussels, 1847.

Wilson, Charles H., *Anglo-Dutch Commerce and Finance in the Eighteenth Century,* Cambridge Studies in Economic History, Cambridge, 1966 reprint.

"Dutch Investment in Eighteenth-Century England: A Note on Yardsticks," *Economic History Review,* XII, no. 2, ser. 2 (1959–60), 434–9.

"The Economic Decline of the Netherlands," *Economic History Review,* IX, no. 2 (May, 1939), 111–27.

"Taxation and the Decline of Empires, an Unfashionable Theme," *Bijdragen en mededelingen van het historisch genootschap,* LXXVII (1963), 10–26.

Winter, Pieter J. van, *Het aandeel van den amsterdamschen handel aan den opbouw van het amerikaansche gemeenebest,* Werken uitgegeven door de vereeniging het Nederlandsch Economisch-Historisch Archief, 7 and 9, 2 vols., The Hague, 1927–33.

American Finance and Dutch Investment, 1780–1805, trans. by Mrs. C. M. Geyl and Irene Clephane, 2 vols., New York, 1977.

Wit, C. H. E. de, *De strijd tussen aristocratie en democratie in Nederland, 1780–1848,* Heerlen, 1965.

Witt, Johan de, *Waerdije van lijfrenten naer proportie van losrenten,* The Hague, 1671; French trans. by P. J. L. de Chateleux, *Le rapport de Johan de Witt sur le calcul des rentes viagères,* The Hague, 1937.

Woude, Adrianus Maria van der, *Het Noorderkwartier: Een regionaal historisch onderzoek in de demografische en economische geschiedenis van westelijk Nederland van de late middeleeuwen tot het begin van de negentiende eeuw,* 3 vols., Wageningen, 1972.

Zappey, W. M., *De economische en politieke werkzaamheid van Johannes Goldberg (1763–1828),* Alphen aan den Rijn, 1967.

Zillezen, Cornelis, *Wijsgeerig onderzoek, wegens Neerlands opkomst, bloei, en welvaard . . .*, Amsterdam, 1796.
Zimmermann, Eberhard August Wilhelm von, *A Political Survey of the Present State of Europe . . .*, London, 1787.
Åmark, Karl, *Sveriges statsfinanser, 1719–1809*, Stockholm, 1961.

INDEX

Index

Index

Index

Index

Index

Index

Index

Index

Index

For EU product safety concerns, contact us at Calle de José Abascal, 56–1°, 28003 Madrid, Spain or eugpsr@cambridge.org.

www.ingramcontent.com/pod-product-compliance
Lightning Source LLC
LaVergne TN
LVHW090304210926
848480LV00001B/126
* 9 7 8 0 5 2 1 1 0 1 1 0 3 *